MW00511268

ˇ THE ˇ
ARCHITECTVRAL
RECORD

AN ILLUSTRATED MONTHLY MAGAZINE OF ARCHITECTURE
AND THE ALLIED ARTS AND CRAFTS.

INDEX TO VOLUME XLVII

JANUARY—JUNE

1920

PUBLISHED BY

THE ARCHITECTURAL RECORD CO.

115-119 West Fortieth Street, New York City

341 Monadnock Building, Chicago   1821 Chestnut St., Philadelphia
Bessemer Building, Pittsburgh   114 Federal Street, Boston

THE ARCHITECTURAL RECORD
INDEX

Volume XLVII   January to June, 1920

TYPES OF BUILDINGS ILLUSTRATED.

ILLUSTRATIONS OF DETAIL.

ARCHITECTS REPRESENTED.

THE ARCHITECTVRAL RECORD

CONTENTS

Vol. XLVII. No. 1   JANUARY, 1920   Serial No. 256

Editor: MICHAEL A. MIKKELSEN   *Contributing Editor:* HERBERT CROLY
Business Manager: J. A. OAKLEY

*Yearly Subscription—United States $3.00—Foreign $4.00—Single copies 35 cents. Entered
May 22, 1902, as Second Class Matter, at New York, N. Y. Member Audit Bureau of Circulation.*

PUBLISHED MONTHLY BY

THE ARCHITECTURAL RECORD COMPANY

115-119 WEST FORTIETH STREET, NEW YORK

F. T. MILLER, Pres.   W. D. HADSELL, Vice-Pres.   J. W. FRANK, Sec'y-Treas.   E. S. DODGE, Vice-Pres

Photographs by Kenneth Clark.

ENTRANCE—THE JAMES J. HILL REFERENCE LIBRARY,
ST. PAUL, MINN. ELECTUS D. LITCHFIELD, ARCHITECT.

THE
ARCHITECTVRAL
RECORD

VOLVME XLVII

NVMBER I

JANUARY, 1920

THE
JAMES J. HILL REFERENCE LIBRARY
AND THE ST PAUL PUBLIC LIBRARY
ST PAUL, MINN.

ELECTUS D. LITCHFIELD — ARCHITECT

By R. Clipston Sturgis

IT is one of the popular delusions about architecture that buildings of a certain class are all alike and that the architect's task is simply to put an exterior on a plan determined by previous experience; a school is simply a school, and one differs from another only in its appearance; and so a library is a library, and the chief difference is a matter of size.

Another common delusion is that architects may to advantage specialize as physicians do, and one be an expert on hospitals and another on libraries. As a matter of fact, no two problems are alike and may often differ in fundamentals; and one architect cannot devote himself exclusively, or even largely, to one class of building without acquiring a narrow and limited point of view which unfits him to render the best architectural service even in his own special field.

Each problem is a new one and must be studied with a mind fortified with experience, which makes sound judgment possible, but also open and ready to receive, and give due consideration to, all problems that are local and peculiar.

In the library at St. Paul Mr. Litchfield had a quite unusual situation, and the problems arising from it were peculiar to this one library, for it was a combination under one roof of a public library, built and administered by the city, and a reference library, built and administered by the generous gift of a private citizen. A building designed as a memorial or simply as the gift of a public spirited citizen is not infrequently made an opportunity for a lavish expenditure which in a building built at public cost would not be justified. Here the two were parts of a whole; and not the least difficult of Mr. Litchfield's tasks was to keep to the simplicity and directness of plan and elevation which was the right keynote of the public building, and yet not have anything which seemed inadequate or ungenerous even as an expression of the beauty and significance of Mr. Hill's great gift.

The popular view of extravagance in a building is expensive materials, carving and ornament without and within. These things do affect the cost, but the greatest extravagance is generally found in a diffuse plan, containing areas which serve no practical purpose but for show only. This library exhibits the true economy both of plan and of design. The plan is simple, straightforward, adapted to the definite uses of the two libraries, public and reference, contains no spaces that are not essential for work or for thoroughfare; and the exterior expresses this plan in a straightforward way, based on the simpler types of North Italian Renaissance, and reminiscent of the great palaces of Florence, Genoa and Rome.

The building is in the shape of a hollow square, again reminding one of these Italian palaces, but is open on the fourth side, the south; and here, enclosed by the wings of the library, is a park overlooking the river. One sees it, when developed, as an open air reading room, a wonderful adjunct to a library. The disposition of the building on its site is one of the fine achievements of those who planned this library. Using the plural in connection with any architectural problem is a statement of fact. None of us stands alone, and as we can generally pass the blame for mistakes to someone else, so we can always share with others the credit of what is good. In the case of this library Mr. Litchfield had the advantage of working with Mr. Soule, a recognized authority on library planning, and undoubtedly he contributed much to the excellence of the plan. Mr. Soule was a Brookline, Massachusetts, man and one recognizes the characteristic feature of Brookline, the open reading room, in the big room on the first floor.

Cooperation between architects and the authorities of the library is evident everywhere in this building; whether in the public library or in the reference library the same thing holds good, the building is planned for a perfectly definite work, thoroughly organized, clearly understood, and expressed in a simple, straightforward way in a plan that is necessarily unusual because the conditions are unusual. Credit therefore should be given to all of those connected officially with this work for its admirable performance.

The exterior is constructed of pink Tennessee marble, one of the most durable and also the most beautiful of our native marbles, excellently adapted for exterior work, both on account of its natural tone and the color it takes when exposed to the weather. It is to be hoped that it will not be subjected unduly to coal smoke, which would seriously injure its appearance. The great simplicity and restraint of the exterior are its keynote. The building expresses on the outside very clearly (1) its double character, in two entrances; (2) the great reading room running through from north to south, lit from both sides with large windows; (3) the reference library with its overhead light and its unbroken walls, and (4) the stack room, which, although it is expressed in the usual way with windows marking the aisles between stacks, is so handled on the outside as to carry through the motif of what might be called the *piano nobile* of the building. The two doorways on the north front have between them the entrance that goes to the lower level where the children's library is located. In addition to these main entrances on the front there are also the garden entrances on the south, and one may hope, perhaps not unreasonably, that this beautiful area, overlooking the river, will be so developed as to make it possible to use it as an outdoor reading

MAIN FRONT, FACING RICE PARK—THE JAMES J. HILL REFERENCE LIBRARY AND THE ST. PAUL PUBLIC LIBRARY, ST. PAUL, MINN. ELECTUS D. LITCHFIELD, ARCHITECT.

The long panel at the second story level on the side of the Hill Library is to be carved in low relief or to contain an appropriate quotation from Mr. Hill's writings.

room, or an open air hall where lectures and pageants and other educational activities might be given a beautiful and appropriate setting.

Entering the building one finds, as has already been intimated, that every space is occupied by nothing that has not its direct use in connection with the library itself. The lobby and the staircase hall are part and parcel of the same architectural feature, and are neither unduly large nor unduly lofty, and yet

the ceilings decorated plaster, and the marble is in simple, large, plain fields, with ornament well designed and well placed, but used as accents only. There is a business-like straightforwardness to the delivery room, and there is in the great reading room a sense of homeliness which gives it just the character that such a room should have.

One does not feel that the furniture is as excellent in design as is the building itself. The chairs and tables, rather

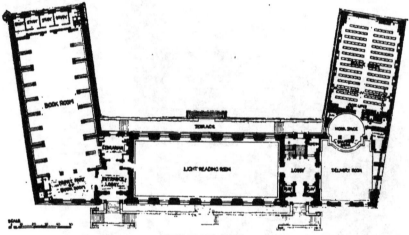

FIRST FLOOR PLAN.

ample so that there is no sense of crowding. On one side of the public library lobby is the delivery room, and on the other the room for light reading; so conveniently located are the two spaces that are most constantly used. The delivery room is large enough for its work, but none too large, so that here, as elsewhere in the library, you feel the restraint dictated by sound common-sense that has made posible this fundamental economy in space. When, however, it comes to a question of the finish of this space, a wise economy has dictated that only the best material should be used, and everything is substantial and permanent, requiring the least annual outlay for maintenance.

In general the walls are marble and

than following excellent established precedent, have a note of innovation, which injures instead of helps the beauty of the room.

One illustration shows the main stairs. Again simplicity has been the keynote of the design, but in some ways neither design nor workmanship are on the same plane as the marble and its carved ornament. The combination of turned spindles and balusters partly composed of twists, and panels of wrought iron, are not on a par with work of this sort that has been done elsewhere in this country.

Passing from the Public Library to the Hill Reference Library, one does not find the same convincing character in plan, perhaps due to the fact that this building is planned for a very great ex-

6

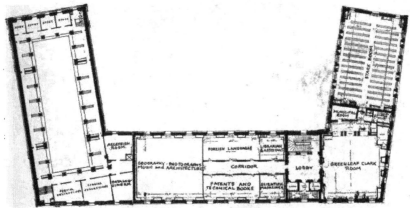

SECOND FLOOR PLAN.

tension of its book capacity, but at present it is a great, open three-story hall, top-lighted, with books arranged along the walls instead of on the alcove system, and with the open floor space now occupied very conspicuously by radiators, temporary one hopes. Studies occupy the southern end of the main book room, and the north end alone reaches an outside wall where outside light is possible, and there it has but two windows out of an exterior composition of three; the centre window of this composition not being *en axe* with the room, nor indeed parallel with the northerly colonade of the room, is a somewhat restless architectural unit in the composition, and one feels that it would have been better to have confined the lighting of this room entirely to the overhead light. There was probably some special reason for lighting the room in this way; generally speaking, however, where side light is available, as it was in this case, it is much pleasanter than overhead light. The room is dignified and well proportioned, and requires only complete occupation and use to be entirely convincing.

One illustration shows a corner of the librarian's room, which is a very charming example of the use of the early

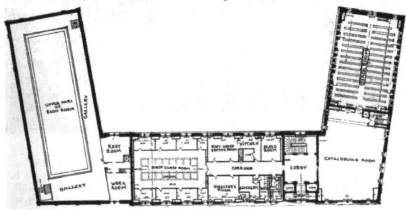

THIRD FLOOR PLAN.

7

REAR ENTRANCE — ST. PAUL PUBLIC LIBRARY, ST.
PAUL, MINN. ELECTUS D. LITCHFIELD, ARCHITECT.

COURT ELEVATION AND STACK WING—ST. PAUL PUBLIC LIBRARY; ST. PAUL, MINN; ELECTUS D. LITCHFIELD, ARCHITECT.

DETAIL OF DELIVERY ROOM—ST. PAUL
PUBLIC LIBRARY, ST. PAUL, MINN.
ELECTUS D. LITCHFIELD, ARCHITECT.

ONE. END OF THE DELIVERY ROOM, SHOWING THE
DELIVERY DESKS—ST. PAUL PUBLIC LIBRARY,
ST. PAUL, MINN. ELECTUS D. LITCHFIELD, ARCHITECT.

DETAIL OF ENTRANCE LOBBY—ST. PAUL
PUBLIC LIBRARY, ST. PAUL, MINN.
ELECTUS D. LITCHFIELD, ARCHITECT.

WINDOW IN LIGHT READING AND PERIODICAL
ROOM—ST. PAUL PUBLIC LIBRARY, ST. PAUL,
MINN. ELECTUS D. LITCHFIELD, ARCHITECT.

LIGHT READING AND PERIODICAL ROOM—ST. PAUL PUBLIC LIBRARY, ST. PAUL, MINN. ELECTUS D. LITCHFIELD, ARCHITECT.

GREENLEAF CLARK REFERENCE ROOM—ST. PAUL PUBLIC
LIBRARY, ST. PAUL, MINN. ELECTUS D. LITCHFIELD, ARCHITECT.

DETAIL OF STAIRWAY — ST. PAUL
PUBLIC LIBRARY, ST. PAUL, MINN.
ELECTUS D. LITCHFIELD, ARCHITECT.

ENTRANCE TO THE JAMES J. HILL REFERENCE
LIBRARY FROM LIGHT READING AND PERIODICAL
ROOM—ST. PAUL PUBLIC. LIBRARY, ST. PAUL,
MINN. ELECTUS D. LITCHFIELD, ARCHITECT.

ENTRANCE VESTIBULE—JAMES J. HILL
REFERENCE LIBRARY, ST. PAUL, MINN.
ELECTUS D. LITCHFIELD, ARCHITECT.

LIBRARIAN'S ROOM — JAMES J. HILL
REFERENCE LIBRARY, ST. PAUL, MINN.
ELECTUS D. LITCHFIELD, ARCHITECT.

ENTRANCE HALL OF GREAT BOOK ROOM—
JAMES J. HILL REFERENCE LIBRARY, ST. PAUL,
MINN. ELECTUS D. LITCHFIELD, ARCHITECT.

GREAT BOOK ROOM—JAMES J. HILL REFERENCE LIBRARY, ST.
PAUL, MINN. THE DISFIGURING RADIATORS ARE A TEM-
PORARY MAKESHIFT. ELECTUS D. LITCHFIELD, ARCHITECT.

DETAIL OF GREAT BOOK ROOM, SHOWING ARRANGEMENT OF STACKS—JAMES J. HILL REFERENCE LIBRARY, ST. PAUL, MINN. ELECTUS D. LITCHFIELD, ARCHITECT.

LOOKING FROM GREAT BOOK ROOM TOWARD ENTRANCE
HALL — JAMES J. HILL REFERENCE LIBRARY, ST.
PAUL, MINN. ELECTUS D. LITCHFIELD, ARCHITECT.

Italian Renaissance, having the same naif quality as is characteristic of our New England colonial work.

Taken altogether the library is a very notable addition to the group of fine libraries that has been growing up since McKim, in the Boston Library, and Carrere and Hastings, in New York, began to establish standards far above what we had known before their time; yet they were not so far ahead of a few things that had been done in earlier times: the old Athenaeum of Boston, now most beautifully extended and amplified, has served as an example for our later library work. We may therefore feel proud of the record made in this country, and yet at the same time remember that the generation that preceded us did much to make our success possible.

SECOND FLOOR GALLERY IN GREAT BOOK ROOM—JAMES J. HILL
REFERENCE LIBRARY, ST. PAUL, MINN.
Electus D. Litchfield, Architect.

PHILIP L. SMALL'S
ARCHITECTURAL SKETCHES

By

LEON V. SOLON

IN the September issue of The Architectural Record, the writer dealt with the lithographic work of David Roberts as a model for technique in rendering certain types of architectural design. It was maintained that the majority of rendered drawings lacked the elements of artistry, both in the presentation of the subject and in the artisic methods whereby it is represented; that they exhibited little appreciation of the adjustment of tone values, of the importance of a focal point in composition, of the massing of shadows, or the action of light; also, that the state of aesthetic undevelopment which is indicated by the absence of such essential qualities might be ameliorated by study of the work of Roberts and those contemporaries who pursued similar objectives. While the article on David Roberts was in the printer's hands, the sketches of Philip L. Small were brought to the writer's notice, who found that they embodied many of the characteristics of the British school of the early nineteenth century; had they come to hand earlier, they might have served as an example demonstrating the practical value of the Roberts school as a model for certain kinds of architectural notation.

The characteristics that form the compendium of qualities in the Roberts and Prout school exist in the work of Mr. Small to an extent rarely found after a lapse of so many years. The resemblance is all the more interesting by reason of the fact that the sketches of Mr. Small are obviously of spontaneous expression.

Precise definition encounters complication when attempting to confine the vagaries of any artistic term to a prescribed sphere of significance; the term "sketch" is no exception to that general rule. In the case of the architectural

sketch, we might demand certain qualifications from the standpoint of its value as a reference for accurate information. The most elemental requirements are accurate representation of the relative proportions of the integral parts of an architectural design, indication of scale in detail, and depth in projection. If the sketch is to qualify as a work of art, not merely as a notation of architectural data, additional qualities must be present, such as composition, chiaroscuro, texture in tone or line, atmospheric depth, and other attributes too many to enumerate or too abstract to define.

If we analyze the component qualities of Mr. Small's work, we find a faculty for contributing to effect in composition by subordinating secondary items; a skilful and precise touch, capable of expressing a wide range of feeling, and a tone sense. In the first illustration (Sketch No. 1), a lithographic proof, these qualities figure prominently. The towering mass of masonry dominates the composition, the deeply slitted windows emphasizing its solidity by the skilful indication of their recessed depth; the surface decoration of the tower is delineated with delicate precision. A tone suggestion of color in the roof structures is accessary to the impression of atmospheric depth of the heavens. The composition is excellent, proceeding from the vigor of strong pictorial perception, stimulated by a grandiose subject which did not depend on forced effects for dramatic presentation. The drab lack of interest which brands the façade of the typical stucco house of the by-ways of French towns serves, as ever, the purposes of an ideal foil for a neighboring masterpiece.

It is surprising that, in French provincial cities, civic movements should not have been instituted for the purchase and demolition of the wretched dwellings that so frequently obstruct the ground immediately surrounding magnificent ancient buildings. The purchase of such land and property would, in many cases, at a comparatively small cost, permit an unobstructed view from the clearing, which would add materially to the beauty of effect. There are many proofs that, previous to the war, civic pride was equal to the burden of such an undertaking, but it is probable that the necessity was not felt, through familiarity with the existing view. It is difficult for natives to visualize an improvement from the point of view of the stranger, whose imagination is not handicapped by old acquaintance.

In a side street of Chartres (Sketch No. 2) the artist's pencil has disported itself over the loss of verticalness which affects inferior structures as they gain in years. Bulging façades with ominously overhanging pediments, leaky roofs, decrepit doorways and warped window-frames, for a moment lure the sketcher's fancy by the harmonious disorder of their varied planes; but the architect in the artist comes to attention when he undertakes to transmit to paper the stately transept, whose picturesqueness and beauty are the product of a deliberate calculation of genius which could only be depreciated by the subsidence of decay that endows the banal with picturesque interest. In this sketch there is a remarkable correspondence of feeling to that which characterizes the old British lithographs, both in the interpretation of detail and in the choice of the centre of composition.

In Sketch No. 3, the subject is a church and street in Nice. The development of transparency in deep shadows by the use of reflected light gives this sketch a particular technical interest. The moment is well chosen; and the effect is one peculiar to the Riviera at certain seasons, when the sun shines on fleeing clouds, chased across the sky by the piercing mistral. The tone quality of the study is rich and suggestive, handled skilfully to the development of contrast. The classic character of the church design is indicated with exquisite delicacy;

the form of caps, columns, architraves and other features is conveyed by a species of suggestion which can proceed only from an intimate knowledge of the precise conformation of the detail rendered. One feels that amplification of detail is merely a matter of scale in Mr. Small's studies, and that in this instance its subordination is calculated to attain atmospheric quality, which has been realized without sacrificing those subtleties of proportion in masses held as vital attributes of structural beauty by the architect.

A side street in Nice (Sketch No. 4) was evidently attractive as an architectural divertissement, in which freedom of line and tone quality were the motif developed. Disrepair in latticed window shutters and the family laundry, always at the artist's professional disposal, atone for an almost negligible interest by the admirable manner in which these objects invariably fulfil a pictorial function.

In Sketch No. 5, a church and tower in Nimes, Mr. Small has attempted to translate into a black and white equivalent the charm of ancient masonry. The classic doorway is delightfully indicated; but the treatment of the square tower is detrimental to the value of this study— a criticism prompted by appreciation of the artist's capacity, rather than by the spirit of censure.

The Pont du Gard (Sketch No. 6) is an excellent type of architectural notation, direct, accurate and simple in execution. The principle of structure is legible in the concisest statement which in no way detracts from the dignity of that noble span of superimposed arches. The effect of light upon the aqueduct arches, which are detached against the sky, is conveyed by quality of line; sharply projected shadows, with a minimum degree of definition of the masses catching the sun's rays, conveys an impression of sunshine; the reflections in the water are less sympathetically handled.

Another method of treatment, inspired by the round tower of Carcassonne (Sketch No. 7) reveals the professional instinct of the architect for precise statement of structural conditions acting as

SKETCH NO. 1. BY PHILIP L. SMALL.

SKETCH NO. 2. BY PHILIP L. SMALL.

SKETCH NO. 3. BY PHILIP L. SMALL.

SKETCH NO. 4. BY PHILIP L. SMALL.

SKETCH NO. 5. BY PHILIP L. SMALL.

Le Pont du Gard - Nimes - Dec.1915.

SKETCH NO. 6. BY PHILIP L. SMALL.

CARCASSONNE · DEC · 25 · 1916

SKETCH NO. 8. BY PHILIP L. SMALL.

CARCASSONNE.
DEC·25·1918

SKETCH NO. 7. BY PHILIP L. SMALL.

Church - Souzay
Sept 3, 1918.

SKETCH NO. 9. BY PHILIP L. SMALL.

Church at Les Lutteaux
On the Loire
Aug 15, 1918.

SKETCH NO. 10. BY PHILIP L. SMALL.

a stabilizing influence to the exuberance of the artist, whose enthusiasm for an inspiring subject, abetted by manual dexterity, only too often reacts to depreciate the value of the sketch as a reference document.

The rendering of the ramparts (Sketch No. 8) is weak in composition, but is reproduced for the clever indication of detail in the machicolated tower.

The churches of Souzay (Sketch No. 9) and of Les Tuffeaux (Sketch No. 10) are rendered in a manner which is primarily architectural in feeling. There is a delicacy of detail treatment in the former sketch which is necessarily destroyed by reduction and a process screen; the detail of the spire windows is so truthfully and clearly recorded, despite freedom in transcription, that it would be almost possible to reconstruct them accurately from their indication.

In these sketches we welcome particularly the spirit of research into the elements of effect and a complete freedom from those hackneyed methods in technique which impress the brand of monotony upon so many of the more pretentious renderings of today. Mr.

Small obviously prefers to regard an ancient wall, discolored by disintegration and hoary with lichen, as a subject for study in tone gradation, enriching areas of subordinate architectural interest; it is not to him an irresistible temptation to foist Herbert Railton's little diversion again upon us, which, delightful in its original novelty, has degenerated through innumerable borrowings into an irritating shop worn formula.

When studying the play of light on architectural members, Mr. Small has earnestly sought to depict effect as he saw it before him, shunning the superficial and mechanical method of parodists of the Whistler manner, who assume that light eliminates form and detail and that projected shadows should be the only evidence of the presence of solid bodies. Such methods are barriers to progress, and are the marks by which the copyist is recognized. In the practice of the graphic and plastic arts an invariable law controls the development of individuality in interpretation: it is the reward for a conscientious avoidance of ready-made fashions, when knowledge is being sought in nature.

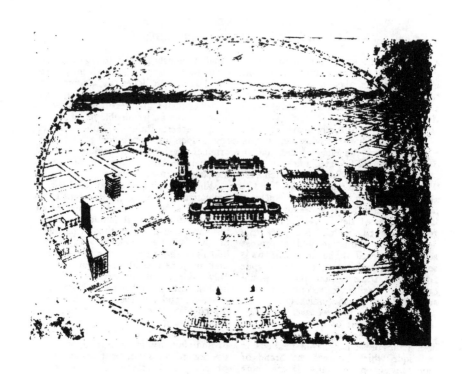

PROPOSED MEMORIAL CIVIC CENTER, SEATTLE, WASH.

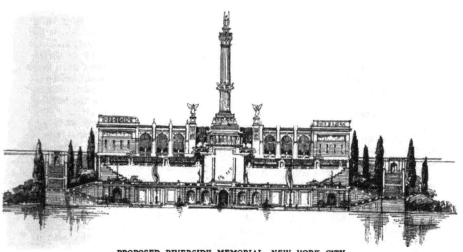

PROPOSED RIVERSIDE MEMORIAL, NEW YORK CITY.
Donn Barber, Architect.

WAR MEMORIALS

PART II

Community Buildings for Large Cities

By
Charles Over Cornelius

THE community idea has taken so firm a hold upon the popular imagination that not only in the smaller communities do we find evidence of its influence but in the larger cities as well community movements show definite activity. Since community houses of the usual type — centers for social, recreational, and educational activities—depend largely for their effectiveness upon a close personal interest on the part of their supporters, this effectiveness varies in inverse proportion to the size of the community, with the result that in great cities it is necessary either to change the form and use of the community building or definitely to break up into smaller groups the

public which will use such buildings, furnishing each local group with its own community or neighborhood home, which may or may not be affiliated with other similar houses in the same city.

We see therefore in the larger cities two things happening where the desire is present for a community memorial in honor of the dead of the recent war.

First, there is the ambitious project of some sort of community center for the whole city; and this by reason of the large number of people who will use it must perforce take the form of a great arena or auditorium, capable of seating thousands of spectators. This great hall, in some cases, forms the nucleus of a new city plan in localities where it is still possible to change or develop the city layout in conformance with a pre-arranged scheme. Again, it may be possible within the limits of a park or on a waterfront, to erect a stadium whose use will be free to all and whose seating capacity may be adequate. But in any case where a whole city is to share in the creation of a utilitarian memorial, it must of necessity be on a monumental scale which will render it a fitting memorial to large numbers of the dead as well as of use to greater numbers of the living.

The second form of memorial is the neighborhood house in which a limited number of persons within a small radius share in the creation and use of a building whose characteristics partake largely of the nature of the usual community house. The method of raising the national army has created a natural foundation for these organizations, for the community spirit shown in the "block festivals" and the service flags dedicated to groups of men from restricted localities which were blessed and hung in the thoroughfares in various sections of American cities are all symptoms of this community spirit which is so strongly marked in American life today.

There is a subdivision of this second group which forms almost a category of its own, buildings erected by certain organizations as memorials to their members who have fallen in the war.

In certain communities these groups are too small to finance separate and self-sustained buildings for themselves and may find a place in the general community house. But in large cities such organizations as the American Legion or local army divisions, whose memberships, numbering thousands, are comparatively well concentrated, frequently will desire to erect memorial clubhouses where the memories and traditions of their service may be perpetuated.

The forms which urban architecture customarily take render the characteristics of dignity and formality not difficult of attainment in the design. And in the arrangement of the building the prob-

lem comes down to an efficient and practical scheme for use. In the large buildings first mentioned the more simple the scheme and the less complicated its functions the greater will be its usefulness. Such varied functions as it may be necessary to combine should be closely related or their accommodation so ingeniously arranged as to make the building work to its full extent.

City plans, of which some such memorial building forms a nucleus, are of particular pertinence in the West and Middle West, where cities are still growing by leaps and bounds and may yet be directed into the proper channels of growth by care and forethought. Such schemes are suggested for cities of so varying a size as St. Louis, San Francisco, La Crosse, Wisconsin, and Seattle, Washington. In St. Louis this plan involves a complete reorganization of the city's public works, including river-front and water-supply improvement, public building and group plans, park and playground systems, bridges and viaducts, a municipal auditorium, markets, hospitals, and housing. An ambitious scheme, but one of the utmost promise for St. Louis and for the future of other American cities who follow in her train before it is too late. Part of this scheme has already been carried out. An equally ambitious plan is that of San Francisco, which would establish an office for the study of the future growth of the city in all of its ramifications, economic. industrial, and artistic.

At La Crosse the Memorial Commission, in discussing an immediate Peace Memorial, found in its study of the subject a need of expert advice in the solution of a general city plan which should include not only the placing of the new memorial but also the relocation of the railroads, depot and public building groups, and the fixing of a zoning system of building regulations.

At Seattle the scheme for development is principally concentrated upon the erection of a noble group of municipal buildings, forming a memorial civic center.

Foremost of the schemes for a great arena or convention hall is the tentative

PROPOSED RIVERSIDE MEMORIAL, NEW YORK CITY.
Donn Barber, Architect.

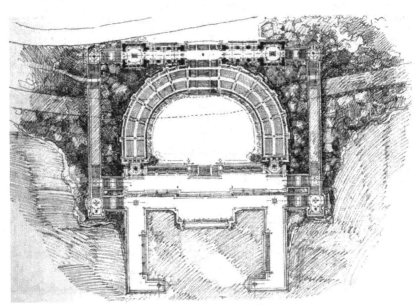

PROPOSED RIVERSIDE MEMORIAL, NEW YORK CITY.
Donn Barber, Architect.

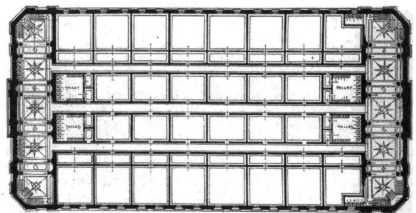

UPPER FLOOR, WITH MEMORIAL AND CHAPTER ROOMS—PROPOSED VICTORY
MEMORIAL, NEW YORK CITY.
Henry Beaumont Hertz and T. Markoe Robertson, Associate Architects.

suggestion for such a structure in New York City, urged by one of the members of the Mayor's New York City Memorial Committee. The location of the building as at present conceived is at the corner of Park Avenue and Forty-second Street, facing the Grand Central Station, on the site which has already been called Pershing Square. Undoubtedly all New Yorkers would prefer to see that and the opposite corner made into an open park which would allow at least a decently spacious, although not adequate, approach to the Terminal; but since such a scheme seems totally outside the realm of probability, the next best use for the ground would be for this great memorial hall. The plan devised covers the whole block between Park and Lexington Avenues, Forty-first and Forty-second Streets and contains three stories. On the ground floor would be an exhibition hall, 320 feet long by 200 feet wide, with entrances from all sides and foyers to

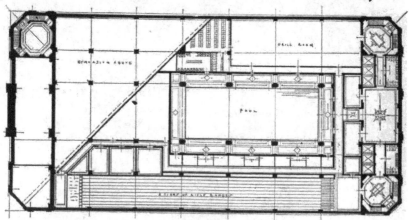

BASEMENT—PROPOSED VICTORY MEMORIAL, NEW YORK CITY.
Henry Beaumont Hertz and T. Markoe Robertson, Associate Architects.

PROPOSED VICTORY MEMORIAL, FACING THE GRAND CENTRAL STATION, NEW YORK CITY.
Henry Beaumont Hertz and T. Markoe Robertson, Associate Architects.

the east and west. In the basement would be a huge swimming-pool, a gymnasium, rifle ranges and every device needful for athletic and military recreation. On the second floor, thirty feet above the Forty-second Street level, would be the arena or convention hall, covering the whole block. It would be surrounded by tiers of seats and bear in its architectural form all the elements of a great coliseum. The seating capacity at its maximum would be of about ten thousand people without the use of balconies.

The floor above this arena, subdivided by the gigantic trusses necessary to support the roof, would be cut into rooms for the many activities which would suggest themselves, while the roof itself, enclosed with wire netting, would form

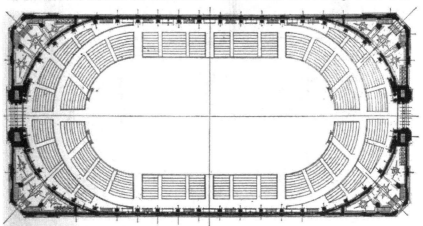

GRAND ARENA ON MAIN FLOOR—PROPOSED VICTORY MEMORIAL, NEW YORK CITY.
Henry Beaumont Hertz and T. Markoe Robertson, Associate Architects.

43

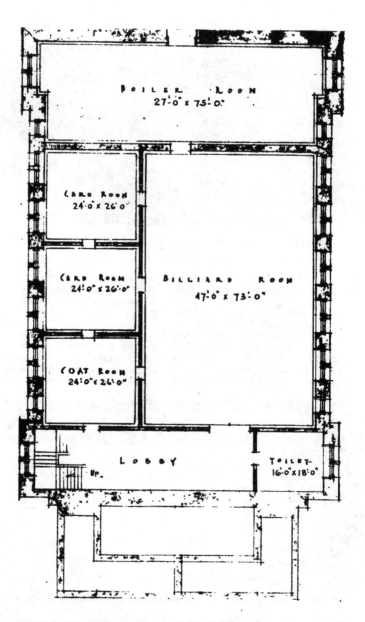

BASEMENT—PROPOSED MEMORIAL BUILDING FOR THE AMERICAN LEGION, BRONX BOROUGH, NEW YORK CITY. STARRET & VAN VLECK AND WILLIAM F. DEEGAN, ASSOCIATE ARCHITECTS.

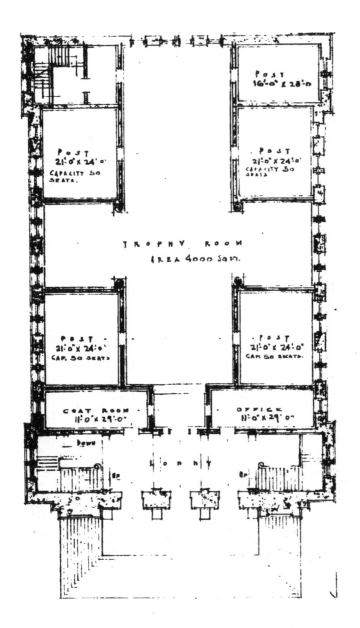

FIRST FLOOR—PROPOSED MEMORIAL BUILDING FOR THE AMERI-
CAN LEGION, BRONX BOROUGH, NEW YORK CITY. STARRET & VAN
VLECK AND WILLIAM F. DEEGAN, ASSOCIATE ARCHITECTS.

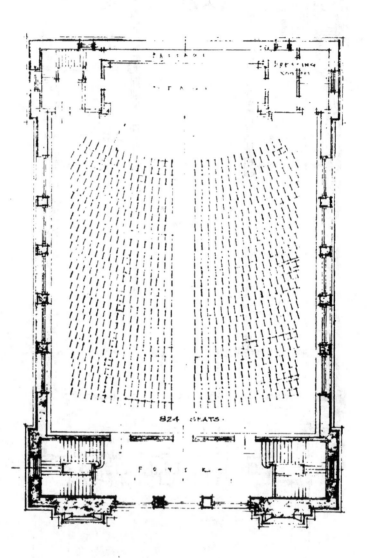

SECOND FLOOR—PROPOSED MEMORIAL BUILDING FOR THE AMERI-
CAN LEGION, BRONX BOROUGH, NEW YORK CITY. STARRET & VAN
VLECK AND WILLIAM F. DEEGAN, ASSOCIATE ARCHITECTS.

PROPOSED MEMORIAL BUILDING FOR THE AMERICAN LEGION, BRONX BOROUGH, NEW YORK CITY. STARRET & VAN VLECK AND WILLIAM F. DEEGAN, ASSOCIATE ARCHITECTS.

a spacious playground, which is much needed in this part of the city. The style of the building would harmonize with that of the Grand Central Terminal, whose base and cornice levels would be carried out in it, thus giving a homogeneity to the group and affording connection with the viaduct leading to the esplanade before the Terminal. The project contains so many superlatives— the "largest" convention hall and swimming-pool in the world, for instance— that it might appear to be too pretentious an effort to memorialize anything

A plan for a convention hall not dissimilar from that suggested for New York comes from Seattle, Washington. This building forms part of the memorial civic center about which will be grouped the usual municipal buildings and museums of science and art. The center of the whole will be a great plaza with a suitable monument or fountain in the center and flanked on one side by the Memorial Auditorium. This building is planned to contain both a large auditorium and a smaller theatre or opera house. Both of these rooms are

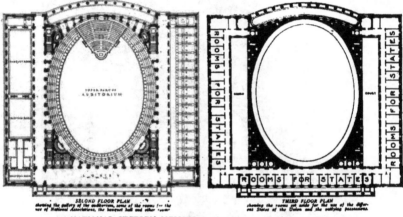

NATIONAL VICTORY MEMORIAL BUILDING, WASHINGTON, D. C.
Tracy & Swartwout, Architects.

but vainglory. But with reflection upon the urgent need for such a convention hall and the convenient access which would be had to the building from all parts of the city and surrounding country, it would seem to be a project worthy of the highest commendation and encouragement.

Another New York improvement of a monumental nature is the Riverside scheme of Donn Barber for the locality just north of Grant's Tomb. This contemplates the erection of a great monumental staircase, stadium and boat landings and, while serving a much more limited use than the memorial hall, is a magnificent and dignified memorial, in which a nice balance has been struck between beauty and utility.

served by the same stage, of a size which would allow it to be subdivided to suit various performances. The plan is simple and straightforward, with no effort to incorporate space for unrelated activities.

The Seattle scheme for a festival hall is very similar in its essence to the auditorium at Oakland, California. This latter building is not a war memorial, but since it contains so many points of interest and suggestion for memorial committees, its mention here may not be inappropriate. In plan it will be seen to contain both a large auditorium or arena and theatre, with one large stage between. The long exhibition corridor is lined with booths from which some revenue may be derived. On its upper floor are

PERSPECTIVE VIEW FROM THE MALL—NATIONAL VICTORY MEMORIAL BUILDING,
WASHINGTON, D. C.
Tracy & Swartwout, Architects.

an art gallery and a ball-room with dependencies and a small stage. The seating capacity of the arena is increased by a broad balcony as well as removable seats on the floor.

The National Victory Memorial Building in Washington, D. C., while similar in many respects to the two buildings which we have just considered, by virtue of its location in the capital and its dedication to all the heroes of the war, partakes of an especial impressiveness. On

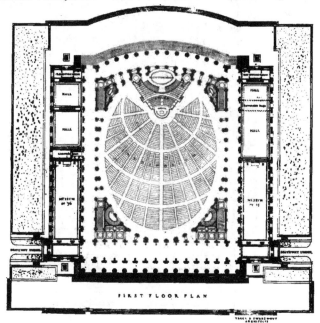

FIRST FLOOR PLAN—NATIONAL VICTORY MEMORIAL BUILDING,
WASHINGTON, D. C.
Tracy & Swartwout, Architects.

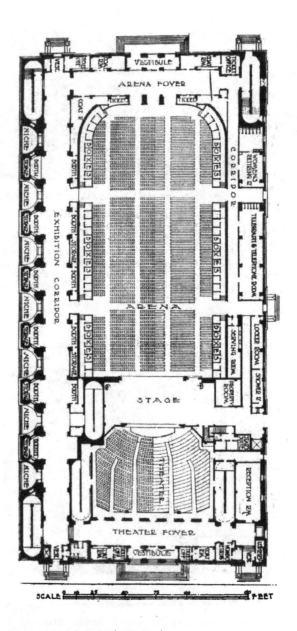

FIRST FLOOR PLAN—AUDITORIUM, OAKLAND,
CAL. JOHN J. DONOVAN, ARCHITECT; HENRY
HORNBOSTEL,   CONSULTING   ARCHITECT.

AUDITORIUM, OAKLAND, CAL.
John J. Donovan, Architect; Henry Hornbostel, Consulting Architect.

its main floor is an auditorium, elliptical in plan, surrounded by spacious corridors and flanked by war museums. To the left is the Museum of '76, in which will be displayed relics of the War of the Revolution, while to the right is the Museum of '17 where similar relics of the World War may be collected and displayed. There seems to be a particular appropriateness in bringing together under one roof collections of objects reminiscent of two distinct crises in the history of the United States and in placing in the midst of these collections a great auditorium which will serve as a meeting-place for the discussion and resolution of the movements which must be solved in a democracy by the meeting of many minds. In upper stories of the building are various rooms for national association headquarters, a great banqueting hall, with reception rooms, and, in the attic story, rooms set aside for the use of the different States of the Union and outlying possessions. This memorial, which should enlist the interest and support of every citizen of the United States, has been allotted a fine site on the north side of the Mall, where it will be fittingly surrounded by monumental buildings in a proper setting of trees.

Three buildings of the auditorium type, but designed for smaller cities than those already considered, are the Soldiers and Sailors Memorial Building at Newark, New Jersey, and two proposed Memorial Buildings for Mankato, Minnesota. These all contain an auditorium, a memorial hall or museum, and certain features which give them some of the facilities of a community house. All these are tentative schemes, but show at least that the memorial committees in these towns have decided upon utilitarian memorials as appropriate for their local purpose.

Typical of the class of building falling partially within our second group is the proposed clubhouse of the American Legion Post of the Bronx. This very pleasing design incorporates some of the features of a clubhouse in a building dominated by its large auditorium. The exterior has much of the monumental and memorial character, which is imperative, and in itself is a satisfying piece of design. The high arched windows of the auditorium dominate the façades, the first floor forming merely a strong base-

51

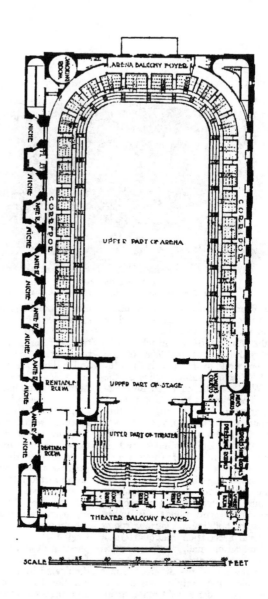

SECOND FLOOR PLAN—AUDITORIUM, OAK-
LAND, CAL. JOHN J. DONOVAN, ARCHITECT;
HENRY HORNBOSTEL, CONSULTING ARCHITECT.

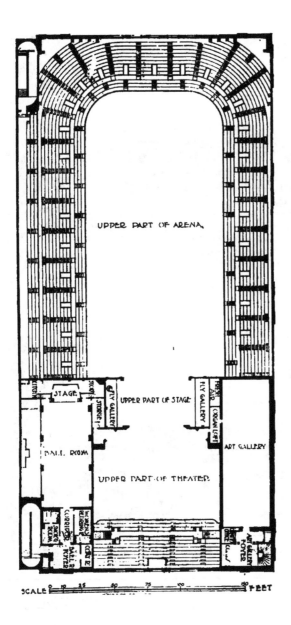

UPPER PART OF ARENA

STAGE FLY GALLERY UPPER PART OF STAGE FLY GALLERY ORGAN LOFT

STORAGE

BALL ROOM

ART GALLERY

UPPER PART OF THEATER

DRESSING ROOM CORRIDOR WOMENS RETIRING BALL ROOM FOYER ART GALLERY FOYER

SCALE 0 10 25 50 75 100 150 FEET

THIRD FLOOR PLAN — AUDITORIUM, OAK-
LAND, CAL. JOHN J. DONOVAN, ARCHITECT;
HENRY HORNBOSTEL, CONSULTING ARCHITECT.

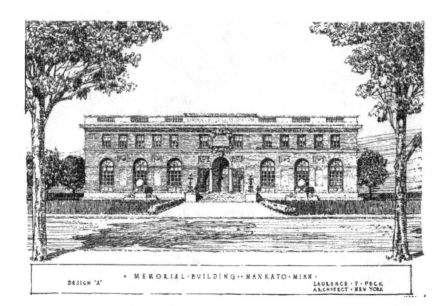

· MEMORIAL · BUILDING · MANKATO · MINN ·
DESIGN "A"
LAURENCE · F · PECK
ARCHITECT · NEW YORK

· MEMORIAL · BUILDING · MANKATO · MINN ·
DESIGN "B"
LAURENCE · F · PECK
ARCHITECT · NEW YORK

ALTERNATIVE DESIGNS FOR ME-
MORIAL BUILDING, MANKATO, MINN.
LAURENCE F. PECK, ARCHITECT.

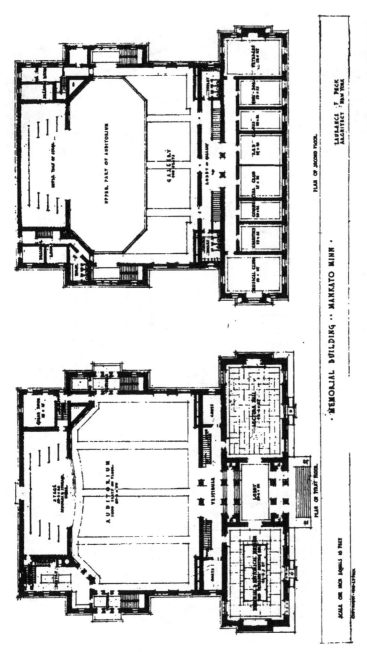

PROPOSED MEMORIAL BUILDING, MANKATO, MINN. LAURENCE F. PECK, ARCHITECT.

PROPOSED MEMORIAL BUILDING, MANKATO, MINN.
Mann & MacNeille, Architects.

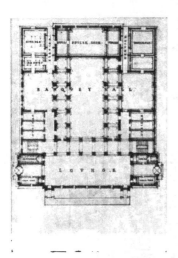

BASEMENT.

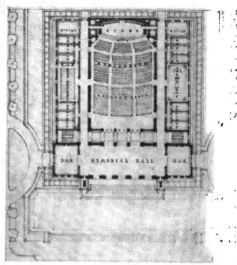

FIRST FLOOR.

ment story. On the interior, this auditorium occupies the entire second floor and is served by the lobby on both floors, through which access may be had to it without entering the club portion of the building. The first floor is given over to a trophy room, which would form in a way a memorial museum, and from it open four meeting rooms for the posts of the association. In the well lighted basement are billiard and card rooms, forming the club element in the scheme.

It is altogether an eminently workable plan; little that is unessential appears, and the whole is treated with breadth and simplicity.

These, then, will serve to illustrate the general types of memorials which are taking form in the larger cities of America. Their adoption is being urged, particularly by the War Camp Community Service, whose Bureau of Memorial Buildings has constituted itself a clearing house of information for architects

56

PROPOSED MEMORIAL FESTIVAL HALL, SEATTLE, WASH.

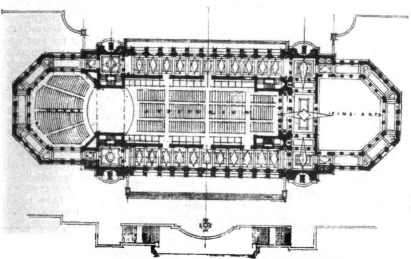

PLAN—PROPOSED MEMORIAL FESTIVAL HALL, SEATTLE, WASH.

and committees interested in the erection of permanent memorials. The Bureau's collection of photographs has furnished the illustrations accompanying this and the preceding article, and the literature which it publishes contains much of helpful suggestion in the practical details which enter into the establishment of community buildings. Many special subdivisions under these two general types will be found, but all unite in establishing primarily a dignified memorial to the dead, with some very important portion devoted to a commemorative hall in which inscriptions may be placed or trophies hung, and in all of them we find a space for a large concourse of people in keeping with the social and democratic idea of community life.

A theatre or opera house, provision for dramatic or musical enjoyment, is found in many of these buildings; and all these units, with such additional features as economic arrangement or local necessity demands, mingle in producing a dignified whole, serving the two-fold purpose of a memorial to the heroic dead through the constantly renewed tribute of the living.

57

SOME PRINCIPLES OF SMALL HOUSE DESIGN

PART III ～ PLANNING

By

JOHN TAYLOR BOYD, Jr.

THE first two articles of the series dealt with the principles of design of the plot of land on which the small house is located. In planning the house itself, these principles of the laying out of the lot should not be forgotten. The lot arrangement of roadways, paths, service, and of drying yard, of terraces, lawns, gardens, outbuildings, largely decides the essential location of the main rooms of the house and the placing of entrances. For these reasons, to plan the house without constantly thinking of the sub-division of the lot is to begin at the end and work towards the beginning.

The neglect of lot-planning is a main defect in the design of American small homes. Before entering too closely into the details of the arrangement of the house itself, it is worth while to ask, Are there other fundamental defects in house design that might be avoided? Does the American small house of today meet fully our ideal of the American home?

Such questions may seem remote from the technical side of architecture, yet they should have full weight in any treatment of the principles of planning. Not only are we apt to view architecture too technically, but we have need of a clear ideal standard to aid in measuring our work. Unless there is some good standard, writing about house design will degenerate into disputes concerning the relative value of details or the merits of current formulae. ·

If one considers American houses as a whole, there is no doubt that they possess many admirable qualities. The best of them answer their purposes well. They satisfy practical needs, and in re-spect to art, they possess the architectural virtues of correct mass and proportioning, well-executed details, of harmonious color and texture. Still, great numbers of them could be better than they are; and even among the best one may note that motives are repeated mechanically, and that a tendency exists toward formula and recipe. Now, it may seem a severe judgment, but it is true, that in many ways our houses lack inspiration. Rarely do they embody true imagination, and rarely are they creative works of art. These shortcomings are better appreciated by such artists as are not architects, by painters or sculptors; for these view architecture broadly and clearly, are not confused by difficulties of technique or of detail, nor are they prejudiced by custom. I have often pointed out how architecture suffers because designers do not take the artists' point of view in mass and color and details of decoration; how in such matters the painter is apt to have a truer eye. This is a fault that can hardly be wondered at, because today the different arts are so separate and so professionalized that each is apt to be one-sided, and thus it may float off from the main current in the stream of art. When it does drift away, the other arts note its turning off the course before it notes it itself.

It should be realized that many artists feel that architecture lacks inspiration, that it imitates rather than creates in the modern spirit. They seek an American style. This last irritates architects, be it said, and opens up a controversy that I do not intend to enter upon here, except to remark that American house architecture is nearer the idea of a national

58

American style than is usually admitted. What can be said fairly is this—there must be some reason in the view that much contemporary architecture is commonplace and lacks inspiration, for if it were truly inspired it would fit conditions and meet demands made upon it in that extraordinarily successful, exquisitely sensitive way of a perfect work of art. Then the American style of architecture would be here, and there would be no further argument about it.

Therefore, house designs should be tested to see if they cannot meet conditions and demands made upon them in a more perfect way, in fine, free and full measure. They should express the fundamental principles of art and decoration and not become sidetracked in professional technique. If they are to meet this ideal, they must seek inspiration, attaining it first in the plan. The plan is the big thing in architecture. It really embodies art more than do either elevations or the decoration—a truth which architects know better than either fellow-artists or the public. The elevations are only the looking-glasses through which the art of the plan is seen; they are the geometry created before the eye by raising the planes up on the lines of the plans. It is the art-forms of the plan that furnish most of the art of the elevations. This is a principle that is fundamental, and the difficulty of carrying it out in practice has ruined many a design. It is naturally most difficult for a client to read a plan—he has trouble enough to grasp details of practical arrangement and of mechanical appliances of heating, lighting and plumbing—and see beyond the obvious details of axes, vistas and of such placing of openings and wall spaces as will allow certain schemes of decoration to be carried out in an elevation or in a room. What escapes him is the hidden import of the plan, those great essentials of mass, proportion, variety, interest, charm, the qualities that secure creative art and personality in a plan, all those combinations and adjustments made in order to attain success, and which, if ruthlessly disturbed, will throw out of balance the whole mechan-

ism of a true work of art—adjustments that effect the design outdoors as well as indoors, the form and color of walls and roofs and chimneys and projections and terraces, elements which must be coordinated with walls and outbuildings and large trees and with the accidents of the surface of the ground. This natural handicap of the client probably causes to a large extent the prevalence of formal and symmetrical art, for symmetry and geometrical balance on an axis is the most obvious form of art there is, readily accepted by the public because it is so easily understood. Thus the plan is the thing. Its essential hidden qualities or art should ever be kept in mind if the design of our houses is to achieve inspiration.

Therefore, the aim should be to test the plan to see how far it measures up to the American ideal of a home. The house plan is a symbol of American life —of American life in its most intimate and elemental relations. It is in fact bound up with the twentieth century American conception of the family, our native symbol of one of the most primitive facts in society, the ancient idea of the hearth-fire. In this moulding of our national hearth-fire many factors have a hand. The more remote ones may have only a brief notice, for they are fairly well understood by architects, who have learned them in the professional schools and have run against them betimes in their practice. First among these factors come geographical and climatic necessities, practical needs, fixing use of materials and methods of construction, determining how the hearth shall be protected against extreme heat or cold or storms. Out of construction needs and local materials at hand grow artistic expression and form in decoration, surfaces, color and textures. Prof. Fiske Kimball has shown in The Architectural Record (October, 1919) how the house plan is compacted in northern parts of the country, where deep foundations and steep roofs are expensive, and where a cellar is necessary for a heating plant. In the south the house may spread over the ground, without much cellar, with the comfort of shaded courts and terraces and loggias and sleeping porches. Roofs may be flatter in the south. Windows may be smaller, with thicker walls and higher ceilings to keep out excessive heat, though this manner of protection against heat is not yet so widely developed in the far south of the United States as in other hot areas of the world, except in California, where the influence of climate is apparent in the best house plans.

Equally important are the effects of sunshine and of landscape on the house plan. They are all too little appreciated by architects and are ignored except in a few rare instances. They affect the elevations of course, but are fundamental in the plan, for they help decide proportions of mass and color, contrasts of broad wall spaces with openings. They influence the important decision whether the exterior is be a design highly worked up in itself, a diversified unit dominating its surroundings, enframed by the landscape and by the foliage; or whether it is be plain, serving as a screen or foil for foliage—a bold mass of color in a landscape of dramatic character, like the rustic villas of Italy. If one desires a more thorough explanation of this painter's principle, he will find it in the November issue of The Architectural Record under the title of "Color of Architecture in Sunshine." It may be said that the house conceived as a simple mass of color in a neighborhood will figure more and more, because houses are being built in groups for the sake of economy, and this means that group design will develop. It is an essential factor, this neighborhood beauty. It is the charm of those wonderful old American villages that still remain, where one sees that the houses are remarkable, not so much through great individual merit, but because their builders, in a perfectly naive, simple

PLAN OF MARMION, KING GEORGE COUNTY, VA. LATE SEVENTEENTH CENTURY.
Reproduced from "Brick Architecture of the Colonial Period in Maryland and Virginia" by Permission.

way knew how to fit them harmoniously into the picture made by the neighborhood. Group design will influence the house plan, for it affects both the character and shape of the mass of the house and the placing of its walls.

Clearly, though these factors seem remote, there is much chance to improve the house plan in these four respects—in remembering the art of the plan, in making it respond to climatic conditions, in viewing with the painter's eye landscape and sunshine and atmosphere, and in making the house a unit in the group design of the neighborhood.

When we consider the house as but a unit in a neighborhood, we are very near the American ideal of family life that must be expressed in the plan. Here it is worth while to hold the mirror up to the ideal of the American home, trying to picture it more clearly in order that the house may be a perfectly expressed symbol of it. Now what are the traditions of an American family? Our national characteristics which mould these traditions are now well-defined, the war has made us more conscious of them, and designers are striving with increasing success to incorporate them in homes. The American family ideal demands much of a house. It requires satisfactions that are practical and others that are emotional. On the practical side there are twentieth century standards of utility, comfort, convenience of arrangement, and the use of mechanical equipment for economy of labor and for sanitation. The American wishes his house to be as efficient as possible, and to this extent he looks upon it as a business organization and a machine.

Under pre-war conditions, the practical side of the family ideal was realized pretty well as the result of three generations of improvement. Unfortunately,

EAST FRONT—MOUNT AIRY, RICHMOND, VA. BUILT IN 1750.
Reproduced, by Permission, from "Brick Architecture of the Colonial Period in Maryland and Virginia," by Lewis A. Coffin, Jr., and Arthur C. Holden; the Architectural Book Publishing Company, Publishers.

the war has brought such changes that much further improvement and readjustment may be needful. As barely a year has passed since the military operations stopped, it is too early for us to realize the full meaning of the new conditions, though some of their possibilities may be pointed out. Whatever the result of post-war changes turns out to be, the practical side of the home will be no great problem, for mechanical difficulties never stump the American for long. It is the part of the home that is not so strictly practical which should be clearly grasped, as clearly grasped as intangible things may be.

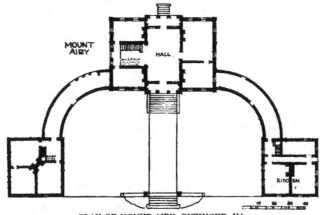

PLAN OF MOUNT AIRY, RICHMOND, VA.

What are the emotional demands that the American family ideal require to be satisfied in a home? A difficult question, indeed, but it demands some answer. As far as tradition goes, the ideal of the American is founded on the ancient biblical virtues which his unyielding Puritan ancestors have bestowed on him. They are the virtues of the Ten Commandments and of the Sermon on the Mount. On this simple ideal of the elementary virtues he has built the powerful ideal of the Anglo-Saxon pioneer, of the worth of vigorous men, who seek opportunity on a new continent. Strength, freedom, optimism and generosity are his. Direct, broad, self-reliant, intelligent, ingenious—he is a true individualist. He is much a child of nature, a boy of a new race, eager for health and play. The bald sternness of the earlier Americans is now clothed with a lighter side; and he loves good cheer, humor, gayety, coming and going, sunlight, outdoor charm of space, of landscape, of trees and flowers, of gatherings and sports. Although he is an intense individualist, he is at the same time an essential democrat. He feels himself a part of his neighborhood, and strict ideas of the privacy of his home still allow him to receive his friends there. In fact there will be occasions when his house will never be large enough for his hospitality, yet ceremony and formality —real formality as it obtains in some other parts of the world—have no attractions for the American. With characteristic irreverence, he is apt to associate them with funerals. He has, however, a true understanding of the value of kindliness and good manners. These are some of his most striking qualities, of which the world is well aware, but there is a further one that marks him from the rest of the races of mankind more than any other, one which is well understood, but for which so far no better term has been found than "pep."

All these characteristics of the individual American combine, with social customs and habits and such fashions as prevail at the moment, to mould that ideal of the American family that should be clearly and imaginatively symbolized in our homes. To the extent that this ideal is finely interpreted, our homes become real works of art. This they are coming more and more to do, for they are taking on increasing form, which is another American quality not so well understood. In early times our forefathers had an exquisite, if very simple, love of form and color in both architecture and furnishings. Their descendants lost this faculty through most of the nineteenth century, but the last two generations have seen it retrieved. American women show it keenly, or perhaps more frankly. Thus, in view of this inherited and redeveloped capacity for form, it seems safe to conclude that Americans will evince an increasing interest in the artistic side of their family life, that they will seek more art in their homes. They will demand an art that meets their needs practically, that expresses their hearth-fire ideal, and each year with surer and surer instinct they will reject the false and the superfluous.

Consequently, designers must instil into themselves the American ideal, while those of them to whom architecture is principally a dealing in wares must take account of what is on their shelves, lest they suddenly be left with a large stock on hand for which there is no sale. They may find that Americans will be content less and less with mediocrity and imitation and formula, but instead will seek art of the house that has personality and inspiration in it. Thus some attempt should be made to picture the American household ideal, because in the imaginative, harmonious and accurate development of this ideal is the real object of house design.

With an ideal standard—however faulty—thus established, specific types of plan may be tested to decide their worth. Here a fact should be noted, which will help in judging the myriads of plans of houses. That is, that when a designer attempts to plan a house, he runs against such a variety and conflict of requirements that he must either eliminate or compromise. He solves the problem finally, and, as might be expected when hundreds of thousands of problems are solved under much the same conditions and their solutions are known among designers, his particular solution may be like the rest. Thus it is not surprising that one plan is found so often in American houses, with such little change, that it may be called typical. We may call this the stock plan. It will be better to examine carefully this stock

oped in England and America in the eighteenth century, first among the gentry, who liked to be easy and elegant and precise; at a time when culture and education took after English notions of Italian and French Renaissance, and was coming under the spell of classic Greece and Rome. Life was less dynamic then than it is now, and the courtly manners of royal France spread over the world.

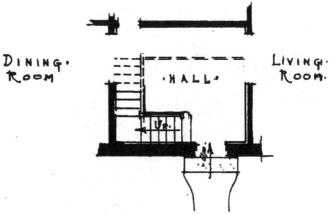

DINING. ROOM

·HALL·

LIVING. ROOM.

TWO-STORY ENTRANCE HALL IN A SMALL HOUSE IN PHILADELPHIA.

plan, and to understand its virtues and its limitations, than to spend time discussing the variations of detail to be found in contemporary house designs.

An excellent example of the stock plan is shown on page 68. It is the familiar formal, balanced arrangement of plan within four walls, a box with simple roof and smaller boxes added for wing or porch where necessary. There is a symmetrical front, center entrance, central hall inside, usually displaying a big stair to view as one enters; and left and right open off dining room on one side, and living room or little reception room on the opposite, according to best exposure outdoors. The situation on the lot varies this arrangement somewhat, but in its essentials it never varies. Porches or loggias or glazed porches are added to suit the case. If there is a wing, it contains kitchen and service. The stock plan is historical, too, for it was devel-

Under such circumstances did the stock plan develop, and it is pertinent to determine exactly how far this eighteenth century ideal meets the twentieth century American ideal of today.

On the practical side, much is said in favor of our stock plan. It is compact, its four walls are easily laid out by the builder, easily subdivided, easily roofed. Details are frequently repeated. The workmen have done the same thing before many times, and mistakes are not made so easily as in a new scheme. Since it is compact, the stock plan is good for the mechanical appliances. It should be admitted, too, that the stock plan overcomes in large measure that great obstacle in house design—the human factor, the difficulty of cooperation between client and architect. For with the stock plan there is not much doubt as to what the final result will be. In the case of an architect undertaking a large volume of work, the stock plan is quickly turned out by clever young draughtsmen, with a little supervision as to details, and house design becomes then largely a problem of business routine and superintendence of construction.

The limitations of the stock plan for modern conditions are decided ones. Even from a practical viewpoint its value may be easily exaggerated. Unsymmetrical houses may be as compact, as simple in construction and as easily roofed as symmetrical ones. The English house shown on page 70 is an example of this. As to the claim of the easy subdivision of the stock plan, it looks true in theory, but in practice such plans are so broken up with closets, baths, etc., so minutely figured to the inch for mechanical details such as pipes and ducts, that one may well be skeptical as to their ease of construction. Besides, anyone who knows the intricate working out of its entrance and stair and porch details knows how easily mistakes are made on the job.

The artistic worth of the stock plan is in controversy. Those who favor it claim a modern trend towards formality in living and in art, towards symmetry and geometrical balance. They dislike individuality in architecture, asserting that the history of architecture is one of slow development. In practice some of them carry this theory so far that architecture becomes a study of correct proportioning and of details. Artists who oppose it voice the same objections that I have mentioned before. Painters and sculptors think our symmetrical plans commonplace, and many architects would say that they emphasize the eighteenth century at the expense of the twentieth. Here it is well to avoid the old controversy between formal and informal architecture. It is enough to say that each has its uses under certain conditions. It is simply a question of how accurately and imaginatively does the stock plan of eighteenth century inspiration meet needs of the small house today, under post-war conditions.

As remarked above post-war conditions are still undetermined, but it is safe to say that, as never before, they impose strict limitations of cost in houses both in construction and in labor of maintenance. The first effect of these restrictions is to cut down the space in the house plan. It is a fact that the dimensions of houses built in the past year are so small that the precious quality of spaciousness once sought in our houses threatens to be lost. A few figures will illustrate this point. In old houses, a main hall ten feet wide, a a dining room seventeen feet square with study nine feet by seventeen behind it, and a living room seventeen feet by thirty, effected a fine impression of roominess, ease, of spacious and hospitable proportions. These are the dimensions of an old Dutch house in New Jersey, measured drawings of which are found in The Architectural Record for July, August and September, 1914. Other old houses may show smaller dimensions that are still satisfactory, but these occur with a ceiling as low as eight feet or less, and their small scale is aided by the exquisitely small and delicate eighteenth century furniture. One of the most beautiful examples of small rooms is in an old house in Cornwall, Conn., in which the main rooms are barely fourteen feet square, and yet they do not seem cramped. But here the ceilings are not much over seven feet six inches high, and the walls with delicate old paneling, beam ceilings or wood cornices, small windows with panes six inches by eight inches and fine old American furniture, petite in scale—all ensure satisfactory results. Probably also, the small size of these rooms seems more acceptable because they afford a cozy relief from the half-wild landscape that may be viewed for miles high up in the great Connecticut hills. Thus, when the width of dining and living rooms is less than seventeen feet or fifteen feet, and when the main center hall of the stock plan is less than nine feet, there is great danger that these important parts of the stock plan—or of any other plan—may seem cramped. These ground floor spaces are the most important features of the small house, most of the life of the family and all its entertaining take place there, and if they are not satisfactory, the whole design is a failure. If they are cut down to dimensions as small as thirteen feet and eight feet respectively, only very low ceilings and exquisitely small and delicate scale of details and furnishings may redeem them—a requirement that cannot always be met in practice. There is a great difference between rooms that seem cozy and rooms that seem cramped. In recent houses rooms are often only fourteen or twelve feet wide. For such dimensions the stock plan seems unfitted. It divides the house into booths and boxes, all about alike, without character, and thus it emphasizes instead of alleviating the smallness of the house. The house then looks like a toy. It is a tiny copy of a large house, and it loses the respect due it if it were honestly designed for what it is, a small house. Stated in other words, the space relationships of most of these very small symmetrical plans are out of balance. The minor features are reduced to the lowest dimensions, yet they are too large in proportion to the main rooms, and the small size of these latter is accented. The rigid restriction of dimensions now imposed on the house plan calls for modifications of accepted types. Accordingly it would seem that the stock plan must either be modified or else be given up, if it is to be used with a house of very small size.

It is not necessary to list here all the possible ways of modifying our symmetrical plans to retain in them some air of roominess and scale, but the process may be briefly hinted at. One form lies in opening out the entrance and stairway space. Where this feature of a house is cramped, the effect is apparent whenever one enters the house or moves about in it or uses the stairs. On the other hand, where this entrance hall is broadened out at once the plan acquires ease and "scale." The most perfect illustrations of this truth are found in the old houses of the south, in Virgina and Maryland, in which the entrance hall was usually as large as any of the principal rooms. On pages 60 and 61 are shown the ground floor plans of Mount Airy and of Marmion, in Virginia, and it will be seen that their great entrance halls mirror the southern tradition of

hospitality that has taken such a firm hold on the American imagination, a tradition, moreover, which is peculiarly appropriate to modern American temperament. It would seem impossible to put the expansiveness of these old southern plans into the limited space of the small house of today, yet I have seen it done most successfully in a little house in Philadelphia. In that house the entrance hall was two stories high and about twelve feet square, and the stair was placed with the lower flight against the wall at the front door, and the upper flight against the side wall. Thus the hall gave spaciousness both to first and second floors. The first floor plan seems symmetrical, though really it is not. A diagram of this entrance hall, sketched from memory, is shown on page 63. Of course, even this arrangement takes up much space, and is best suited, as this Philadelphia plan was, to a small family of adults. A large family could hardly spare so much space. In the very small house for a Long Island group development (House No. 1) on page 73 the effect of a roomy entrance has been gained by another extreme, that of making the entrance so tiny that it is merely a vestibule to the living room. One really enters into the living room.

For a large family in a small house, the restricted dimensions and narrowed hallway of the conventional stock plan are not fitting, and its minute subdivisioning shows at its worst. With all the spaces about alike in size and in shape, the interior of such a house is difficult to decorate with any individuality. Even in large houses, the constant use of the conventional plan in recent years was making interior decoration commonplace. Two or three formulae had grown up for hall and stairs, living room and dining room, executed in routine manner— a situation pleasing only to commercial designers, and distasteful to able designers like Mr. Baum, who has done much excellent work in a freer style than the example here shown. In a word, it is no exaggeration to say that constant, often ill-judged use of symmetrical plan has caused something like a deadlock in small American houses, in all their es-

65

sentials—not only plan, but lot design, elevation and interior decoration. One must conclude that, if the remarkable progress of our national house design during the last generation is to be maintained, if our houses are to interpret the American family ideal, a way out of this deadlock must be found.

The way out of this deadlock in house design should come through elimination. Compromise has been overdone. I am inclined to welcome elimination, for I believe that it will cause designers to face the issue squarely instead of dodging it. Then the small house will come into its own, for it will be designed to meet specific conditions freely and imaginatively. There will be nothing false about it, for above all it will not be, as so many houses are now, an impossible attempt to copy in miniature all the features of the big house. The detailed statement of how this process will occur will be left for the fourth article, but certain larger aspects of the matter may be considered here.

Elimination should have two results in the house plan. It will abolish or reduce certain features, and the space saved will be used not only in order to enlarge the really essential features to their proper importance, but it may also allow, minor elements to be added to the plan that have not hitherto been thought of. No rules can be laid down to govern such a process. Elimination should take place according to the various needs of different cases, and this is something to the good, for it should result in more variety and charm and character and personality in our houses. However, certain possibilities of the process, may be indicated. First, the main entrance could be simplified. The tiny coat and toilet rooms that sometimes encumber the entrance, may well go. The main stairs should not give the effect of a hotel, inviting the guest upstairs to the sleeping rooms where he is not desired, but should instead be much reduced and made less conspicuous. The little reception room for visitors should either be abandoned or its function worked out as an alcove off the living room. A more radical solution, one that

I believe will come into favor, will be to gain ease and space in the entrance in the following way: The entrance hall could be opened out into a squarish space, say seven or eight feet by nine feet, furnished to receive callers who cannot be immediately taken into the living room. The furnishing of the entrance room will make it cheerful, and it will be large enough to avoid that detestable cramping of entrance mentioned above. This entrance may open into a large living room, from which the stairs ascend to the second floor, small but interesting in design, perhaps set in an alcove. The space saved in the conventional stair hall and reception room could be added to the living room to make it much larger. The usual dining room arrangement might be modified by using the living room for eating, or else by making the dining room continuous with it, which is the same thing. Or else the dining room might become an alcove in the living room. The two little house plans on pages 73 and 74 illustrate these ideas practically.

Thus, by making our ideas of small house planning more flexible, yet honestly admitting its limitations, at once the door of the American small house opens up a picture of comfort, roominess, of beauty and distinction hitherto denied it. The living room, enlarged, is a living room, big enough for a family of many children and with real possibilities in art and decoration. It would be a room seventeen feet to twenty feet wide, thirty feet to forty feet long, and it might be even twelve feet or fifteen feet high; and, with its varieties of alcoves or other details from the stiff planes and cubic lines of the usual box-like living room, would have an unusual character, one capable of great variety of design. Such a living room in its bigness and beauty would really express the American idea of home, with its tradition of hospitality, and in it the life of the American family might well take on dignity and enrichment as never before. It would be a perfect room for festivity. The living room of Mr. Colby's home, in the first article of this series goes far toward realizing this possibility. Every other fea-

RESIDENCE OF MRS. TEN EYCK ELMENDORF, FIELDSTON, NEW YORK CITY.
Dwight James Baum, Architect.

ture of Mr. Colby's plan is subordinated to the living room, which transcends most other living rooms of small houses. In its proportions and decorations it is such a room as is thought of only in very great houses. Other examples of planning for a living room are in The Architectural Record for October, 1919, Fig. 75, page 356, and Fig. 79, page 359.

But it is not the interior of the house that is solely benefited by making the house plan flexible. Further than that, features may be added, particularly on the exterior, that may be the making of the whole design. An example of these possibilities appears on page 71 in a design submitted in a competition by Messrs. C. H. Umbrecht and L. J. Kaley. The lot plan is excellent, though the house is located too near the street, and the service yard seems almost too big. The plan of the house itself is really masterly. The main living parts are toward the south, overlooking the garden, in the case of the bedrooms upstairs; and downstairs the three main rooms are placed in a row with a fine

air of bigness and space—a disposition perfect for entertaining. The entrance hall opens out nicely, with the stair less conspicuous than usual, and here the difficulty of entrance, coatroom and toilet is admirably solved. The porch off the living room and the square one off the dining room are well placed. But the chief virtue is the beautiful way in which the garage is grouped with the house and connected to the front door by a covered passage. The result is an exterior very simple and entirely charming, but bold and imaginative, with the roof masses dropping down and making the design of the house harmonize with the horizontal lines of the level site. This is real house architecture.

An English example, on page 70, shows further illustration of the use of features in plan to complete the exterior. In the house at Biddenham, the long gable of the roof, with its stylish chimneys, is carried down towards the ground, in a fine sweep, which ties the roof lines to the garden details of drying-yard wall and lattice. In the plan this result is

67

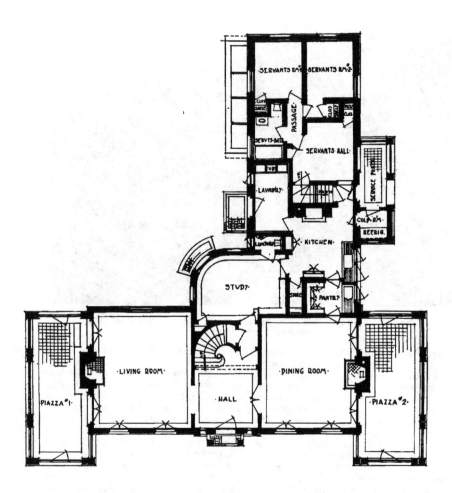

FIRST FLOOR PLAN—RESIDENCE OF MRS. TEN
EYCK ELMENDORF, FIELDSTON, NEW YORK
CITY. DWIGHT JAMES BAUM, ARCHITECT.

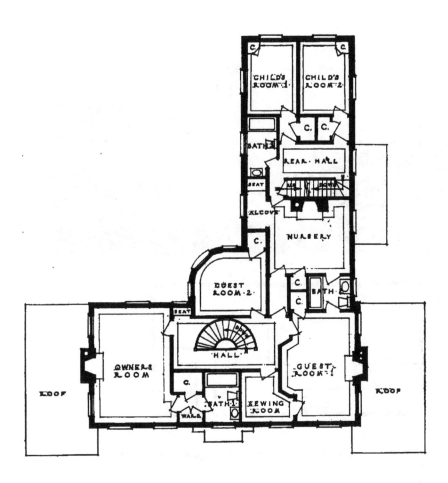

SECOND FLOOR PLAN—RESIDENCE OF MRS. TEN
EYCK ELMENDORF, FIELDSTON, NEW YORK
CITY. DWIGHT JAMES BAUM, ARCHITECT.

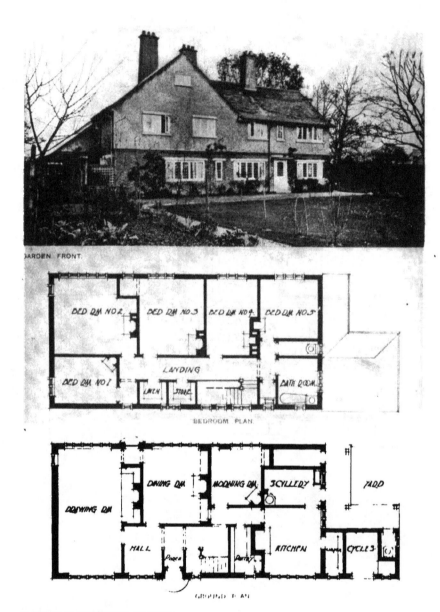

GARDEN FRONT.

BED RM NO 2 · BED RM NO 3 · BED RM NO 4 · BED RM NO 5

LANDING

BED RM NO 1 · LINEN · STORE · BATH ROOM

BEDROOM PLAN

DINING RM · MORNING RM · SCULLERY · YARD

DRAWING RM

HALL · Porch · Larder · Pantry · KITCHEN · CYCLES

GROUND PLAN

COTTAGE AT BIDDENHAM, BEDFORD-
SHIRE. C. E. MALLOWS, ARCHITECT.
Reproduced, by Permission, from "Country
Cottages" by J. Elder Duncan; John
Lane Company, Publishers.

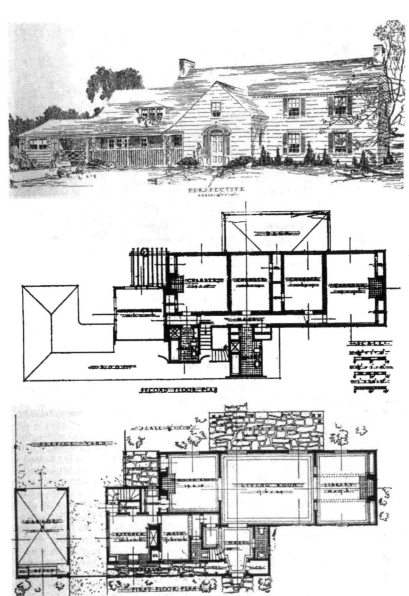

DESIGN FOR A SUBURBAN HOUSE AND
GARAGE OF WHITE PINE. CHARLES H.
UMBRECHT AND L. J. KALEY, DESIGNERS.
Reproduced, by Permission, from "The White
Pine Series of Architectural Mono-
graphs," Vol. II, No. 4.

HOUSE NO. 1. HOME COMMUNITY CORPORATION, BALDWIN, L. I.
Polhemus, Mackenzie & Coffin, Architects.

accomplished by adding a little room lettered "Cycles" at the service end of the house. In England, houses are usually built without cellars, and this limitation forces minor features which in American houses are found in the cellar, up on the ground, when they may be combined with the other features of the plan in most happy fashion. Some English houses have a long, low, picturesque wing of nothing but laundries, sheds for tools, coal, vegetables, toilets, etc. This is but another instance where designers have turned the limitations of a plan to good advantage. The interior of this house is planned well, particularly the long drawing room with fireplace in a big alcove. Another good feature is the use of chimneys, which is one of the excellences of English houses. Probably much of their character and the consistency of their plans are due to the chimney stacks that carry up through the floors at frequent intervals. The service arrangements are somewhat less compact than an American might desire, but they are designed for different conditions than ours. The fine, broad, simple proportions of this house appeal particularly to our taste. In its form and details it has splendid style, but does not belong to any particular style of architecture, as the word is commonly used. It is simply a vigorous honest meeting of a problem that is the stamp of a real work of art.

Sometimes, in order to get a desirable effect in roofing or in a gable, a few square feet of floor space more than is absolutely necessary, may be needed in the plan, and it should not be begrudged. Mr. Colby's plan is well compacted, but he did not hesitate to make the pantry a few feet larger than required, in order to give his roof and gable the right proportion on the exterior. Such sacrifices must sometimes be made in the plan in

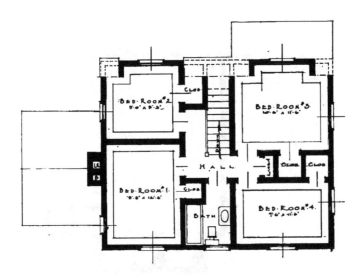

SECOND FLOOR PLAN

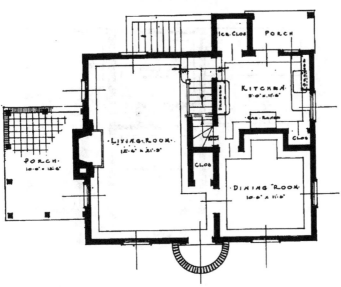

FIRST FLOOR PLAN

FLOOR PLANS—HOUSE NO. 1, HOME COMMUNITY CORPORATION,
BALDWIN, L. I. POLHEMUS, MACKENZIE & COFFIN, ARCHITECTS.

FIRST FLOOR PLAN

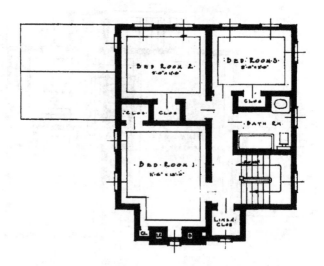

SECOND FLOOR PLAN

FLOOR PLANS—HOUSE NO. 2, HOME COMMUNITY CORPORATION,
BALDWIN, L. I   POLHEMUS, MACKENZIE & COFFIN, ARCHITECTS.

HOUSE NO. 2. HOME COMMUNITY CORPORATION, BALDWIN, L. I.
Polhemus, Mackenzie & Coffin, Architects.

order that art may not suffer on the elevation. This principle, of course, cannot be carried to extremes; but if a sacrifice of this sort be reasonable, and is once made, the house built and lived in, who will regret it?

The three designs last considered were all of them conceived before the war. If they were built nowadays for people of the same means, they would probably be reduced and simplified. How this is done appears in the two houses shown on pages 73 and 74 (Houses Nos. 1 and 2, Home Community Corporation).

They are very small structures indeed, cheap to build and cheaper to maintain, manage and clean, and they show elimination of all but the bare essentials, following in many respects the principles of elimination set forth above. The first of these is an interesting modification of the symmetrical stock plan and shows a specific example of the flexible ideas of planning described above where both the entrance and the stairs are al-coves in the living room, giving the latter a spaciousness of width that its dimension of twelve feet six inches would not otherwise permit. It will be noticed, also, on the second floor, that the most compact planning has still nevertheless allowed a little space at the head of the stair well. The stock plan has been so modified in this case that it has really no symmetry left in it, except on paper, and except for the exterior. Actually, inside it would seem perfectly informal and picturesque, as befits its very small size.

The other plan is entirely unsymmetrical, but with good arrangement of axes. The hall is narrow, but, not being long, will probably not appear cramped. Here the dining room and living room are practically one, and the designer has imparted a creative touch to their planning by the interesting feature labelled "Nook," which is the making not only of these two rooms, but the front of the house as well.

75

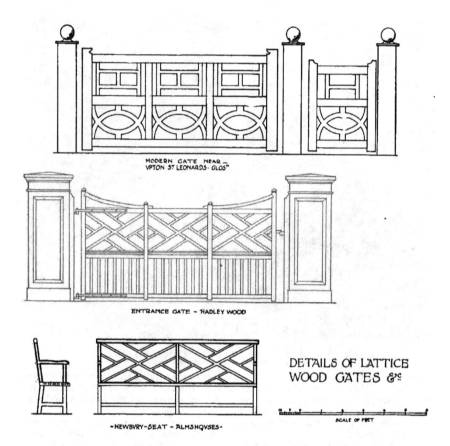

MODERN GATE NEAR –
VPTON ST LEONARDS · GLOS

ENTRANCE GATE – HADLEY WOOD

~ NEWBVRY ~ SEAT ~ ALMSHQVSES ~

DETAILS OF LATTICE
WOOD GATES &c

SCALE OF FEET

Measured and Drawn
by Albert E. Bullock.

English Architectural Decoration
Text and Measured Drawings by Albert E. Bullock

Part XII. Porches and Treillage Design.

IF I may be permitted a slight divergence from the strict interpretation of the title in the present article, it will be to present a few details of porches which exhibit some artistic taste and necessarily require special designing either in iron or wood upon the principles adopted for treillage.

There are in England a variety of very interesting entrances to the smaller houses which give an element of grace and charm to the village green. In the last article the fanlight was the topic, which is observable both from within and without, whether incorporated with a lamp or merely a design of fancy in wood, lead or iron.

The light lathwork in treillage design is particularly suitable to garden architecture, being applicable to the gate, seat or porch, or blank wall treatment beneath a larch-covered pergola adjoining one side of a house.

There are also several types of verandas in similar vein, and the instances illustrated are taken from Hertford, Watford, Southampton, Newbury and other towns of England, or the environs of London, as well as in London City.

The Adam Brothers were pre-eminently designers of artistic merit, and whether it was furniture, decoration, lighting or building in its several branches, they always brought the subject into the light of their criticism and endeavored to improve upon past methods.

Imitation being the sincerest form of flattery, there were many replicas of their work varying much in their degree of excellence.

As regards the fanlight to overdoors, the origin was certainly dated from Tudor times, of which there is an excellent example extant in the Close at Gloucester Cathedral, where the space between the top of the door and the soffit of the decorated arch is filled in with lead-glazing forming triple lancet arches with quatrefoils over. The main lines of this design are to be seen in many more modern overdoors, only usually executed in wooden bars.

The example I gave in my last article from Sussex House, Watford, is a metal casement having traces of lead-glazing which is of considerable interest, and in principle is not unlike the one formerly at Great Ormond Street, and now in the Victoria and Albert Museum.

These various types justly serve to show the variety of play and inventive genius which emanated from the minds of the designers of the late eighteenth century, for it is from that period whence most of the examples appear to date where delicacy of treatment is the theme of their design.

It was natural that porches and gates should come within the purview of the artist called in to advise his client upon the embellishment of the interior where a house was not brought into being as one grand conception. The eighteenth century was largely an age of additions when old work shouldered new types in adjacent rooms. I call to mind Brympton D'Evercy, with its Gothic Porch, Jacobean Hall, Monks Parlor and Charles I period rooms, which is on a par with Forde Abbey,—an ancient monastery converted to a residence and having within many periods, including an oak panelled hall with small Adam period drawing room and carved Charles I staircase, with a chapel having an early Georgian screen.

However humble be the cottage, a wonderful grace pervades its external appearance when a delicately designed porch forms its main entrance. Moreover, such a porch harmonizes well with most materials, whether brick and stucco,

77

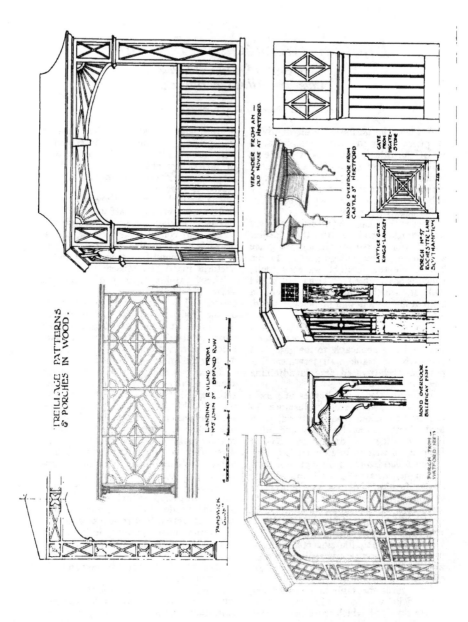

TREILLAGE PATTERNS & PORCHES IN WOOD.

VERANDER FROM AN — OLD HOUSE AT HERTFORD.

HOOD OVERDOOR FROM CASTLE ST HERTFORD

GATE FROM INGATE-STONE

LATTICE GATE KINGS·LANGLEY

PORCH N° 57 ROCHESTER LANE SOUTHAMPTON

HOOD OVERDOOR BILLERICAY ESSEX

PORCH FROM WATFORD HERTS

LANDING RAILING FROM — N°5 JOHN ST BEDFORD ROW

PAINSWICK GLOS

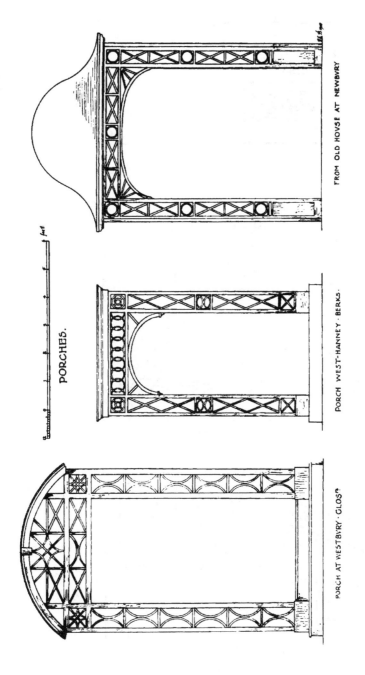

PORCHES.

PORCH AT WESTBVRY · GLOS?

PORCH WEST-HANNEY · BERKS.

FROM OLD HOVSE AT NEWBVRY

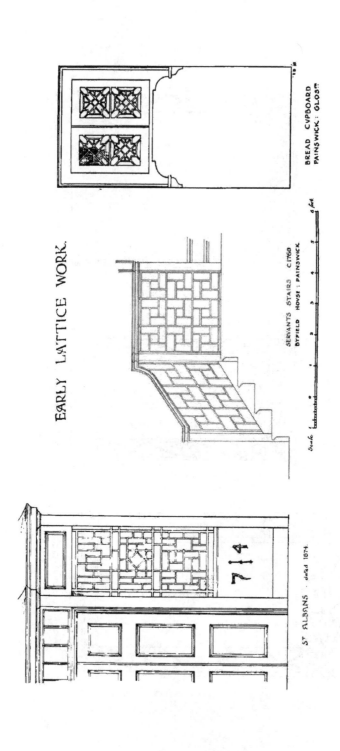

EARLY LATTICE WORK.

BREAD CVPBOARD
PAINSWICK: GLOS⸵

SERVANTS STAIRS C1760
BYFIELD HOVSE: PAINSWICK

Scale   6 feet

S⸵ ALBANS · dated 1674.

714

WROT & CAST IRON
PORCHES : BALCONIES &c..

SOVTHAMPTON

THE CLOSE : LICHFIELD

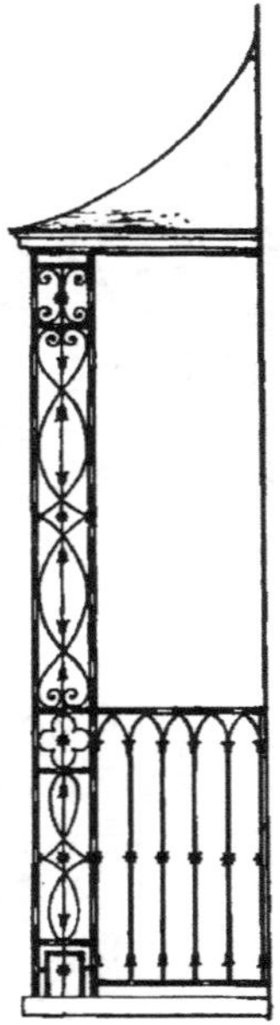

SPA ROAD : GLOUCESTER.

stone, or half-timbered work, and looks as well with thatched roof as with tiles or stone slates.

The laths are for the most part quite slender, being when in wood about ¾-inch by 1¼ inches deep in section, the main uprights rarely exceeding 2 inches square. With wrought and cast iron the dimensions are naturally reduced, owing to the added strength of this material, being usually ½-inch thick by ⅞-inch deep with 1¼-inch standards.

There is a light footbridge over the main road near Shere, Surrey, connecting two gardens, designed upon a similar principle, and the staircase to No. 5 John Street, Bedford Row, London, follows corresponding lines.

By a variety of interlacing curves or circles considerable play is obtained when designing in bronze, while many of the Adam pierced steel fenders exhibit qualities of taste and refinement.

In the porches mentioned, the finish of the curved lead roofs are features of interest, as also the construction of the framing supporting the canopies.

Interlaced circles in designs of iron work and pierced steel were common in work of the late eighteenth century, while gates of squared laths upon diagonals obtained in many villages in Hertfordshire and elsewhere.

In wrought iron work the scrolls are frequently ornamented with leaves, especially in support consoles to piers. The effect of such ornamentation when disposed at salient points is to enhance or enrich the general appearance of the continuous bars. The wrought ironwork to the railed enclosure of the Bishop's Court at Westminster Abbey, and the railing of the main staircase at Hampton Court Palace have features of considerable interest.

At Painswick, near Stroud, Gloucestershire, there is a comparatively small house with sumptuous internal decorations dating from about 1760. The general spirit of early George III work pervades the whole place from the staircases to the cupboards.

The servants' staircase rail is of lath work and illustrated here with the ex-

ample of treillage from the porch of a house at St. Albans. A feature of note lies in the treatment of the small bread cupboard with its openwork lath joinery.

Although ironwork presents a sphere of greater freedom with the power of curving the forms of the design, there is a distinct charm about many of the examples of simple lath work.

As applied to garden architecture and winter garden ornamentation some very ambitious designs are frequently to be seen in country seats, and even the plain walls of small enclosed yards at the rear of houses in Park Lane. These are frequently worked upon architectural lines with cornices, architraves and columns, the paneling being formed upon a perspective basis with radiating lines to a focal centre.

Much elaborate work can thus be attempted, mostly founded upon the old French principles, of which there are many designs in books of the period by Daniel Marot and others.

The interest which centres upon the veranda and pergola is not without advantage, except that for external work the materials are largely perishable and liable to rot in damp situations unless carefully treated at definite seasons. It is, however, a disadvantage to overdo treillage work. To come suddenly upon a gem of an example is of far more worth than to find a lavish display running over a great area.

The cottage with its porch, the kitchen with its cupboard, the charm of the back stair or the seat in the entrance to the Almshouse, all with isolated examples of the taste of the century of their origin mark them as distinct by comparison with works of greater importance but less taste.

While a certain design may be the keynote to the rhythmic display of any theme, distinct contrasts frequently make for the correct rendering of an idea when the treatment falls short of a recognized comprehensive style. These contrasts are either accidental or occasioned by reason of the artist's code of harmony and proportion. Therein lies the true merit of a successful interior based, as it should be, upon the laws of selection within the scale and limitations of its definition.

This abstract of the theoretical principles of design must necessarily be followed in practice by a careful choice of detail. This, after all, is the essential element in all things and especially in decoration. Nothing is more disappointing than to find a house or room that has been "restored" by someone out of sympathy with or lacking knowledge of the style with which he is dealing. Such restoration only leads to disaster. Had I time and space I could illustrate this point with comparative enriched moldings. As it is, I have in mind a small bedroom in a large house belonging to a noble lord in one of the western counties, who, discovering by accident some fine early Georgian paneling beneath the canvas of the walls, decided to have it restored. While the original paneling is good, of the additions little can be said with pleasure. The door paneling and architraves are wrong in detail, and the

Tudor arch to the chimney breast (with the exception of the molding to the mantel architrave) is entirely out of keeping with the remainder of the room.

The same applies to other features, namely, the rim locks and furniture of a room, the lighting arrangements, and even the frames of the pictures hanging upon the walls. Each item reveals clearly the inferior taste either of the owner or of his advisers.

The charm of good French work is its completeness in every detail, down to the door-knocker. Which last reminds me that there are a great variety of brass door-knockers, escutcheons, bell handles and wrought iron bell-pulls of great interest in England. They date from Georgian and Adam times, while earlier ironwork of the Jacobean period is of equal artistic merit.

I hope at no distant date to illustrate some of these, together with the chasing adopted on some examples of early polished brass furniture.

DINING ROOM — FELDEN HURST, BOXMOOR, HERTS.

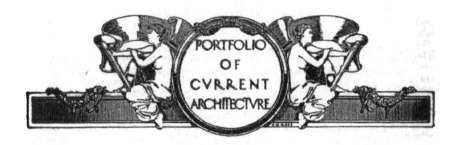

CHRIST LUTHERAN CHURCH, FORT WAYNE, IND.
J. W. CRESSWELL CORBUSIER, ARCHITECT.

ASCENSION EPISCOPAL CHURCH, LAKEWOOD, OHIO.
J. W. Cresswell Corbusier, Architect.

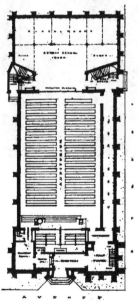

PLAN OF CHRIST LUTHERAN CHURCH.

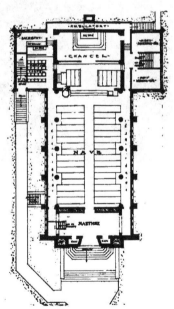

PLAN OF ASCENSION EPISCOPAL CHURCH.

ASCENSION EPISCOPAL CHURCH, LAKEWOOD,
OHIO, J. W. CRESSWELL CORBUSIER, ARCHITECT.

RECREATION BUILDING ERECTED BY THE CITY OF EVELETH, MINN. ELWIN H. BERG, ARCHITECT.

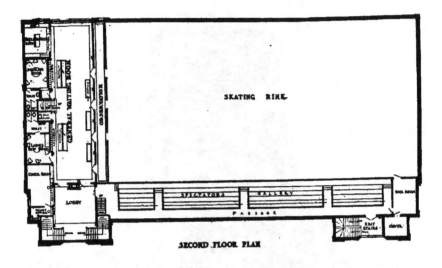

SECOND FLOOR PLAN

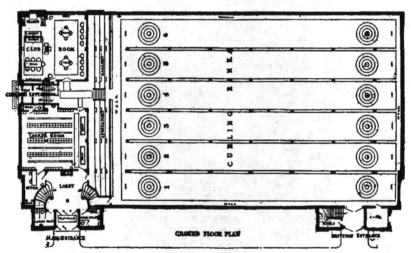

GROUND FLOOR PLAN

RECREATION BUILDING ERECTED BY THE CITY
OF EVELETH, MINN. ELWIN H. BERG, ARCHITECT.

THE ARCHITECT'S LIBRARY

INDUSTRIAL HOUSING REPORTS
By JOHN TAYLOR BOYD, Jr.

THE publication of the *Report of the United States Housing Corporation* (Vol. II. Houses, Site-planning, Utilities. Washington, Government Printing Office, 1919) must be considered an event in the literature of American architecture. It will be welcomed by a much wider circle than our profession—by town planners, engineers, manufacturers, labor interests and agencies devoted to social betterment, philanthropy and civic improvement. In fact, the vast work undertaken by the Government in order to house its war workers has a significance for the whole nation.

The two characteristics of this volume are its thoroughness and its interesting makeup—qualities which would indicate that its sponsors knew well the importance of the report. The more one digs into it, the more one finds there; and we may hope that the reader will thoroughly master its text, instead of treating it simply as a fascinating picture-book of plans and perspectives.

This war housing is really the beginning of industrial housing in America. It is rare that a new movement is introduced on such a vast scale, striving for the highest professional standards, and,

considering the haste and waste of war effort, so exceptionally well organized. Only one question may be asked concerning its extraordinary success. How far was it efficient?

It is indeed a tough question, and I shall not attempt to answer it, notwithstanding the accepted convention that seems to prescribe that a reviewer of a book should pose as a higher authority than the writer. I think it enough to point out that war conditions are not favorable to efficiency, not only because it is difficult to carry out an improvised program, but also because that program must be constantly readjusted to other programs and policies of the great war organization. Criticisms which ignore this fact are unfair, and they tend to discredit a movement which, if studied sympathetically, should form the basis for a tradition that might redeem the town-planning, engineering and housing of American communities from their present unhappy condition. Already it is being noted that in the reaction against the war activity many of its real benefits are being ruthlessly scrapped. Therefore, lest the lessons of this war housing be lost, a thorough, unprejudiced appraisal of it should be made from all points of view, in order that we may determine how its principles could be applied to peace conditions, and to what extent its errors and shortcomings might be avoided in future work. Such an appraisal would be mindful, as the editor's preface of the Housing Corporation report states, that before the war industrial housing was practically a new field for Americans, since English precedents did not fit our conditions and since but little information was available about the few pioneer projects that had been launched in America. It should further be realized that the policy of industrial housing in this country is not yet settled. The disagreement as to policy will, I think, be found to rest mainly on the financial side. That is to say, the war housing has established the work securely on a technical basis, but there is great difference of opinion as to how much money should be spent on these improvements in order to make them practicable. This, again, is a question that town planners, architects, engineers, may hardly decide. They have worked out their part of the vast problem—of course many points are yet to be decided and much experience is to be gained in further work—and it now remains for the manufacturer, the laboring men and the general public to determine labor's standard of living. This determination of the standard of living is, as we all know, the vital need of the whole world, one of the great problems of industry and of the war that society is now about to liquidate. When the labor problem is so liquidated, the missing links in industrial housing will be supplied.

At different times you may hear architects who took part in the war housing criticize it as being too luxurious. Too much design or plumbing wasted on people unable to appreciate it, they say. Such criticisms are not technical criticisms at all; the critics make them, not as architects or as engineers, but as lay citizens or sociologists, or, in some cases, merely as sufferers from class prejudice. Of course, criticisms as to cost are pertinent, for an industrial housing project

should certainly be sound financially or it will fail. But it would be better if professional critics of war housing understood that, so far as the future is concerned, standards of living are yet to be established. The professions should take their stand on the remarkable technical solution of industrial housing that they have provided and then say to the public —capital, labor, consumer — "once you determine wage scales and standards of living so that we may know what amounts the different classes of citizens may pay for rent, we are ready to go ahead with construction. We have the knowledge and the experience to provide what you want in a far better way than ever before."

The results of taking such a position before the public should be of vast benefit to the professions involved. . . . .

The policy of the Government in regard to housing projects is clearly set forth in the first three chapters of Vol. II. There is little to add or to subtract. Vol. II deals with design, especially architectural, with townplanning, and with engineering. Vol. I will cover the work of the Real Estate. Transportation, and Homes Registration Divisions of the Housing Corporation. Chapter IV of Vol. II contains a short, clear account of some of the principles adopted in the treatment of topography, drainage, planting, etc. It is well to note that planting was sparingly used in the housing schemes, and this should be kept in mind in judging the completed work. The editor deserves the greatest credit for Chapter V, for while he has dealt with the limitations of design, materials, and policy imposed by the war program, he had refused to take refuge under this shelter, and treats frankly of mistakes that were made. This unusual attitude is continued throughout the book in the short summaries that accompany the illustration of each of the individual projects. In Appendix XI, one fault appears, repeated elsewhere. While siteplans, construction and details of elevations of individual houses are carefully considered, the treatment of the individual house plan is superficial. The plans vary greatly in excellence. Some, notably standard plans K, L, M, O, on pages 56 and 57, are better than others, for they bring out the important principles of saving steps to the housewife, and of allowing her easy surveillance of entrances, stairs, etc. This is especially desirable where upstairs rooms are rented to boarders. Also, there is a great scarcity of plans of L-shaped kitchens, where the cooking, etc., is carried on in a kitchenette space, of, say, eight by fourteen feet, and to which is attached an alcove, about eight feet square, where the meal table may be placed, helping save thus extra work in serving, and possibly a dining room.

Of course, the interest of most people will be centred in the projects themselves, with the excellent renderings of site plans, individual houses and pen-and-ink perspectives. They show a splendid standard of achievement in a great variety of examples. In the work 21,005 families were housed at a cost of $5,398.11 per family—on the basis of figuring adopted by the corporation—$4,374.70 representing the cost of the house itself and the remainder, $1,024.40, covering land, land improvements, site utilities and the occasional community buildings. Altogether not an extravagant showing for war work.

In the elevations, here and there, are to be noted the usual faults of contemporary small house design—monotony, together with self-conscious attempts to relieve it by trickiness, imperfect scale and proportions, particularly of windows, too many windows looking spotty against too little wall space, angularity, too many roof peaks. In viewing some of the desperate attempts to force art on these little boxes, one is forced to conclude that, unless local conditions and prejudices absolutely forbid it, group houses and semi-detached houses are better than single ones. They may be made more interesting and more artistic in design, they may cost less in themselves, and they bring down the cost of land, roads, paths, sewers, planting, etc., because they permit more people to live on an acre of ground without overcrowding. The strongest argument against the isolated house is the group housing at Bridgeport, Conn. Fortunately, it had for its architect Mr. R. Clipston Sturgis, than whom no architect in the country could show better the possibilities of this type. His exquisite sense of proportion, of small scale, of refinement, of restraint, of the value of broad wall surfaces, together with his imaginative sense of interest and of charm, provide a rarely successful model for the industrial housing of the future.

The housing undertaken by the Emergency Fleet Corporation was the other great venture into the field of industrial housing undertaken by the United States Government during the world war. Since it ran parallel to the work of the U. S. Department of Labor, the same significance may be attached to it, the same observations made regarding it, and the same questions asked. The board was, in the best sense, of course, a rival of the corporation, and we may infinitely regret that its report (*Types of Housing for Shipbuilders.* United States Shipping Board Emergency Fleet Corporation. Passenger Transportation and Housing Divisions) is so much less complete. It deals almost entirely with individual houses, their plans, elevations, perspectives, with only here and there part of a site plan or a whole site plan. No explanations of policy, of organization employed in the program, of technical details used, or any of that so generous admitting of mistakes that is found in Vol. II of the Housing Corporation report. Nor is any indication given in this report that this precious information withheld will later be supplied to us. Such shortcomings are to be deplored. The various professions and the part of the public interested in industrial housing should bring pressure to bear to have the desired information given out before it is lost or becomes obsolete. We cannot take the report of the Housing Corporation, however fine it may be, as a substitute for that of the Shipping Board, for no matter how capable two great organizations are, each is bound to develop a differing point of view, emphasize certain aspects, more than others. Particularly true is this in the case of two such improvized organizations as war organizations are bound to be. Indeed slight differences of divergence are apparent in the illustrations in the two reports. The shipping experts seem to have an individual attitude toward the house plan and they seem to prefer a very simply treated elevation. In the scant data on their site plans provided us, they seem to prefer deeper setbacks of houses where some houses are varied in depth from their neighbors. In this last particular, the Housing Corporation gentlemen take pains to explain that a setback of two feet is usually sufficient. The Shipping Board, in its admirable site plan of Newburgh, N. Y., adopted interior courts in the house blocks around which "community garages" are grouped. Here are some of the points of technical import yet to be decided and on which the public is entitled to be enlightened in the name of future progress.

All in all, the significance of the war industrial housing lies in the future. We are interested in its as architecture, not as archaeology. If rightly taken, it could inspire a great movement, of benefit not simply for the professions concerned, but for American civilization. It opens to the professions a field hitherto denied them, and, as one studies such reports as are here reviewed, one is convinced of the appalling waste, of the opportunities neglected in contemporary housing, which continues to proceed contrary to the experience of several professions. Now, over a year after the signing of the armistice, a national housing crisis confronts us. We should apply the knowledge gotten in the war, in which, in a few months, under the pressure of the conflict, we gained years of technical practical experience measured in terms of peace time progress. The activity of the war industrial housing was cut short, but not before a number of completely executed, working projects were provided in various parts of the country, to serve as models.

Architects have a peculiar responsibility in this effort to perpetuate these beginnings. While they are not the only professional men interested in industrial housing, it is the only great work in which their profession was called upon to serve. Many complaints are voiced that architects lost prestige from this indifference of the public. But if this share of the housing was all that was given to them, they should make the most of it in a concerted effort to understand the war housing, comprehend the applications of its principles to peace time, and then persuade the public of the national benefits that proper housing will bring. Unless the architects do make the most of what was given them, they can scarcely claim that they were entitled to a larger share in the war work.

John Taylor Boyd, Jr.

NEW BOOKS RECEIVED FROM PUBLISHERS.

University of Illinois Bulletin. No. 108. Analysis of Statically Indeterminate Structures by the Slope Deflection Method. By W. M. Wilson, F. E. Richart and Camillo Weiss. 218 p., 9 by 6 inches. Published by the University of Illinois, Urbana.

The Broadway Engineering Handbooks. Volume I. Elementary Principles of Reinforced Concrete Construction. A Text-Book for the use of Students, Engineers, Architects and Builders. By Ewart S. Andrews, B. Sc. Eng. (Lond.) 57 ills., 225 p., 4½ by 7½ inches, numerous worked examples, and the L. C. C. regulations for reinforced concrete construction. London: Scott Greenwood & Sons. New York: D. Van Norstrand Co.

"The Studio" Year-Book of Decorative Art, 1919, With Special Articles on Cottage Design, Decoration and Equipment. Edited by Geofrey Holme. Many ills., 136 p., 8½ by 12 inches. London: Paris: New York: The Studio Ltd.

Timber—Its Strength, Seasoning, and Grading. By Harold S. Betts, M. E. Forest Service, U. S. Department of Agriculture. First Edition. Many ills., 234 p., 9½ by 6 inches. New York: McGraw-Hill Book Co., Inc. Price $3.00 net.

NOTES AND COMMENTS

The Creation of an American Style of Landscape Architecture. Occasionally attention is called to an article on garden craft in which the writer makes the statement that there is now an American style; but in no article has that assertion been backed up by evidence; in no claim of that kind has there ever been submitted the analysis of a design distinctive enough to be recognized as different from the other styles, distinctive enough to be admitted as a new style. Until the analysis of an American garden shows originality of ideas, as well as of design, we cannot reasonably claim the creation of a new style—the American style. That it is only a question of time until American ability does create a national style, few will doubt; but before that important event occurs we shall have to recognize the real difficulties to be overcome, as well as investigate and fully understand the importance of certain factors—factors that have always played a leading part in the creation, if not in the actual composition, of a new style in garden art.

It is not my intention to show in this article how to compose new designs and styles, but merely to indicate the factors of influence active in the invention of designs and styles—factors of influence to be thoroughly studied and weighed by the landscape architect. If I am not mistaken the factors of influence in the creation of a new style are, in the order of their importance, the taste and temperament of those for whom the gardens are laid out; the natural contour of the land; the climate, and plant materials. It must be plainly understood that I am now speaking of the factors of influence, not of the elements, nor of the principles of garden composition.

It was principally the taste and temperament of the Italians of the Renaissance, assisted by the natural contour of their land, which produced what we know today as the Italian style of gardening. And the artists who created that style labored not only with brilliancy of ideas, with originality of design, but also with acuteness of intellect which told them that the making of a garden was but half the problem, the other half being suggestion, the imagination, the mind of the beholder, upon which sentiment and emotion would assist in creating an esthetic impression. The same is true of the French style, which came into being as the result of the taste and temperament of Louis XIV, and the treatment of a wide, flat surface of land by Le Nôtre. And the creation of the Dutch style and the English style are also due primarily to these two factors—taste and temperament, and land contours. Climate and plant materials have been secondary influences, but not secondary elements, as they are of first importance when we consider the composition and the decoration of a garden.

If we examine closely the Italian gardens of the Renaissance we shall see in them the influence of taste and temperament on garden art, as those gardens reflect not only the personalities of those for whom they were created, but also the characteristic desires of society at that time. Italian gardens were designed for opulent and proud leaders of secular and ecclesiastic affairs, and their love of display, of peace, comfort, and seclusion demanded artistic and luxurious surroundings in the garden as well as in the house; although we must remember that not in all cases were the gardens used for pleasure alone, nor for recreation entirely. During the summer's heat they afforded the most comfortable places for conferences on church, state, or

93

personal affairs. Some of them were often courts of justice where laws were interpreted or made, where men of affairs went and came, where priests and lawyers, architects, painters and sculptors, doctors and men of letters met to discuss affairs of importance, or were guests, the gardens affording change, rest and amusement.

Such a garden was that at Villa D'Este, laid out about 1550 by Ligorio for Cardinal Ferrara, then governor of Tivoli. And there we have a good example of those influences—taste and temperament and the natural contour of the land in the creation of artistic features and enchanting effects in the garden; and the contour of the land afforded the very opportunity for the gratification of the Italian love of looking out upon the distant view, or down upon the garden design, where, at Villa D'Este, we see the splendid treatment of a steep slope deep enough to carry five great terraces of artistic design. The terrace in the Italian garden became a feature of first importance, adding beauty and dignity to both garden and house. And there we see that contour of land aided by taste and temperament produced the terrace. And the same is true of the creation of other features and effects in the garden—pools, fountains and cascades; water theatres and water galleries; architectural, sculptural and floral decorations; hedges of evergreens; variety in the texture of foliage; the picturesque forms of trees; light and shadow effects; and the flash or the splash, the soothing, somnolent sound and musical tinkle of water in action. Those were some of the features and effects that delighted or appealed to the Italians of the golden age of art, whose designers took the above facts and factors into consideration before planning their little five to ten-acre gardens, rich in mysterious, elusive charm.

In the creation of the French style we find the same two influences operating for the composition of a distinctly new style. The taste and temperament of Louis XIV was favorable to pomp and brilliancy, and a magnificent garden like Versailles or Chantilly, where he might hold splendid fêtes, would dazzle and enchant the court, surprise the nation, and impress the ambassadors of other countries with the importance, the wealth, and the lavish entertainment of the sovereign of a mighty nation. And those were the principal motives for the laying out in France of six grand gardens on new plans with original ideas by André Le Nôtre, whose genius was equal to the occasion of converting hundreds of acres of flat, uninteresting land into a new style of gardening. In those great gardens Le Nôtre might spread his long clipped alleys and richly decorated parterres; his groves full of architecture and gilt trellises; his immense canals, cascades and fountains; and his profusion of statues, vases and urns over a plot of land a hundred times the size of Villa D'Este. And here again the same two influences, taste and temperament, and contour of land, were responsible for the creation of the peculiar features that distinguish the French style.

It would be easy to show how those two influences, differing in their character, however, account for the creation of the Dutch and the English styles also, but I feel it will not be necessary.

The great importance of climate and plant materials has always been apparent in the decoration of gardens rather than in the invention of styles, where those two factors have played a secondary part in comparison with taste and temperament, and land contours.

In the creation of an American style it will be necessary to take certain facts and factors into careful consideration. To begin with, the difficulties to be overcome by the landscape architect are arduous, and numerous, some of which are the very factors I have been discussing—as a taste often uncultivated, and a temperament usually without ideals; contours of land of great variety; a climate running through the scale from sub-tropical to cold temperate; and a flora vast and imperfectly understood. Then the landscape architect must realize at once that he cannot longer design superficial schemes without injuring himself and worse still the profession. He must have not only valuable ideas, but original ideas if he hopes ever to invent a new design—an original design. Now as we all know that design is the distinguishing feature of a style, the feature which differentiates one style from another, it is quite apparent that it is to garden design we shall have to give profound thought; to garden design we shall have to bring new ideas. But where can we get new ideas, original ideas? I have already given the clues to the creation of the Italian and French styles—taste and temperament, contour of land, climate, and plant materials; and as they may possibly furnish a clue to a new style, let us examine those factors in America.

What are the characteristics of taste

and temperament of Americans in comparison with the Italians of the Renaissance, with the French of the time of Louis XIV, with the Dutch and the English of the seventeenth and eighteenth centuries? I might devote columns to that comparison, and to the analysis of American taste and temperament, but this is a magazine article, and more than that it is for Americans whose taste and temperament demand facts, effects, results, economy of time, of effort and of financial outlay, and as a quick solution of every problem, and as I am now discussing a problem I presume I should give either the answer at once, or suggest the process of solution in as short a space as possible. As I cannot give the answer to this problem of the creation of an American style, I shall try to indicate the process of solution.

Italian, French, Dutch and English gardens were created for certain purposes, with definite objects in view, and to satisfy certain desires, which were so dominant that unusual results in the shape of new designs were produced, and those designs were so pronounced that they were considered new styles. Keep that well in mind because there we have one of the clues to the invention of styles. Now with definite objects in view, with distinct ideas in mind, the landscape architect should create gardens in America for certain purposes and effects, by reason of certain desires; and here, owing to the difference in the character of American taste and temperament, climate, and plant materials from European factors of influence, there should be a design produced distinctly different from those of European designs. And when such an American design becomes sufficiently pronounced it will constitute a new style, which up to the present time is not an accomplished fact.

While European land contours were especially influential in the creation of the different styles, it is doubtful if that factor will be of as much importance in the creation of an American style as will climate and plant materials. It is, therefore, to those two factors that we must turn for aid in the development of a new style, and then possibly not so much to climate as to plant and foliage varieties. In this locality where there are few hardy evergreens, we shall have to give more attention to the possibilities of deciduous plant materials, which for the summer home will answer quite well. Perhaps in the end we shall see that in the creation of a new

style it is more a matter of how to use available materials than what materials to use. The European designers took the materials which they found at hand for the creation of their several styles, and why should we not do likewise?

Perhaps the most important factors of influence in American garden design will, after all, prove to be taste and temperament, and plant materials; and the landscape architect who can handle the first factor with tact, feeling, and clear perception, and the last factor with ability, with skillful treatment, and with a knowledge of the artistic effects to be created, will be the one who will produce the most charming results, and perhaps the most original results, in both features and design. But in striving for originality of design the very worst mistakes are often made. A desire for diversity in garden designs results frequently in variety being carried to excess, and when that happens simplicity and beauty are lost completely. Originality does not mean excessive variety. Variety becomes puerility when carried to the extreme; and it is in that very respect more than in any other that in all ages the gravest damage has been done to the arts of design. Variety is the chief tool with which the mediocre artist works most, the one tool that is the most difficult to control, the one that when improperly used has had the most pernicious effects by deterring the development of the arts of design. When properly used variety is a valuable principle in art, but unless handled with care and feeling, with taste and moderation, with skill, it acts as a boomerang. Those are some of the difficulties and facts to be considered by the landscape architect in America.

At present garden art in America is merely attracting the attention of the masses, although a lively interest is becoming evident among the progressive classes, while among some of our wealthy citizens a most commendable patronage is manifest. With the advent of the motor car another characteristic of taste and temperament appeared which in time will have, no doubt, an additional influence on garden design. Persons of wealth and wisdom are now going out beyond the noise and hurry and worry of city confinement to the beauties of the country, where they are giving the landscape architect an opportunity to create new gardens, new designs, and possibly a new style. What will be the final result on garden design of this increasing interest in rural life depends wholly upon the desires of wealthy Americans and upon the ability of landscape architects to satisfy the taste and temperament of their clients. This is the awakening of garden art in America and the landscape architect has now a great field of endeavor before him, a splendid opportunity to create magnificent gardens, or on the other hand the very opportunity to discredit the profession by creating gardens of puerile design. Another interesting fact to remember is this, that garden art in America is in its nascent stage and it was while still in that stage in Italy, France and Holland that those countries invented their national styles.

WILLIAM E. BLIZ-ZARD.

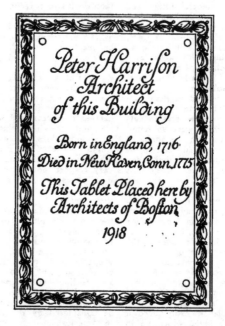

Peter Harrison
Architect
of this Building

Born in England, 1716
Died in New Haven, Conn. 1775

This Tablet Placed here by
Architects of Boston
1918

A Tablet to Peter Harrison

In June, 1918, there was published in these columns a brief account of the life of Peter Harrison, a pioneer American architect. At about the same time, June 14, the 202nd Anniversary of the birth of this early American designer, who was perhaps our first professional architect, there was placed in the vestibule of King's Chapel, Boston, a memorial tablet commemorating his work as designer of that building. This is a rare instance of modern American good will toward early American good work. Those who laid the foundations of our architectural practice deserve at least passing notice at a time when that practice has achieved an amazing complexity, and when the stolid, sturdy forward striving pioneer who designed fortifications and chapels by turns — possibly trading in rum as a side issue in respectable practice—has been replaced by the designer of office building canyons.

It is worth recording that architects of Boston arranged this tribute to Peter Harrison, Architect, 1716-1775. The tablet is about eighteen inches by twenty-six inches, and is of green slate with incised lettering and carved border. The work is most delicately executed. The tablet was designed by Theodore B. Hapgood, and carved under the direction of Edwin J. Lewis, Jr., as architect.

RICHARD F. BACH.

THE
ARCHITECTVRAL
RECORD

CONTENTS

Vol. XLVII. No. 2   FEBRUARY, 1920   Serial No. 257

Editor: MICHAEL A. MIKKELSEN   *Contributing Editor:* HERBERT CROLY
Business Manager: J. A. OAKLEY

Yearly Subscription—United States $3.00—Foreign $4.00—Single copies 35 cents.   Entered May 22, 1902, as Second Class Matter, at New York, N. Y. Member Audit Bureau of Circulation.

PUBLISHED MONTHLY BY
THE ARCHITECTURAL RECORD COMPANY
115-119 WEST FORTIETH STREET, NEW YORK

F. T. MILLER, Pres.   W. D. HADSELL, Vice-Pres.   J. W. FRANK, Sec'y-Treas.   E. S. DODGE, Vice-Pres.

ASTOR DOORS OF TRINITY CHURCH.
BY CHARLES H. NIEHAUS.

PANEL ON THE LIBRARY OF J P MORGAN. ~ Adolph Weinman

NOTABLE DECORATIVE SCVLPTVRES OF NEW YORK BVILDINGS

BY

FRANK OWEN PAYNE

NEW YORK CITY is peculiarly the art center of America. Her museums, both public and private, and her innumerable galleries where works of art are displayed, are among her chief institutions. But art has not made its abode alone within the confines of the Metropolitan nor about the purlieus of millionaires' palaces. There are works of distinguished merit to be found here and there about the city, mere details of the decoration of vast temples of trade, which would be treasured as masterpieces in the foremost art museums of the land.

It is the purpose of this paper to present to the reader some of the more interesting works which adorn our city's business houses and private dwellings—works really worth seeing and yet seldom seen in the crowded thoroughfares. A mere list of the names of the artists who have contributed to the decoration of these edifices looks like a list of the

masters whose works are on view in the galleries of great museums. This discussion has no reference to the decorative features of public parks, such as monuments and other memorials.

Lower Broadway presents a great number of imposing façades, many of which have been superbly decorated. The Exchange Court Building has four heroic statues of Hudson, Stuyvesant, Wolfe and Clinton, the works of J. Massey Rhind. The same artist has given us the beautiful group of symbolical figures on the American Surety Building, which is one of the most splendid façades in the city. Again on the domed towers of the Park Row Building we see eight slender graceful statues silhouetted high above the street. But the works of Rhind are not confind to business houses. There are the north doors of Trinity Church which depict scenes from the Old Testament, and farther uptown, on the Church of

St. Mary the Virgin in Forty-sixth street there are several fine examples of Rhind's ecclesiastical art.

Few if any sculptors have created a larger number of decorative works on New York buildings than Philip Martiny. His works may be found in every part of the city. The bronze doors of the Importers and Traders Bank at Warren street and Broadway present two excellent illustrations of Martiny's work in low relief. On the Chamber of Commerce one of the familiar groups is also from his hand. The lintel over the door of the old Mail and Express building at Fulton street and Broadway represents the four continents. These figures still arouse our admiration in spite of the fact that two of them have been mutilated to make way for the construction of a hideous show-window. Martiny's most conspicuous work is to be found on the Hall of Records. The figures representing New York and Greater New York which grace the Park Row side of that edifice are presented here. Martiny also collaborated with French, Adams and O'Connor in the façade of St. Bartholomew's Church, in Park Avenue.

The late Karl Bitter left many characteristic examples of his art about the city. His are the three tremendous titans which bear on their shoulders the lintel of the St. Paul Building at the corner of Broadway and Fulton Street. Over the entrance of the Chamber of Commerce are two recumbent figures suggestive of the similar works by Michael Angelo. The great front doors of Trinity Church show what Bitter could do in ecclesiastical art. The private residence of Mrs. Cornelius Vanderbilt, facing the plaza and the mansion of Mrs. Hungtington at Fifth Avenue and Fifty-seventh Street, have charming illustrations of Bitter's pleasing work. The only sculptures hitherto placed on the Metropolitan Museum of Art are worthy the great building which they so fittingly adorn, and the Tombs Angel in the Criminal Courts building is full of tender feeling. All these works illustrate the great versatility of one of our foremost sculptors.

Paul Manship's unique art has become a fad, especially in the realm of garden sculpture. He is not known as the creator of the decorative features of buildings either public or private. Yet Manship's work may be found on the Fulton Street façade of the Western Union Building, in a place where the marvelous technique of the sculptor may be studied to advantage.

Frederick MacMonnies is best known through his numerous monumental works about the city, especially in the borough of Brooklyn. We know of only two exemples of his purely decorative sculptures on buildings. These are the spandrels on the Bowery Savings Bank, works executed with a delicate touch which unfortunately can not be seen to advantage either from the opposite side of the street or from the platform of the Third Avenue Elevated Railway. MacMonnies also made the two wall-fountains which flank the main entrance of New York Public Library. The finished works in marble have not yet been put in place, but their representatives in plaster have been much admired.

Of all New York's public buildings, the Appellate Court House on the east side of Madison Square is the most ornate. Indeed, it has been declared to be greatly over decorated. It bears the works of many sculptors and some of them seem to be rather out of scale. Others are decidedly commonplace. But there are at least two works which redeem this elaborately decorated structure and lift it high among the finest sculptural features of the city. These are the pediment by Charles H. Niehaus and the group which surmounts it by Daniel Chester French. Neither of these artists has contributed much to the decoration of New York Buildings. The pediment of the Court of Appeals and the south doors of Trinity Church are the most noteworthy works by Niehaus. But there are several very fine and characteristic examples of his art on the façade of the University Club on Fifth Avenue. These are the ideal portraits of the great leaders of the world's thought carved on the keystones of the arches of the windows. Few there be who pause to regard these splendid creations among the throngs which pass them every day.

Mr. French has created several masterpieces about the city. The symbolic groups which flank the entrance of the Custom House at Bowling Green are

pendous work was executed by John Quincy Adams Ward and Paul Bartlett. To study it properly, one must ascend to the fifth floor of the Mills Building on the opposite side of Broad Street, where an excellent view of the work can be had. At that point of vantage one discovers that there is very fine symbol-

PANEL IN ASTOR DOOR, TRINITY CHURCH.
By Charles H. Niehaus.

familiar to all. The beautiful groups which typify the boroughs of Manhattan and Brooklyn at the eastern approach of the Manhattan Bridge, the great pediment of the Brooklyn Institute Building on the Eastern Parkway, and Alma Mater, which dominates the terrace before Columbia University Library, are characteristic examples of Mr. French's art. In collaboration with Adams, Martiny, and O'Connor, French also designed the doors of St. Bartholomew's Church recently removed from Madison Avenue to Park Avenue.

Probably there is nothing finer in the way of decorative sculpture in New York than the imposing pediment of the New York Stock Exchange. This stu-

ism in this great work. In the center stands the figure of Integrity, which should dominate all business transactions. At her left are Agriculture, represented by a man bearing a sack of grain and a woman leading a ram. Farther to the left are miners at work. At the right of Integrity are two figures representing Manufacturing and Electricity, while at the extreme right are reclining figures representing Building and Constructive Design. To the writer there is nothing finer of the kind among the decorative sculptures in America.

As one advances further uptown, there seems to be a region in which the decorative features of buildings are for the greater part the work of foreign ar-

PANELS IN NORTH DOOR OF TRINITY
CHURCH. BY J. MASSEY RHIND.

MAIN DOOR AND TYMPANUM, TRINITY
CHURCH. BY KARL BITTER.

tists, chiefly Germans. The statues of Franklin and Gutenberg which adorn the Staats-Zeitung Building are the works of Max Plassman, the same whose statue of Franklin dominates Printing House Square. It was Plassman also who made the Indian which surmounts Tammany Hall. The most pretentious work is the pediment on the old New York Central Freight Terminal in Hud-

time. One of the most noteworthy of all these decorative features belonged to the Arion Hall, now the Anderson Galleries in Fifty-Ninth Street and Park Avenue. The strong lamps at the entrance of that building are still to be seen there, but the really interesting figure of Arion which topped that edifice was taken down when the Arion Club went out of existence. These sculptures

PEDIMENT OF MADISON SQUARE PRESBYTERIAN CHURCH.
By Adolph Weinman, in Collaboration with Mowbray.
After Designs by Louis Tiffany and Stanford White.

son Street. This imposing work is not easily seen except from the trains of the Ninth Avenue Elevated Railroad.

On the building which stands at the south-west corner of Broadway and Fourteenth Street are some very decorative figures well worth study. These are the work of W. Kuntz, who also made several other sculptures of a similar character on business buildings of the better sort of fifty years ago. It is said that Kuntz was not able to obtain enough work to support him and that he practically died of starvation. Kuntz, like Plassman, was one of a number of sculptors of German and Austrian birth who came to America. Their works may

were the work of Alois Loeher. No. 6 East Twenty-third Street bears a pleasing figure representing Photography which is the work of one Hess, another of the German artists already referred to.

Isidore Konti has given us a superb relief in the façade of the Gainsborough Building in Fifty-Ninth Street near Broadway. Here we have a festival procession, which takes up the entire front of the second story. It is a most fitting decoration for a building which is devoted to art studios.

Augustus Saint Gaudens left many examples of his transcendent art in the parks and museums of the city. But so

FIGURES AT ENTRANCE TO HALL OF RECORDS. BY PHILIP MARTINY.

is but one of his creations to be found on a building in New York. That is the Diana which tops the Madison Square Garden tower, known as the "Diana of the Tower." This was originally executed much larger, but when it was found to be too large for the place chosen for it, a reduced copy was substituted on the Garden tower and the larger original was taken to C h i c a g o, where it was the finial on the Agricultural B u i l d i n g of the W o r l d's Columbian Exposition in 1893. We believe that that work was destroyed w h e n the building was burned after the close of the Fair.

G u t s o n Borglum has not made any of the decorative features of New York's business houses. So far as we are informed, his Beecher statue and his Lincoln tablet, which are on Plymouth C h u r c h, Brooklyn, a n d t h e Angel with a trumpet which crowns t h e apse of the Cathedral of St. John the Divine are all from his hand.

FINIAL ON TOWER OF WESTERN UNION BUILDING IN FULTON STREET.
By M. Evelyn Longman.

No finer business house exists in New York than that of the Gorham Company in Fifth Avenue. Here one may see the delicate art of Andrew O'Connor displayed in the beautiful spandrels on the two exposed sides of the building. These, together with the impressive sculptures on St. Bartholomew's Church, are the only significant decorative works of O'Connor in the city.

Caspar Buberl is the author of the charming figure of Puck which was the distinguishing feature of the building of that name when "Puck" was the leading humorous periodical of the land. It is a good piece of work and it well deserves

to be preserved when the building on which it stands shall be razed.

For the greater part the decorative features of New York buildings are either historical or allegorical in character. The churches very naturally furnish more or less excellent specimens of ecclesiastical art. Trinity, Grace, the Paulist Church, St. Patrick's Cathedral, and other houses of worship furnish good illustrations. L e e Laurie is the foremost sculptor of such work. His reredos in St. Thomas' Church is now rapidly approaching completion.

Artists who have devoted their time to animals have little place in the decorative sculptures o f New York buildings. To view works of animal sculpture, one must resort to the Zoölogical Garden in Bronx Park, where many excellent studies by Proctor, Knight and Eli Harvey may b e s e e n. Potter's lions are found before the Public Library. Through the courtesy of the New York Zoölogical Society, we are permitted to publish pictures of some of the houses in the Zoölogical Garden; one of these shows A. Phimister Proctor at work on the elephants which adorn the Elephant House. The Lion House furnishes good examples of the work of Eli Harvey.

In ceramic art there are numerous beautiful examples to be found in the encaustic tiles and other ornamentations of the subway stations. Wall Street, Fulton Street, Astor Place, Columbus Circle, and many other stations furnish suggestions of some historical fact connected with the immediate neighborhood. The delightful art of the late Olin War-

ONE OF FOUR COLOSSAL GROUPS BEFORE NEW YORK
CUSTOM HOUSE.
By Daniel Chester French.

GROUP TYPIFYING BROOKLYN AT EAST APPROACH
OF MANHATTAN BRIDGE.
By Daniel Chester French.

CENTRAL FIGURE IN PEDIMENT OF
SUPREME COURT HOUSE, APPELLATE
DIVISION. BY CHARLES H. NIEHAUS.

SUPREME COURT HOUSE, APPELLATE
DIVISION. SCULPTURES BY FRENCH,
NIEHAUS, RUCKSTUHL AND OTHERS.

SPANDRELS ON GORHAM BUILD-
ING. BY ANDREW O'CONNOR.

NEW YORK HERALD CLOCK.
BY ANTONIN JEAN CARLES.

PEDIMENT OF STOCK EXCHANGE, BY J. Q. A.
WARD, IN COLLABORATION WITH PAUL BARTLETT.

DECORATIVE PANELS OF GAINSBOROUGH
BUILDING.   BY ISIDORE KONTI.

A. PHIMISTER PROCTOR AT WORK ON SCULPTURES OF
ELEPHANT HOUSE IN ZOOLOGICAL GARDEN.

DETAIL FROM ZOOLOGICAL GARDEN.
By A. Phimister Proctor.

114

ELI HARVEY'S SCULPTURES ON LION
HOUSE IN ZOOLOGICAL GARDEN.

CARYATIDES ON THIRTY-FOURTH
STREET FRONT OF MACY'S DEPART-
MENT STORE. BY J. MASSEY RHIND.

ner may be seen in the medallions on the Long Island Historical Society Building in Brooklyn. Here there are excellent portraits of Franklin, Columbus and other celebrities.

The creations of Adolph Weinman are among the finest art treasures of the city. The most conspicuous of these are the reliefs and finial of the Municiapl Building. The Pennsylvania Terminal clock is wrought with masterly technique. The pediment of the Madison Square Presbyterian Church, which is soon to be taken down, is a thing of great beauty. This was done in collaboration with Mowbray after designs by Louis Tiffany and Stanford White. But the most exquisite of all the works of Weinman and, as we think, about the finest decorative pieces of their kind in the city, are the panels of the Morgan Library. These are charmingly expressive and dainty creations.

In addition to the pediment of the Stock Exchange, which he did in collaboration with Ward, Paul Bartlett also carved the frieze sculptures on the Public Library, about the only works worth mention on that ill-fated building. Miss M. Evelyn Longman is the creator of the golden figure of Modern Zeus or the Genius of Telegraphy which tops the tower of the Western Union Building in Fulton street.

There are also many good sculptural works about the city whose authorship is not known. Among these are the medallions on the Edison Building in Read street, which portray the likenesses of Franklin, Edison, Morse and others. The house of Eimer and Amend in Third avenue, at Eighteenth street, possesses good likenesses of Liebig, Darwin, Lavoisier and others, heroes of the world of science.

French artists are not very largely represented by works of a decorative character in New York City. The most conspicuous are the Herald Clock, which is the admiration of all who visit the vicinity of Herald Square at the beginning of the hour. This most unique clock consists of a beautifully modelled figure of Minerva, who presides over a great bell at each side of which stands a workman armed with a huge hammer. In striking the hour, each of these men swings around and smites the bell. The Herald Clock is the work of Antonin Jean Carlès of Paris. The bell was cast in the famous bell-foundry at Troy, N. Y.

Another artistic clock may be seen on the Grand Central Passenger Terminal. Here we have an imposing group symbolizing the purposes of the railway. The design is the creation of Coupin, the famous French decorative sculptor, and the carving was done by John Donnelly.

Louis Richard is the author of the simple and beautiful pediment sculptures on the Duveen Brothers' store in Fifth avenue. This work fitly decorates the façade of New York's foremost art concern.

To one who looks for works of artistic merit about the thoroughfares of the metropolis, a walk in almost any direction will prove an inspiration. Daily we stand in the presence of marvels of architecture, engineering and art. How few of us take time to regard them. Truly Gotham is one of the wonders of the modern world. Whether we see it at rosy dawn, or through pearly mists, or tinged with golden light at sunset, or indeed projected against the dark sky at evening with all its myriad lights asparkle like a huge constellation, it is a marvelous thing of beauty.

SKETCH FOR FLAGPOLE BASE, CLERMONT, CAL.
MYRON HUNT, ARCHITECT; BURT JOHNSON, SCULPTOR.

WAR MEMORIALS

PART III
MONUMENTAL MEMORIALS
BY CHARLES OVER CORNELIUS

THE preference as between a purely votive and a utilitarian war memorial is largely a matter of temperament and a question of taste. In view of the character of the recent war, a struggle between autocracy and democracy, little help in the way of inspiration is to be gained from a study of the great memorials of the past. For these are as a rule products of social conditions existing in autocratic governments, conditions whose roots were laid in a unified or, at least, a definitely classified state of society; as yet our own democratic state is in a flux, the resolution of which belongs to the future. However, although the usefulness of the great memorials of the past is merely nominal in one sense, it is all important in another—that of furnishing standards of comparison for our own creations. Since these ancient monuments, which we admire for their excellence and fitness for their purpose, originated in motives so foreign to our commemorative impulse, we should view them mainly as a point of departure; sensitive to the evolutionary processes of artistic development, we must create our own memorials if we are to speak to future generations of our own ideals and in our own language.

The architectural expression of historic periods in which mental outlook and spiritual experience approximated those of our own age, may offer suggestions to the designer, but suggestions only, for the various forces that entered into the expression of past periods are variable quantities which may be, and probably are, largely absent in our own scheme of life. Inspiration must be sought in our present day life and in the emotional appeal of which we, as a people, are conscious.

The utilitarian memorial does not address itself so directly to the emotions as does the purely votive memorial. Its appeal is often sociological or economic; and in equal measure as this is true come opportunities for diverting the real purposes of the memorial, for subordinating the commemorative idea to less exalted ends, so that in the last analysis the work epitomizes the materialism of its living creators instead of the ideals of the dead whose honor it is supposed to proclaim. There is danger of employing this commemorative impulse as a vehicle to bring into being innovations making for the comfort and convenience of the public, innovations whose presence that public may have every right to demand as its due without the introduction of the memorial element as a reason for their being. With the purely votive memorial, expression is more direct, the language through which it speaks is less obscure and better understood. The arguments in its favor are more intangible, yet the ultimate expression of its purpose is likely to be understood by a much greater number of interested observers.

119

Let us consider dispassionately what our own experience tells us of the actual appeal to the emotions of certain types of memorials which we know. Take, for instance, a building such as a library, a dormitory or a settlement house erected in memory of some one whose intensest interest during life was associated with the immediate activity fostered in the building. As we approach, do we not think of it first of all as housing a particular activity? When we enter, if it is properly fulfilling its function, are we not primarily interested in the actual operation of the activity whose home it is? We may have asked ourselves whether this is not a memorial building as our eye was attracted by some detail of decoration or some votive tablet. But in the end our attention is occupied by the purely physical organization and embodiment to the exclusion of any thought of the man or woman to whose memory this pile of masonry has been dedicated.

With the purely votive memorial this is seldom true. Whether it be a dignified outdoor monument or a window of glowing stained glass, the appeal is direct, attention is not distracted from its message. As in a medieval mass, the employment of a combination of the arts unified by one impulse may heighten the emotional appeal and give pause to the average man for a moment of serious thought of the dead thus commemorated, introducing a touch of sentiment referred directly to the single and unescapable object of our thought.

There must, however, be no presupposition that the utilitarian and commemorative ideas are in any way mutually exclusive; but where both are present the demand upon those to whom is entrusted the expression of both elements in terms of architecture is of such difficulty as to call for a touch of genius in addition to the well trained talents of which we may presume the author to be possessed. And, in a country by no means notable for the dignity and quality of its memorial art, is it not well to choose in the earlier stages of the development of that art the least complicated and the more surely excellent

terms in which to express the desire of commemoration?

To point out really successful votive memorials, successful in the sense that they carry their personal message of deeds nobly done through beauty of conception intrinsic in form and detail, we find our choice limited indeed. More than half a century after the event, memorials to the personalities of our Civil War are beginning to take on a commensurate excellence of artistic diction. It is probable that a nobler result would have been achieved if at the time when poignant feeling was still crying for expression, artists of inspiration and training had been at hand ready to interpret. Today we find ourselves infinitely better placed in this respect and with a glance at the very few results which have already shown themselves we may feel encouraged for the future.

The memorials which are shown in the accompanying illustrations all obviously bear the mark of twentieth century conception. In use of architectural form they are eclectic, while in choice of subject and its presentation they mark a tendency toward generalization which is a characteristic of the time. They are all, however, an appeal direct to the emotions, an appeal never sentimental, always dignified and frequently rich in historical or dramatic suggestion.

The larger group is composed of outdoor monuments placed in positions chosen to heighten their effect, somewhat aloof from the rush of city life. Nothing could be simpler or finer than the memorial to Major Clarence T. Barrett by Sherry Fry and the architectural setting by T. Sillett is original and bold.

The Albany memorial shows an adaptation of the Renaissance sarcophagus motif to a twentieth century usage. The effect of the combination of materials and the individual treatment of each is distinguished and rich.

In the flagstaff base the architecture by Cass Gilbert and the sculpture by Paul Bartlett harmonize with rare perfection. Seldom can we point to a work where the essential qualities of the ma-

MEMORIAL FLAGPOLE BASE, MINNEAPOLIS, MINN.
CASS GILBERT, ARCHITECT; PAUL BARTLETT, SCULPTOR.

LAFAYETTE MEMORIAL—NINTH STREET ENTRANCE
TO PROSPECT PARK, BROOKLYN. HENRY BACON,
ARCHITECT; DANIEL C. FRENCH. SCULPTOR.

MEMORIAL TO MAJOR CLARENCE TYNAN BARRETT, STATEN ISLAND, N. Y. SHERRY FRY, SCULPTOR; T. SILLETT, ARCHITECT.

MEMORIAL TO SOLDIERS AND SAILORS OF THE CIVIL
WAR, ALBANY, N. Y.: HERMON A. MAC NEIL, SCULPTOR.

MEMORIAL TO SOLDIERS AND SAILORS OF THE CIVIL WAR, ALBANY, N. Y. HERMON A. MAC NEIL, SCULPTOR.

MEMORIAL VESTIBULE AT YALE UNIVER-
SITY. SCULPTURE BY HENRY HERING.

MEMORIAL VESTIBULE, NASSAU HALL, PRINCETON
UNIVERSITY. DAY & KLAUDER, ARCHITECTS.

MOSAIC PARAPET RAIL IN ST.
THOMAS' CHURCH, NEW YORK CITY.
BERTRAM G. GOODHUE, ARCHITECT.

RHEIMS CATHEDRAL—MOSAIC PARAPET RAIL IN ST. THOMAS'
CHURCH, NEW YORK CITY.

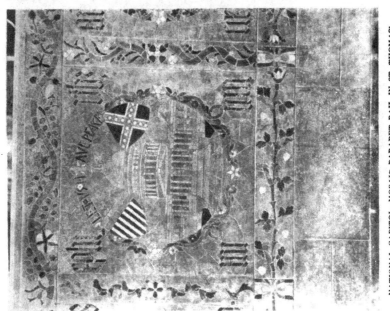

NATIONAL CAPITOL—MOSAIC PARAPET RAIL IN ST. THOMAS'
CHURCH, NEW YORK CITY.

4

WINDOW IN MEMORY OF CAPTAIN NATHANIEL
SIMPKINS, CHURCH OF ST. JOHN THE EVANGELIST.
BEVERLY FARMS, MASS. BY CHARLES J. CONNICK.

terial (in this case Minnesota granite) have been so perfectly preserved both in sculptural and architectural treatment. The bronze, too, confesses this appreciation of material on the part of the designer and possesses a sparkle and brilliancy frequently lost in similar work.

Three interior memorials are shown. The first, the Memorial Vestibule which is being erected in Nassau Hall, Princeton University, marks the dedication of one room in a most important position as a memorial to those who fell and those who served in the World War. The building in which it is placed is in no sense a memorial building. But the whole impressiveness of a memorial has been concentrated into this marble room. English in scale and feeling, it harmonizes with the provincial tradition which it follows and finds a particular appropriateness in its location in a building so closely identified with the struggle for American independence.

Related to this memorial is the vestibule at Yale University, part of which takes the form of a broad archway flanked by Henry Hering's fine reliefs, and in which architecture, sculpture, mosaics and metal-inlay unite in the final effect. The broad wall space treated with lettering has a decorative quality quite unexampled.

Not the least interesting of the interior memorials is the Captain Simpkins window by Charles J. Connick. Simple in its composition, powerful in its leading, resonant and symbolic in its color, these three lancets seem to answer all of our demands for the appropriate war memorial—direct and strong appeal to the emotions, a suggestion of the sadness of early death, the glory of power and the beauty of sacrifice. The effect of such a memorial is of course intensified by its location in a dim and quiet church.

A record, rather than a memorial, is seen in the mosaic parapet rail newly placed in St. Thomas' Church in New York. In the detail of the whole choir is an abundance of suggestive imagery telling the story of the years of its erection. In this portion of the choir furniture, which separates the nave from the choir, is the story of church and state in America to the year 1919. On the left three panels present the church as a refuge, a ship and a lighthouse. To the right we have the first settlement at Jamestown in 1607, Independence Hall in Philadelphia, and the Capitol at Washington. The two remaining scenes, which flank the steps to the choir, introduce the World War, marking the end of one era of church and state and the beginning of a new. To the left the grain of mustard seed has grown into a tree where perch the eagle and the dove. Beneath it lie down in peace the lion and the lamb. The inscription, "League of Nations 1919," may seem a trifle premature, but there it stands. To the right of the steps the panel shows Rheims Cathedral, with the date 1915.

The colored marble is soft in tone and the values are kept so nearly equal that the surface is not disturbed. The mosaics, which are unusual in scale and technique, are successful decorative treatments, and the contrast with all the work which surrounds them is very fine.

The various forms of these memorials of a votive nature, some of which by reason of their position as portions of buildings may well be termed utilitarian, suggest a few of the many expressions which the memorial impulse may take. They are, first of all, compositions of few elements, so that their message comes direct. They show the effect of modern intellectual approach in the choice of subject and in the eclectic nature of their detail. They express, above all, the desire to commemorate the ideals which inspired the heroic dead rather than the confused events of the war itself. In these very facts we seem to see an attitude toward the subject of memorial art different from that of centuries preceding, an effort to render permanent an impression of individual sacrifice and personal ideals, in contradistinction to the commemoration of victorious battles and physical prowess. Our country is well equipped with artists and architects capable of carrying out the work while still the memories of the war are fresh in mind; and the only necessary additional factor is an intelligent and active public interest.

ENTRANCE—RESIDENCE OF DR. T. J.
ABBOTT, CORNWALL-ON-HUDSON, N. Y.
PARKER MORSE HOOPER, ARCHITECT.

SOME PRINCIPLES OF SMALL HOUSE DESIGN

By John Taylor Boyd, Jr.

Part IV - PLANNING - Continued

THE first three articles of this series have dealt closely with the architectural side of the design of the small house. This is their purpose, for they aim to set forth clearly certain principles of the household art. However, there are several important features of cost and of construction that must be briefly noted in so far as they influence planning and decoration.

Taking up the economic side, the financial problems of the American family—income, household expenses, service—were becoming more complicated before the war, until today they are really in a critical state, as everyone knows. Prof. Kimball, in an admirable summary of family economics in the October number of the Architectural Record, presents tables which show that, for a family whose yearly income is $3,000, the sum of $6,000 is a reasonable investment in a house (and land); and for a family of $6,000 income, $12,000 should be a proper expenditure for a small house. In addition, in the budget of the first family, $450 is available per annum for running expenses and $900 is available in the budget of the second family. When a family employs a maid, the expense of providing her with room and bath should be included in the cost of her hire; and this leads Prof. Kimball to conclude that, at present prices, only families of $6,000 to $8,000 may afford to keep even one maid.

These figures set forth, in terms of arithmetic, the plight of the family of "limited income" one year after the troops stopped fighting in the Great War. "Limited income" means professional and salaried workers above the class, economically speaking, of skilled wage-earners and clerical employees. The figures tell why homes are not being built extensively enough to relieve the unprecedented shortage of homes throughout the country. Thus the man who wishes to build finds himself blocked by world conditions. He realizes that the tremendous forces of civilization have been thrown out of gear, and he sees that they must either come back to their old adjustments or else reach a new balance before all the work of civilization can proceed. Of course, in such a situation, speculation is useless. One may say, however, that the unfortunate economic relationship presented by Prof. Kimball cannot last a very long time: certainly, the American family must be decently housed, and the American people will find a way to do it even if the way is not altogether clear at the moment. It may well come to pass that rentals for houses—or their equivalent in yearly cost of owning a house—may hereafter require a larger share of the family income than formerly.

Whatever the future may bring, common sense would decide that we are likely to live in smaller houses than we were accustomed to before the war. They are not only cheaper to build and to furnish,

133

but they are cheaper to maintain, to repair and to run. So far as construction goes, for some years expert builders and architects and engineers have looked forward to introducing into house construction the economies of business organization and of use of machinery. Such methods have been developed in the building of great office buildings and factories. But houses are erected much as they were in the time of Moses, when, as now, each brick and stick of framing was handled many times by hand labor in its progress from claybank and trees to its final place in a building. However, even if construction of houses be made cheaper, that other most important side of their cost—operation—can hardly be much reduced. Repairing always means hand labor, which is expensive; and the other factors of maintenance, cleaning, operation, service, etc., even if simplified and cut down in some respects by greater use of machines, may grow more costly in others. It may be always difficult to get maids. Each year business and industry expand at a greater

rate than population; they absorb more and more of the young women of the country, paying them well, and seeking the intelligent workers. The hapless housewife must compete with business for her labor. The result of this unfortunate situation is, as everyone knows, that more and more houses are run with fewer maids than formerly or with no maids at all, and nearly all houses are run without maids a part of the time.

The scarcity of domestic workers forces people to plan their homes as simply and as economically as possible. This is not to say that we are yet at a point where maid service is only for the rich and that houses should be planned to be operated without maids. There are times in the history of every family when domestic service will be needed or desired.

One more possible economy has to do with the mechanical equipment of our homes. The installations of plumbing, heating and lighting are costly in themselves, costly to construct and to repair and to operate. They cut up the walls with pipes and ducts and are unpopular

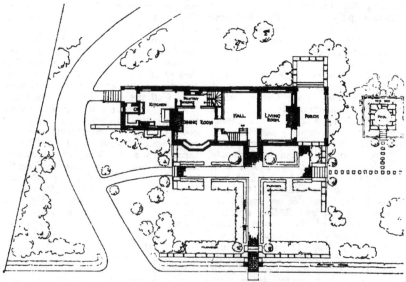

BLOCK PLAN—RESIDENCE OF GEORGE WILLING, ESQ., CHESTNUT HILL, PHILADELPHIA, PA.
Charles Willing, Architect.

with the designer. One may well ask, Is not all this mechanical equipment too complicated? If only a single agent—electricity or gas or oil—did all the work of heating, heating water, cooking and lighting, one or more of the various systems of piping that are now required in a house might be eliminated. Gas does much of the work needed in a house; and electricity can do more, with the added advantage of using small motors, nearly automatic, to operate labor-saving devices. But, unfortunately, electric heat consumes a great amount of current. Coal is a nuisance in a home; it is being driven out of the kitchen by gas, and we would like to see it put out of the cellar, too. This may be done by using central power plants for groups of houses, but this method still leaves the complicated system of heating pipes in the walls. Altogether, the most unsatisfactory features of the mechanical equipment are the complicated pipe and duct systems, and the use of coal. It is to be hoped that technical experts will find how to eliminate those two defects of household mechanics, and furnish us with simpler devices which, even if not so much cheaper in themselves, will at least be cheaper to repair and to operate.

Such is a brief summary of some of the economic and mechanical features of the house, in their bearing on its design in the broadest way. I have considered them only enough to show that they are undergoing changes in this post-war period, and that the results of this change cannot possibly be predicted. All that may be gathered is that houses should be planned in restricted dimensions, and as simply as possible. Designers are being forced to eliminate some features entirely, or else make them more subordinate than was formerly thought desirable. They must be ready to reclassify the essentials.

With this short excursion into the no-man's-land of economic and mechanical principles ended, more specific features of the architecture of house plans may be considered. Here one is writing at a disadvantage. For, in striving to understand the adaptations of house plans required by post-war conditions, one must depend on illustrations drawn from houses built before the war, few of which meet existing conditions perfectly. Thus a great variety of types and sizes of houses appears in these pages, and yet the whole collection does not give as clear a picture of a

135

RESIDENCE OF GEORGE WILLING,
ESQ., CHESTNUT HILL, PHILADELPHIA,
PA. CHARLES WILLING, ARCHITECT.

SOUTHEAST FRONT—RESIDENCE OF GEORGE WILLING, ESQ., CHESTNUT HILL,
PHILADELPHIA, PA.
Charles Willing, Architect.

small house as one might desire—as clear a picture as will be obtained two or three years from now, after many houses have been built under the new conditions. To this extent the discussion has played around the small house rather than centered in it. What is needed is a more specific statement of the planning of the small house, in order to make the ideal more vivid.

The first thing to be decided about the small house is its size—the number of rooms. Here is a standard to which we may repair with a little more confidence than in the case of shifting costs. Formerly, as we have seen, the "small house" was permitted to contain many of the features, even if reduced in scale, of the great house. It was also allowed service wings with quarters for three servants if needed. But today such space it is almost impossible to pay for and to operate. Hence it is not sur-

prising that many houses built since the war, in 1919, have been nine-room houses; "nine rooms" meaning three or four rooms (including kitchen), on the first floor, and four or five bedrooms, (including maid's room) above. Since one more bedroom is easily added on the third floor, or in a wing, many ten-room houses have been built. If the first floor is to be planned flexibly, in ways I have described in the third article, this room standard may need to be differently expressed. Where, for example, the dining room or the reception room is thrown into the living room, it may be better to measure the room standard by the number of bedrooms. Accordingly, the average small house will have its ground floor planned flexibly to suit the individual family, and above will have five bedrooms and probably two baths, including one room and a bath for the maid. Small families of adults may be

137

content with fewer rooms, and larger families may add more bedrooms and baths. Still another way of arriving at the standard of the small house is to realize that the five-bedroom house, or the nine-room house as it is better known, is a house that is only a little larger than the five and six room house of skilled mechanics and of the better class of clerks. In this latter type of house one room is often both dining and living room, leaving three or four rooms for bedrooms. These skilled wage earners' houses are operated without maids, and it will be seen that they are only a little smaller than the small houses of the professional man and salaried worker. Their rooms are not much smaller in dimensions and are only one or two less in number; and where the family maintains a maid the actual bedroom space

at its disposal is hardly greater than that which the wage earner's family—in the economic class just below—possesses in its higher standard house.

Thus it may be said that five and six bedrooms are a fair index of the size of the small house, a standard which economic conditions, construction costs and costs of service, maintenance and operation, all tend to fix for the "average" family. It is a house a little larger and somewhat finer than the house that is coming to be the standard for the skilled employee. And since the "average" family is not always average, the small house may slightly vary from this figure, above or below, according to the size of the family and its income and the economics of the neighborhood.

With the size of the small house more definitely decided, materials must be con-

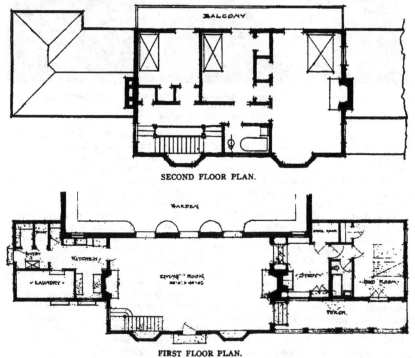

SECOND FLOOR PLAN.

FIRST FLOOR PLAN.
RESIDENCE OF DR. T. J. ABBOTT, CORNWALL-ON-HUDSON, N. Y.
Parker Morse Hooper, Architect.

RESIDENCE OF DR. T. J. ABBOTT, CORNWALL-ON-HUDSON, N. Y.
Parker Morse Hooper, Architect.

sidered. Building costs vary all over the country, and at present relative costs of different materials even in any locality are not easy to establish. Before the war, all-wood construction was cheapest in most localities. Wooden houses with exterior stucco or brick walls came next in figure. But now the supremacy of wood and brick are threatened by high labor costs. Wood is becoming scarce, although, with good forestry regulations, the United States should have a sufficient supply of good building lumber. Wood may be high-priced for some years. Another drawback of wood that is coming to be better understood is its high maintenance cost. Wood construction deteriorates rapidly after five or six years. Mr. Prescott F. Hall has gathered some figures on depreciation of brick and wood buildings. He quotes the report of the Lloyd Thomas Co., a firm of appraisers, made to the Chicago City Council, that brick has a "life" of from eighty to one hundred years and frame thirty-three to forty years; that in the better class of residences brick has no depreciation during the first five years and one per cent yearly after that. Mr. Hall quotes a canvass of twenty-two insurance companies, agents, builders and architects, advising that brick dwellings have an average depreciation of one and one-half per cent and wood two and one-half per cent. Some estimates ran as high as five per cent for wood. Mr. Hall concludes that wood depreciates two to three times as rapidly as brick. He prepared his figures before the war, and it is possible that today wood may compare more unfavorably, because wood must be repainted every few years, and painting is now very high in comparison with the cost of other items in building. Altogether, it would seem that houses will be built more and more of stucco or brick for exterior walls, except in those fortunate regions like Philadelphia, where a beautiful, easily worked, local stone is available. Stucco is particularly acceptable to designers because of its possibilities of treatment for texture and color; with respect to color, it is far preferable to brick in our hot American sunshine, in which ordinary brick is out of key. Many designers understand the color limitation of brick and some of our keenest architects have painted or whitewashed the walls of their buildings in light colors, with striking success.

Coming now to the acual planning of the house, the matter of location, according to compass points, exposure, topography of the site and outlook, is important. While some of these factors are apt to be conflicting, they may usually be reconciled.

In the eastern part of the country the north is the least desirable exposure. Here are located kitchens and as much as possible of entrance, service and minor features, such as halls, bathrooms, closets, etc. The east—and also the south—is a good place for the dining room because daylight meals of breakfast and lunch are favored by sun-

RESIDENCE OF DR. T. J. ABBOTT, CORNWALL-ON-HUDSON, N. Y.
Parker Morse Hooper, Architect.

RESIDENCE OF DR. T. J. ABBOTT, CORNWALL-ON-HUDSON, N. Y.
Parker Morse Hooper, Architect.

light. The living room goes well on the south, southwest, or west, with a porch or awning on the most exposed south or west side to alleviate the heat and glare of light. After spaces for living and dining rooms have been arranged on the plan, other rooms, such as the study, reception rooms, etc., take what is left, usually on the north or northwest, but often on the east. It is usually not difficult to harmonize these requirements with the best direction of outlook. In this connection, one regrets that so many Americans still place the best part of the house—the dining and living portion downstairs and the best bedrooms upstairs—along the street front, instead of overlooking the garden, where, if the garden is presentable, they certainly belong. The plan of Mr. Colby's house in the first article of this series is a fine example of accurate orientation. He had the advantage of a lot on the south side

of an east and west street and made the most of the opportunity. On a lot on the opposite side of the street from Mr. Colby's the kitchen may be east. If it is to the rear, northeast, it runs into the garden. This may not be desirable; the kitchen may come towards the street, as in the admirable plan shown on page 359 (fig. 79), of the October Architectural Record. The dining room should have some east light, and the living room should be well lit on the west.

Where the lot is on the west side of a north and south street, the kitchen comes easily on the north; but in order to place the dining room on the garden and at the same time give it east light, it must run through the house from east to west. This might cause it to be too large, besides adding other complications, a situation which would naturally favor the dining room as an alcove, opening east off a living room that runs north

141

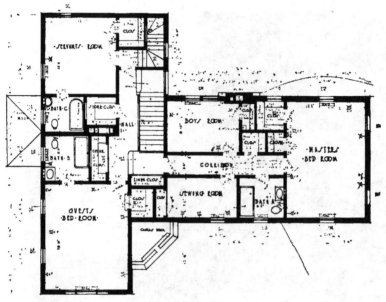

SECOND FLOOR PLAN.

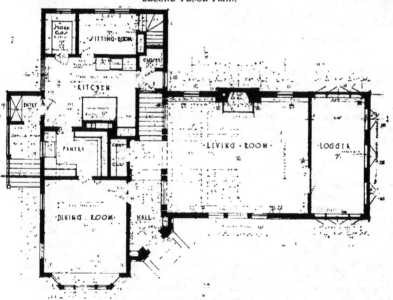

FIRST FLOOR PLAN.

RESIDENCE OF FRED LAVIS, ESQ., HARTSDALE,
N. Y. PARKER MORSE HOOPER, ARCHITECT.

RESIDENCE OF FRED LAVIS, ESQ., HARTSDALE, N. Y.
Parker Morse Hooper, Architect.

RESIDENCE OF FRED LAVIS, ESQ., HARTSDALE, N. Y.
Parker Morse Hooper, Architect.

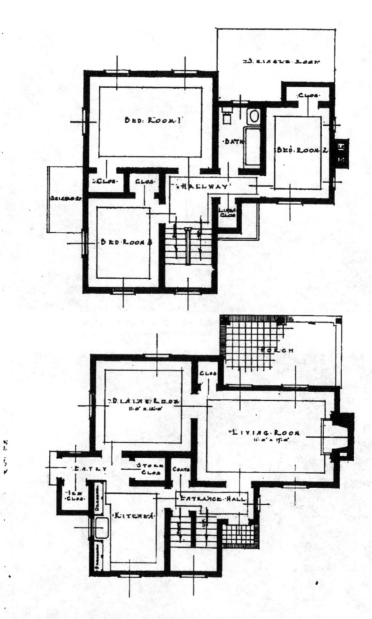

HOUSE NO. 1 FOR HOME COMMUNITY
CORPORATION, BALDWIN, L. I. POLHEMUS,
MACKENZIE & COFFIN, ARCHITECTS.

HOUSE NO. 1 FOR HOME COMMUNITY CORPORATION, BALDWIN, L. I.
Polhemus, Mackenzie & Coffin, Architects.

and south. The living room is easily placed on such a lot. In the case of an east lot on a north and south street, there is a fine location for a dining room southeast on the garden, with a long living room running north and south. It is evident that this location favors a dining room continuous with the living room. On a north and south street, of course, kitchen and garage offer no difficulty. This situation—an east lot in a north and south street—is the best situation for the "stock" plan, considered in the third article, since the dining room may have south and east exposure on the garden, with a little breakfast porch or loggia opening off it. The stock plan goes well on the south side of an east and west street. Its weakness on the average small suburban lot is that the living room usually runs along the end of the house and thus not along the garden.

After exposure is well in mind, the matter of entrances is to be settled. At this point the automobile threatens the small house. It demands either a turn seventy feet or more in diameter or else a roadway in the shape of a semicircle. These features are expensive to construct and to maintain, and they ruin the expanse of the lawn of small lots. Mr. Colby was careful to maintain the breadth of his hundred-foot wide lawn by keeping it unbroken by either path or road, using instead dull-colored stones set in the greensward, two rows to the garage, as tracks for his car. These great spaces for automobiles are out of place in any but large estates. A circular turnaround is particularly obnoxious, for its seventy-foot expanse presents the somewhat comic effect of an entrance to a house that is bigger than the house itself. There are various excellent substitutes, particularly the charm-

145

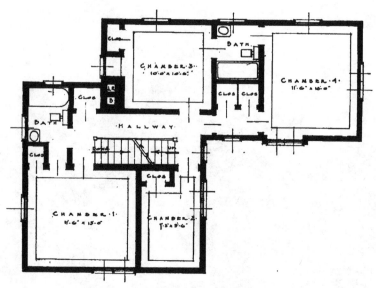

SECOND FLOOR PLAN

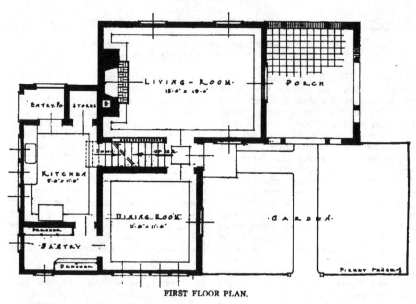

FIRST FLOOR PLAN.

HOUSE NO. 2 FOR COMMUNITY HOME
CORPORATION, BALDWIN, L. I. POLHEMUS,
MACKENZIE & COFFIN, ARCHITECTS.

HOUSE NO. 2 FOR HOME COMMUNITY CORPORATION, BALDWIN, L. I.
Polhemus, Mackenzie & Coffin, Architects.

ing covered way to garage from front door illustrated in the third article. One should not hesitate to back and turn a car in a narrow roadway on one's own lot just as one does on the public street. One may also construct little parking spaces or switch tracks at right angles to the garage roadway which will allow the car to be turned with a single backing.

All these matters of orientation, outlook, entrances, etc., are, of course, bound up with lot planning, which precedes and reacts on the planning of the house. The division of the house into family and service portions is next to be considered. Some time ago the practice of placing the maids' bedrooms on the third floor came to be thought undesirable in many cases. It brought the maids too much in contact with the family, caused them much stairclimbing, and on the exterior made the house look top-heavy. As a result there was developed the service wing, where kitchen and maids' rooms were set apart in a unit which was really a separate little house in itself, connected to the main house only by the pantry between the kitchen and the dining room. This is of course an excellent arrangement, particularly for two maids or more, and it should be retained so far as possible in the future. It may be practicable to place the maid's room so near the family that it may be occupied by the family if no maid is to be had. Also, in many cases the secondary service stair from kitchen to maids' bedrooms, is being eliminated. In the elevations, any distinction between the main house and the wing need not be made if the house is already so small that its appearance would suffer if it were cut into two pieces. Some people may wish to eliminate the pantry between kitchen and dining room as unnecessary, where there is no maid, but this is a radical step that should be well considered, for it might hurt what is called the "real estate value" of the house.

The other aspects of the arrangement of the first floor plan have been covered

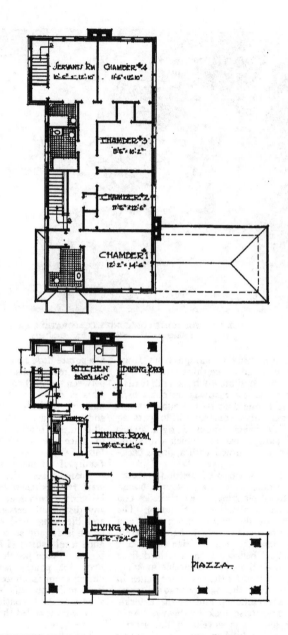

HOUSE AT SCARSDALE, N. Y.
EUGENE J. LANG, ARCHITECT.

HOUSE AT SCARSDALE, N. Y.
Eugene J. Lang, Architect.

in the third article of the series. Therein the possibilities of a flexible subdivision into principal rooms and minor spaces were described; how simplification and combination might make plans not only more practical and more economical to build and to operate, but also, on the creative side of household art, would render the plan a more perfect symbol of the ideal of the American family; how imagination, cheerfulness and beauty of decoration might be obtained in our homes, outside in the plot of land, and inside as well, centering chiefly in the living room; how this living room might be made larger in size and endowed with distinction in a way formerly thought possible only in great houses.

From this alluring side of the ground-floor plan it is but a step into the kitchen and service. Their details will be considered later, but it may be said here that elimination may take place in this part of the house as well as elsewhere. Before the war, maids were being provided with their own dining rooms, pan-

try, porch, etc. These features are not so necessary where there are only one or two maids and their expense may be too great. Their effect may be gained by ingenuity in planning. For instance, to a small kitchen, say nine or ten feet by twelve or fourteen feet, might be added a small alcove for the meal table, which would preclude the impression of dining in the kitchen. Laundries are not thought so desirable as formerly, particularly in the basement. The above considerations therefore leave the service part of the house—reduced to its lowest terms—to consist of a small kitchen, perhaps with alcove for a meal table, a small pantry between it and the dining room, a stair down to the cellar, a small porch or entrance loggia, a little room for supplies and for the ice-box, which may be iced from the outside. And then such features of garage, covered ways, tool and garden sheds, as add to the utility of the plan and the beauty of the elevations.

Only the bedroom floor remains to be

149

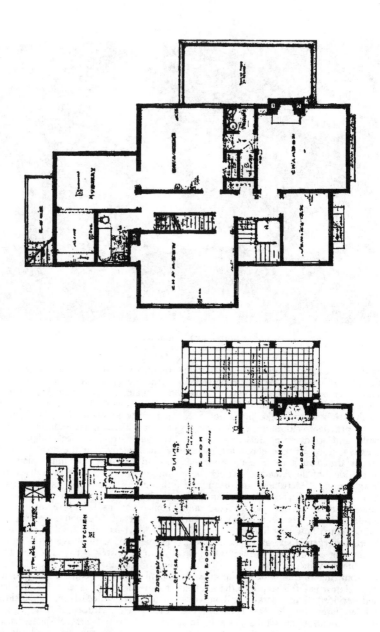

RESIDENCE OF DR. EDMUND F.
CURRY, FALL RIVER, MASS. PAR-
KER MORSE HOOPER, ARCHITECT

RESIDENCE OF DR. EDMUND F.
CURRY, FALL RIVER, MASS.
PARKER MORSE HOOPER, ARCHITECT.

RESIDENCE OF DR. EDMUND F. CURRY, FALL RIVER, MASS.
Parker Morse Hooper, Architect.

considered in this summary of the typical small house of today. Not so very much is to be said about it. In these days no one need be told how best to subdivide a second floor into bedrooms, bathrooms, halls, closets, etc., in order to get maximum value of space, exposure, cross ventilation, access, and of such details as the proper placing of the furniture. Only one defect should be warned against. That is the too-usual cramped hallways, long and narrow tunnels. Long three-foot wide halls with no open space at the head of the stairs give the bedroom floor an air of the staterooms on a steamer.

It is seldom that one may find a group of houses more inspired by the ideals of the small house than the examples that appear in this article. They are the work of younger architects and display extraordinary artistry and imagination, boldness in decoration and color in sunlight, yet they are tempered with all the expert skill and perfection of detail that is the worth of the older and more book-

ish school of architecture. They are at once dramatic works of art and livable American homes. I should like to confront with these houses those critics who claim attention by crying out for American art and should like to ask them if these houses are not works of art and American.

These houses portray the differences in style of New York and Philadelphia, the two regions where American house architecture is at its best. In Mr. Willing's design are the strength and harmony of Philadelphia, bold, strong capacity in massing, mastery of roof, ability to make landscape paintings out of building materials, the modern freedom which somehow sticks to two centuries of tradition. In details, Mr. Willing's house ranks with the best Philadelphia practice, which is often heavy; for it has the delicate brilliancy of mouldings of the early American work. His details give that touch of sparkle and gayety, and vividness so characteristic of twentieth century

152

America. It is well arranged on the lot, on a sloping hillside, overlooking at the rear a lovely valley and its solid walls and strong roof slopes make it seem built into the landscape, an effect which is aided by the details and shapes of outdoor terraces, walls and planting. Its plan repays study. It is for a small family and much space is allowed the entrance, affording on a small scale that air of openness and hospitality that, as I pointed out in the previous article, are so perfectly mirrored in the plans of the old Southern mansions.

It is interesting to see how Mr. Hooper's three houses possess the same extraordinary qualities as Mr. Willing's, yet are entirely different in character. Taken as Philadelphia houses, they illustrate how personality may bring variety into art and yet follow the same traditions. The house at Cornwall-on-Hudson is a splendid outdoor house, situated on the famous Storm King Mountain, with entrance on the west. Its plan is lengthened out, most of it on the ground floor, home-like and perfect for entertaining. As will be seen, its arrangement is flexible. Mr. Hooper has a fondness for changes in level, which add so much to the charm of a house; in this case the living room, on the lower level, is all the more quaint because of its low ceiling. On the exterior, the house has a splendid bold massing, high, vertical centre part and tower-like chimneys balanced against low wings with horizontal accents. It reveals both the painter's eye for mass and color and the sculptor's feeling for strong modelling in places and relief of surfaces, combined with perfection of details. Note the perfect proportioning of the windows, the exquisite scale and oblong shape of the window panes, which are not too square. Mr. Hooper's house at Hartsdale shows another characteristic, free plan, "L"-shaped, with entrance in the angle and with change of level, in this case up to the dining room.

Two charming little houses to be built at Baldwin, Long Island, prove that tiny dimensions and compact plan do not of necessity forbid imagination. These

houses are about as small as even a small house may be.

Mr. Hooper's house at Fall River and Mr. Lang's house at Scarsdale solve a difficult problem—that of a house on a narrow street front. In such cases it may be advisable to turn the end of the house toward the street. The gist of Mr. Lang's compact plan is that the lot is on the east side of a north and south street and the principal rooms are strung along the south. The maid's suite is another interesting point in this plan. These lengthened plans bring out the difference as regards floor area between plans that are long and narrow and those that are more nearly square. The squarish plan is thought to be more economical, because more compact. This cannot be denied, but I think that its importance is exaggerated. There is no great difference in the ground floor economy of the two types, particularly if the longer plan is planned freely. Upstairs, in the longer plans there is apt to be more length of corridor than in the square plans, where nearly all the rooms open off the head of the stairs. Still this waste may be exaggerated, for supposing an extreme case of twenty extra feet of corridor three feet six inches wide in the long plan, this is a cubage of only about 700, costing $350 at a liberal allowance under present prices. There are people who will always be willing to pay a few hundred dollars more in a small house when this expenditure yields charm and personality and artistry in the final effect.

Mr. Hooper's plan shows the added complication of business quarters on the ground floor, in this case a physician's suite. Incidentally, this house was built at a very low cost. The elevations of both these houses are excellent. Mr. Lang's simple, vigorous and fine in scale, and Mr. Hooper's bold in the decorative modelling of walls in planes and projection. The detail of the front of Mr. Hooper's house shows that this modelling is not a whim but is intimately connected with the plan. It allows on the first floor the fine bay window, and on the second floor, four feet to be added to the bedroom above.

Photo by F. R. Taylor.

DOORWAY LEADING TO MAIN
STAIRCASE, ASHBURNHAM HOUSE.

English Architectural Decoration
Text and Measured Draw-ings by Albert E. Bullock

Part XIII.

INTERIORS of carved pine wood became common about the middle of the eighteenth century. Of these the Victoria and Albert Museum at South Kensington possesses two excellent examples removed from old houses in London. One is from No. 27 Hatton Garden, a street rich in good panelled interiors, and the other from No. 5 Great George Street, Westminster. The former is a work of quite exceptional merit, possessing many features of interest, not the least of which are the bold carved cartouches to the overdoors. The chimneypiece design is reminiscent of work by Inigo Jones, having female heads crowning the flanking pilasters (similar to those in one of the rooms of the Queen's House, Greenwich), while on either side are sunk niches with scroll pediments.

The general effect is rich, although the original painting is now pickled down to the ordinary wood surface, giving a cold effect. Owing to the lapse of years these carved pine rooms usually have so many successive coats of paint applied that the enriched moldings become choked with the color mastic, and much of the sharpness of the cutting is lost.

The adjoining room, which is similarly treated, is of later date, towards the close of the reign of George the Third. In this there are several features characteristic of the period, notably the Greek fret pattern to the dado rail, the carving of the friezes to the overdoors and the general nature of the smaller panel molds comprising the walling. The overmantel of the chimneypiece is flanked by boldly carved pendant drops, which are a salient feature contrasting well with the quieter tone of the other decorations. Both these rooms have sunk moldings, differentiating from the earlier practice of the William and Mary or James the Second periods, when the bolection molding was in vogue. The moldings of the example in question are enriched, and the whole room is a complete scheme in simple vein embracing elements of much refinement.

There are two instances of William and Mary rooms at Westbury Court near Newnham-on-Severn, Gloucestershire. One is the interior of the classic pavilion on the boundary wall of this charming garden, at the end of a long narrow lake lined with low broad yew hedges; the other is a room on the first floor of the older portion of the house formerly covering a loggia to an earlier mansion. The house is owned by Mr. Colchester Wemyss, but is tenanted at the moment by Mr. Backhouse, whose interest in the garden and house is quite keen.

The small but lofty room, which is about fourteen feet high, is similar in character to work of the same period at Hampton Court Palace. The windows have heavy bars and small panes, while the mirror over the marble architrave is divided into two bevelled squares separated by a narrow strip of glass of Venetian design, cut and bevelled with a series of floral patterns chased on the surface; the panelling is bolection molded.

The pavilion was evidently erected at the same time, as the character of the moldings of the interior panelling is similar but of simpler nature, the stiles being sunk with ovolo moldings and fielded panels. The exterior is in stone, the entrance door being flanked by Corinthian pilasters.

About two miles west of this house is the residence of Lady Paget, known as Unlawater, Newnhamn-on-Severn. The house is small but of early foundation, facing the north bank of the river. Additions from time to time have altered the plan and nature of the interior. In the hall, of late Georgian date, one gets

155

a glimpse at one side of the chimney-piece of a portion of a carved stone Jacobean lintel; and between the columns is seen an Adam period leaded fanlight which was over the original entrance but now forms the entrance to the combined library and drawing room built out towards the river front. The painted decorations to this room are by Lady Paget, who, having spent some thirty-six years in Italy, is imbued with the spirit of that warmer clime. Another of her Ladyship's painted rooms is entered from the hall, the scheme of which is blue and white, with Austrian silver candelabra and embossed silver mirror to the over-mantel. The staircase is a particularly fine example of mid-Georgian character, being molded through to the wall strings on the soffit of each tread, as in examples at the Victoria Hotel, Newnham, and at No. 5 Clifford Street, Bond Street, London, of which I hope to treat in my articles upon staircases.

Before leaving this house mention must be made of a small angle chimneypiece on the landing of the first floor. It is ornamented by large flanking carved scrolls, past which a flight of steps leads to a small room utilized as a chapel and having a beamed ceiling painted in imitation of that from Santa Cruz.

The Victoria Hotel at Newnham contains, besides the staircase mentioned, several panelled rooms, some of which were painted by the former owner in the Badminton Hunt colors—French blue, white and brown. The large dining room on the garden front has a vaulted or coved ceiling, a fine chimneypiece and windows with thick bars and mid-Georgian carved scrolls to the architraves where they meet the dado rail. This room was formerly a Catholic chapel, probably part of the house before it became a residential hotel.

After visiting this hotel I went on a mile, and up a steep incline, to the residence of Lieutenant Kerr, but found little of architectural interest. The view over the Severn from this altitude is particularly fine, and the house contains some good furniture and a great sword said to have been carried by the Bishop before

King John. It was repaired in the sixteenth century, and is incised with the date and a description.

Cirencester House, the residence of the Earl of Bathurst, has an eighteenth-century staircase of some interest in the hall, which is long and narrow and contains four large marble columns carved with Corinthian capitals, probably placed in their present position by the preceding Earl. The history surrounding their introduction is obscure, but they were doubtless brought over from Italy about the time of the Elgin marbles.

There are some recently discovered simple panelled rooms, both Jacobean and Georgian, on the bedroom floor; but there are not any reception rooms of antiquity. Such additions as have been made are comparatively modern.

Two good chimneypieces, which the present Earl found in an outhouse, have been incorporated in the interior, the one in the large dining room being a good example of late Georgian design. The ceiling of the dining room has been raised at the expense of the comfort of the rooms above. The carved woodwork has been brought from another old house and adapted to the room. The mahogany veneered doors look well in their white deal enriched architraves.

The charm of the exterior lies in the great park and in the fine circular yew hedge, enclosing the principal front, which has a height exceeding twenty-five feet in a continuous sweep, horseshoe fashion, the classic stone front of the mansion joining the extremities. Compared with many another English example, there are few large yew hedges as fine and in as good condition as this one at Cirencester House.

The decorations at Byfield House, Painswick, are of the mid-eighteenth century. The ceilings and wall adornments are important, since many houses of the period were without ceiling adornment. On the wall of the rear passage communicating between the main and servants' staircases the panelled decorations are worked on the plaster, and the small shell pattern is notable for its originality of design.

CEILING OF DR BUSBY'S LIBRARY,
ASHBURNHAM HOUSE, WESTMINSTER.

CARVED DOOR HEAD FROM NO. 27
HATTON GARDEN, LONDON. IN
VICTORIA AND ALBERT MUSEUM.

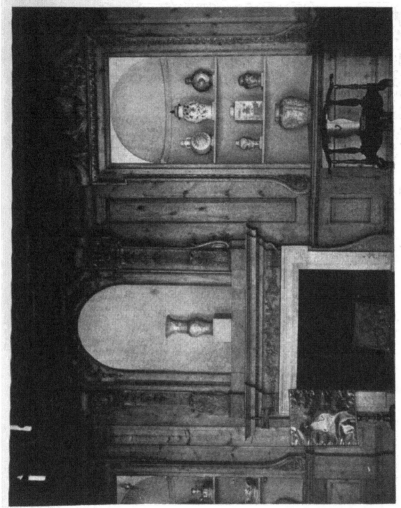

CHIMNEYPIECE FROM NO. 27
HATTON GARDEN, LONDON. IN
VICTORIA AND ALBERT MUSEUM.

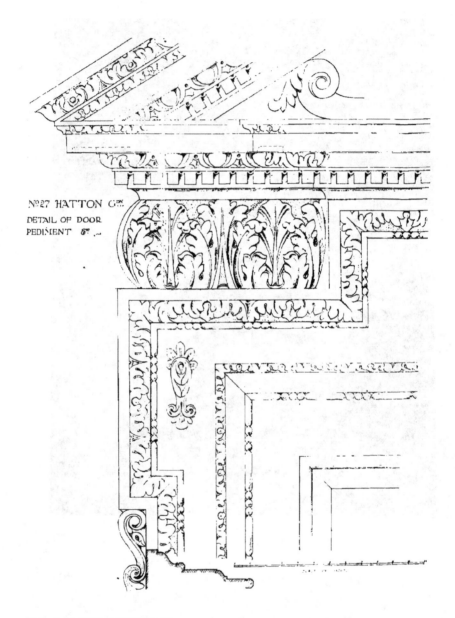

Nº 27 HATTON Gᴰᴺ
DETAIL OF DOOR
PEDIMENT 6" →

**DETAIL OF DOOR PEDIMENT—NO.
27 HATTON GARDEN, LONDON. IN
VICTORIA AND ALBERT MUSEUM.**

SCALE OF FEET

DETAIL OF DOOR CASING—NO. 27
HATTON GARDEN, LONDON. IN
VICTORIA AND ALBERT MUSEUM.

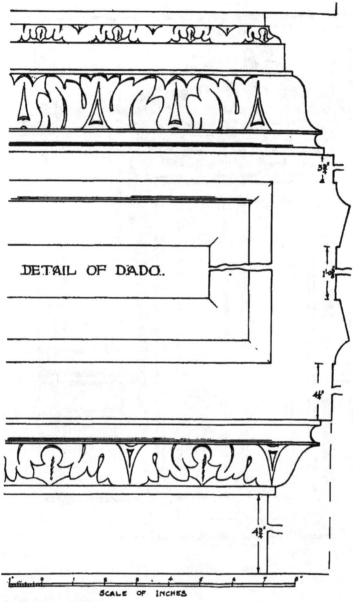

DETAIL OF DADO.

SCALE OF INCHES

DETAIL OF DADO—NO. 27
HATTON GARDEN, LONDON. IN
VICTORIA AND ALBERT MUSEUM.

ROOM FROM Nº 27 HATTON GARDEN - LONDON.
NOW IN THE VICTORIA & ALBERT MVSEVM.
(SOVTH KENSINGTON)

PLAN ABOVE MANTEL

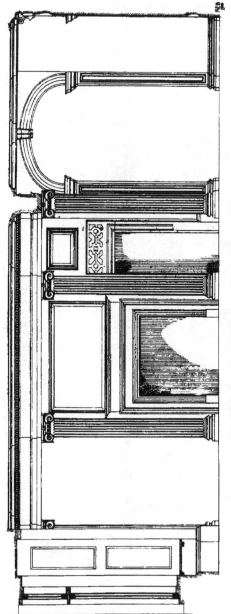

THE HALL AT UNLAWATER · NEWNHAM·ON·SEVERN.

SCALE OF FEET.

THE HALL AT UNLAWATER.
NEWNHAM-ON-SEVERN.

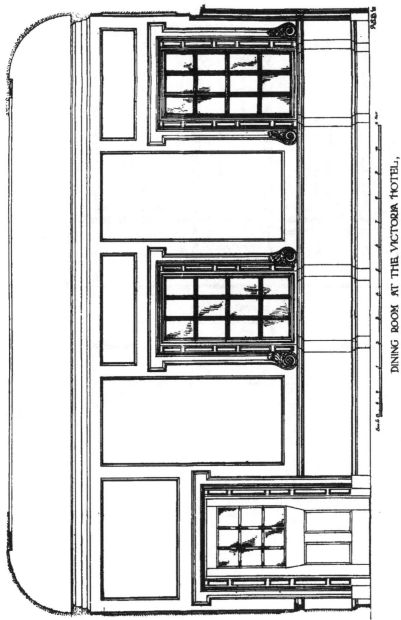

DINING ROOM AT THE VICTORIA HOTEL,
NEWNHAM - ON - SEVERN.

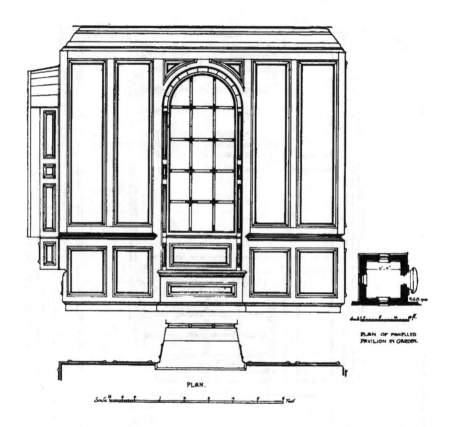

PLAN.

Scale ⁱ² feet

PLAN OF PANELLED
PAVILION IN GARDEN.

GARDEN HOUSE, WESTBURY
COURT, GLOUCESTERSHIRE.

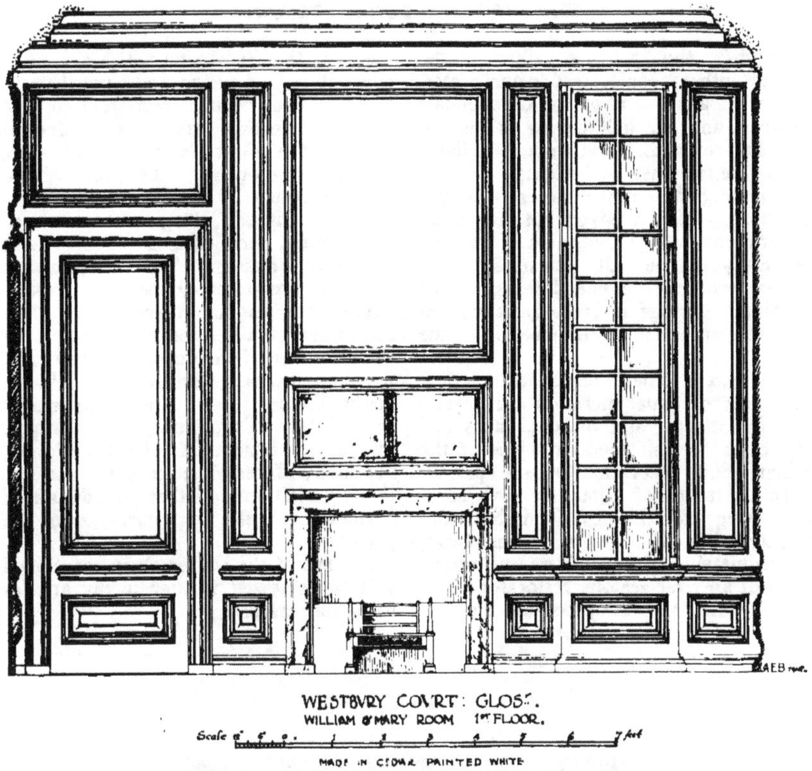
AEB mes.
WESTBURY COURT: GLOS'.
WILLIAM & MARY ROOM 1st FLOOR.
Scale 1 2 3 4 5 6 7 feet
MADE IN CEDAR PAINTED WHITE

WILLIAM AND MARY ROOM ON FIRST FLOOR,
WESTBURY COURT, GLOUCESTERSHIRE.

Further, the staircase ceiling is designed with an eagle crest in the center. The walls are typical of the Chippendale manner, and the hall ceiling is divided into squares with Doric soffit medallions lining the staircase well edging.

The original chimneypieces have unfortunately been removed, but the plaster decorations to the overmantels remain, especially in the hall, which is typical of work of the Chippendale era. The adjoining passage is vaulted, having interesting ornament at the meeting of the ribs.

There are other rooms with ceiling ornament of equal merit on the ground and first floors; and the cupboards and staircases furnish good examples of the joinery and decoration of the period.

In the town of Gloucester are some interesting old houses, including the Conservative Club. The others have, unfortunately, suffered from the attentions of an over-zealous restorator.

There are some late Jacobean chimney-pieces at the Bell Hotel which are, however, of coarse design and clumsily executed. The wood street-front is the most interesting carved and panelled Charles the First design I have seen, and in a good state of preservation.

A room usually shown to visitors, existing at Fisher's Restaurant, is pieced up from old panelled examples and lacks continuity of design. The Georgian sash windows are probably the most genuine part of the original room. These show rooms are usually inserted to attract and catch the eye of the unwary. They exist in most towns. The Sparrow House, Ipswich; the Treaty House, Uxbridge; the Buttery, Dartmouth, etc., all have undoubted elements of original antiquity, but have suffered either from bad restoration or additions of other periods out of harmony with the first conception of the place.

Several of the houses above mentioned will be reviewed further in my articles upon staircases.

CARVED CHIMNEYPIECE, SEVENTEENTH CENTURY.
In Victoria and Albert Museum.

PORTFOLIO
OF
CVRRENT
ARCHITECTVRE

UNIVERSITY CLUB, SYRACUSE, N. Y.
TAYLOR & BONTA, ARCHITECTS.

MAIN ENTRANCE—UNIVERSITY CLUB, SYRA-
CUSE, N. Y. TAYLOR & BONTA, ARCHITECTS.

LOGGIA—UNIVERSITY CLUB, SYRACUSE,
N. Y. TAYLOR & BONTA, ARCHITECTS.

MAIN ENTRANCE—UNIVERSITY CLUB, SYRA-
CUSE, N. Y. TAYLOR & BONTA, ARCHITECTS.

LOGGIA—UNIVERSITY CLUB, SYRACUSE,
N. Y. TAYLOR & BONTA, ARCHITECTS.

LOBBY—UNIVERSITY CLUB, SYRACUSE, N. Y.
Taylor & Bonta, Architects.

LOUNGE—UNIVERSITY CLUB, SYRACUSE, N. Y.
Taylor & Bonta, Architects.

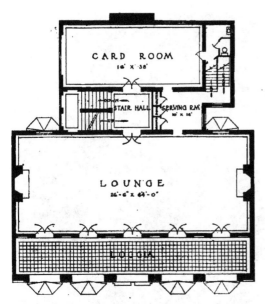

SECOND FLOOR PLAN—UNIVERSITY CLUB, SYRACUSE, N. Y.
Taylor & Bonta, Architects.

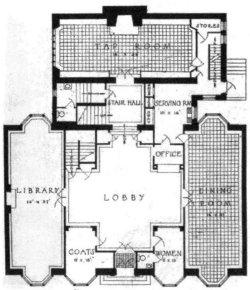

FIRST FLOOR PLAN—UNIVERSITY CLUB, SYRACUSE, N. Y.
Taylor & Bonta, Architects.

173

HOTEL CLEVELAND, CLEVELAND, OHIO.
Graham, Anderson, Probst & White, Architects.

HOTEL CLEVELAND, CLEVELAND, OHIO.
Graham, Anderson, Probst & White, Architects.

174

HOTÈL CLEVELAND, CLEVELAND, OHIO. GRAHAM, ANDERSON PROBST & WHITE, ARCHITECTS.

GUARANTY TRUST COMPANY'S BANK OF ASIA, NEW YORK CITY.
Alfred C. Bossom, Architect.

GUARANTY TRUST COMPANY'S BANK OF ASIA, NEW YORK CITY.
Alfred C. Bossom, Architect.

GUARANTY TRUST COMPANY'S BANK OF ASIA, NEW YORK CITY.
Alfred C. Bossom, Architect.

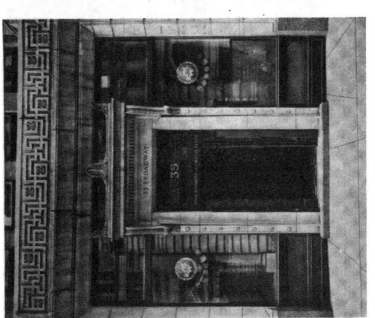

GUARANTY TRUST COMPANY'S BANK OF ASIA, NEW YORK CITY.
Alfred C. Bossom, Architect.

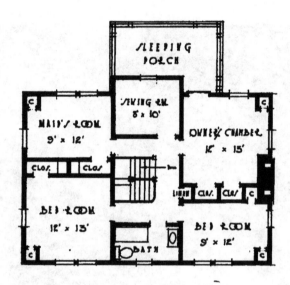

· SECOND FLOOR PLAN ·

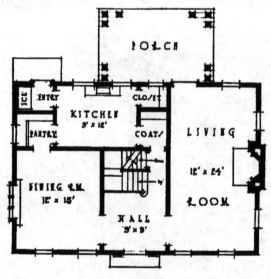

· FIRST FLOOR PLAN ·

RESIDENCE OF DR. R. B. TAFT, BELMONT,
MASS. GRANDGENT & ELWELL, ARCHITECTS.

RESIDENCE OF DR. R. B. TAFT, BELMONT, MASS. GRANDGENT & ELWELL, ARCHITECTS.

DOOR DETAIL—RESIDENCE OF DR.
R. B. TAFT, BELMONT, MASS. GRAND-
GENT & ELWELL, ARCHITECTS.

ST. PHILIP'S CHVRCH
BRVNSWICK COVNTY, N.C.

A Typical Colonial Meeting House of the South Atlantic Coast —

By N. C. Curtis

SITUATED in a pine forest near the west bank of the lower Cape Fear River about twelve miles below Wilmington, North Carolina, adjacent to the colonial plantation of Orton, may be seen the ruins of the ancient parish church of St. Philip and in the adjoining churchyard some historic tombs of a type interesting to the student of early American architecture. The curious and romantic history of this old parish and of the long abandoned town of Brunswick, where were located the homes of the churchgoers, is a matter of record and has been set down in the annals of the lower Cape Fear by Dr. James Sprunt and others. To the studious disciple of architecture, the materials, workmanship and manner of design practised by our forefathers and acceptable to their taste are no less significant and worthy of notice.

This church was built about 1730 with bricks, which, it is said, were brought over from England by the settlers of that region. Although this assertion is often made about a large majority of our colonial brick buildings when there is little evidence to support it, in this particular instance there can hardly be any doubt, since the superior quality and peculiar character of the bricks used to face the walls bear ample witness to the truth of the statement.

The strength of the masonry walls of St. Philip's Church is really remarkable. One would think, considering its great age of close upon 190 years, and the fact that up to a few years ago it has been a totally neglected ruin, that much of its walls would long since have crumbled to the earth. But the very opposite is true, for apparently not a single brick has fallen or loosened from its bed.

Every vestige of woodwork has, of course, disappeared; but, even so, it has not been a difficult task to make a restoration of reasonable accuracy. In the accompanying measured drawings I have attempted to suggest such restorations as are warranted by the evidence, but the chief merits of the building must be discovered in such features as proportion, quality of brickwork, etc., as there is little indication of any studied ornamental detail.

The brickwork is beautiful and interesting in character. The face bricks, which are laid in Flemish bond, are backed with an excellent quality of small common bricks laid with rather thin mortar joints. The face bricks themselves vary in shade from a rich, dark maroon to purplish red, and with the exception of the surface, which is hard and smooth, though uneven, resemble very closely the variegated bricks now manufactured. The most interesting thing about the bond is found in the headers, which are all coated on the exposed end with a dark bluish-green enamel. This is a genuine surface glaze and is not due to vitrification of the bricks, as might at first be surmised. The mortar joints are rather thin, varying from three-eighths to one-half inch. The joints are struck flush and are of a light yellow color. The actual dimensions of the brick units is a point worth noting. Their size is considerably larger than the present-day standard brick, being three by four by nine inches, exact measurement. The mortar used is of a most excellent quality, showing not the least sign of crumbling. No doubt it was made of shell-lime, burned on the spot and mixed and seasoned with the greatest care.

The tombs of William Dry, Esquire, and of Mistress Mary Quince illustrate a characteristic type of design which was very generally used for funerary monuments in the early days. It is a type also closely reminiscent of contemporaneous work of the same nature in Georgian England. This has been pointed out by Carl C. Tallman, writing of the tombs of Bruton Parish Church, Williamsburg, Virginia; who concludes from the excellent stone-cutting of mouldings, bas-relief work and beautiful lettering, that these monuments must have been executed in the mother country. This conclusion is further borne out by a comparison of the Governor Nott tomb at Bruton with such English tombs as the example in the churchyard, Braintree Essex, England, illustrated in Mervyn Macartney's "Practical Exemplar of Architecture." Here are noticed the same arrangement of squat corner pilasters or balusters, interrupted by side and end panels, and the characteristic thumb-moulded rim around the top slab. The tomb of William Dry is entirely of marble, stained and mellowed by time; while that of Mrs. Quince has a sandstone base and bluestone slab. In both examples the lettering of the inscriptions is excellent.

Some years ago the ladies of the North Carolina Chapter of Colonial Dames were instrumental in having the churchyard cleaned up and fenced in, and a few necessary repairs to the church and neighboring tombs were intelligently carried out at that time.

St. Philip's Church, while not of outstanding architectural significance, is historically interesting and noteworthy, since it represents a type of the brick colonial church or meeting-house of moderate size, of which many were built at various places along the South Atlantic coast by the early settlers. Among these may be mentioned Jamestown Church; Ware Church, Gloucester County, Virginia; Pompion Hill Chapel, near Charleston, South Carolina; and old churches at Edenton and Bath, North Carolina.

As indicated above, there was little attempt at planning or development of special features, but it is evident that what the early builders did they sought to do well. Moreover the proportions of a single room, as here, fifty by seventy feet by thirty feet high are by no means insignificant. The construction of the roof on a clear span of fifty feet was probably not very difficult, for abundance of yellow pine timber of virgin quality stood close at hand, and walls three feet thick and so well built could easily bear the load. It is further interesting to note that the sides of the oblong plan are in the ratio of the side of a square to its diagonal — a relation which has been frequently cited by theorists as being a close approach to ideal proportions.

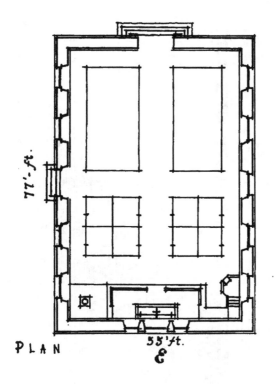

PLAN

77'-ft.

55'ft.

E

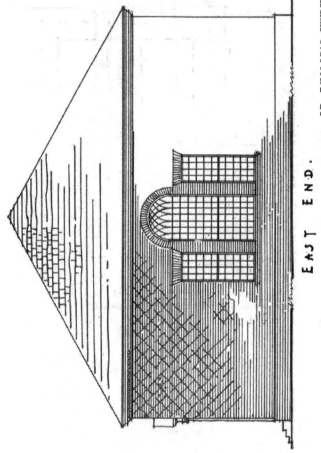

EAST END.

ST. PHILIP'S CHURCH,
BRUNSWICK COUNTY, N. C.

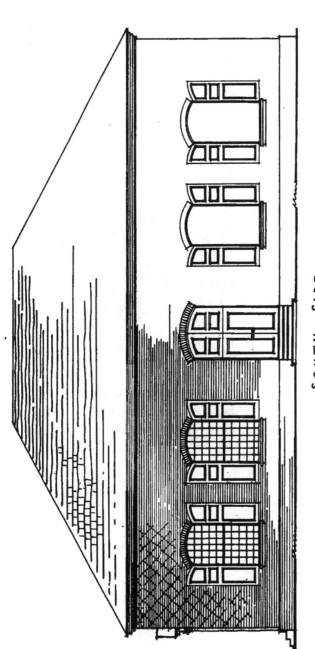

SOUTH SIDE

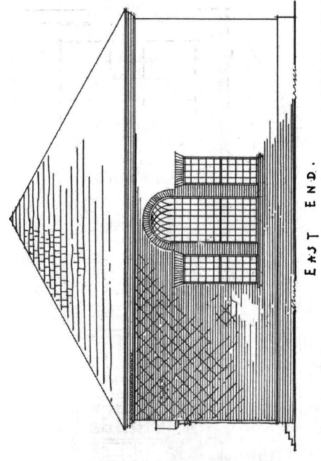

EAST END.

ST. PHILIP'S CHURCH,
BRUNSWICK COUNTY, N. C.

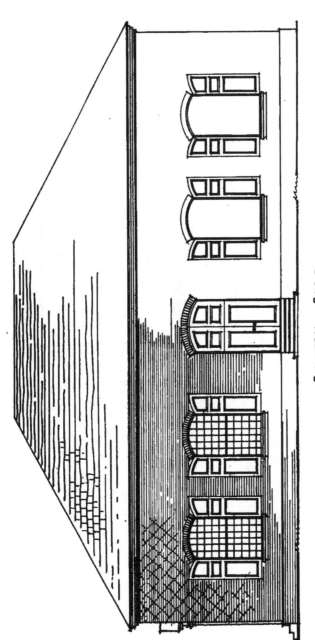

SOUTH SIDE

ST. PHILIP'S CHURCH,
BRUNSWICK COUNTY, N. C.

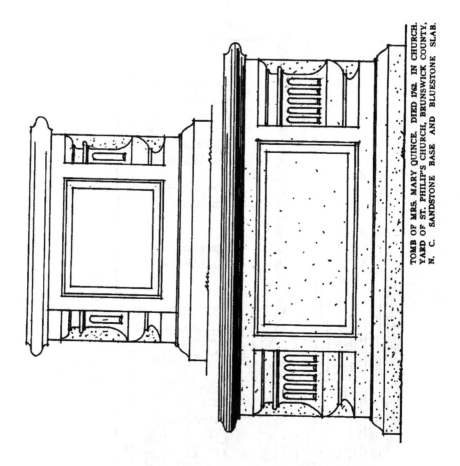

TOMB OF MRS. MARY QUINCE, DIED 1762, IN CHURCH.
YARD OF ST. PHILIP'S CHURCH, BRUNSWICK COUNTY,
N. C. SANDSTONE BASE AND BLUESTONE SLAB.

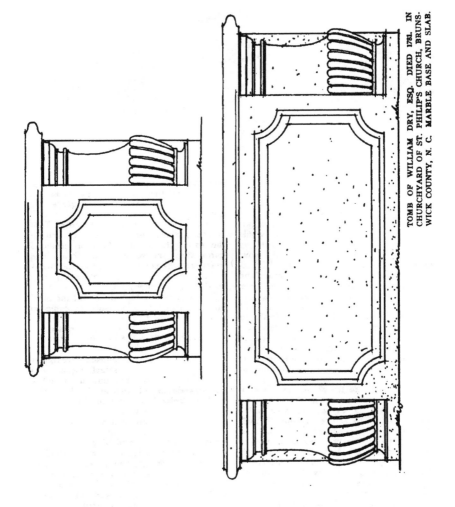

TOMB OF WILLIAM DRY, ESQ. DIED 1781. IN CHURCHYARD OF ST. PHILIP'S CHURCH, BRUNS-WICK COUNTY, N. C. MARBLE BASE AND SLAB.

Gentlemanship. As a child I imagined the house of every gentleman to stand alone by itself and to be surrounded by beautiful gardens; I fancied the whole world to be peopled by gentlefolk. And now, even, I do not see why it could not be so. It would require only some reflection and forethought on the part of town builders. My sympathy with the ideal of the "garden city" is not to be questioned. But precisely because I believe so firmly in the development of all vacant land on the principle of the garden city, I must call attention to the danger of reproducing under a fresh coat of paint the evils of the ancient slums we are seeking to abolish.

Going directly to the point, there is now a tendency to lay out garden cities or villages in such a way as to revive building in rows. The errors common to such building have been avoided, I admit, in certain cases of urban development like that designed by Messrs. Murphy and Dana and published in the Architectural Record for July, 1918, by Mr. Lawrence Veiller; here the rows are not deep, and there are no long rows, nor are the rows of equal length, and the taste of the whole is perfect.

But to see long rows at Garden City, in Letchworth, England, seems to me contradictory to the spirit of the place. In the September, 1918, number of "Garden City" magazine, p. 55, is a photograph of the district-council's war cottages. It all looks very well because of the fresh paint, but it will not last. There is no privacy, no intimacy—the primordial requirements of a house.

Let the home stand by itself, have its own individuality, its own voices, songs, silences and life. Every family its house; every house its garden, every garden its flowers.

Cost? I am not counting the cost. That is the business of the architect and of the manufacturers of building materials. I know they are ready to put brain and heart into the solution of the matter, waiting for the people to meet them half way on the road of education.

The time is ripe for this study; the ideal of the garden city is ready to come to fruition. Do not wait too long.

GEORGES BENOIT-LEVY, Director,
Association des Cités-Jardins de France.

A Façade in Three Units. An unusual treatment of a street façade was worked out in the office of George B. Post and Sons for the Euclid Building in Cleveland. The problem was not an interesting one at first sight. It was a remodelling job such as every architect detests. The old building was ugly in design, had never been completed and for years had been an eyesore in the busiest part of the city. A portion of it had been cut off and rebuilt as a separate structure and its structural steel work had to be partially rebuilt; in fact, its only redeeming feature seemed to be that it was of good size and offered an excellent opportunity for a façade with the customary three or four story basement of plate glass and terra cotta, the infinite stories of face brick wall and the capping stories of terra cotta.

Instead of following the obvious lead, however, the façade was considered in terms of three units, each given an individual treatment, but all tied together as

Lithograph by John Vincent.

EUCLID BUILDING, CLEVELAND, OHIO.
GEORGE B. POST & SONS, ARCHITECTS.

a harmonious ·group; harmonious in size, scale and style, but differing in detail. Terra cotta was used as a facing material, and this was accented by a varied use of marble and ornamental bronze.

This triple effect can not be criticized on the score of affectation, for the building itself was also divided into three parts corresponding to the front.

The customary idea of producing an imposing skyscraper was ignored, and instead there was worked out a straight forward illustration of restraint and uniformity in street architecture and sky lines. As one's eye takes in the chaotic effect of the neighboring buildings, each one of which seems to proclaim aloud its inalienable right to be what it pleases to be, this dignified little group makes one wonder whether some restraint should not be placed on the present unbridled abuse of architectural freedom.

The accompanying illustration deserves especial mention, as the original from which it was taken is a lithograph. Water color, pencil, pen and ink and even pastel have long been the architect's medium of expression, but the lithographer's stone has seldom been requisitioned for this purpose in late years. As one recalls some of the work executed in this medium a generation or two ago, interesting possibilities are suggested in a revival of this neglected medium.   I. T. FRARY.

MAIN EDUCATIONAL BUILDING OF THE MASSACHUSETTS INSTITUTE OF TECHNOLOGY.

The Massachusetts Institute of Technology Endowment Fund.

The Massachusetts Institute of Technology has been vitally connected with the development of American architecture. The first permanent school of architecture in the United States was founded at the Institute. Nearly a score of architectural departments throughout the country have Technology graduates at their heads or in important positions. Moreover, the recent successful culmination of Technology's $8,000,000 endowment fund campaign sets her free to contribute even more amply to architecture in the future than she has done in the past.

The plant of the Institute itself is a remarkable architectural achievement. Technology was fortunate, three years ago, in being able to move to an entirely new site with a splendid water front position on the Charles, where fine new buildings had been erected with her especial needs in mind. The most important part of the plant now completed consists of the Main Educational Building, which encloses an area of about thirteen acres with a floor space of about fifteen acres. As the need arises, additions will be made to the Main Educational Building until ultimately it will enclose an area of about thirty acres with a floor space of thirty-five acres. The low buildings center about a great dome, giving unity to the whole group. A great technical school consists for the most part of laboratories and drafting-rooms, and from this point of view the Institute's plant presents a most remarkable combination of beauty and service. The plans are the work of W. W. Bosworth, '89. The man who made Technology's new plant on the Charles possible by gifts totalling $7,-000,000 at the time the move was planned some years ago, was for a long time known only as "the mysterious Mr. Smith."

Last fall when Boston Tech's $8,000,000 endowment fund drive was officially launched, it became known that "Mr. Smith" had again come to the rescue. He promised $4,000,000 and another $4,000,000 was raised by alumni and friends, the $8,-000,000 goal being reached shortly before the Technology Alumni dinner, January 10, 1920. Over a million dollars came in as retainer fees from industrial concerns under contract, in connection with the new Technology plan of cooperation with industry. At the Alumni dinner the late Dr. Richard C. Maclaurin, president of the Institute, officially announced that George Eastman, of Kodak fame, was the "mysterious Mr. Smith."

CHARLES STONE.

Revising Our Notions of War Memorials.

Among the ultra-conservative notions which we are fortunately gradually discarding is the idea that war memorials must be arches or columns or fountains or, worse yet, set images in uniforms that promptly go out of date. The conception of a memorial as nothing more than a monument is antiquated. It is out of tune with the time.

Generally speaking monuments are useless things. They are set up at considerable cost, out of all proportion to the net return as values go in this busy day. They are points of concentration for the surging enthusiasm of a grateful moment; then they are left to the usual oblivion that so readily results from short memory, when the structure in point has no other than a purely memorial purpose.

Size, value or beauty will not remove a monument from the danger of this forgetfulness on the part of the very children of those who erected it, children brought up in awe of their splendor and of the deeds which they record. The Parisian walks past the Arc de l'Etoile, wonderful monument that it is, as free from impressive memories as are we ourselves when we pass the numerous monuments that have been placed in public squares

and parks, such as the Worth monument, or even—to our disgrace, be it said—the Washington Arch itself. It is open to question whether the Roman still sees the egregious monument to Victor Emanuel and really regards it as more than a pile of masonry.

A way must be found to oblige us to keep fresh the memory of the deeds of our men in the World War. What shall it be?

If the monument is given a purpose, however slight, that of a flagpole, of a lamp standard, of a public fountain, there is some hope that its usefulness will occasionally bring to mind the reasons for its existence. If the monument falls in the field of sculpture, and assuming that it is as good at least as the Sherman equestrian figure at the Plaza, or the Shaw Memorial in Boston, or the Trask Memorial at Saratoga, we have the advantage of life and movement, of the satisfaction of real beauty, and memory at once gets busy, thus preventing the musty staleness of inscription loaded columns and obelisks, or of arches straining to support the lengthy account in poor lettering set in their attic story. The festive spirit that gives life to the many decorative structures on Fifth avenue for the welcome procession of the New York Division would soon wear off, were all of these to remain and become part of the set architecture of our city streets. For this reason we cannot view with enthusiasm the prospect of the permanent arch as projected in Madison Square. Its novelty will soon pale—except of course for the visitors from beyond the walls—and it will fall into the class of the useless monumental dirt-collecting obstacles in an over-encumbered city.

A better solution is seen in a different direction—that of the useful memorial. In other words, not a monument at all, but a building or other structure with a definite daily utilitarian purpose for all of us, a building that will serve a distinctive purpose as well as preserve a record of fine deeds well done. Our smaller towns by the thousand need a point of concentration of public interest, let that be a community house erected as a memorial to the sons given to the cause. Let each such house contain a memorial hall or corridor, so placed in the building that all who enter must pass through this place of memory, or else so that foregatherings of the people take place in the presence of trophies and other visible emblems of the struggle. The community house offers an excellent solution for the problem of the appropriate memorial and the essential purpose of a record is provided for in either of the distinctly memorial features mentioned. And the same principle can be applied to other groups; what is effective for the village or small town is also feasible for the district or ward, or even the block, in the large city.

Something of the kind has in the past been done in churches, but here the idea of the tomb and the type of design which that requires and inspires has usually been uppermost. The customary conception of the memorial in the past, so far as the chief Christian styles are concerned, has been the votive church. The various pagan styles erected numerous monumental memorials, almost invariably structures of utilitarian value. A list of votive churches would extend into the hundreds and thousands. In more modern times, we note the increased use of memorial halls, memorial libraries, memorial gates and clock towers, and the like; such memorials are chiefly the work of the last century.

With regard to present practice, there are in addition to the community house as such many other types of structures amenable to current purposes but still eligible to serve a memorial end. In the university group, for instance, the students' building could be assigned to such an object; instead of a room for trophies won on the baseball diamond, the running track or by the varsity crew, let there be an appropriately decorated hall for trophies gathered on Flanders Fields and record of good work done in the Argonne by the sons of the university.

In a great city, why not a memorial stadium, driveway or park? Why not a memorial playground or recreation structure for the children of those who fell in battle? Why not memorial library branches or bridges or municipal towers or art galleries? Or, on a small scale, a pair of metal gates or doors, or even a stained glass window? Why not a public square as a memorial; surely no more effective public recognition could be bestowed. Why not, indeed, a memorial skyscraper, the greatest yet erected, devoted to public uses?

We recently had occasion to ask Professor Hamlin to indicate a few buildings, not monuments, that had served as memorials while rendering account along other directly useful lines. The first five examples that he mentioned give proof of the feasibility of such a combination and of the value of making memorials earn their cost in a return to the public. They were: Memorial Hall, Harvard University, dated 1876, serving the various purposes of dining hall, convention auditorium and memorial hall proper; Westminster Memorial, Westminster, London, dated 1910, a Methodist building combining the memorial purpose with current use as an auditorium, denominational offices, and other requirements; The Escorial, near Madrid, Spain, a sixteenth century battle memorial of the votive type, combining the purposes of monastery, university, church and palace, with that of the memorial; the Victoria Tower, connected with the Houses of Parliament, London, dated 1857, a splendid memorial for a whole nation, built as part of a capitol building; the Memorial Bridge, Hartford, Conn., dated 1883, combining with the memorial purpose indicated in an arch the useful purpose of a bridge.

Need any further evidence be adduced to show that a memorial should be made useful, that it should be made to work for the people, that it should do good? Surely its message can be most firmly fastened in our minds, clinched in the thoughts of our children, if its constant use keeps the deeds of our heroes fresh. Let us have done with monuments unless they cannot be avoided because of money restrictions; and even then let the memorial be at least a lamp post or a flag standard. Let us have memorial buildings, structures with a lasting purpose. If, then, the idea of memorial is properly understood by the architect and adequately incorporated by him in the useful structure, this lasting purpose of the building will insure the lasting memory of the men and deeds that made its erection worth while. RICHARD F. BACH.

A CORRECTION.

The authorship of the High School at Southampton, L. I., illustrated in the Architectural Record for December, pages 584 and 585, should have been attributed to the firm of Hewitt & Bottomley, now dissolved, instead of to William Lawrence Bottomley individually.

THE
ARCHITECTVRAL
RECORD

CONTENTS

Vol. XLVII. No. 3   MARCH, 1920   Serial No. 258

Editor: MICHAEL A. MIKKELSEN   *Contributing Editor:* HERBERT CROLY
Business Manager: J. A. OAKLEY

*Yearly Subscription—United States $3.00—Foreign $4.00—Single copies 35 cents. Entered
May 22, 1902, as Second Class Matter, at New York, N. Y. Member Audit Bureau of Circulation.*

PUBLISHED MONTHLY BY
THE ARCHITECTURAL RECORD COMPANY
115-119 WEST FORTIETH STREET, NEW YORK
F. T. MILLER, Pres.   W. D. HADSELL, Vice-Pres.   J. W. FRANK, Sec'y-Treas.   E. S. DODGE, Vice-Pres

ENTRANCE—RESIDENCE OF F. W.
WOOLWORTH, ESQ., GLEN COVE,
L. I.   C. P. H. GILBERT, ARCHITECT.

THE
ARCHITECTVRAL
RECORD

VOLVME XLVII **NVMBER III**

MARCH, 1920

RESIDENCE OF THE LATE F.W.WOOLWORTH, ESQ.

GLEN COVE, L. I.

C.H.P. GILBERT ~ ARCHITECT

By HERBERT CROLY

SINCE well-to-do Americans began to build costly country houses during the ninth decade of the last century the style and character of these houses has passed through a number of different phases. The first type consisted of the villa, erected usually on a rather limited site and situated on the sea-shore. It was, of course, the country house of a city business man, intended for occupancy only during a few months in the year. When these villas began to be built soon after 1880, conditions of life, even among rich people, were comparatively simple. The American millionaire was still much more interested in making money than in spending it. He did not maintain a very large establishment, and his sea-shore residence was usually an informal rambling structure, belonging to no particular architectural style, surrounded at most by a few acres of land and in every way lacking in pretension and in social self-consciousness.

This particular phase did not last very long. American fortunes quickly increased during the eighties in number and in amount; and the increase was immediately reflected in domestic architecture. The typical country residence of the New York millionaire during the

WEST TERRACE—RESIDENCE OF F. W. WOOLWORTH, ESQ., GLEN COVE, L. I.
C. P. H. Gilbert, Architect.

GARDEN AND TEA HOUSE—RESIDENCE OF F. W. WOOLWORTH, ESQ., GLEN COVE, L. I.
C. P. H. Gilbert, Architect.

BELVEDERE, FROM FRONT ENTRANCE—RESI-
DENCE OF F. W. WOOLWORTH, ESQ., GLEN
COVE, L. I. C. P. H. GILBERT, ARCHITECT.

MANTEL IN HALLWAY—RESIDENCE OF
F. W. WOOLWORTH, ESQ., GLEN COVE,
L. I. C. P. H. GILBERT, ARCHITECT.

DETAIL OF HALLWAY—RESIDENCE OF
F. W. WOOLWORTH, ESQ., GLEN COVE,
L. I. C. P. H. GILBERT, ARCHITECT.

MUSIC ROOM—RESIDENCE OF F. W.
WOOLWORTH, ESQ., GLEN COVE,
L. I. C. P. H. GILBERT, ARCHITECT.

DETAIL OF MUSIC ROOM—RESIDENCE OF
F. W. WOOLWORTH, ESQ., GLEN COVE,
L. I.   C. P. H. GILBERT, ARCHITECT.

DINING ROOM—RESIDENCE OF F. W. WOOLWORTH, ESQ., GLEN COVE, L. I.
C. P. H. Gilbert, Architect.

PORCH—RESIDENCE OF F. W. WOOLWORTH, ESQ., GLEN COVE, L. I.
C. P. H. Gilbert, Architect.

MANTEL IN BEDROOM—RESIDENCE OF
F. W. WOOLWORTH, ESQ., GLEN COVE,
L. I. C. P. H. GILBERT, ARCHITECT.

DOORWAY IN BEDROOM—RESIDENCE OF
F. W. WOOLWORTH, ESQ., GLEN COVE,
L. I. C. P. H. GILBERT, ARCHITECT.

like a picturesque and informal effect, and it almost forces the architect to use stone in the structure of the building rather than brick. Flat-roofed houses tend, consequently, to be palatial and they also tend to be dull. The Woolworth house is saved from dullness only by its successful formality. Its exterior is conceived and executed in the grand style.

Notwithstanding the large number of rooms the plan is simple and convenient. The visitor enters through a spacious hall which runs through the house and leads straight to the formal garden on the other side. As you enter there is a foyer hall on the left which leads to the music-room. This is the largest and the most important and the most elaborately designed room in the house. This same foyer hall also provides an approach to the library. On the right of the entrance hall is the dining room and to the right of the dining room the kitchen, pantry and offices. The interior design preserves the grandiose character of the exterior; but except for certain rooms it has not preserved the same simplicity. The design of some of the apartments is hurt rather than helped by the amount of ornamentation, but it should be added that the ornament is always correct and the house contains some very interesting examples of modern woodwork.

The interest of the Woolworth house is increased rather than diminished because of the fact that it belongs to a type of domestic architecture which is destined to disappear. In the future it is improbable that even very rich men will want or can afford a big grandiose formal residence of this kind. The high rate of income taxation will diminish the number of those who can build them, and the enormously increased cost of service will cut down the number who can operate and maintain them. Moreover, it is probably that families who occupy buildings with more than a limited provision for the accommodation of servants will eventually have to put up with special burdens. There is a tendency to tax luxuries which may in the end include dwellings with a certain number of servants' rooms in its scope. The country residence of the American millionaire of the future will, we may confidently predict, again become a smaller and more informal and a less pretentious building.

THE GARDEN—RESIDENCE OF J. J. GILBERT, ESQ.,
LITTLE FALLS, N. Y.

A city plot with a walled-in garden adjacent to the living room porch, the high wall shutting out undesirable views, but ramping down to a low wall at the left to command a wonderful outlook over the Mohawk Valley. The planting near the wall obscures the roofs of the buildings below. The wall fountain is on the axis of the living room.

LANDSCAPE ARCHITECTURE IN THE MIDDLE WEST

SOME RECENT WORK
of WILLIAM PITKIN, JR.

BY PHILIP LINDSLEY SMALL

IN the Middle West the population is so cosmopolitan, in all classes of society and walks of life, that it might seem impossible to make a definite statement as to the predominance of any one source of precedent in our artistic tastes. Nevertheless, it is evident that in the matter of culture, the Anglo-Saxon element predominates, imposing its traditions of art upon our Americanized foreign-born citizens.

The architect, the landscape architect, the decorator, the artist, is therefore confronted with the problem of satisfying an Anglo-Saxon or an Anglicized temperament. It is due to this fact that our domestic architecture is for the most part English in origin, whether we are translating it first-hand or are revising in turn what our Colonial forefathers in their day translated.

Much of the charm of old English gardens and English landscape lies in their atmosphere of age, in their stability, in the feeling they produce of having long been just where they are, matured by time and nurtured by the care of generations. Our gardens cannot have this aspect; with us property changes hands rapidly, the old is soon discarded to make room for the requirements of another generation. And the requirements of this new generation are that the house, the garden, the estate, must be created entire.

I recall a certain day in June in a little village in Oxfordshire, not far from Banbury. I had left my "bike" at the inn and was prowling about the lanes at the outskirts of the village. Attracted by the lines of a thatched roof through the trees, I was soon looking over an old stone wall; and there before me, flanked by the cottage and backed by a dense mass of forest green, was the most satisfying little garden I have ever seen. It was very tiny, not over fifty feet in length, and only as wide as the main part of the cottage. In this main part, which had two shed wings, was a wide central door and on either side a group of low casement windows, all part of the one large room which looked out upon the garden and whose floor was a trifle lower than the walk outside. The door gave on the main axis down which led a walk of flagging, irregular in shape and wide-spaced, with grass growing in the joints. At the center was a round pool, into which trickled a fine thread of water, carried in a narrow groove in the middle of the walk from a basin in the stone wall at the far end. At the pool was a cross-walk that extended from a recess in the wall where I stood to a gate into a tiny vegetable garden opposite me. The entire rectangle was surrounded with roses interspersed with a few perennials not yet in bloom. The ground under the roses was thickly covered with a vine which crept up and over the top of the enclosing wall. In the far corner, bending over her roses and busy with a pruning knife, was a little old lady, without whose presence the whole scene would have lost much of its charm: she seemed so much a part of it and the garden seemed so much a part of the cottage and the landscape and the day and the life about me.

I tried to analyze its charm and decided that, so far as materials were concerned,

THE TERRACE—RESIDENCE OF J. B. CROUSE, ESQ.
CLEVELAND, OHIO.

The house is on a comparatively small property, with adjacent buildings close to it. Screening is therefore a very important detail in the study of the problem. It has been effectively carried out, as may be seen from this view looking toward an adjoining property line.

THE FRONT ENTRANCE—RESIDENCE OF. J. B. CROUSE, ESQ.,
CLEVELAND, OHIO.

An interesting example of near-the-house planting, subordinate to and yet supplementing and enhancing the charm of a bit of architectural detail. The layout of the planting is formal, but softened
by the manner of its application.

ENTRANCE TO THE SUN PORCH—RESIDENCE OF J. B. CROUSE, ESQ.,
CLEVELAND, OHIO.

A screen enclosing a vista from a much-inhabited room of the house. An effective combination of hardwoods, low evergreens, shrubs and ground coverings.

ENTRANCE TO FORECOURT—RESIDENCE OF MRS. HENRY STEPHENS,
GROSSE POINTE, MICH.

The architectural formality of the court was recognized in the arrangement of the planting by the use of cedars and other evergreens of architectonic value, grouped in compositions harmonizing with the lines of the walks, piers and ironwork, and at the same time revealing and emphasizing the architecture rather than burying it. The severity of the planting is softened by leaving the cedars untrimmed and facing them with carefully restricted rounding masses of evergreen and deciduous material, thus blending the planting into the lawns and tying both planting and architecture snugly to the ground. The center panel is left open to permit of the view through the court and is unplanted except for four perfect Mugho pines. The layout was planned by the architect, Mr. Charles A. Platt. The planting was designed by Mr. Pitkin.

VIEW ACROSS THE GARDEN—RESIDENCE OF WILLIAM S. WALBRIDGE, ESQ.,
PERRYSBURG, OHIO.

One of many charming glimpses of the house, the unfortunate features of whose design have been very cleverly and effectually obscured by the planting.

THE GARDEN—RESIDENCE OF WILLIAM H. MURPHY, ESQ., "DEEP DALE,"
BIRMINGHAM, MICH.

A small and very simple garden enclosed by a light picket fence of Colonial design. The planting is quite new and the vines are not yet over the garden house. The tower is a converted silo. The garden house forms a terminal to the path and serves as a screen to hide the stable yard beyond.

THE FOOT BRIDGE—RESIDENCE OF WILLIAM H. MURPHY, ESQ., "DEEP DALE,"
BIRMINGHAM, MICH.

This view shows how the banks of the stream have been left in their natural state and the real
beauty of the existing tree growth emphasized by proper clearing and by the addition of a few large
trees and shrubs of the same character.

THE GARDEN—RESIDENCE OF C. G. EDGAR, ESQ.,
DETROIT, MICH.

The living room and sun room open directly upon this main part of the garden. The grass panel is on the axis of the living room and is bordered on each side by a ten-foot bed of perennials which produce a succession of flowers from early spring until late fall. The panel is terminated at the property line by a wall fountain, which, though not tied into the scheme by walls, is sufficiently substantial to appear well located.

WALL FOUNTAN—RESIDENCE OF C. G. EDGAR, ESQ.,
DETROIT, MICH.

Showing flagstone paving and steppping stones each side of grass panel, connecting with the house and providing a dry-shod way of reaching the flowers. The alley leads to the rose garden.

4

ENTRANCE TO MUSIC COURT—RESIDENCE OF SENATOR TRUMAN H. NEWBERRY,
GROSSE POINTE, MICH.

Another example of near-the-house planting, charming in its own color and composition, yet
subordinate to and enhancing the qualities of the architecture.

THE OLD-FASHIONED GARDEN—RESIDENCE OF SENATOR TRUMAN H. NEWBERRY,
GROSSE POINTE, MICH.

A small and very intimate garden in a wood, where sunlight and deep shade are strongly contrasted, giving an air of quiet and seclusion amidst an ever-changing though subdued color scheme
throughout the season.

THE ROCK AND WILD GARDEN—RESIDENCE OF SENATOR TRUMAN H. NEWBERRY,
GROSSE POINTE, MICH.

Occupying a position between nut trees, where plants suitable to both sunlight and shade are used in a natural way. Several varieties of forest trees are planted as slender saplings to supplement the nut trees and to produce the effect of coppice growth. In the partial shade thus produced enough shrub undergrowth, shady growing herbaceous plants and ferns are introduced to afford protection to tender plants. Into this general ground-work the more interesting varieties of wild flowers are set as nearly as possible in the manner of their natural growth. The music of falling water is obtained by the introduction of a naturalistic pool partly in the shade of the filberts and partly in the open sunlight. The water wells up slowly as from a spring in the hollowed-out bowl of a picturesque rock, and pours over into a shallow pool, bordered by ferns and water-loving wild flowers.

THE ALLÉE—RESIDENCE OF SENATOR TRUMAN H. NEWBERRY,
GROSSE POINTE, MICH.

The allée is the connecting link between the music court and the flower garden and passes
through a wood of large elms and maples, beneath which an undergrowth planting of rhododendrons,
azaleas, hemlocks and white dogwood has been so arranged as to form a well marked vista between
the court and the garden, with subordinate byways on either side. The whole region is thus given a
closed-in, shaded effect between two open sunny areas.

THE WINTER GARDEN—RESIDENCE OF CHARLES J. BUTLER, ESQ., DETROIT, MICH.

A sheltered, compact little garden adjacent to the porch and living room of a house on a one-hundred-foot lot. The vine-covered wall back of the bird bath shuts out the street, while the red cedars at the right completely obscure the service wing of the house on the adjoining lot, which is within ten feet of the line. On the street side of the wall large evergreens are added to give further privacy and to make a good background. The planting within the garden is composed mostly of fine-textured evergreens, with here and there such varieties as rhododendrons, azaleas and mountain laurel to give a bit of bright color in the spring. Very few deciduous shrubs are included, such as spirea and the lilacs, against the porch to the left. Daffodils and Darwin tulips, naturalized between the plants, add their color in the spring, while a very few perennials are in the planting to give a touch of color throughout the summer and especially in the fall, when the white anemones are in flower at several points. The whole scheme is enclosed and given definite outline by a dwarf hedge.

cottage and garden could be reproduced at home, but however clever or accurate the copy there would always be something lacking. That garden belonged just where it was, and in no other place could it be the same, its atmosphere, its whole vitality would be gone.

One may see near a certain American city a little garden very similar to the one in Oxfordshire—the same outlook from the house, the same walks, the same grass plots, the same border of roses and vine-covered wall, the same thread of water, and with a very well simulated atmosphere of age. But the whole air of the place is, somehow, affected and convinces one that the only person who ever enters it is the gardener. It has no place in the life of the owner or his household, no particular connection with the house or the landscape or the community, no merit as a part of the setting for the house, no reason for being.

One seldom sees the reproduction of an old-world garden set down in our modern American landscape but what one inevitably feels that, even though charming in itself, still as an integral part of the *ensemble* of the home it is incongruous. We do not reconstruct our civilization to meet the requirements of a new art; our art is merely one of the many ways in which our civilization manifests itself. Should we change our home-life in order that an expatriated garden shall not be incongruous? Quite the contrary. We are twentieth-century Americans and we could not be anything else.

It is gratifying to note, in the examples of work being done today, the number of landscape architects who are working with this thought in mind. Mr. William Pitkin, Jr., of Cleveland, is one of them. His work is the result of thorough study: each problem is attacked frankly as new and unique, and the solution is consequently American, as well as individual.

WESTERN END—RESIDENCE OF RICHARD
M. GUMMERY, ESQ., HAVERFORD, PA.
WILSON EYRE & McILVAINE, ARCHITECTS.

SOME PRINCIPLES OF SMALL HOUSE DESIGN

❦ By ❧
JOHN TAYLOR BOYD, Jʀ.

PART V - ELEVATIONS-STYLE

THE elevations of a house must be considered as part of the design of the lot of land and of the plan of the house itself. For this reason, in the preceding articles on plot design and house plans, it has been necessary to refer often to the design of small house elevations; and, in addition, many excellent illustrations of exteriors have appeared which themselves portray principles of design more vividly than text could do. Were it not true that precepts disappear in practice, there would be no need of pointing them out. But in architecture, as in many another field of modern civilization, we have become so used to complexity that we find it hard to think of the obvious. It is the obvious that baffles, and so it may sometimes be worth while to deliberate on fundamentals, in order to keep to the path.

In architectural exteriors, it seems clear that two main factors govern their design. The first of these is the principles common to all the arts, aesthetics, and the second is the technique of architectural design. It is in regard to the first of these, the general aesthetic principles, that reference has been made in the preceding articles, and they may be briefly summarized before considering architectural technique.

As I have already noted, the small house is at its best when it seems to be a pure work of art, something more than merely a pleasing bit of architectural design. It looks best when it satisfies the painter as a picture and satisfies the sculptor as a sculptured mass in light

and shade and decoration, besides meeting the architect's wish for fine proportions and exquisite details and textures. The ablest designers have this ideal in mind, and most of the failures in houses occur through ignoring it.

What are the elements which make architecture a work of art? This is too deep a question to answer fully, beyond saying that the house exterior should display those world-old ideals of color, mass, shape, proportion, of harmony, balance, rhythm, in the solid geometry and in the planes of space and measurement. All this it should be in addition to being an excellent product of the architect's drawing board. Indeed—and this is the root of the matter—the three arts of architecture, painting and sculpture are largely modern abstractions, assumptions adopted for convenience in our complicated twentieth century. They are due to twentieth century extremes of specialization and professionalization, which to a certain extent arbitrarily cut off the different arts one from another. Today the arts are distinct, each a little world where its followers work apart from other artists, whereas formerly the arts were one great activity, a single profession or craft, and each artist was a craftsman, a designer, practising as many kinds of art as he was able. Even where he "specialized," he worked in closest collaboration with other kinds of artists.

The modern artist would progress faster if he realized, in practice, that the complete separation of the arts is a conception of business and economics rather than of art itself. He would then grasp the wonderful possibility of small house design and know how significant a field it covers in modern art. For in the modest dimensions of the small house and its simple technical problems, a full separation of the arts becomes a little absurd. Not only do lot plan, house plan, house elevations, house interiors and furnishings fit naturally into each other, but the owner cannot be expected to employ a whole squad of specialists and experts to supply him with his art, as he might do if he were building a public library. In this light one may conceive of small house design as the "household arts."

The "household arts" are the whole art of the household. It is highly diversified, it is true, but no part of it is so elaborately specialized as to be a field worth cultivating by itself or one forbidding outsiders to enter into it. A capable designer should be able to master all of the household arts, one as well as another. If he does he will be far along in the higher road of art. He then will cover a wider field, like the masters of an older time; his view will be deeper and truer and his experience will be richer. It will draw nearer the unique inspiration of craftsmanship. And his work will be sound and normal, since it will be done directly in the intimate life of the American home, which is at the root of all American civilization. The designer will be less apt to succumb to those perils of the modern art-world — the influences of propaganda, of "schools," literary or foreign or "intellectual." He will be less influenced by isms. Thus, being truly natural and direct and honest, art will swiftly become national. In fact, it is not exaggerating to say that the art of the household offers really the greatest opportunity of art in America today, for, in the present confusion of the "major" arts, it holds the future of the American style.

All the above may seem visionary, yet one can prove that the theory is already in large part fact. Particularly is the first of the assertions true—that all the arts which center in the home are one and that one man should be a designer

of them all. Nearly all the designers whose work appears in these pages design gardens and furnishings as easily as they design plans or elevations. Some can even carry their design into craftsmanship's art, and in odd moments themselves work out all household details, from planting to full-sizing furniture, choosing hangings or painting decorations. As to the second assertion—that our household art is bound to develop a national art—this may sound strange to some minds, but in further pages I shall present certain facts which are too commonly overlooked.

As mentioned before, examples are not wanting of American houses that come close to the ideal of works of art. As pictures they appear beautiful bits of architecture, perfect in mass and proportion and outline, exquisite in scale and in the pattern of their details, harmoniously fitted into the landscape, directly, simply, yet imaginatively and with inspiration. They combine modern ideas of rich, free decoration and are cheerful and gay in sunlight. They are as dramatic as domestic art could be and yet be liveable and in good taste. In short, they will bear comparison with any modern house architecture in the world.

It must be said that our better houses need better color. This does not mean that they are bad in color, for they are harmonious by well blended colors of materials. Their color simply does not go far enough. It is designed as "local" color, often too dull and sombre, and it does not flash or vibrate in our intense sunlight, which is hard and searching in the north, and mellow and golden in the south. What strong coloring may be in house architecture can be seen in an old mansion in Georgetown, in the District of Columbia. This old house is on the crest of a hill, a fine classic design of bold forms—round headed, wide windows and semi-circular entrance porch of columns and half-dome roof—contrasted against great breadth of wall. Its long walls are of stucco, of the richest orange, slightly faded, relieved by the shadow of entrance porch and by white wood details, the

GARDEN FRONT—RESIDENCE OF RICHARD
M. GUMMERY, ESQ., HAVERFORD, PA.
WILSON EYRE & McILVAINE, ARCHITECTS.

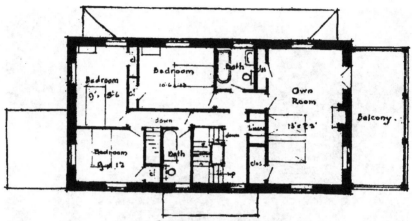

Second Floor Plan.

mass standing out against the blue southern sky, and enframed by large blackgreen pines and cedars and tall oaks, with their reddish trunks and branches, and by a brilliant golden green slope of lawn in the foreground—all flooded with blinding sunshine. No modern colorist could help admiring this effect of clear, rich colors blended in the vibrating sunlight. Other such pictures may be seen in the south, in mansions of two-storied porch or tall portico—without the incredible orange of the Washington house, it is true, but having walls of light

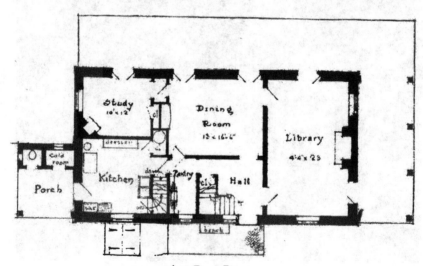

First Floor Plan.

RESIDENCE OF RICHARD M. GUMMERY, ESQ., HAVERFORD, PA.
Wilson Eyre & McIlvaine, Architects.

236

salmon brick burnished in the sunlight and heightened by the deep or brilliant green of the luxurious vegetation. This tradition of color is one of which America may well be proud. It could not import anything more inspiring for its house architecture.

In our contemporary architecture we have a few—extremely few—examples of this vivid coloring. Such is the larger residence of H. H. Rogers at Southampton, L. I., described in the Architectural Record for January, 1916. The coloring of the Rogers' house is keyed to the more mellow light of the sea and to the color of dunes and sea grasses. Its walls are a light grayish-yellow. Mr. Colby's house at Hartsdale has a coloration somewhat like that of the Rogers house, but more subdued, with warm light gray walls and a soft claret color of shingle roof. A fuller discussion of the principles of color will be found in the Architectural Record for November, 1919, in "The Color of Sunshine in Architecture." One may say that, in contrast with these southern examples and with the Rogers house, nearly all American designers try to get along with as little color as possible on the exteriors. In the south their architecture looks sombre and out of the key of the golden sunlight, and in the north it often shows up sombre with hard edges in the searching glare. Instead of meeting the harsh light and breaking it up with bright colors and strong shadows that blend over edges, designers seek to avoid its ruthless emphasis of details by drawing in projections of cornices and belt courses and mouldings, and making these as flat and as tiny as possible. In larger buildings the running bands and members have been so reduced vertically and horizontally that they have lost all character and vigor and emphasis and modelling. That is why so much of our civic architecture is overrefined, even effeminate. Such delicacy is not so out of place in small architecture, but even there the obsession of designers for "flatness" has damaged many a good design.

This brings us to those principles of design that are developed in their highest form in sculpture. Architecture, too, offers a great field for modelling in planes, in relief, in decoration, in light and shade and sun. Such modelling is most easily come by in stone work, as the Philadelphia architects have perceived. The designs of Messrs. Mellor and Meigs, of Mr. Willing, and of Mr. Wilson Eyre in these pages are examples of sculpturesque as well as of pictorial qualities. In wood architecture, this sculptor's art is not often thought of, and it may be the reason behind some criticisms to the effect that early American architecture is too thin, is not vigorous enough to express the twentieth century. Undoubtedly some of our wooden houses are thin, in spite of fine modelling of cornices and of door, window and porch details. It seems to have remained for Mr. Parker Morse Hooper to discover what an extraordinary vigor may be put into a wooden wall, even enough to satisfy a "modern." Scarcely anyone so well as he, has modelled wood in advanced and receded planes of overhanging stories and bay windows, or has emphasized this vigor by extreme sparkle and delicacy in sunlight of that ornament which is peculiar to wood forms. One of his houses appears in these pages, and two were shown in the last issue. Most designers have hesitated to go so far, cautioned by those clumsy failures, found all over the United States, made by architects who have attempted strong modelling in wood architecture. This latter type of architecture is familiar enough. It really results from deep ignorance of form, particularly of how to draw architectural details at full-size.

In short, whether in regard to color and pictorial qualities, or in regard to modelling and sculpturesque qualities, the designer cannot hope to cheat the American sun. Unless he meets it on its own terms his architecture is apt to be in color, cold and drab, out-of-key, and in form, flat and skinny—paper architecture.

All the foregoing factors in design are important in themselves, but they have a further significance, which is this: They show that, even when archi-

NORTH FRONT—RESIDENCE OF RICHARD
M. GUMMERY, ESQ., HAVERFORD, PA.
WILSON EYRE & McILVAINE, ARCHITECTS.

GARDEN FRONT—RESIDENCE OF RICHARD
M. GUMMERY, ESQ., HAVERFORD, PA.
WILSON EYRE & McILVAINE, ARCHITECTS.

tecture is viewed in the fundamental principles of aesthetics, of art in all ages, native American conditions decide the problems of design of elevations in form and light and shade and color, just as they decide the arrangement of plans, or fix the construction, or determine the economics or the houshold customs, or the ideal of the family. They illustrate again the fact that the more American a designer can make his art, the finer it will be. This means, therefore, that in the broadest way, American conditions of climate and landscape and sunshine and foliage, just as much as conditions of economics and traditions and customs and national temperament, have a big part in determining architectural style. Here again—and one cannot emphasize it too strongly—is the obvious. Here is a whole set of conditions, of principles, not clearly understood whenever the question of style of buildings is determined. Here the obvious proves the folly of that indiscriminate "borrowing" of foreign art-forms which has so confused our architecture.

In the matter of style it is common knowledge that American designers have offered their public a variety of architectural languages or "styles." How far is this practice a sound one? How many of these styles are good ones to use in America? In answering these questions, it will be helpful first to eliminate forms that are clearly unsuitable. What is certain, is that the last twenty years have seen a fortunate killing-off of many of the styles used in the United States. We are much better off than a few years back, when all the styles and most of the sub-styles known to man were cultivated in this country. Architects, more plausible than sound, toured Europe seeking out exotic forms to "make a hit with" in America. Designers went into the import business. Wealthy citizens boasted of "exact copies" of Italian villas or French châteaux or English manors which they had seen in Europe. It was a ludicrous time, as we look back at it now, even though this clumsy pioneering was an inevitable stage in progress.

Importation still continues, but now it is mostly limited to details, which is a perfectly sound practice if not carried too far. European architecture now comes in as an unfinished product, to be worked up by Americans as they see fit, and these importations are being carefully selected. So much every designer will admit. Thus it may be agreed that the bringing into the United States of foreign art-forms has almost ceased, and American designers are concerned with the "domesticated" product only. The problem of style is to decide the value of these domesticated styles.

As to the domesticated styles of architecture in America, if the variety of styles used by the best architects be compared with that of twenty years ago, it is seen that a number of styles have been eliminated. These are the styles of continental Europe. There is very little of pure French art in American houses, except an occasional single sophisticated room in a large mansion. Here and there are forms and motives of French origin, but even those are not many. Americans were once interested in the palatial types of French architecture; but these do not enter into the scope of American small houses; and furthermore, their unique French character cannot be grasped by the American personality. Our debt to France lies rather in the teaching of the principles of design of the Ecole des Beaux Arts, and the more clearly Americans perceive these principles, the more are they likely to develop their own native form.

Of the north European styles other than French, such as Swiss, German, etc., only a weak attempt was ever made to establish them here and it has long since been given up. Only Italian and Spanish forms have ever gained foothold in America. Spanish is not found except in California and in the southwest, although in some ways Spanish conditions —sunlight, landscape, and the free virile richly decorative art they inspire—resemble American more than do others. However, even in the southwest the Spanish type—Spanish Colonial—is not predominant. On the whole, it is evident that the Italian influence is the only

GENERAL VIEW, SHOWING SERVICE AND GARAGES—
TWO HOUSES FOR THE MORRIS ESTATE, OVERBROOK,
PHILADELPHIA. MELLOR, MEIGS & HOWE, ARCHITECTS.

ENTRANCE SIDE—TWO HOUSES FOR THE
MORRIS ESTATE, OVERBROOK, PHILADELPHIA.
MELLOR, MEIGS & HOWE, ARCHITECTS.

ENTRANCE DETAIL--TWO HOUSES FOR THE
MORRIS ESTATE, OVERBROOK, PHILADELPHIA.
MELLOR, MEIGS & HOWE, ARCHITECTS.

ENTRANCE SIDE—TWO HOUSES FOR THE
MORRIS ESTATE, OVERBROOK, PHILADELPHIA.
MELLOR, MEIGS & HOWE, ARCHITECTS.

ENTRANCE DETAIL—TWO HOUSES FOR THE
MORRIS ESTATE, OVERBROOK, PHILADELPHIA.
MELLOR, MEIGS & HOWE, ARCHITECTS.

one that remains from the continent of Europe, and it is now a much diluted one. The most Italian of our "Italian" villa-houses, whatever they may seem to an American, would not deceive an Italian if he saw them set down in an Italian landscape. Their American lines, confusion in architecture without increasing it through careless use of terms. When we speak of "Italian villas," "Italian feeling," "Italian," in connection with small houses, we usually mean no such thing. What we have in mind is a *slight Italian influence.* For we may

GARDEN SIDE—TWO HOUSES FOR THE MORRIS ESTATE,
OVERBROOK, PHILADELPHIA.
Mellor, Meigs & Howe, Architects.

their lower story-heights, porches, plentiful windows, their other Americanisms that are now so bred into our designers that they cannot avoid them if they wish, would betray the imitation. It takes more than a low tile roof, stucco walls and an arch or two to make an Italian villa. As a rule, this is the recipe that is advertised as Italian. We have enough acknowledge that Italian forms are now so thoroughly Americanized that soon all that will be left of them will be but a few odd motives and an appreciation of what breadth, dignity, perfect proportions and pure lines mean in architecture.

A charming little example of the Italian influence is the house designed by Mr. William Edgar Moran at Glen Ridge,

244

N. J. It is an alteration, resulting in an effective plan, particularly in respect to the spacious, hospitable entrance hall, from which the stairs ascend under an arch. Its color is fine, indeed—a brownish roof, walls of pinkish stucco made from sand similar in color to the red sand-

In fact, to the question, What foreign styles are important in house design in the United States today? the answer is: None but British. The question of styles in houses is reduced, in this year of 1920, to a choice between English styles of architecture and their early American de-

FRONT LAWN—TWO HOUSES FOR THE MORRIS ESTATE,
OVERBROOK, PHILADELPHIA.
Mellor, Meigs & Howe, Architects.

stone of New Jersey, with details of light tan, trim window frames and green shutters and railing. But the point of this design is that its mass and shapes are American. Its roof is akin to the old Connecticut standard, with an overhang. Examination shows that really the only pure Italian features are the details of the entrance and first floor windows.

rivatives. Twenty years have simplified the confusions of styles, and only two or three out of a dozen are left. It seems therefore that the time has come to appraise the few remaining, to decide between them, to determine the best one to use. For until one style is used, American architecture will not be entirely satisfactory.

In deciding between our styles, there are but three English ones—the medieval, the Renaissance or Georgian, and the modern. Among them one notes the same process of evolution, of elimination, that has almost wiped out the styles of continental Europe in this country.

ited to the large mansion type of house. Apparently, American designers have preferred the early American forms of Georgian origin. Georgian was thoroughly domesticated on this side of the ocean a hundred years ago, so why repeat the process? Therefore, it is fair

FROM DINING ROOM DOOR—TWO HOUSES FOR THE MORRIS
ESTATE, OVERBROOK, PHILADELPHIA.
Mellor, Meigs & Howe, Architects.

The medieval and Elizabethan types are no longer copied, not simply as a matter of taste, but because they are so largely intricate craftsman's art, and are thus too expensive to be practical. Hence these medieval English types are found only occasionally among the houses of the wealthy. The Georgian style of Great Britain is disappearing. It, too, is lim-

to say that, with the medieval and Georgian types of England eliminated, only two styles appear in American small-houses—the early native American style and the modern English style—to some extent influenced by a faint breeze that still blows from Italy.

Thus the process of elimination of architectural styles, of bringing us out of

246

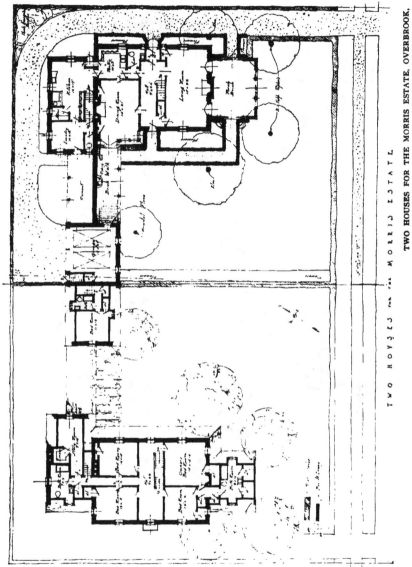

TWO HOUSES FOR THE MORRIS ESTATE, OVERBROOK,
PHILADELPHIA. MELLOR, MEIGS & HOWE, ARCHITECTS.

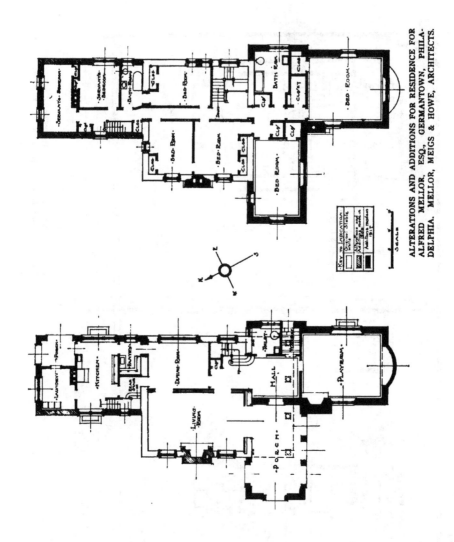

ALTERATIONS AND ADDITIONS FOR RESIDENCE FOR ALFRED MELLOR, ESQ., GERMANTOWN, PHILADELPHIA. MELLOR, MEIGS & HOWE, ARCHITECTS.

WEST ELEVATION—RESIDENCE OF ALFRED MELLOR, ESQ., GERMAN-the chaos, has allowed only two to survive. Now, before it is safe to conclude that evolution has ceased and that we should fasten on these two styles, American and British, it is desirable to appraise the English style carefully, to see whether or not it, too, will go by the board and of breadth and freedom and directness. It is also very flexible, which is just the quality that a good deal of American house architecture has lacked, largely because designers have allowed themselves to become hampered by the formula of the stock plan. Many designers

VIEW FROM ACROSS THE STREET—RESIDENCE OF ALFRED MELLOR,
ESQ., GERMANTOWN, PHILADELPHIA.
Mellor, Meigs & Howe, Architects.

leave only our native tradition to survive. The latter alternative is the law of the development of art in history. As national characteristics develop in a people so does the art develop, growing out of vernacular forms.

Much is to be said for the English style in theory. It is practical and it is inspired, conceived in the modern spirit wish to work in a free way and they turn, naturally enough, to English houses. But it is in practice, unfortunately, that the English style in America does not come up to the expectation of its followers. Its real successes are rare. It often does not suit its American setting, and seldom does it embody that fine personality and exquisite good breeding of the English standard. Not only are its details poor and heavy and unstylish, its window spacing crude and spotty in many of our American imitations, but the more essential factors of mass and harmonious sweep of roof lines, arrangement of walls and gables and bays—which are the heart

forms. The design of an English country house is, in its way, as simple and pure and harmonious as an Italian villa; yet, because it is apt to be more imaginative, it is far more difficult.

This brings us to the root of the difficulty of using the free British style in

CHIMNEY ANGLE—RESIDENCE OF ALFRED MELLOR, ESQ.,
GERMANTOWN, PHILADELPHIA.
Mellor, Meigs & Howe, Architects.

of this style—usually just miss the mark in even the better examples and, in the less successful ones, present a series of jumbled walls and jagged roofs, jerky peaks and spotty dormers, without coherence or meaning. Designers do not seem to realize that the laws of design of unsymmetrical, free forms are just as severe as are those of symmetrical classic

the United States. The American likes this style because it is imaginative and he feels that he can imagine this work as well as the Englishman. The American may be right in this faith in his imaginative powers, but the point is that the Englishman does not "imagine" the style, so far as inventing it goes. It is not generally realized in America that in

251

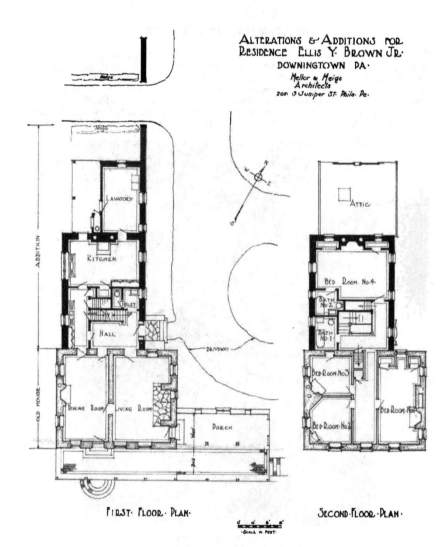

ALTERATIONS & ADDITIONS FOR
RESIDENCE ELLIS Y. BROWN JR.
DOWNINGTOWN PA.
Mellor & Meigs
Architects
205 S. Juniper St. Phila. Pa.

LAVATORY

KITCHEN

CLOSET

HALL

DINING ROOM LIVING ROOM

PORCH

DRIVEWAY

ADDITION

OLD HOUSE

ATTIC

BED ROOM No.4

BATH No.2

BATH No.1

BED ROOM No.3

BED ROOM No.2

BED ROOM No.1

FIRST · FLOOR · PLAN·

SECOND · FLOOR · PLAN·

Scale in Feet

ALTERATIONS AND ADDITIONS FOR RESIDENCE
OF ELLIS Y. BROWN, JR., ESQ., DOWNINGTOWN,
PENNSYLVANIA. MELLOR & MEIGS, ARCHITECTS.

SOUTH ELEVATION—RESIDENCE OF ELLIS Y. BROWN, JR., ESQ., DOWNINGTOWN, PA.
Mellor & Meigs, Architects.

EAST ELEVATION—RESIDENCE OF ELLIS Y. BROWN, JR., ESQ., DOWNINGTOWN, PA.
Mellor & Meigs, Architects.

VIEW FROM NORTHEAST—RESIDENCE OF ELLIS Y. BROWN, JR., ESQ., DOWNINGTOWN, PA.
Mellor & Meigs, Architects.

their apparently free, untrammeled home architecture, the British designers are simply putting a new turn on a very old tradition. It is the tradition that has come down to them from medieval, Gothic England. They have revived it after the Victorian eclipse. Many Americans do not know that some of its most "original" forms and details are but practical expedients of adapting the complicated, expensive details of medieval craftsmen to modern workmanship. For instance, in chimneys the light and shade of medieval examples have been retained, but they have been translated into simpler forms, and in windows the stone mullions and sills and jambs have been replaced by wood. Roof details have been simplified. It should be remembered, moreover, that such changes are only superficial; they do not much affect proportion and size and scale of details which have remained the same for five centuries. So it is evident that the British designer has all the advantage of the American when it comes to

that final step that makes or breaks a design—I mean the full size details. If an English architect or draughtsman is in doubt as to how a detail may look on the building, he can walk along the street and probably see several ancient examples which will set him right. The American has no such help, he must guess on paper and experiment on the building, something fatal to accuracy in the full-sizing. Young American draughtsmen have no examples of medieval details at hand to follow, no perfect examples patiently and exquisitely worked out by master-craftsmen to use as models and standards. In most parts of America they see only poor, ignorant imitations of English types at best, and their design thus perpetuates abuses not only with regard to details, but in the more difficult problems of mass and perspective they flounder in the maze of irregular groupings. The American is dazzled when the Englishman scores a bull's-eye with some daring motive of roof or gable, not realizing perhaps that

254

RESIDENCE OF LAWRENCE F. ABBOTT,
ESQ., CORNWALL-ON-HUDSON, N. Y.
PARKER MORSE HOOPER, ARCHITECT.

RESIDENCE OF LAWRENCE F. ABBOTT,
ESQ., CORNWALL-ON-HUDSON, N. Y.
PARKER MORSE HOOPER, ARCHITECT.
(The Dormer Window in a Later Addition.)

RESIDENCE OF LAWRENCE F. ABBOTT, ESQ., CORNWALL-ON-HUDSON, N. Y.
Parker Morse Hooper, Architect.

the Englishman has simply adopted something he saw out of his office window, and knew exactly how the motive would look from all points of perspective before he drew it on paper. The modern Englishman is not given to imagination, he is the most realistic, matter-of-fact man on earth, and even if he is creative, he is as sound and thorough as he can be. He knows the value of centuries of race experience and is not prone to abstract invention. He uses the vernacular of his country, not a personal language of his own.

Not only do the difficulties of office practice in this free British style tend to make it fail with American designers. It is in essence and spirit Gothic, and its subtle medieval beauty is as alien to

the American temperament as the luxurious, complex style of royal France which could not be made to flourish over here. Everyone knows that Gothic has been the most signal persisted failure in American architecture. Only a half-dozen architects have triumphed in it.

It should be clear that, outside a small minority of designers in the eastern cities, most American architects are at a hopeless disadvantage in attempting the picturesque English architecture in America. This minority are unusually gifted men, bred in English traditions, who have trained a special office force for this style of work. Their work is done in the most painstaking fashion with as much study and travel in England as is possible. They know that, no matter

257

DETAIL OF FRONT—RESIDENCE AT HARTSDALE,
N. Y. FRANK ARNOLD COLBY, ARCHITECT.

RESIDENCE AT HARTSDALE, N. Y.
Frank Arnold Colby, Architect.

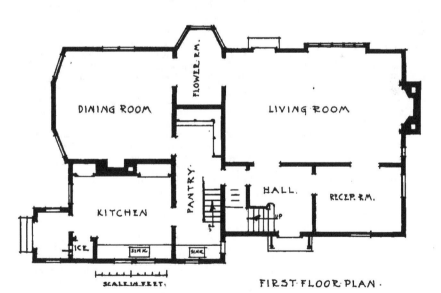

FIRST·FLOOR·PLAN·

RESIDENCE AT HARTSDALE, N. Y.
Frank Arnold Colby, Architect.

RESIDENCE AT HARTSDALE, N. Y.
Frank Arnold Colby, Architect.

how creative a man may be, he can only make his design successful by acquiring an accurate vocabulary of forms and details and by entering thoroughly into the spirit of a tradition. Even these men are giving this British style an American turn. They are more or less consciously adapting its forms and colors to American conditions.

The above considerations are offered to explain the weakness of the picturesque English style in America. Practical difficulties stand in the way of using it; it was developed to suit conditions entirely different from ours, and Americans broke with the medieval tradition three centuries ago, and cannot retrieve its subtle Gothic spirit. I believe that it, too, will pass, in the way of the other foreign styles, or else be so modified as to merge into native types. Even now it is not often met with in pure form in small houses. Soon all that will remain of it will be a faint, exquisite aroma of inspiration, vigor and freedom, and perfect breeding and stylish manners. It will then take its place beside the bal-

ancing Italian memory of simplicity and perfection and grace, and only our own early American tradition will be left.

I have shown two houses of American design which have evidences of the English influence. One is the house of Mr. Alfred Mellor, an alteration by Messrs. Mellor, Meigs and Howe. It has one of those long, narrow plans which are so effective in elevation. The first floor arrangement is very charming, unusual, and admirable for entertaining. Most effective is the situation and character of the porch, which is really a loggia or outdoor wing. Upstairs the hallway is long and narrow, but its unexpected openings out into the stair hall and anteroom make this less noticeable. Outside, the attraction of the house is evident in the photographs. It is altogether a part of the neighborhood and goes well with adjacent houses. If it seems at first sight English, in its larger windows and comfortable, ample proportions, it is quite American. Even in detail much of its elements could be found in some of our old houses, and they are kept fine in

260

scale and well modeled for clear sunlight. Mr. Frank Arnold Colby's home is different in character, with its English elements still less apparent. Its windows are thoroughly American and its roof details are well designed for intense light. It has, in addition, a pronounced individual character, an unusual touch of gayety, even humor. Both its lot plan and its floor plans have been discussed in Part I and Part IV. of this series as models of architecture.

Thus the decision of style in small houses rests upon the worth of our national forms. This should not be difficult to determine. The trend of the times seems to set stronger each year towards the historic American tradition, towards the forms of household arts developed early in Colonial days and carried well into the nineteenth century, and submerged in most parts of the country—but not everywhere—for fifty years, from 1840 to 1890. Other types there are, but they are meeting with less favor. The more they are analyzed the more they are rejected by our ablest designers as clearly unfit. Either they are Victorian relics, barbarism, or crude interpretation's of European models, or else merely the result of ignorance of design. An exception is a type developed early in the century by a few gifted men in Chicago. Its progress was watched with sympathy in the east, but its early promise was not fullfilled and it is being turned again into the stream of the early tradition. In only a small area of the country is clearly found.

Fortunately, it is not necessary at this date to defend at length the early American tradition. Nearly all the foremost designers favor it. When they attempt other forms it is either through necessity or else as an occasional diversion. They believe that it holds great possibilities artistically, architecturally, and nationally. They are fascinated by its extraordinary variety, which new researches among old houses and buildings in districts hitherto neglected, is always increasing. It was developed to fit American conditions and life and manners at a time when people had plenty of leisure to study how to express the ideal of the American family and hearth in the household arts. Our ancestors all over the country, from Canada to Florida, worked nearly two hundred years on this task, and they carried it to complete success.

It was folk-art, the art of craftsmen. Although there were no architects in the modern sense, most of the design was done by craftsmen, carpenters and masons, who designed right on the building. They thus came to adapt simply and naively the forms and details in wood and stone to American conditions of climate and sunlight and landscape. Samuel McIntyre, the great architect of Salem, Mass., whose masterly details of entrance porches and doorways and mantels are famous, began as a carpenter and woodcarver. This instance was repeated indefinitely. In many regions this long process of craftsmanly adaptation of forms to American conditions was carried so far that European forms were finally eliminated. For instance, in the old New Jersey houses of the Holland descendants, even columns and entablatures do not appear in the pure type of this region, and except for an occasional detail of trim or door paneling, they do not contain a form found outside America. Our native style is thus a true vernacular, which accounts for its endless charm and interest and for its vitality of local variations.

American designers feel that this beautiful old native style not only expresses American ideals, but as a practical matter it is easy to design with. There are countless masterly old examples along the Atlantic seaboard and west to the Mississippi to profit by—perfect standards for design and models for details. Architects and draughtsmen are always studying, visiting, measuring, memorizing the forms of these buildings. They have thus all the models for a vocabulary which they could not exhaust in the busiest practice, and this advantage they do not possess with any other style. These forms are a simple series, suited to our methods of construction, in contrast with the forms of other

RESIDENCE AT GLEN RIDGE, N. J.
William Edgar Moran, Architect.

styles which are less direct and therefore more expensive. They were ingrained in our people—among all ranks, democratic—as thoroughly as any part of American culture, and it is absurd to think that fifty years of Victorian ugliness could have broken the tradition. Its spirit remains as vigorous as ever.

In truth, the failure in past years to appreciate the value of our early artforms was largely due to a confusion of terms. The word "Colonial" was spoken as carelessly as the word "Italian." The first students of our native style did not know that its greatest period came in the nineteenth century, long after the United States were colonies, and that it flourished all over the country for over sixty years after the Declaration of Independence. In some rural countrysides and villages it never died out. It is thus as absurd to call it "Colonial" as to call the early works of Emerson "Colonial," or to claim Poe a "Colonial." Whitman wrote "Leaves of Grass" only a few years after Victorianism poked its ugly face into the beautiful picture of the old American hearth, and it should be realized that he, and all his contemporaries in American literature grew up in the atmosphere of a native, nationwide, homogeneous, exquisitely perfected household art. The visitor to Concord will see that, even to the end of the nineteenth century, Victorianism was never able to gain a hold in that historic town. To the extent that they have ignored the significance of our native art tradition, the literary and intellectual circles of America have overlooked the obvious.

Of course, we should not copy our early forms mechanically. We may continue to modify and to develop them according to our taste and circumstance, and we may emphasize certain aspects of its spirit as more symbolic of the twentieth century. Using a style does not forbid progress. But we might as well give up our language or our law or education as to cast aside this native art, for it is the one that our designers use with the greatest, most consistent success.

Only two doubts remain in some minds as to how far this early American tradition fits architecture today. One

262

comes from certain designers who wish to work in a free, picturesque style. They believe that the symmetrical balanced design and neo-classic details of many old houses are out of place in certain special conditions of landscape or neighborhood. In fact, a few designers have tried to lay down the principle that site and situation govern style. They assert that the American tradition is meant only for formal town conditions or for a quiet farmland; but that a picturesque style modeled after the modern English country house should be used in an informal neighborhood or in rough, picturesque country. This I believe to be a fallacy. To say nothing of the difficulty

of using the English style in the United States, it is contrary to all the teachings of the history of architecture to develop two or more styles just because different physical conditions are met with. Here, again, one need not depend on theory. The most recent studies of old houses show that it is an error to think that the old American style means prim, balanced, neo-classic design. Such was undoubtedly the impression when, a generation ago, architects began to explore the resources of our architecture in New England towns and cities, where the more sophisticated mansion type first met their eye. Later, however, a more thorough knowledge of the style, particularly

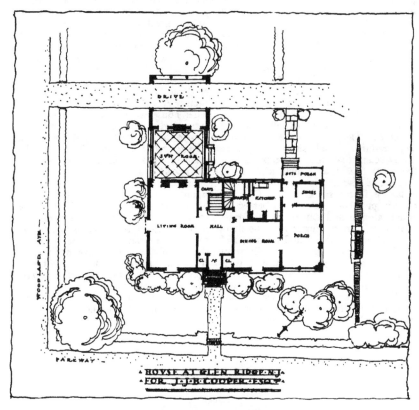

RESIDENCE AT GLEN RIDGE, N. J.
William Edgar Moran, Architect.

that gained in the last five years, has turned up an extraordinary amount of the freest sort of architectural expression in massing, groupings, roofs, gables, details. There is still immense material for our vocabulary of this picturesque type of design yet to be collected, particularly south of New York. There is much of it even in New England, and I have encountered a fine field in southern New Hampshire.

These discoveries are welcomed by designers, because the lack of picturesque, informal motives had been the one flaw in their enthusiasm for our early architecture. Now they know that they have all the types of models—without which architectural forms are guess-work—needed for all kinds of design. They prefer this type of freer forms to the variations of the modern British style, because it is thus not abstract design on paper, and, even more, because its picturesque vernacular aesthetically fits our natural conditions. Its fuller, more horizontal proportions, its porches and sheds and outbuildings, its simple, direct lines and construction, its large, cheerful windows, its sunlit details, its lively, cheerful, hospitable, simple, open character, are all characteristically American.

All in all, every fact that influences the choice of style points to the use of our own tradition. And, since no style of art is sound that does not express perfectly the life of the people who use it, this native tradition is the only one that is honest in the small house. Our ancestors gave two centuries to perfecting American life and expressing its ideals in this art, harmonizing it with the literary tradition of Poe and Emerson, and the fifty years interlude in the Victorian period is not of great moment. It is certain that the elemental life of the family and the society which was based on it have not changed much in our American countrysides and villages and town neighborhoods. They are wealth-

ier, more comfortable, have more machines; that is all. We need not wait for a new "nationalism," a new society, or a "new social era" in order to achieve a new style. The art-forms that mirror our national, rural and small community life are the only ones that really are worthy of small house architecture today.

So much for one of the two prejudices still existing against the native American style. The other has been hinted at before. That is the criticism of certain artists and "intellectuals" that our old forms are too thin, too prim, too cold—too uninspired—to express the twentieth century, which is dynamic, powerful, symbolized by splendor and daring. To such ideas there is no great need to reply. The quiet, simple, household art of town and country is in question here, not the architecture of our confused, unplanned cities; nor even the architecture of our great residences, some of which are but eccentric advertisements for their owners, who clearly do not know how to make homes out of them. It is enough to say that such assertions of critics as to the out-of-date character of the American tradition are based on ignorance of facts. Again it may be said that many older houses show much imaginative design, particularly in stone architecture, and in the architecture of the south, design as "modern" in its boldness and dramatic effect as people could live with year after year.

In conclusion, may not this be agreed upon: Do not the very best modern houses designed in the native American tradition attain nearly all the possibilities of a national style of architecture? Even those who hesitate to agree must feel that if our architects have not yet perfected an American style in small houses, they are so far on their way towards their object that there is no turning them back. And, in view of their great achievement, who would care to stop them?

SOLDIERS & SAILORS MEMORIAL HOSPITAL

PENN YAN   NEW YORK

EDWARD F STEVENS, ARCHITECT

PHILANTHROPIC foundations are fitting memorials to the men who served the cause of humanity in the World War, and not a few foundations of this nature are taking the form of hospitals. Such a memorial is planned in Penn Yan, N. Y., to the boys who went out from Yates County. Public spirited citizens have contributed generously that it might be of the greatest good to the county, and the site is one of the finest in the town, with splendid oaks and maples shading the approach.

The entrance is through a "Memorial Hall," commodious and inviting, speaking welcome to all. The walls, panelled to the top of the doors, will bear bronze tablets containing the names of the 650 soldiers, sailors and marines who served in the war. The memorial hall will have cabinets for war relics and will be large enough for the holding of commemorative meetings, etc. From the hall, one enters the hospital office and the staff room; this administration unit is therefore cut off from the hospital proper. While the capacity of the hospital is only eighteen beds, it is so subdivided as to provide for the segregation of diseases and of the sexes.

On the first floor, besides the memorial hall and offices just mentioned, there is a complete operating department, with operating room, sterilizing and work room, surgeons' dressing and locker room, anaesthetizing and supply room.

At the south end of the first floor is a small but complete maternity department with a two-bed ward and three private rooms, a delivery room, creche and toilet facilities, together with an airing balcony on the south. Centrally located are the staircase and elevator, together with the ambulance entrance to the rear.

As the ground falls off toward the south, sufficient height is obtained in the basement for the kitchen, dining-room, heater room and X-Ray department, with ample storage capacity.

Provision for the general patients is made on the second floor, which is so divided as to allow for eight patients in wards and five in private rooms, with ample provision made for toilets, bath, linen and medicine to make the hospital complete. An airing balcony extends across the south end, affording room for many of the patients to be in the open air.

The exterior will be of the Mission type of architecture, constructed of tile blocks with "rough cast" plaster finish and red tile roof. While this will be a complete hospital in itself, it is so arranged that future additions may be made without affecting the usefulness of the first building.

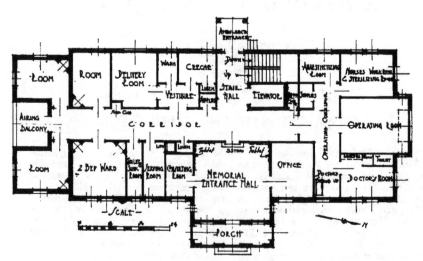

FIRST FLOOR PLAN—SOLDIERS' AND SAILORS' MEMORIAL HOSPITAL, PENN YAN, YATES CO., N Y.
Edward F. Stevens, Architect.

266

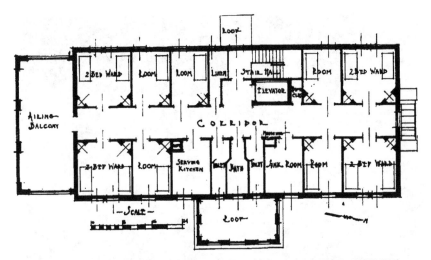

SECOND FLOOR PLAN—SOLDIERS' AND SAILORS' MEMORIAL HOSPITAL, PENN YAN,
YATES CO., N. Y.
Edward F. Stevens, Architect.

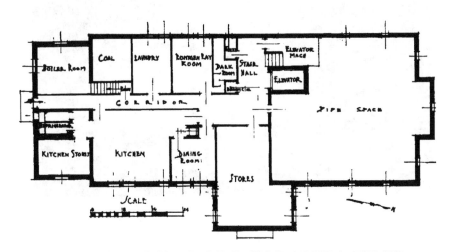

BASEMENT PLAN—SOLDIERS' AND SAILORS' MEMORIAL HOSPITAL, PENN YAN,
YATES CO., N. Y.
Edward F. Stevens, Architect.

267

DOORWAY FROM NO. 5 GREAT GEORGE
STREET, WESTMINSTER, S. W. IN
VICTORIA AND ALBERT MUSEUM.

English Architectural Decoration

Text and Measured Drawings by Albert E. Bullock

Part XIII'. Carved Overdoors, Chimneypieces, Etc.

THE details relating to the rooms illustrated in my last article give a clear idea of the elaboration and richness of the carving put into work executed during the first half of the eighteenth century. The room from No. 27 Hatton Garden is particularly bold with regard to the chimneypiece, niches and overdoors. This example has curved, scrolled and enriched cornices to the pediments of the niches, while the cartouches occupying the center feature to the broken pediments of the overdoors are well carved and of good design. The inverted husk ornament will be noticed at the mitered angles of the door architraves, as well as the scroll drop which finishes the breaks against the vertical sides of the architraves. This doorway is of pleasing character and typical of many rooms executed during the reign of George II.

The adjoining room at the Victoria and Albert Museum, which comes from No. 5 Great George Street, Westminster, is a later example carved with that French touch associated with the name of Chippendale. The style is most in evidence in the design of the frieze to the overdoor and the nature of the carving to the chimneypiece. The Greek fret pattern to the dado rail and to the picture frame of the overmantel was in vogue during the closing years of the reign of George II, but it is quite possible that the room was executed within a few years of the accession of George III. The carved pendants at each side of this frame are free of all convention, exhibiting much skill in execution.

Another feature of interest lies in the carved wood brackets on either side of the frieze to the chimneypiece reminiscent of the marble examples of the time of Wren as exemplified at Belton House. The picture harmonizes well with the simple character of the room.

The apartment is tastefully designed. It has the advantage over the Hatton Garden room in having the four panelled walls intact, including the window shutters, but neither example possesses an enriched plaster ceiling. One imagines that the windows were the usual sash or guillotine type with thick ovolo molded bars common at this time, and it is a pity they were not also preserved and inserted in position. Both rooms are in deal and have modillioned main cornices crowning the panelling to the walls.

Throughout the realm of interior decoration the want of original ceiling ornament is very marked in many otherwise excellent examples of panelled rooms. There exists at Westminster one enriched ceiling of this period in a small house situated at the back of North Street, said to have been once occupied by Lord North, whose bust is supposed to be modelled in one of the ceiling panels. The design is based upon the constructional principle of cross-beams enriched with a Greek fret pattern and having an elliptical molded center panel. The square angles have large rosettes, and the side panels have the bust referred to, enclosed by ovals with foliated scrolls.

The tendency to a severer classical ideal is noticeable in most of the plaster work of this age, but the moldings and ornament were for the most part bold and of full relief. The work of James Gibbs at the Radcliffe Library, Oxford, and St. Martin's-in-the-Fields Church near Charing Cross in London give instances of the character of the ornament of this period. The latter example is rich in detail, the soffit of the gallery having semidome shaped sinkings for the circular window heads to give fuller light, the center of these sinkings being ornamented with a large shell and accompanying ornament of appropriate nature.

269

At this time the rooms were not so lofty as those common to the William and Mary period, and this fact often makes the ornament appear somewhat heavy. Realizing this defect with its tendency to coarseness, the Adam Brothers sought to obviate the difficulty by the *finesse* of their purer Greek methods. Their Flaxman type of relief work was of fine line and graceful pose. In common with Wedgwood they endeavored to depict the mythological subjects of Pagan history in all the salient positions favorable to the completion of their designs. There are several ceilings of this character in London, notably in some of the older houses in St. James' Square, Argyll Place and Adelphi Terrace, while the libraries at Belton and Nostell Priory

and the decorations at Sion House are a few instances of good examples outside the capital.

The Adam designs for chimneypieces were particularly happy, with fine marble inlay and carving, of which there are examples at Stratford House, the town residence of the Earl of Derby, and at Kedleston, the seat of Lord Scarsdale. The wood carved mantels of this era were frequently rather more lavish of detail, especially those designed by Pergolesi. The Adam ceilings exhibit an enslaved attachment to geometrical formation, of which the ornament was often so finicky as to rob the example of much value and jeopardize the grandeur of their larger reception rooms. This is very noticeable at Lansdown House

STAIRCASE CEILING, ASHBURNHAM HOUSE, WESTMINSTER, S. W., CHARLES I. PERIOD.

SALOON CEILING, ASHBURNHAM HOUSE, WESTMINSTER, S. W., CHARLES I. PERIOD.

where the dining room ceiling is subdivided, with the smaller panels worried with essays in geometry.

The assistance of George Richardson —who issued a book of ceiling designs at the time—no doubt contributed to the failure of this section of the work, as his designs are not very inspiring, the redeeming features being the many delightfully painted panels of Kauffman and Zucchi.

The mechanical triumph of the compass over the artistic tendency of the mind, the sense of making as many variations of intersecting and adjacent curves in juxtaposition as will conveniently vary a given pattern to avoid complete monotony—these are the impressions one feels upon examining many of these ceilings from a critical aspect.

One cannot imagine that Pergolesi ever yielded to this temptation, and possibly Van Gelder and Spang were left a free hand to devote their energies to carving the many chimneypieces which will live to the renown of the school. The draughtsmanship of C. L. Clérisseau

certainly contributed to much of the delicacy of the work where it related to metal ornaments and fittings, no less than the Wedgwood cameos or small painted panels of the artists employed. Robert Adam had struck a firm friendship with Piranesi, whose engravings are still the wonder of his age.

The greatness of the Adam Brothers' work lies chiefly in the clever planning and grandeur of form of many of their mansions, as well as those of their school, such as Boodle's Club in St. James' street, and other houses in the London area. The detail of the decorations are of secondary importance, although essentially typical and necessary to the style, and therefore inseparable from it. Lightness and grace were the keynotes of each theme, and they attained their object to a remarkable extent.

By comparison with earlier styles one notices that detail forms a much more essential part of the general conception in preceding ages. The large cavetto of the cornices of the James II period, the bolection moldings of the age of William

271

FIREPLACE FROM NO. 5 GREAT GEORGE STREET, WESTMINSTER, S. W. IN
VICTORIA AND ALBERT MUSEUM.

and Mary, the tendency to classic forms during the reigns of the first two Georges, and the free rendering of plaster work in the early years of George III, based upon the French Régence style, culminated in the development of finer qualities of expression. The work of the Chippendale school was really a hybrid taste grafted on an old English principle. It helped to promote a desire for something different and apart from previous thought. Thus the discoveries of early Roman and Greek work which transpired at Herculaneum and Spalato gave the motifs required and the impetus to the development of a new and original style adapted from an ancient source. In addition, the intercourse with France—where the fine work of the era of Louis XVI was in full swing—could not fail to have a beneficial influence upon the practice in this country, and the later Adam work synchronized with that of the French Empire style which was developing at the time of the Revolution.

Many are inclined to look upon the death of Robert Adam as the climax or end of the development of decoration in England, and to a certain extent, from a historical standpoint, this is so; but there is a sequel in the work of Sir John Soane and Sir Charles Barry, which I shall hope to deal with at a later date. The latter architect was responsible for many important edifices, including Bridgewater House, the Travellers' and Reform Clubs in Pall Mall and the interior of Stafford House (now the London Museum), all within the vicinity of St. James's Palace.

The disposition of panelling upon the wall surface usually presents some difficulties where the chimneypiece or door is not placed centrally in the full width of the side of a room. Upon the bisymmetric principle a chimneypiece or door may be made central by reconstruction,

272

NO. 27 HATTON GARDEN, LONDON, E.C. IN VICTORIA AND ALBERT MUSEUM.

No. 5   GREAT GEORGE ST. WESTMINSTER.

(NOW IN THE VICTORIA & ALBERT MVSEVM.)

No. 5, G⸱ GEORGE S⸱ S.W.
(NOW IN THE VICTORIA & ALBERT MVSEVM.)

DOORWAY SIDE OF ROOM.

SCALE OF INCHES & FEET

DETAILS.

ENRICHED MOLDING
TO PANELLING

DETAIL OF MAIN CORNICE:
Nº 5, GT GEORGE STᵀ SW.
V.&A.M.

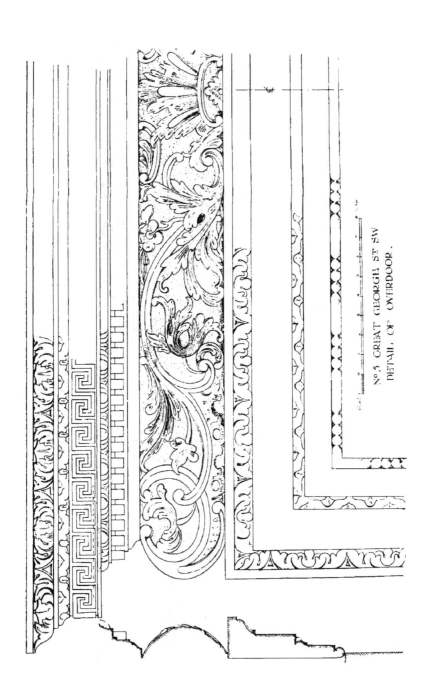

Nº 5 GREAT GEORGE ST SW
DETAIL OF OVERDOOR.

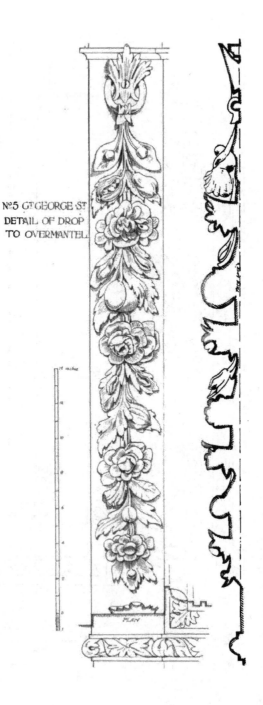

N?5 G! GEORGE S!
DETAIL OF DROP
TO OVERMANTEL

Nº 27 HATTON GARDEN · E.C. *from work*

DETAIL OF ORNAMENT OVER NICHES.

GEORGIAN PANELLED ROOM
CIRENCESTER HOVSE · GLOS.

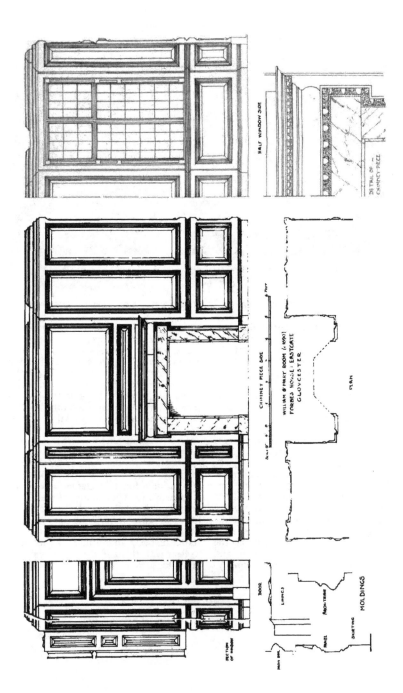

WILLIAM & MARY ROOM (c.1690)
FORBES HOUSE · EASTGATE
GLOUCESTER

HALF WINDOW SIDE

DETAIL OF CHIMNEY PIECE

CHIMNEY PIECE SIDE

PLAN

SECTION OF WINDOW

MOLDINGS

ADAM PERIOD CAST-LEAD FANLIGHT IN VICTORIA AND ALBERT MUSEUM.

where such is possible, but it does not always so occur. Take, for example, the comparison of the door side of the room from No. 5 Great George Street. Westminster, with the chimneypiece side of the room from Forbes House, Gloucester. The latter example is of the early William and Mary period, before the introduction of the sash window into this district. Although the chimneypiece is practically central, there is an unequal distribution of panelling on either side of the chimney breast. Each side is. however, so designed that a compensating balance results, which is quite harmonious. This is not seen in the side of the room from Great George Street. The door here is awkwardly placed, and the panelling consequently irregularly spaced. Fortunately, one does not look at the side of a room in direct elevation, and upon entering this room. the chimney-

piece side, which is equally balanced, demands the first notice. A room is always seen in perspective, and the main feature, which is usually the chimneypiece, attracts the eye immediately, before it travels around in quest of other items of interest. Irregularities in the panel distribution can therefore be softened by the judicious disposal of articles of furniture.

It is possible there existed a definite reason for the projecting feature seen to the left of the chimneypiece in the instance cited from Forbes House, as it was built for an ecclesiastic who was responsible for the building of the church opposite. A number of the better houses in this town were built for prelates. Canon Maden's House, with its fine staircase, being an example. I shall hope to deal with this and the Foresters' Hall in a later article.

HOUSING UNSKILLED WORKERS

By JOHN TAYLOR BOYD, Jr.

THIS* is one of three American books that treat comprehensively of the housing problem. One other is the Report of the U. S. Housing Corporation, of which Vol. II. was reviewed in the January issue of the Architectural Record. Architects will find that the two works supplement each other. The Housing Corporation's Report furnishes a wealth of technical data on building projects, but it does not cover the whole field of housing. The non-technical aspects of the subject are the real crux of the existing housing crisis; and it is in the sound comprehensive exposition of the non-technical factors that the chief value of Mrs. Wood's book lies. The third book is Mr. Lawrence Veiller's "Housing Reform."

In much of the writings of the architectural profession on housing there is a wide gap; the subject matter deals with the two extremes of technical details and of vague generalities on sociology, and leaves out the solid intermediate field between. That is the field of promotion and of organization: It is the building up of a public opinion to support good housing, which means inspiring prominent citizens to organize to

*"The Housing of the Unskilled Worker." By Edith Elmer Wood. New York: Macmillan Co.

obtain legislation which shall protect good housing against the ruinous competition of bad housing; and then the forming of corporations that will undertake the practical duties of finance, construction and the management of actual housing enterprises. If architects will master the principles of this undeveloped side of housing, they will be better able to exert the influence to which their position entitles them. No doubt they will leave this side to others to handle, but they should certainly understand its workings in order to achieve full co-operation in housing work.

Despite the title of her book, Mrs. Wood has not restricted her subject to the unskilled worker. Inasmuch, however, as his housing troubles are the hardest part of housing, and as their solution concerns all the factors of the subject, they form the central theme of the discussion.

The first chapters contain a most intelligent short history of bad housing, together with a classification of its various types and of the moral and physical kinds of deterioration that slums cause. These opening chapters are invaluable for an architect, because he should be able to recognize the ancestry of any spurious schemes of relief that will be placed before the public. They will be offered with the crafty excuse that, in the crisis, we must do the best we can, and cannot expect too much. Had San Francisco been able to replan her city after the great disaster, she would not now be faced with a housing problem in the devastated area, only a dozen years after the great catastrophe. Halifax, N. S., on the other hand, after a like calamity in 1918, is replanning her ruined districts under the auspices of an experienced town planner.

The importance of the legal side of housing runs all through the book. The author does well to attach such significance to the legal and administrative system of housing and town-planning that has grown up in Massachutetts under the state's Homestead Commission. Those who know anything of the rapid progress made by the Massachusetts commissions, their sound, sure sense, the wisdom of their policies, how they win popular support and establish themselves firmly in the fundamental law and administration of the state, and how their example spreads in other states—such observers will eagerly watch the work of the Commission, for out of it may come the solution of the difficulty. Already the Homestead Commission has obtained from the voters two amendments to the state's constitution in aid of its policies.

This absense of a legal system and of agencies of political administration indicates how great is the task confronting those who would see good housing established throughout the nation. Any great activity, in order to succeed, must root itself in customs and habits and good will of the people, who then write it into their laws. In housing, the void is a big one to fill up. At present one state, Michigan, and two cities in the United States, New York and Chicago. have effective restrictive housing legislation and administration. On the constructive side there is chiefly only the Massachusetts Homestead Commission with its rudimentary system of co-operation with towns and cities. But under pressure of the shortage of homes, public interest is awakening as never before.

Older methods do not seem to fit the situation and new ones are being sought for.

EARLY BRICK ARCHITECTURE.

THERE is always space on the architect's book-shelves for additional works on the subject of early American architecture and the appearance of *Brick Architecture of the Colonial Period in Maryland and Virginia** is warmly welcomed. Study of our early architecture and decorative arts has passed the stage of discursive and general treatment and has reached the point where a thorough investigation of particular localities or types of material is in order.

No portion of the original colonies can boast a richer tradition of beautiful building in permanent material than Maryland and Virginia. Settled under more favorable economic auspices than the New England states, these great properties granted by the crown were laid out and developed by men of taste and wealth who were conversant with much of the finest Georgian architecture of the mother country. Their intercourse with England was continuous and the wealth which was derived from their extensive landed holdings found ready outlay in the sumptuous surroundings from the midst of which they dispensed their generous hospitality.

The use of brick is rather the rule than its exception in this country. Brickmaking was one of the earliest trades extensively practiced in Virginia and in the seventeenth century we find records of contracts let for brick buildings which should follow in all respects the brick building methods of England. In the appreciative introduction to the book a description of the use of brick, particularly in Maryland, is interesting. Its color, texture, methods of laying and joint pointing are important in reproducing as closely as possible the wall effects of the originals, such for instance as the Brice and Ridout houses in Anna-

*"Brick Architecture of the Colonial Period in Maryland and Virginia." By Lewis A. Coffin and Arthur C. Holden. New York: The Architectural Book Publishing Company.

polis, where the whole wall surface is made up of headers, breaking joints, and where the use of molded bricks laid on edge and forming the water tables is noteworthy. The chimneys are striking in their height and in the thinness of their lesser dimensions, and their form was evidently considered a necessary element in the composition of the gable elevations, as is witnessed in the Baltimore town house of Charles Carroll, where these chimneys are without use and of little more than the thickness of the walls, the actual chimneys rising at some distance within the end of the gables to serve fireplaces on the inside walls of the rooms.

The detail of the exterior woodwork, of which numerous measured drawings appear in the book, is often beautiful in scale and form and its whiteness contrasts well with the soft-hued brick. There are legends of more than one fine lead cornice in Annapolis, whose existence, however, no one is willing at present to vouch for, but which furnishes an interesting object for architectural search.

Attention is also called to the window treatment, which plays a large part in the design—the frames, simply molded, are set flush within the brick openings, and are almost without exception devoid of shutters.

The interior woodwork in many of the houses is elaborately carved, its effectiveness as a whole making up for imperfections in certain cases in the technique. The measured drawings of this carved and molded work, both interior and exterior, serve their purpose of scientific accuracy, supplemented by photographs which explain the relief and gradations of surface. Throughout much of the carved detail runs a slight French feeling—a bit of the *rocaille et coquille* as

interpreted by the hands of English trained workmen.

An interesting detail of many of these houses not noted in the book is the use in frequent cases where paneled walls occur of raised and beveled panels of hard plaster within molded stiles and rails of wood. It would seem to have been utilized where wide panels were desired and wood of sufficient width unobtainable, for wooden and plaster panels of identical detail are apt to occur in the same house. In the later houses much very beautiful stucco ceiling ornament is found, which leads us, from its perfection, to believe that European workmen were imported for this careful work.

The arrangement of comparative plans is interesting and emphasizes the popularity of the great central hall, which runs through from front to rear, relict of the seventeenth century country house plan. Another striking feature is the infrequent occurrence of the monumental stairway. The stairway is usually relegated to a subordinate position and in some cases practically hidden away.

The book presents an unusually interesting collection of material, plans, photographs, and measured drawings of details, with useful and interesting notes attached to them. Several of the houses, strictly speaking, are not of the Colonial period, but date rather from the early Federal times. The bibliography, too, should be of service, although the list of the early carpenters' guides, which were widely used, might be greatly augmented. The most striking omission in the present edition is that of any index, an item which would add much to the usefulness of the work, but whose absence cannot impair the interest attaching to the fine selection of material chosen with a trained architectural taste.

CHARLES OVER CORNELIUS.

One rarely finds in a Spanish church a window **The Carved Window of San José.** that has been developed into an ornamental feature, unless it forms part of a larger composition. This statement does not apply of course to Gothic churches, which are essentially French importations. The Spanish architect keeps down the size of his windows, because of the blazing sunlight of his country, and gives scant thought to their enrichment.

It is therefore interesting to come upon such a feature as the baptistery window of Mission San José de Aguayo, near San Antonio, Texas. One discovers it unexpectedly on a side wall that is otherwise quite devoid of embellishment and which provides no special structural setting for this gem of ornament.

The character of the work is quite like that upon the west front of the church, florid and in high relief, displaying a marked baroque influence. The framework of the design is strong and well defined and is softened by scroll and leaf work of that irresponsible and irrepressible character so roundly denounced by stylistic purists.

The simple iron grill which occupies the opening is reputed to have been made in Spain and brought here by the padres. Local tradition relates that the window was the crowning achievement of the artist whose skill contributed so much to the beauty of this mission; that it was a labor of love dedicated to the memory of the woman whose fickleness drove him to a monastic life, that upon the completion of the window he languished and soon died, to be buried beside the mission walls.

The window merits the reputation it bears of being one of the most beautiful examples of Spanish architectural detail

left by the padres, of whose skill so many traces are to be found in our Southwestern States. I. T. FRARY.

———

One of the problems in town planning not yet solved concerns the pro- **A Gathering Place in Town Plans.** vision that is to be made for a public gathering space, a central square or forum which shall be the theatre for such public functions as may take place in the life of the community. In designs for town plans published from time to time, two tendencies may be noted. Town planners of architectural training often display open squares or plazas based on well-known European examples, while those whose training is in landscape architecture hesitate to open out such a center anywhere in the design, preferring instead informal parks, where the attraction lies in decorations of green lawns and foliage. The latter consider empty asphalt spaces to be artificial, uninteresting in execution. the result of an overtechnical emphasis on formal design. They point with pride to their splendid facilities for outdoor recreation, both in little playgrounds scattered through the town and in the large parks on the outskirts, where every sort of sport and gathering may take place. They provide assembly spaces and outdoor theatres. They ask, with much reason, what more could be done?

Like many another problem, the important consideration is the problem itself, rather than individual preference or historical analogy. The point may be made that modern town planning, especially in the minds of many of its leaders who are gazing far ahead to a highly socialized community, means a community extra-

SOUTH WINDOW OF BAPTISTERY, MIS-
SION SAN JOSÉ, SAN ANTONIO, TEXAS.

ordinarily organized. That means towns entirely humanized and humanitarian. It means towns akin to the old Greek and Latin civic ideals—towns self-conscious in civic life, proud, powerful, models of co-operation. As one aspect of the life of such communities we have countless public meetings, where people foregather collectively, not to transact business directly, but for celebration and stimulation; with ceremonies, addresses, commemorations, inaugurations, pageants, in which the whole people formally but democratically and spontaneously, delight to join. Indeed, such activities have greatly increased in American life within the past few years. Now, may we not conclude that town plans must provide for such an important social feature? Will an informal park or outskirt meadow answer the purpose? In such gatherings the emphasis is on man, not on nature. What is really wanted is a setting for a human picture, for crowds kaleidoscopic in color, for decorations of drapery, of pageants, of flags and banners, contrasted in sunlight and in the deep shadows of walls. The painter should be asked for an opinion as to the setting for such pictures. He might say that during half the year the trees are leafless, the lawns are straw, and a drab background is thus provided for a public function. Any great masses of green cut up the crowds, and they detract from the impressive effects of that colorful pattern of crowds and processions, that endless fascination we find in massed and moving humans. The simpler the setting, the better. Neither elaborate architecture nor elaborate naturalistic parks are needed. Differences of level might be found—if not too frequent—so as to provide great elevated spaces as platforms on which the chief part of the spectacle could take place.

In discussing this feature with a city planner, he agreed with me, and, in return, made the significant remark that the reason for the hesitation and disagreement on this focal point in town plans was that communities themselves have not yet developed clear ideas as to how they may use such a forum, or broad avenues leading to it. Once they make their demands known, he said, town planners will soon meet the demand. Although my friend made a good point here, it is also true that designers should be forehanded. Note that where such a gathering place has been provided, even with a limited purpose, soon a wider and broader usage for it has grown up. I refer to the immense stadia provided for football contests at our universities. They form great settings of bare grass and barriers of monumental architecture. They are preferred to informal parks and shaded campuses for every kind of entertainments, pageants, celebrations, dramatics. In fact, our universities are our only planned towns that actually exist at the present time; not only architecturally but socially.

It is to be regretted that the true function of geometry in civic architecture is not understood by all. Fundamentally its use comes in where the human element, the element of collective organization, is emphasized. In the controversy between two schools, one school is apt to worship geometry for its pomp and display and artificiality, while the other dislikes it as reaction. It is liked or disliked for its own sake, rather than appreciated as an expression of a human need.

JOHN TAYLOR BOYD, JR.

THE
ARCHITECTVRAL
RECORD

CONTENTS

Vol. XLVII. No. 4　　　APRIL, 1920　　　Serial No. 259

Editor: MICHAEL A. MIKKELSEN　*Contributing Editor:* HERBERT CROLY
Business Manager J. A. OAKLEY

Yearly Subscription—United States $3.00—*Foreign* $4.00—*Single copies* 35 *cents. Entered
May 22, 1902, as Second Class Matter, at New York. N. Y. Member Audit Bureau of Circulation.*

PUBLISHED MONTHLY BY
THE ARCHITECTURAL RECORD COMPANY
115-119 WEST FORTIETH STREET, NEW YORK
F. T. MILLER, Pres.　W. D. HADSELL, Vice-Pres.　J. W. FRANK, Sec'y-Treas.　E. S. DODGE, Vice-Pres.

EARLY AMERICAN DOORWAY, DAN-
BURY, CONN. ABOUT 1805 OR 1806.

THE
ARCHITECTVRAL
RECORD

VOLVME XLVII

NVMBER IV

APRIL, 1920

SOME PRINCIPLES OF
SMALL HOUSE DESIGN

◧ *By* ◧

JOHN TAYLOR BOYD, Jʀ

PART VI - ELEVATIONS-STYLE

THIS part of the series contains specific illustrations of the principles of design of elevations that were set forth in part V. It concerns the technical methods of architectural design through which are expressed those principles common to all the arts, and which should be at the basis of any design.

In a given problem, as noted in the previous articles, the first step necessary is to form a clear conception of the arrangement of the lot and of the precise scheme of house plan that develops from that arrangement and from the practical needs and the ideals of the family. In this fundamental scheme, the plan of lot and house are imagined with the purpose of creating an artistic picture in the landscape setting or, if the lot is a small town lot, of creating a picture in the neighborhood. The aim as regards the design should be to attain an inspiration that is akin both to painting and sculpture—an effect of masses and spots and shapes of color in light on one hand, and an effect of geometrical form in perspective of relief, of modelling in different planes, and of decoration in light and shade and shadow. Otherwise, if the design is worked out in the routine way, all too common, it will be merely design on paper. The design of the elevations, the pretty one-eighth inch scale sketches that attract the client, will steadily lose quality with each step as it develops through working drawings and full sizes into the final forms of the constructed house. When the fundamental scheme—or *parti* as it is known in the slang of the architect's office—is once settled, the application of the principles of design is more strictly a matter of architectural technique. Design thereafter becomes a matter of how to make the most of the artistic and practical possibilities of the preliminary scheme in the mechanics and materials of building construction.

Among the technical principles of the particular art of architecture, the most fundamental element of all is style. The preceding article was devoted to this subject which has so baffled American architects and confused their clients, the American people. It was found that, whatever may be the confusion of styles in the architecture of our misshapen, half-planned, half-understood, heterogeneous and discordant cities, the problem of style in domestic architecture is solved. The style to use is that which is founded on early American architecture. It is the simple, exquisite household art of our farmland, village and town neighborhood—the native American style that was developed through two centuries of craftsmanship to express the simple American society which has not changed much in one hundred years. This art flowered out in the first half of the nineteenth century, in the formative period of the United States, when the great traditions of Americanism took lasting shape. It was the art of the hearth that nurtured Lincoln and Grant and Marshall and Emerson and Poe and Whitman and Henry Adams. It has come back strong among us, and has nearly driven out whatever foreign importations it could not easily assimilate. Even the modern British picturesque style of direct Gothic ancestry is vanishing. Practical difficulties stand in the way of using this British and other styles, and furthermore they neither respond to the conditions of American climate and landscape and light and atmosphere, nor do they express the in-

stincts of American civilization. It should no longer cause surprise to say that the temper of American design is coming to a point where it can hardly accommodate itself to any foreign spirit in form. The struggle of native architecture against foreign still goes on in the cities and in the great residences of the wealthy, though these latter contain many victories for our own tradition. Our intellectual people have overlooked the obvious fact of this conflict of forms, and also the obvious result of it. They dwell in the incoherent cities, with "isms" coming at them from all directions at once, like the motor-cars, and, in their excitement over their narrow escapes, imagine, some of them, that their agility is developing a new art—the expression of a new era—that will revolutionize the countrysides. But cities never revolutionize countrysides. This is one of the simplest principles of history. What neither Rome nor Paris nor London could do, New York, in its present unformed state, cannot hope to do. It can never force an alien or exotic art upon the people of the villages and countrysides, above all an art of the household that is an intellectual abstraction which does not vitally express the traditions of that society of small neighborhoods that forms the backbone of the country. When the small communities have developed an art that meets their needs, the cities may take this vernacular and create with it a great civic architecture.

Therefore, it seems safe to conclude that, in the matter of style as in most other respects, the small house has come into its own. We have now an American style suitable for any type of design, formal or informal, severe or free, classic or picturesque, symmetrical or not. Besides, and this is one of its greatest virtues, it is adapted to the flexible system of planning which both twentieth century economic conditions and the modern spirit force upon us. In the third and fourth articles, design was pictured as the problem of reconciling two conflicting powerful forces. One was economic —modern conditions of cost and maintenance, limiting the size of small houses

SOUTH ELEVATION—COTTAGE IN CON-
NECTICUT. MURPHY & DANA, ARCHITECTS.

DETAIL—COTTAGE IN CONNECTICUT
MURPHY & DANA, ARCHITECTS.

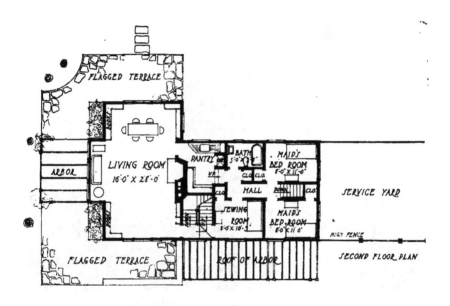

FLAGGED TERRACE

LIVING ROOM
16'-0" X 28'-0"

ARBOR

PANTRY
BATH
5'-0"

MAID'S
BED ROOM
8'-0" X 11'-0"

UP
CLO. CLO.

CLO.
HALL
ROOM
CLO.

SEWING
ROOM
8'-0" X 10'-3"

MAID'S
BED ROOM
8'-0" X 11'-0"

SERVICE YARD

HIGH FENCE

FLAGGED TERRACE

ROOF OF ARBOR

SECOND FLOOR PLAN

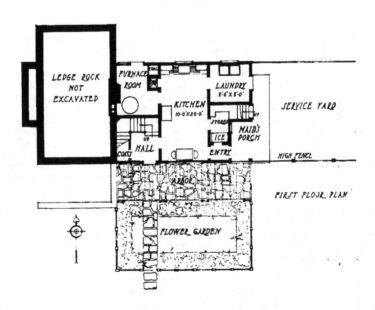

LEDGE ROCK
NOT
EXCAVATED

FURNACE
ROOM
COAL

KITCHEN
10'-0" X 20'-0"

LAUNDRY
8'-6" X 8'-0"

SERVICE YARD

STORE
UP

ICE

MAID'S
PORCH

UP
COATS HALL

ENTRY

HIGH FENCE

ARBOR

FIRST FLOOR PLAN

FLOWER GARDEN

FLOOR PLANS—COTTAGE IN CONNECTI-
CUT. MURPHY & DANA, ARCHITECTS.

RESIDENCE OF MISS ETHEL KETCHAM, BELLPORT, L. I.
Delano & Aldrich, Architects.

and ruthlessly cutting away luxuries, even necessities. The other was the modern art spirit which has stimulated the imagination, and which demands free, full creative design—inspiration. Only great ingenuity can break the deadlock between the two demands. Formulae, customs and habits of design, routine, or bookish inspiration cannot meet the situation. Designers are compelled to reclassify the essentials and to adopt a flexible scheme of planning and design to meet specific cases. This much of a summary of the four preceding articles is necessary before turning again to technical details.

When, as remarked above, in solving a particular problem, the general scheme of arrangement of lot and house and of the picture of the house in its setting has been decided, the next step is to fix upon that type of the American style that best expresses the scheme. One must decide the variety of regional types of architecture to use. Now, before considering some of the good points of the several types, it should be said that the most

experienced designers believe that the soundest practice is to stick to the current of tradition of the region where the house is located. This is, after all, but one of the oldest principles in architecture. Without it, no consistent character of town, no beauty of neighborhood, may be obtained. Even in the field of the American style there is such contrast between the types of New England and Philadelphia, for example, or of New Jersey and the south, that they could hardly be harmonious. This principle should be followed willingly by the designer, nor should he fear that it will hamper his initiative or stifle his personality, to use a catchword of certain modern artists. A thorough knowledge of the regional type should provide him with a vocabulary ample enough to enable him to express all the creative ideas he may possess. It is evident that the imagination of Mellor, Meigs and Howe has been helped, not handicapped, by keeping to the spirit of the Philadelphia type; and this is true in the case of

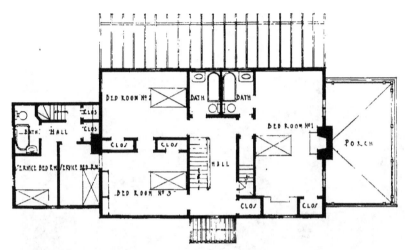

Parker Morse Hooper, who interprets the wood style of New York with a bold originality rare in architecture. Of course, in newer communities where there is no tradition of old houses, a type should be settled upon if possible, and it should be a fascinating enterprise to interpret the ideal which best expresses the local conditions of climate and landscape and light and color and atmosphere as well as the local building materials and the social character of the community.

There is not space in these pages to cover fully the value and characteristics of the various regional types of the United States. Only a few paragraphs may be spared to mention some of their

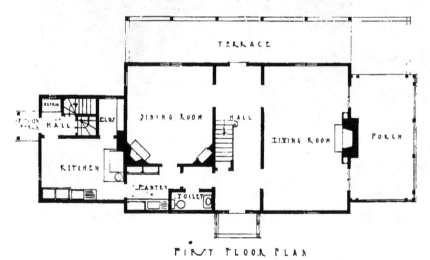

FIRST FLOOR PLAN

FLOOR PLANS—RESIDENCE OF MISS ETHEL KETCHAM, BELLPORT, L. I.
Delano & Aldrich, Architects.

297

DOOR DETAIL—RESIDENCE OF W. N.
HARTSHORN, ESQ., CAMBRIDGE, MASS.
GRANDGENT & ELWELL, ARCHITECTS.

essentials. Among them, as an all-round type, the regional architecture of Eastern Pennsylvania is not surpassed. Splendid in conception, bold and perfect in execution, with extraordinary charm and cheerful personality, the best examples follow interpretively, but closely and consistently, the old fieldstone and stucco houses of Eastern Pennsylvania, whose big, solid, full, spreading proportions, large roofs, fat chimneys, afford an air of comfort, of permanence, of home. equal to anything in the world. Yet, notwithstanding all its strength and big mass, the Philadelphia type is not clumsy. It is beautiful in proportions, excellent in scale, and the houses are set well into their site, the wings and porches being well designed with this object in view, while the low, horizontal effect so necessary in most small houses is aided by the fine use of the projecting hoods over the first-story windows which cast a long horizontal shadow, tying the elements of the elevation together and adjusting them to the elements of the lot. These hoods also facilitate an unsymmetrical spacing of windows. Some times the Philadelphia details are heavy, but in the hands of the best designers they are as delicate as anything in New England, and serve as a fine contrast to the sturdy proportions. The best Philadelphia houses meet the real test of a masterwork, for when viewed in their situation, it does not seem as if anything else could do so well. Nowhere do houses look more homelike. Nowhere do they have a finer air of breeding and good taste. They are symbols of a region that has maintained American traditions of living and manners through the Victorian period, perhaps more vitally than elsewhere. It is therefore not surprising that the Pennsylvania people have recaptured that elusive quality of neighborhood beauty—if, indeed, they ever quite lost it—which is the final achievement of house architecture and the greatest glory of the old American towns.

Coming to the district around New York City, one finds a greater variety of types than around Philadelphia, though the wooden architectures of Westchester County, Long Island and Western Connecticut are much alike. This architecture lacks the sturdy, solid quality of the Philadelphia region, but, like it, has a fine massing and sets well into the site when it uses low wings and porches. Its low roof slope—about thirty degrees—has beautiful angles, and is much admired. In Connecticut this style has the striking merit of many varied groupings in a free, picturesque manner on all sorts of sites, level or sloping or uneven, where houses and wings are combined with out-buildings and low sheds. Good use is made of glazed porches and loggia motives. These afford much charm and a variation of wall planes, alleviating the thinness and flatness of wooden walls. One of the most extraordinary qualities of this style is the perfection of its proportions and shapes, and its grace and gayety, carried out in perfect taste, very simply and moderately. Such artistry is indeed rare in house architecture, especially in free, informal types, which are too often clumsy and unrefined. This New York-Connecticut type has also a series of houses conceived in a more formal, sophisticated manner, which finds favor in ambitious suburbs and wealthy countrysides.

The New York district contains some brick and stucco architecture, on the whole successful, and resembling the wooden type. Unfortunately, the New York architects have not concentrated enough on their local type, though they devote themselves more to it each year. They have been handicapped by working at the Port of New York, which carries on an import business in art as in other things. This foreign influence combines with the constant flow of new people with conflicting tastes into the district to create much confusion in art and decoration. This confusion has wrecked the neighborhood beauty of many communities in the metropolitan district. The situation has not been helped by the popularization of the modern hybrid called "Dutch Colonial," which people have seized upon because

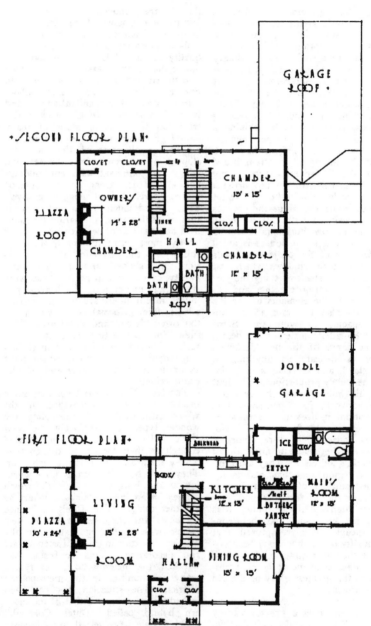

FIRST AND SECOND FLOOR PLANS—RESIDENCE
OF W. N. HARTSHORN, ESQ., CAMBRIDGE,
MASS. GRANDGENT & ELWELL, ARCHITECTS.

RESIDENCE OF W. N. HARTSHORN, ESQ., CAMBRIDGE, MASS.
Grandgent & Elwell, Architects.

+THIRD FLOOR PLAN+

they appreciate that extraordinary e x - pression of hearth- fire—the ultimate quality in a home — so characteristic of the houses of the descendants of the Holland farm- ers in Long Island and New Jersey The "Dutch Co- lonial" has done the true New Jer- sey type harm, for it has ruined the exquisite proportions and beautiful an- gles and lines of the old local gambrel roof, through changing them to get maxi- mum space for the second story and to get maximum light by dormer windows. Only in the rarest cases is the hybrid passable.

In New Jersey it is to be regretted that the local architects have not given their own type the opportunity of a modern expression. Many New Jersey houses are designed in New York City, where neither the value nor the char- acter of the New Jersey tradition is perfectly under- stood. There are three types of tra- dition in the state. Besides the pure "Dutch" type, there is a two-storied type, sometimes with gambrel roof, in Newark and south in Monmouth County, and also the west- ern type which resembles Pennsylvania architecture. The eastern type, whether in stone, stucco, brick or wood, sets well in the flat or rolling land—low in pro- portions, small in scale, and wonderfully homelike. The western type, of brick or frame, is often taller, but is still small in scale. Many are familiar with the fine

301

EAST END—RESIDENCE OF W. N. HARTSHORN, ESQ., CAMBRIDGE, MASS.
Grandgent & Elwell, Architects.

old brick houses in Princeton. They are painted a clear light yellow, which renders them peculiarly attractive in the soft, thick vegetation in the delicate, slightly radiant New Jersey light.

As to the local New England types, they are well known. They are the ones that have borne most of the criticism directed against our native style as cold and thin, too symbolical of the eighteenth century, too uninspired in its rigid "Puritanism" to be pertinent to modern times. It cannot be denied that there are a few houses in Eastern Massachusetts which this description fits. In some of the New England examples the mass sticks up gaunt and blocklike, the roof angles are cruder than in Connecticut, the lines are hard and the walls are cut up with windows set too close together. Their air is prim and somewhat uncompromising. However, this prim, sophisticated kind of house is not typical, although it has some beautiful details. Throughout New England are plenty of another kind, examples which belie the critics. The New England form of gambrel at its best is excellent indeed, as, for instance, in the Wadsworth House at Harvard. The smaller towns contain many free, picturesque examples, and all this architecture of brick and wood is a wonderful mine for a vocabulary of forms and details. New England architects have done some excellent work in their local types, particularly lately. A typical New England home is the house at Cambridge, Mass., designed by Grandgent and Elwell. The front elevation is characteristic, finely interpreted. Note how the tall mass of the main part of the house is harmonized with the level site by the low wing, which is placed at the rear next the kitchen. This arrangement is a case where the plan has fixed the art of the elevation, for it opens the dining-room to the garden on the east and to the morning sun. The end gable is admirably designed, which, with the juncture of the wing, is a frequent failure in house design. The view of the north elevation and garage is especially fine—New England at its best. Characteristic of New England is the whole design of Grandgent and Elwell, who have exercised imagination where it was required and for the rest followed carefully, in faultless proportion, both letter and spirit of their tradition, carrying it out with a restrained, yet very fine, taste. It is clearly the work of gentlemen. This Cambridge house offers an interesting comparison with some of the freer, more imaginative New York and Philadelphia designs shown in these pages.

From New England it is a far jump to the south, where different conditions, a different people, and consequently a different type of architecture are met with. I have mentioned many of the southern characteristics in previous pages. To the south we are indebted for a warmer inspiration, a more luxurious spirit, for ideas of brilliant color keyed to golden sunlight, of a more sensuous, a more lavish use of form, a richer sense of decoration. One must regret that southern architects, like the architects of New Jersey, have not fully appreciated the remarkable value of their local forms, have not developed a modern type of the southern vernacular. We cannot afford to squander any of our heritage, either the hearth-character of older New Jersey or the luxurious spirit of the south in its traditions of hospitality and fine country manners. Both of these influences appeal to the modern American.

This ends a hasty survey of the regional variations of the native style. They should be thoroughly understood, in letter and spirit, not for the sake of historical accuracy, but for the purpose of grasping their meaning. In a recent house designed by a well-known architect, which for evident reasons cannot be reproduced in these pages, is to be seen the result of not knowing architectural styles. The house has a heavy English Georgian cornice, a more delicate, but simple, early American mass and windows, and an Adam entrance porch and window above, this last of a very sophis-

NORTH SIDE AND GARAGE—RESIDENCE OF W. N. HARTSHORN, ESQ., CAMBRIDGE, MASS.
Grandgent & Elwell, Architects.

RESIDENCE OF WALTER CRITTENDEN,
ESQ., CORNWALL-ON-HUDSON, N. Y.
PARKER MORSE HOOPER, ARCHITECT.

RESIDENCE OF WALTER CRITTENDEN, ESQ., CORNWALL-ON-HUDSON, N. Y.
Parker Morse Hooper, Architect.

ticated air. Here are found on the same small house front three sets or styles of forms of opposing spirit and different scales, each perfect of its kind, but not harmonious with the other two. Such a result teaches the principle that one should possess that consistency and knowledge of style which alone will permit one to incorporate variations of motive and one's own individuality with success. It shows also what a difficult task it is really to master a style of architecture. One in a lifetime is enough for most designers. To design in two styles perfectly is as difficult as it is to write in two languages, for, like language, architectural style is a profounder thing than an arbitrary set of forms.

After this summary of style, more specific aspects of elevations are in order. There is the practical matter of choosing building materials. All the different materials have their artistic and practical merits, each its peculiar qualities in which it surpasses the others. They are

well known, and need no great comment. The essential principles are architectural expression, coloring and modelling and decoration and texture, in the mass and form and details of the house, in sunlight and shadow.

Of course, there is nothing superior to stone in building. Everyone envies the Philadelphia architects their supply of beautiful, light-colored, variegated, easily worked, cheap stone. They know perfectly how to use it—how to proportion the sizes and joints to give it strength, color and solidity. A study of this stonework will explain its excellence more than any description could do. The Philadelphia design emphasizes the light colors of this stone, and treats it as one colored and textured mass of many tiny hues mingling as in a tapestry, maintaining a unity of color. The emphasis is neither on single stone nor joint. In many cases the mortar is spread around freely, with a whitish effect and in some recent houses I have noted walls that

305

SOUTH FRONT—PAIR OF SMALL HOUSES NEAR HAVERFORD, PA.
Wilson Eyre & McIlvaine, Architects.

were entirely painted or whitewashed, like stucco. The result is wonderfully beautiful, showing a perfect appreciation of coloration in sunlight. In districts where the stone is of dull color this painting and whitewashing is advisable.

In brickwork, Americans are not so skillful. This assertion will surprise many, because great progress in brickwork has been made in twenty years, since the days of the impossible pressed brick. Architects have developed well-textured brick, well-jointed, of good "local" color and a good tapestry of hues, but they seem to overlook the effect of sunshine on the brick. Dark brick in Europe retains its warm, rich tone in the misty light, but here in the United States its color is neutralized in the bright light, and it looks cold and drab. In many cases bright white joints only serve to make it spotty. It loses the sparkle of shadows and does not catch and reflect the light. If anyone doubts this statement, let him visit the new neighborhoods in New York City in which most of

the houses have been remodeled recently, their brick or brownstone fronts stuccoed and painted in lightest tints of warm grays or gay yellows. He will be astonished in these streets to see the warmth and brilliancy of the sunlight, its luminous shadows, its play of light and color on surfaces and details, all of which will make him feel, when again he returns to the cold drab brick streets, that he has been in a latitude a thousand miles south. He has obtained a new idea of the American sun. However, this is not to condemn brick entirely. It is likely that there will come into use brick of light, clear colors, in a variety of "hot" hues, such a brick as I saw in Hampton Institute, Virginia, which was admirably keyed to the sunlight and landscape. A similar brick is found in the old southern plantation mansions. Only such massing of color and surface will count in our big sunlit landscapes, and no longer will designs pass which are merely an "interesting" pattern of white details of cornice and trims and quoins and doorways,

ENTRANCE COURT—PAIR OF SMALL HOUSES NEAR HAVERFORD, PA.
Wilson Eyre & McIlvaine, Architects.

standing out hard and naked against a dark brick wall, inharmonious with it and both inharmonious with the sun. This latter method is drawing-board design, while the former is architecture.

Stucco and wood are two materials too well known and too well understood by designers to need much comment. The former has been prized by designers since the days of Pompeii. American architects use it admirably, but only a few of them make full use of its possibilities of color. There is no better material for our native light. Of wood, much has been said. No artists in the world have better used wood outdoors than Americans. Our early craftsmen developed a series of wood forms that are thoroughly functional, an organic expression of the construction, in the simplest, most direct way. They also modelled them to make the most of sunlight. In the north the hard, cold, light brings out every form and line of detail with uncomfortable distinctness. This fact led the old car-

penter craftsmen to make their details very simple and delicate and fine in scale, using rounder mouldings to soften the edges, avoiding a machinelike appearance; while to the south, where the light is warmer, mellower, and vibrating with color, it does not accent edges, hence the craftsmen used heavier and bolder detail, with richer decoration in the luminous shadows. The reader may have felt at times that I have a hobby for the early American tradition and that I thrust it forward at every turn. Notwithstanding this, it seems clear that, with all the immense study that we have put on the old buildings, we have not progressed very far beyond form and details. In the matter of essentials we are only beginning to appreciate the value of our older craftsmen and architects, particularly in the matter of form and color of architecture. In fact, I believe that it is no exaggeration to say this: Never in the whole history of architecture did a single people or nation so homo-

307

geneous as the early Americans were develop a single domestic architectural style over such a range of geographical space of climate and of landscape conditions. Thus, in its flexible, imaginative craftsmanship, adapting form and color to such a variety of conditions, it illustrates the fundamental principles of

walls cannot be considered apart from roofs. In a small house the great difficulty is to keep its proportions from appearing poked up, from looking like a box without much relation to its site, with an air of having been moved there from somewhere else, instead of belonging to its site. In roofing, the es-

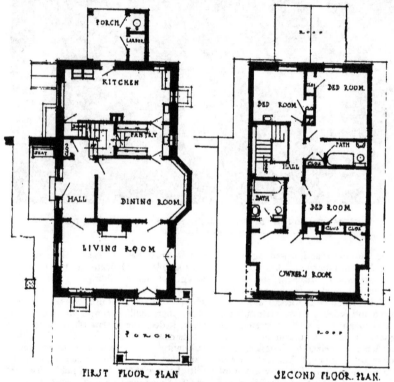

FIRST FLOOR PLAN   SECOND FLOOR PLAN.

PAIR OF SMALL HOUSES NEAR HAVERFORD, PA.
Wilson Eyre & McIlvaine, Architects.

form and color in architecture, as influenced by the conditions of nature, better than any other historical style. It even rivals Gothic in this respect, for the principles of Gothic architecture are complicated by the fact that they were put into practice by several different peoples, of differing temperament and social organization.

Leaving this digression, the design of

sential is to achieve this relation to site, and then to keep its mass and shapes simple without too many jerky peaks and gables and angles and spotty dormers. Those designers whose work shows clearly that they do not believe in simple, harmonious roofing as a matter of art, should at least accept this principle on the ground of economy.

If the house is symmetrical, a low

SOUTH END—PAIR OF SMALL HOUSES
NEAR HAVERFORD, PA. WILSON
EYRE & McILVAINE, ARCHITECTS.

SOUTH FRONT—PAIR OF SMALL HOUSES
NEAR HAVERFORD, PA. WILSON
EYRE & McILVAINE, ARCHITECTS.

wing or shed, aided by terraces or walls or porch, will tie the house to the ground. Many examples of this are seen, and one of the best—in that difficult situation, a flat billiard table site—is the Cambridge house in these pages. If the house is unsymmetrical, the problem of roofing is one of the toughest in architecture, and reveals how real is the artistic power of the designer over form. The laws of picturesque design are as severe as, and far more difficult than, those of balanced design. This type of design is not taught in the architectural schools. Much was said of this matter in the previous articles of this series, in speaking of the characteristics of the modern English free style. Confusion of elements is not picturesque art. As in classic design, simplicity and grace and harmony and perfect proportion are essentials, together with the careful subordination of minor to major elements. Specifically, a single long roof ridge with a single minor peak or gable at one end, and a tiny dormer or two, or one long dormer nestling into the roof, may be all that is needed to achieve a beautiful, picturesque result. Bay windows need not be too much multiplied, and frequently those tricky, clever details of low roof over entrance, and porch gables, which look so clever on paper, may easily be simplified and united with the main roof, thus gaining unity, adding boldness yet maintaining interest. In the walls of a picturesque style, it is well not to cut them up too much with windows, which should have plenty of space around them. Another mistake in American picturesque design is too much variety in window shapes and sizes. While windows need not "line up" in every case, many of them may well be so tied together, and one can hardly deny that they should have an absolute consistency of scale and avoid spottiness. Some of the very finest picturesque houses are extremely simple in mass and roof, with but a few minor features and but a few different sizes and types of windows. Their restraint in minor motives emphasizes the beauty of their mass.

In a free style, the shapes and angles should be thoroughly consistent. How often does one see fat windows on tall thin gables with steep roofed peaks, or the opposite relation. Where a "battery" of windows are used, the shape of each unit should be harmonized with the general character of the house. One great fault of roofing is the use of angles approximately forty-five degrees. This is the crudest form of angle there is—ninety degrees at the peaks and 135 degrees at the eaves. The slope should be either much greater or much less, according to the character of the design, whether it be horizontal or vertical, as determined by the shapes and contours of the site. It may be remarked here that the heavy, clumsy details so often seen in picturesque design are as much out of place as they would be in formal design. They show ignorance of how to draw at full size. Mr. Delano's house, in these pages, contains a picturesque roof dormer; the proportions of the sticks of rough timbers are as beautiful and as accurate as in any motive of column and entablature. Although this house is not a small house, this detail of it is published as a splendid example of how simple form may be, and yet how interesting and very stylish. As in the brick design for the Watson house at White Plains, N. Y., the cornice detail is almost eliminated, leaving the bare mass of the walls with simple openings of windows to contrast with the finely textured roof, sloping at the right angle. The whole effect is prevented from being bare and flat by the interesting dormer and the deep shadows of the porch. The effect is perfectly designed for intense sunlight. Mr. Delano is one of the leading architects in the design of great houses, the author, with Mr. Aldrich, of the Knickerbocker and Colony Clubs of New York City. It is interesting to see his taste as displayed in his own house.

All these many considerations, which advise us to be ingenious in maintaining simple design in small houses, even when they are picturesque, and also to fit them well into their site so as not to appear top-heavy, favor a house plan that is lengthened out, rather than squared, and one incorporating the garage or a shed or two in the house plan. Stated in dimensions and terms of geometry, a compact small house, without garage, will have an area of about thirty feet by forty. This is a box, with little difference in shape between end and side elevations. It is a type sometimes unavoidable on a small lot, and the house designed by Tilden and Register shows how this difficult type may nevertheless be made attractive. It is hard, indeed, to prevent such a house from poking up too high. On the other hand, if this floor area, 1,200 square feet, be a rectangle approaching twenty feet by sixty, it then has a fine long front, contrasting with an interesting narrow end. If the garage be added at one end, the front then becomes sixty-five to seventy-five feet long, possessing endless possibilities of design in interesting groupings. This group design is a natural result of a flexible system of planning. The reader may have noticed that the lengthened type of plan predominates in the houses shown in these articles, and while this choice is deliberate on the writer's part, it is fair to say that the most skillful architects like this arrangement.

In respect to color, there is room for much improvement in roofs. Cold colors are apt to be lost in roofs, since sunlight, particularly when mellow or golden, takes the color out of slate or shingle when they are blue or black or gray or dark green. Much better are the hot colors, either in a mixture of variegated bright colors or in softer colors, such as leathery browns, or soft claret colors or straw color. Where there are variations in the colors of a roof, the variety should not be so great as to cause a spotty effect, but just enough to add life and vibration to a mass of color. Where stained shingles are used, it is easy to decide on an appropriate color. If the designer is doubtful, he may easily find some tone in the landscape, of earth or rock or tree trunk, that will be absolutely safe to use. Slate is beautiful in character and texture, but its colors are apt to lie in the cold side of the spectrum. In such cases the lighter the hue the better. One may see in Spain what roof colors should be in a hot strong sunlight. There, every hue is found, from the rich, incredibly vivid claret and vermilion and scarlet tiles of the north to the softer, more straw colored ones in the south. The reds go with warm tawny or golden walls, and the straw yellows with whitish walls. Beside such coloration, the heavy, dull dark roofs of America seem commonplace.

Walls and roofs and wings form the mass of a house, but porches are features only slightly less important. Formerly they were disliked because, as it was said, they were apt to appear like separate things tacked on to a house, and not an integral part of it. But experience has shown that the trouble was due rather to unskillful design of this feature, than any inherent defect of the motive itself. Besides, the design of the house may be at fault. There are, of course, many ways to make the porch seem a part of the house. One method recognizes the custom of glazing in porches, and designs them as wings or outbuildings, loggias or even bay windows, with sloping roofs and simple solid corners enframing a broad mass of window panes. This is indeed an effective motive. Another scheme also favors simplicity, but of a more open kind. It uses slender uprights and lintels, with no great elaboration of columns or balustrades. There is no longer that heaviness of these details, that excessive grouping of posts and columns, particularly at the corners; and fortunately the ugly short, round columns are nearly extinct. They looked more like garden products than architecture. In very small houses and very small porches a good recent practice is to form the corners of plain solid uprights, two inches by four or four inches by four, about a foot or so apart, filled in between with lattice of simple pattern. The result is a light, graceful porch which is at the same time a solid part of the house. Service porches are more appropriate when picturesque or naive in character.

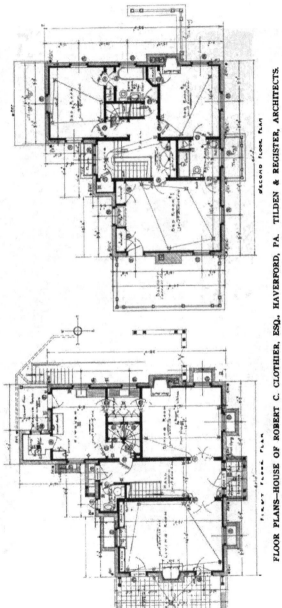

ENTRANCE DETAIL—HOUSE OF ROBERT C. CLOTHIER, ESQ.,
HAVERFORD, PA.   TILDEN & REGISTER, ARCHITECTS.

HOUSE OF ROBERT C. CLOTHIER, ESQ., HAVERFORD, PA.
TILDEN & REGISTER, ARCHITECTS.

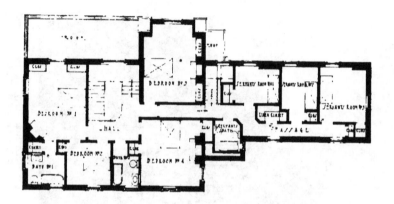

SECOND FLOOR PLAN

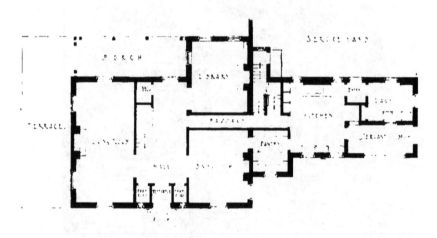

FIRST AND SECOND FLOOR PLANS—RESIDENCE
OF MISS E. A. WATSON, WHITE PLAINS,
N. Y. DELANO & ALDRICH, ARCHITECTS.

RESIDENCE OF MISS E. A. WATSON, WHITE PLAINS, N. Y. DELANO & ALDRICH, ARCHITECTS.

The above are some of the principles of the mass and of the minor features of elevations. Details would require volumes to describe them fully. Chimneys are one of the finest features of the house. None know better how to use them than the British architects, whose houses are heated by many fireplaces and chimneys, modeled on a fascinating array of ancient examples. Americans, too, have a series of excellent old chimneys, different in character, but better suited to our forms and system of proportions. Our modern designers have some splendid effects in them. Excellent are the chimneys of the Philadelphia architects, of Mr. Parker Morse Hooper and Mr. Theodore Blake—the latter in Part I of this series. Usually, the more flues concentrated in a chimney to make it bigger, the better for its appearance outdoors. Incidentally, if the chimney tapers, a very slight batter is all that is necessary, because the slopes are exaggerated in perspective at the corners. Also where chimneys are designed with breaks and offsets, these should be as carefully proportioned in mass, slope angle and line as any other feature of the house.

Perhaps nothing affects the design of a house so much as the windows. They are important in free picturesque design, in the ways noted above; and in a symmetrical elevation, which consists of nothing else than a cornice, an entrance and side porch, the windows either make or break the house. The mistakes common in windows are in shape, size—usually width—and scale. As to shape, a common fault is to see elevations of long horizontal proportions pierced with tall-shaped windows, and the contrary. The combination of window and shutter—usually necessary, both practically and artistically, particularly on wood houses—trips many a designer. The relation of second story windows with those on the first story often cause trouble. In some of the oldest houses—eighteenth century—the windows are the same size on first and second story, emphasizing the interest and importance of the entrance motive, which is large and dominates the whole front. In very small houses this is an excellent scheme. Usually, however, the second floor windows are smaller, but it is not well to exaggerate the difference. This arrangement is most effective in a larger type of small house with wing, when contrasted with the opposite arrangement in the wing or service portion, where the first story windows are small, high up from the floor—which is good practically—and a little narrower than the bedroom windows above. As a rule these three sizes of windows are usually all the general variety that is needed to make an elevation interesting. Sometimes a few second story windows are the larger and there is, of course, the interesting variation of casement windows to the floor. In many designs the tendency is to get the windows too wide. A couple of inches seems little on a ¼-inch or ⅛-inch working drawing, but it is serious at full-size. It is especially serious in third story gable or dormer windows, which are usually best when small. Also if windows are grouped in pairs or in a battery of three or more, a mistake in the width of the unit is multiplied in the width of the group. Windows grouped together are finely effective, particularly casements, and the effect is increased when they are placed in bays, or tied together with some element of design like the overhanging hoods of the Philadelphia style. The placing of windows with regard to the roof cornice is the cause of many mistakes. Too much space between tops of second story windows and cornice usually makes the house too high and causes the windows to "float" in the walls. Particularly in wooden houses, the windows are better tied to the cornice with the top of window trim of window head coming up against the bottom moulding of the cornice. Of course, this arrangement will not go where there is no cornice, as in two of the houses of Delano and Aldrich shown herewith. Dormers should be carefully proportioned—not too large, not top-heavy, not too many of them. The more delicate and compact their tops and jambs, the better.

318

RESIDENCE OF W. A. DELANO, ESQ.,
SYOSSET, L. I. OWNER AND ARCHITECT.

EARLY AMERICAN DOORWAY,
BARRINGTON, R. I. ABOUT 1800.

One of the most frequent failures is lack of harmony between double-hung and casement windows. There is no reason at all why these types of windows should not be used in the same house and even in the same elevation. What is necessary is to attain a certain harmony of sizes and shapes of the two kinds of windows, and, equally important, between the sizes and shapes of window panes.

But all these principles of window design will avail little if the sizes of window panes are not accurate. In the first place they are usually too large. On very small elevations a pane nine inches wide is ample, which means three panes wide for a window two feet four inches or two feet six inches wide, and four panes for a window three feet or three feet two inches wide. In stone walls the panes may look better when wider, but in flat wood walls, the pattern of the glass tells strongly in contrast to the wall, and hence the smaller they are, the more "snap" there is in the elevation. In some of the finest of the smaller New England houses the windows are two feet four inches wide, with twenty-four six-inch by eight-inch panes on the first and second floors, and about one foot ten inches wide, with twelve six-inch by eight-inch panes on the third story gables. Thus the windows are varied in size by changing the number of panes in the window, and maintaining the same size. Of course, in those days the builders may have been able to obtain panes of only one size, but whatever the cause, there is no denying the artistry of the result. If possible, the panes should be of a decided oblong shape throughout, though the oblong need not be mechanically repeated. The best way to make sure of this consistency of window sizes and panes is to draw a ¾-inch scale detail sheet of all the types of windows in the house—especially if there is a variety of windows—and carefully harmonize them with each other. Inches are decisive in this process and are too easily lost in ¼-inch and ⅛-inch scale working drawings.

Entrance porches and doorways are one of the most fascinating motives in design. No house architecture in the world has a greater variety of them than our early architecture. On page 320 of this article is one hitherto unpublished, as beautiful as any that I know of. It is one of a type of the Rhode Island region. It has not only the exquisite grace and perfection of the very best of the American doorways, but also a wonderful personality, an almost mediaeval richness of decoration. Another one, of wider proportions, is that of an old house at Danbury, Conn. With such models to guide the designer there should be little chance for failure in entrances, and certainly no excuse. The greatest difficulty in the choice of a model—for one can hardly invent an entirely new motive which has not already been discovered by the old craftsmen—seems to be to obtain a shape, or modified shape, in harmony with the shapes and the mass of the rest of the elevation. Very appropriate, indeed, is that series of spready, but delicately proportioned and detailed, doorways that look so comfortable and have such a fine cordial, hospitable air of welcome. One fault may be noticed in some of the best modern doorways; that is, they are sometimes too small for the whole front. Some of the small, old houses have fine big doorways, whose top peak or gable reaches well up to the sill of the second-story windows, dominating the whole front.

Besides these major and minor features of the elevation, there is a whole class of very subordinate details of metal work, lamps, window boxes, railings, walls, fences, gateways, trellises, lattice, etc., which may only be mentioned here. As every one knows, they add greatly to the finish and interest and life of the design. Lattice and trellises seem to be the hardest of these to do, as a study of old trellises proves. Exeter, New Hampshire, is noteworthy for countless exquisite old trellis details. These minor details add much sparkle of color and shadow against a light wall, especially stucco. Examples of this are seen in those rows of stucco fronted houses in New York City, referred to above, where these details, particularly of the iron-work, are tinted all sorts of the gayest colors, even vermillion or cobalt. When first applied, such hues may well startle prosaic eyes, but the weather soon softens them without injuring their vivacity.

This ends the discussion of some of the principles of design of elevations. There are many more of them, particularly concerning details, and the discussion of their application never ends during the lifetime of a man. I have mentioned them briefly, and notice principally those in which further improvement in design is needed. But even in this I have wasted time if I have not put forward the vital importance of using our beautiful old American buildings as models of design. They are the best teachers. They alone make design real and inspired. Not until the young graduate of the school of architecture takes to measuring and observing models do his drawings become altogether sound, no matter how clever and facile a draughtsman he may be. Too many young draughtsmen expect to learn entirely from older men whose skill dazzles them. They may indeed learn something of good taste and of the abstract principles of composition; but from early American buildings alone can they acquire a vocabulary and reality in form and color and art outdoors. When the older man works he has clear pictures in his mind of what he is aiming at, which the younger man gets second-hand.

The houses illustrated in these pages are fine examples of design of elevation, especially as developed from the plan. The charming little house of Murphy and Dana has a trace of French influence, with its high backed roof and casement windows. It obeys the scriptural injunction to build upon a rock, which is the chief reason for its interesting scheme. One enters on the ground floor, ascending to the first floor to arrive at the main part of the house, the direct openings, left and right off the stair hall, being another French touch in plan. It will be seen that the principle of one big living-room, put forth in Part III, is here fully carried out, in a room of interesting shape, so arranged as to allow its different functions of eating, lounging and receiving to be easily performed. The exterior is most vivacious and picturesque, yet utterly simple, exquisite in grace and scale. It has a striking color scheme, both indoors and out.

In Miss Ketcham's house, Delano and Aldrich have brought out most effectively the Long Island type of New York with an unmistakable trace of the fisherman's cottage, which is to be recognized all up and down the Atlantic coast. It is of simple plan, without any apparent striving at display. Outside, the softness of texture of the elevation is noteworthy, an object-lesson for so many of our designers of steel-like lines and surfaces.

The Cambridge house, designed by Grandgent and Elwell, has been mentioned above as typical of the small house of the old New England town, as distinguished from the mansion types of Salem, Newburyport and Portsmouth. Another design in wood-forms is the house at Cornwall-on-Hudson, another example of Mr. Parker Morse Hooper's bold, strong design in strikingly modelled wood details.

The pair of small houses at Haverford recall a similar arrangement of Mellor, Meigs and Howe, illustrated in Part V. It reminds one also of the "Dutch-Colonial" type of New York, with the difference, that here, at last, is a perfect example of that marriage of old and new, which has turned out to be a happy one. It is also a fine sample of stonework.

Two brick designs are next given. One is an example of Delano and Aldrich's exquisite proportions and restrained, delicate grace. With the high service wing it is a type of plan much favored several years ago. The other design, of Tilden and Register, is much similar in the main part, but expressed in the characteristic Philadelphia style. Both designs seek to avoid finicky contrasts of white wood details against dark brick walls, by separating the colors into larger and simpler masses.

322

REMAINS OF ROMAN GATE AT LANGRES.

SOME CITY GATES OF FRANCE

BY
JOSEPH PATTERSON SIMS

THERE is an old axiom that types of society are as old as their systems of circulation. Taking this as true, by a careful examination of the landways and waterways, including primarily roads and bridges and, as a natural concomitant, city gates, we arrive at the social conditions of a country during its various stages of development. City gates, aside from their beauty, have a strong appeal which stirs the imagination, for, under these arches, how many types of society, with their various customs, religions, fears, hopes, ambitions, predatory trades and pillaging armies,

must have passed—passed and vanished, devoured by time. In their wake we find an interesting record and many-colored variation, from the medieval gateway, through whose machicolations red hot stones and boiling oil were poured on the heads of the attacking enemy, to those gigantic arches, personal vanities, built in honor of *"Le Roi Soleil"* or the Great Napoleon. Thus, by finding the *raison d'être* of the dominating motives, one can better understand the architecture itself.

Among the earliest city gates of the Christian era in France are those at

RESTORATION OF PORTE ST. ANDRÉ AT AUTUN IN MIDDLE AGES. AFTER VIOLLET-LE-DUC.

Langres, Autun, Nimes and Arles. They are all much on the same plan, consisting of two main outlets for the entry and exit of vehicles, and two for foot passengers, flanked on the outside by two semicircular towers, forming a pronounced projection. At Autun, the Porte St. André, a most complete example of the Roman model, built A. D. 69, is surmounted, above the two arches forming the passageway, by an arcaded gallery, using the Ionic order, serving for communication between the flanking towers and, at need, for defense. The bays were originally closed by wood gates and lacked both portcullis and drawbridge. The towers served as military posts for the garrison, the two top stories being reserved for defense.

This gate is constructed of large sandstone blocks, laid dry, following the Roman method, and on the road are remains of Roman paving in large irregular blocks. The road from the city stretches away, ribbonlike, into the valley, and far enough in plain view to

ENTRANCE SIDE—PORTE D'ARROUX AT AUTUN.

324

EXTERIOR—PORTE ST. ANDRÉ AT AUTUN.

give warning of the approach of enemies. Time has laid an obliterating hand on some of the details, but in mass and proportion this is one of the finest of the Roman gates.

The Porte D'Arroux is similar in scheme, but uses the Corinthian order in the arcade, and is in greater disrepair.

As we proceed toward the middle ages we see an ever-increasing emphasis on defense. It was only with the regular establishment of the feudal regime that the gate development arrived at the point we see in the eleventh century. How-

INTERIOR—PORTE ST. ANDRÉ AT AUTUN.

325

PORTE DES DEGRÉS, BOULOGNE-SUR-MER.

ever, most of the gates before this time, nearly always modified, show that already the art of defense was well understood. It was no longer the question, as in the Gallo-Roman epoch, of having large openings for those coming and going, but on the contrary to make the gates as narrow as possible, thereby do-ing away with the possibility of surprises and facilitating the defense. In all instances heavy projecting towers protected the gates. Two excellent examples of the projecting towers, but with a single entrance, are the Porte des Degrés and the Porte Gayolle at Boulogne.

In the gates of the twelfth and thir-

PORTE GAYOLLE, BOULOGNE-SUR-MER.

PORTE DU CROUX AND OUTER GATE.

PORTE DU CROUX, NEVERS.

GATE AT GUÉRANDE, BRITTANY.

teenth centuries elaborate methods of defense are found, with main towers, outer towers, moats and all the medieval war mechanisms of drawbridge, portcullis, etc. Probably the best and most complete form of this means of defense is to be found at Carcassonne, in the south of France. These gates have been many times reproduced in drawings and photographs and can be studied at length in Viollet-le-Duc's *La Cité de Carcassonne*.

Another excellent example, here reproduced, is the Porte du Croux at Nevers. Built at the end of the twelfth century by Pierre de Courtenay, Comte de Nevers, there remains today only the main gate and its outer gate. Both gates

PORTE DE BOURGOGNE, MORET-SUR-LOING.

were originally defended alike with moats and drawbridges, and the road connecting the two was flanked by a battlemented wall from which archers could shoot. At Loches, in Touraine, the Porte des Cordeliers is a tower of de Bourgogne, and the Postern, show a most interesting variety of treatment. The Porte de Bourgogne is part of an ancient war bridge, and the old ramparts flanking it are still to be seen. An idea of the smallness of the city can be ob-

PORTE DES CORDELIERS, LOCHES.

much the same scheme, only on a smaller scale. It belongs to a much later period, in fact to the fifteenth century; but the similarity is so striking that one cannot help feeling that the Porte du Croux must have been its inspiration.

The city gateway at Guérande is a Brittany example, very charming in its simplicity. At Moret-sur-Loing are the remains of a medieval walled city; the three gates, the Porte de Samois, Porte tained from the view of the Porte de Samois, through the opening of which, at the other end of the street, is seen the inside of the Porte de Bourgogne.

In the period of Henri IV the sturdy character of the architecture was well adapted to defense. It may be seen applied to this purpose in the old gates of Nancy, and in others at Richelieu, that somnolent but not dead creation of the great Cardinal's. Several of the gates

329

PORTE GUILLAUME, DIJON.

of Paris, the Portes St. Bernard and St. Honoré, long since disappeared, were also of this age and character. If the style lacked refinement of detail, it still had vigorous and original decorative qualities.

Shortly after this time city gates lost their original function of defense and became simply a monument and ornament. The arch form was greatly in favor, and all sorts were erected by Louis XIV to impress the public. At Paris the Porte St. Denis, built in 1672, was one of the best examples, and there is no building of the time more inspired, as Ward says, "by the magniloquent spirit of barocco expressed in terms of French rationalism."

There are no orders, no pediment, no rustication, which, by the way, was a favorite device. It is a plain, square mass, seventy-eight feet high, crowned

PORTE ST. DENIS, PARIS.

330

THE POSTERN GATE, MORET.

PORTE DE SAMOIS, MORET.

by a bold cornice and pierced by a single arch. On either side are obelisks bearing trophies in high relief. Everything in the design, from the scale of the sculpture and the laconic inscription *Ludovico Magno* to the minuteness of the openings for foot passengers through the pedestals, conspires to produce an overwhelming impression of power.

Under Louis XVI the designs are more ornate as a rule; excellent examples at Bordeaux, Nancy and the Porte Guillaume at Dijon are here reproduced. As monumental architecture in Napoleon's day, the arch form reached its highest mark in the Arc de Triomphe at Paris. If not a city gate in the sense of forming the boundary on a main city thoroughfare, it is certainly the direct descendant of those earlier gates. The description of it in Ibanez's *Four Horsemen of the Apocalypse* occurs to one as a splendid expression of the "soul" of a piece of architecture:

"This arch is French within, with its names of battles and generals open to criticism. On the outside, it is the mon-ument of the people who carried through the greatest battle for liberty ever known. The glorification of man is there below in the column of the Place Vendome. Here there is nothing individual. Its builders erected it to the memory of 'la grande Armee' and that grand army was the people in arms who spread revolution throughout Europe. The artists, great inventors, foresaw the true significance of this work. The warriors of Rude who are chanting the Marseillaise in the group at the left are not professional soldiers, they are armed citizens marching to work out their sublime and violent mission. Their nudity makes them appear like Sans-Culottes in Grecian helmets. Here there is more than the glory and egoism of a great nation. All Europe is awake to new life, thanks to these Crusaders of Liberty. The nations call to mind certain images. If I think of Greece, I see the columns of the Parthenon; Rome, Mistress of the World, is the Coliseum and the Arch of Trajan; and revolutionary France is the Arc de Triomphe."

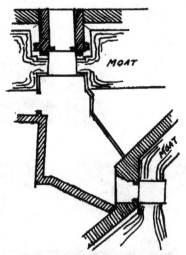

PLAN OF MEDIEVAL DEFENSES OF
PORTE DU CROUX, NEVERS.

English Architectural Decoration

Text and Measured Drawings by Albert E. Bullock

Part XIV. Staircases.

THE design and evolution of the English staircase is one of the most interesting features relating to the adornment of the interior of the English house. From earliest Jacobean times the utmost elaboration of joinery prevails. Much variation exists in plan, treatment and detail of ornament in most of the notable examples. The early oak staircases of the larger mansions, such as Hatfield House, Crewe Hall and Blickling Hall, are heavily carved, with much strap work and other ornament filling the space between the stairs and handrail.

The earliest form of staircase plan was either a straight flight between two walls or a circular form with a big newel going its full height, as at Eastbury Manor, Barking. The smaller stairs were built with the upper and lower flights joining a single newel—known as the "dog leg staircase"—and the larger ones with an open well. In Jacobean days the newels of these open well staircases were frequently continued through to the upper flights or were carved with moldings a foot or two above the handrail level.

Closed strings were common in the earlier examples, and open strings favored from the latter end of the seventeenth century.

The balustrading varied at different periods. In Jacobean times strap work and carving prevailed, followed by heavy pedestal balusters, as at Ashburnham House, Flaxley Abbey and Pump Court, Fleet Street; carving and piercing of solid panel work succeeded, as at Forde Abbey, Guildford and other works of mid-seventeenth century origin; and the close of the century saw the introduction of wrought iron work, as at Chatsworth and Hampton Court Palace. During this period large balusters were reverted to,

as at the Ward School, Love Lane, which in the eighteenth century were gradually reduced in size until it became common to put three balusters to a tread, often varying in pattern, as at Beacon House, Painswick, No. 5 Conduit Street and many others.

Several examples of lath work to the balustrading are extant at No. 5 John Street, Bedford Row, and the back stairs at Beacon House; the spandrel pieces were nearly always carved in console formation either to each stair end or, combined with a sunk panel, to every second stair, as at Ladybellegate House, Gloucester, and Victoria Hotel, Newnham. At Newnham the moldings formed by the carved end are continued under the soffit to the supporting wall, which is a very elaborate and costly form of joinery.

During the Adam period the hardwood stairs were sometimes inlaid on the risers and treads to give additional interest and adornment, which obtains at Claydon House, Bucks.

Wrought iron, which was introduced during the Wren period, was also common from the middle of the eighteenth century, of which a simple example is to be seen at Pembroke House, Whitehall Place, Westminster.

Of the examples illustrated, mention should be made of the staircase at the Museum at Newbury, known as the Cloth Hall, which is a good late Jacobean example with balusters molded on the square, a type of which there have been many modern copies.

The most interesting staircase, from the point of architectural design, exists at Ashburnham House, attributed to Inigo Jones. It is wide and solid, with simple wall decorations combined with Ionic pilasters and a ceiling decoration having an oval center light ornamented with small columns and balusters to the attic dormers, of the most unique and original character. The pedestal balusters are carved with egg and tongue ornament, and carving is executed upon the panelled newels. At the Queen's House, Greenwich Hospital, also by Inigo Jones, the balusters to the gallery handrailing are of similar character, but without enrichment.

At Forde Abbey the balustrading is pierced and carved in the usual Charles II manner, of which there are several other examples, notably at an old house at Guildford. There is preserved at Hampton Court Palace an altar rail of similar type, painted and gilt, probably slightly earlier, say of the Commonwealth period, which formerly adorned the Chapel.

Throughout the realm of joinery there has been no feature where the skill and inventive genius of the craftsman has been so successfully tried as in this matter of staircase construction, and the mason has vied with his brother craftsmen in the formation of oval and spiral stairs in stone, as at St. Paul's Cathedral, at houses in Lincoln's Inn Fields, and many other parts of London. Where stone steps are used the balustrading was invariably of wrought iron work, of which there are several interesting examples. This is the only instance where the smith competed favorably with his compeers in the interior.

One may see in most of the larger towns of England excellent examples of his work, especially in the Cathedral cities, where skilled smiths were in continual demand for making grilles within the fanes situated in the vicinity. Chichester, Yeovil, Bath, Gloucester and a host of other places furnish examples of much skill in wrought iron work, but the joiner has always held his own in the interior because the nature of his medium renders a cheaper and more convenient form of decoration.

It was typical of the mid-eighteenth century examples to have a newel formed of a Doric or Corinthian order, the former type being occasionally ornamented with a series of blockings, as is illustrated at the Victoria Hotel, Newnham, and at North Pallant House, Chichester.

Treating the subject in detail, quite apart from the plan, the formation of the handrail provides a useful guide to the date of a staircase. Early handrails and strings stopped on the newel post, which if square usually had a half baluster attached, and the baluster spacing had little relation to the number of stairs in the flight. The principle of ramping the handrail in graceful curves was not fully developed until the eighteenth century. Early attempts first occurred on the capping to the wall panelling, as the old stairs at Flaxley Abbey illustrate. Later the top members of the handrail were run into the newel capping, which was mitred round the top of the newel and worked into the other portion, the top forming an obtuse angle with the rake of the rail. Some of the early staircases in Whitehall, as that at the rear of the building now occupied by the Paymaster-General, are ramped up to the newel post, although having a solid molded string. Ramping was, however, more usual with staircases having an open string. Various methods were adopted for getting over the necessity of mitering the top of the newel. Sometimes the top member of the Doric capital molding, instead of being square on plan, was made circular, cleared by an inch or so from the soffit of the handrail; and this portion was turned-in in a cavetto mold of reduced width, which would allow of making a much smaller twist to the finish of the handrail at the foot of the stair. In other cases a baluster sufficed, and the handrail was ramped up both ways without mitering at the angle return, as at Hardwick Hall, Shropshire.

The very elaborate carving to the newels of the early Renaissance staircases ceased by the middle of the seventeenth century. The much advertised staircase formerly at Cromwell House, Highgate, had figures of Commonwealth soldiers terminating the newel posts. This house is said by Mr. Lichfield to have been the residence of General Ire-

THE STAIRCASE—
CREWE HALL, CREWE.

STAIRCASE CEILING—THE PYNES.   William and Mary Period, About 1690.   STAIRCASE—THE PYNES, DEVON.

STAIRCASE — THE
MALL, HAMMERSMITH.

STAIRCASE — THE WARD SCHOOL,
LOVE LANE, LONDON. WREN PERIOD.

STAIRCASE — ASTON
HALL, BIRMINGHAM, 1618-35.

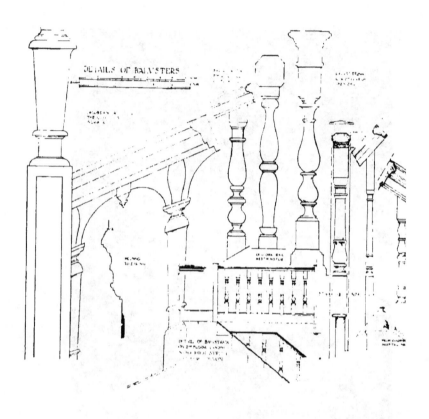

DETAILS OF BALUSTERS

DETAILS OF EARLY SIXTEENTH
CENTURY STAIR BALUSTERS.

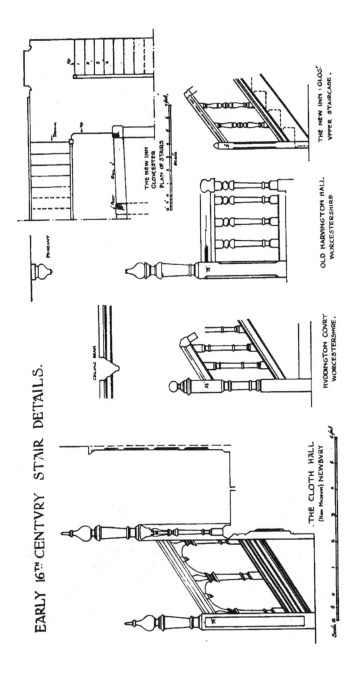

EARLY 16TH CENTVRY STAIR DETAILS.

THE NEW INN
GLOVCESTER
PLAN OF STAIRS

THE NEW INN : GLOS.
VPPER STAIRCASE.

OLD HARVINGTON HALL
WORCESTERSHIRE

HVDDINGTON COVRT
WORCESTERSHIRE.

THE CLOTH HALL
(New Museum) NEWBVRY

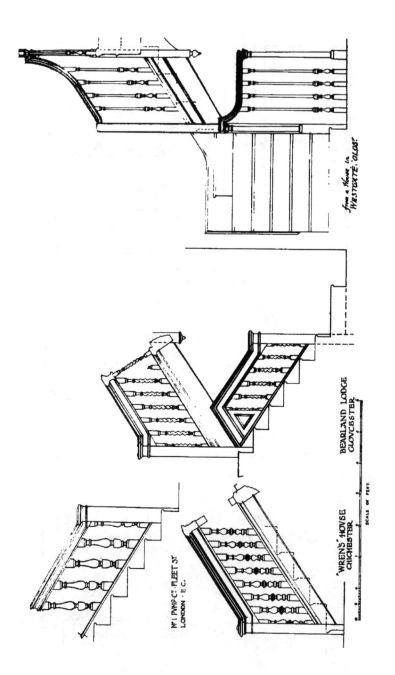

from a House in
WESTGATE: GLOS?

BEARLAND LODGE
GLOUCESTER.

SCALE OF FEET.

"WREN'S" HOUSE
CHICHESTER.

N° 1 PUMP-C? FLEET S?
LONDON - E.C.

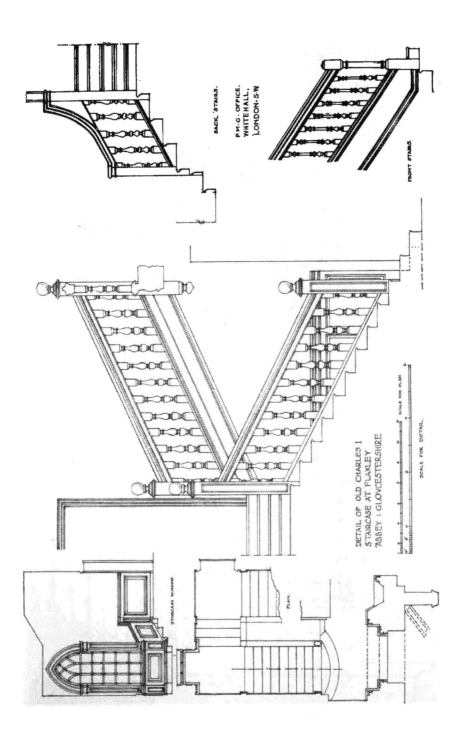

BACK STAIRS.

P.M.G. OFFICE.
WHITEHALL,
LONDON·S·W

FRONT STAIRS.

DETAIL OF OLD CHARLES I
STAIRCASE AT FLAXLEY
ABBEY : GLOUCESTERSHIRE

SCALE FOR PLAN

SCALE FOR DETAIL.

STAIRCASE WINDOW

PLAN.

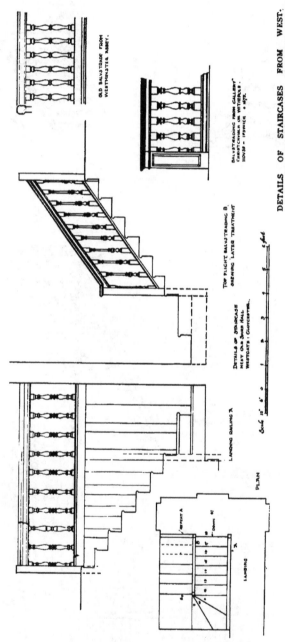

OLD BALUSTRADE FROM WESTMINSTER ABBEY.

BALUSTRADING FROM GALLERY CHRISTCHURCH OR WITHERSFIELD HOUSE - IPSWICH + 1672.

TOP FLIGHT BALUSTRADING & SHEWING LATER TREATMENT

DETAILS OF STAIRCASE NEXT OLD SHIRE HALL WESTGATE: GLOUCESTER.

Scale 1/2" 6" 0   1   2   3   4   5 feet

LANDING RAILING A

PLAN

FRONT A

DOWN 97

LANDING

DETAILS OF STAIRCASES FROM WEST-
GATE, GLOUCESTER, FROM CHRISTCHURCH,
IPSWICH, AND FROM WESTMINSTER ABBEY.

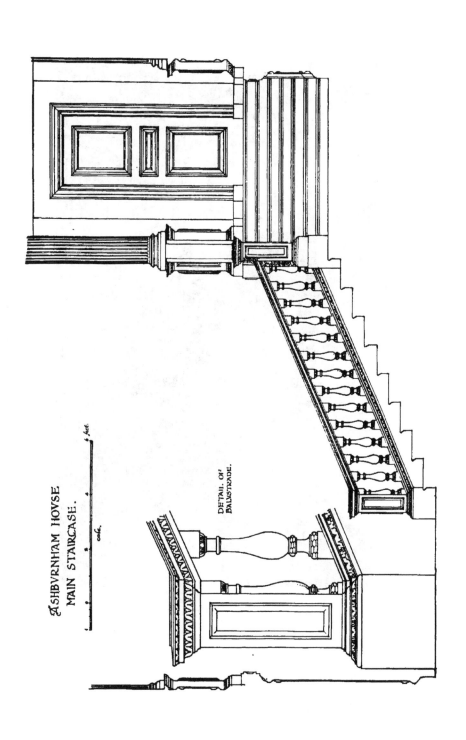

ASHBVRNHAM HOVSE
MAIN STAIRCASE.

DETAIL OF
BALVSTRADE.

STAIRCASE—NO. 25 HIGH
S T R E E T, GUILDFORD.

ton, who married Bridget, daughter of the Protector. At this time there existed several different types of staircases, but all having "closed" or solid strings. There were balusters of the double pedestal formation, some molded like a skittle, as at the New Inn, Gloucester, and a house next the Shire Hall, Westgate, Gloucester; while others were of the Palladian type usually adopted by Inigo Jones and John Webb, as at Ashburnham House, Coleshill and Flaxley Abbey. At Forde Abbey pierced balustrading is adopted with very fine carving, the newels being terminated with a vase holding fruit and flowers in a naturalistic manner. A house in High Street, Guildford, has a similar treatment, which became common with John Webb and his carver Simon Gibbons during the latter years of the reign of Charles I. With Charles II the twisted baluster was introduced both to staircases and furniture. Of the latter instances may be found in Shaw's "Ancient Furniture." The Pynes, Devon, Bearland Lodge and Forbes House, both at Gloucester, and many other houses possess this type when the ramp in the handrail came into general use.

A baluster of three-inch square section was quite common during the reigns of Charles I and Charles II, to which the newel would vary from four inches to eight inches, the latter usually having a sunk or raised panel. When the twisted baluster was introduced a slight reduction in thickness took place. With many of the Wren period stairs a return to the heavy baluster resulted, except where wrought iron was adopted, as at Chatsworth and Hampton Court Palace. These stone stairs, being built up of simple blocks, mark the beginning of the cut string which became common in the early years of the eighteenth century.

Staircases with the soffits molded through to the wall string are to be seen at the Victoria Hotel at Newnham, and "Unlawater," Lady Paget's house hard by. There is an instance of one in London, at No. 5 Clifford Street. Mayfair, but this is a later type. Panelled risers

were not uncommon, the Foresters' Hall (Ladybellegate House) at Gloucester possessing such an example. In this case the landings are carefully joined in a form of parquet. Newels composed of four balusters grouped together are occasionally to be seen, the last mentioned instance being of this nature, but they were more common during the eighteenth century, when the cut string was in vogue. Bearland House has a particularly fine example. This staircase is rich in detail, with molded soffits and clustered newel placed on the second stair, the two bottom stairs being turned beneath the base of the newel. The handrail is ramped and turned in a variety of interesting curves. The hall screen or arched division is pierced with a well carved leaf design. At Winchester there is a house with a well planned hall and an early rear staircase; the main stairs are recessed between the principal rooms and approached through an arched opening.

The illustrations accompanying this article are largely confined to the earlier closed string type of staircase. Our next article will deal with the later examples, some of which are referred to above by way of comparison in describing the characteristic features of the English staircase. Of the illustrations here given the attention of readers is drawn to the examples from Flaxley Abbey and Ashburnham House. The measured drawings of these exhibit the typical, sound bold nature of the later Charles I era.

The staircase window on the landing at Flaxley is later than the staircase, the reason for the pointed architrave being occasioned by an attempt to create a note of harmony with the vaulted refectory now forming the kitchen and offices of the mansion. It is a curious compromise between two opposed periods, the happiness of the blending being open to question.

The example from Ashburn' am House is always regarded as the *chef d'oeuvre* of Inigo Jones, and is among the finest types one can select from the wealth of material at one's hand in England.

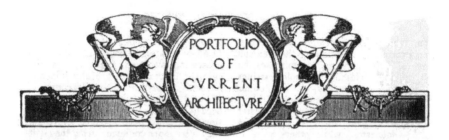

PORTFOLIO
OF
CVRRENT
ARCHITECTVRE

ENTRANCE TO ADMINISTRATION SIDE
- Y. W. C. A. BUILDING, SYRACUSE,
N. Y. TAYLOR & BONTA, ARCHITECTS.

FACADE—Y. W. C. A. BUILDING, SYRACUSE.
N. Y. TAYLOR & BONTA, ARCHITECTS.

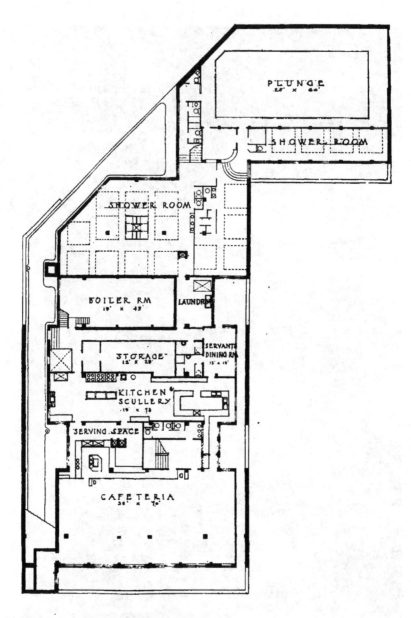

BASEMENT FLOOR PLAN—Y. W.
C. A. BUILDING, SYRACUSE, N. Y.
TAYLOR & BONTA, ARCHITECTS.

LOBBY—Y. W. C. A. BUILDING, SYRACUSE, N. Y.
Taylor & Bonta, Architects.

ROOF TERRACE—Y. W. C. A. BUILDING, SYRACUSE, N. Y.
Taylor & Bonta, Architects.

WAR BOOKS OF THE CATHEDRALS

BY BARR FERREE

PART VIII.

ONE of the most interesting narratives of personal experiences at Verdun is the *Journal du Commandant Raynal*, which carries the subtitle *Le Fort de Vaux*, with which famous fort his name will always be associated. It is the story of a tragedy in the highest sense of the word, the most tragic episode in the whole history of Verdun. At the opening of the war Raynal was a major with troops in Africa; a severe sickness incapacitated him for a time in France, but finally he reached Verdun, and was almost immediately placed in command of Fort Vaux. Long since disarmed, it was used as a shelter for relief troops for the adjoining trenches. The ferocity of the German attack, the heroic defense made by Commandant Raynal, the dreadful sufferings of his men, his appeals for help which never reached him, and his unavoidable surrender, all these are part of the glory of France. It is indeed something to have this tragic story related by its chief actor. It is a story of almost inconceivable suffering and heroism, told in a most engaging manner, and a book well entitled to rank among the most notable relating to Verdun.

The brilliant pages of *L'Angoisse de Verdun* by Pierre Alexis Muenier are saturated with blood and horror. The author was a driver of an ambulance. Unlike some American writers, who thought to keep up the spirits of their families by telling of daily sports and pleasantries, Mr. Muenier is solely concerned with war as it was. He was absorbed in his work, work of the hardest kind, work without relaxation, bitter work among the wounded and the dying. In his pages one gets very close to real war and its utter horror. His book is at once profoundly interesting and profoundly moving. A veritable masterpiece.

A highly distinctive quality is given to books by writers connected with the war in different aspects. Mr. Muenier shows it from the point of view of the ambulance driver. The Abbé Thellier de Poncheville, Military Chaplain at Verdun, naturally viewed the war from the standpoint of his sacred office. His *Dix Mois à Verdun*, is thus not only a narrative of personal experiences, but an interesting summary of the work of a war chaplain during a period of heavy military operations. His ten months at Verdun coincided almost exactly with the great year of Verdun. It is not a cheerful story he has to tell, for much of his work was among the wounded and the dying. He gets very close to the individual soldier, and is only concerned with the great movements at Verdun as they affect the men personally.

Very moving indeed is the story of three months at Verdun as told by the Sous-Lieutenant Raymond Jubert in his *Verdun (Mars-Avril-Mai 1916)*. Born at Charleville he was an advocate at Reims. His book, which has the distinguished advantage of a sympathetic preface by Paul Bourget, is a personal narrative of experiences which the author himself describes as miserably small and restrained in the midst of most formidable events. Yet quite unconsciously he has produced a masterpiece, and writes a book that will surely live. It covers, as the subtitle indicates, the most tragic period of the battle of Verdun. It was completed in a hospital at Brest in 1917. In August of that year he was returned to Verdun, and was almost immediately killed.

Trench life, as distinguished from active war duty, forms the special theme of *Tranchées de Verdun* by Daniel Mornet. He particularly treats of experiences from July, 1916, to May, 1917. The great pleasures of trench life, he points out, are negative: not to be thirsty, not to be hungry, not to be cold, not to be afraid. A chapter on "Quelques notions d'architecture" offers some notes on the construction of second line trenches.

L'Abbé Chevoleau, by Émile Baumann, is a brief biography of a priest who was corporal of the 90th Infantry. He saw much active service in the war, in which he distinguished himself by absolute disregard of danger. He was killed at Verdun shortly after being sent there. *En Batterie!* by Lieutenant Fonsagrive covers a very considerable period of war, including Verdun in 1916, the Somme, the Aisne, and again at Verdun in 1917. Although not unduly long, the author has the art of conveying a great deal of detailed information within comparatively restricted space. His experiences are connected with the artillery. *De Verdun au Rhin* by François de Tessan reproduces the notes of a newspaper correspondent during the time immediately following the armistice. His book is, therefore, quite outside the war period.

The earlier period of the war is admirably depicted by Dr. Georges Veaux in his book entitled *En suivant nos Soldats de l'Ouest.* Mobilized at Rennes, he was connected with Breton troops, and his book is concerned with their adventures over a wide territory. He saw service in Belgium, in the first battle of the Marne, at Reims, Arras, Ypres and many other places. The story moves swiftly and is told in a most interesting manner.

Very considerable, also, are the experiences related by the Commandant Bréant in his book *De l'Alsace à la Somme.* Alsace, Lorraine, the first battle of the Marne, two sojourns in Champagne, at Verdun and on the Somme constitute a career of ample military experience. A true soldier, Commandant Bréant, for after six days' holiday in Paris he returned to his regiment with satisfaction.

La Grande Mutilée de Reims by Georges Ferrero is a lecture given at Toulouse, and summarizes the history of the cathedral. *Les Sacrifices* by Henri Lavedan and Miguel Zamacoïs is a dramatic poem in three tableaux. The final section is entitled Reims, and is in prose; the first two, Les Flandres and Noël, are in verse. The section on Reims is a highly poetic conception, representing events supposed to be taking place within the cathedral. It begins with the coronation of Charles VII under the direct view of Jeanne d'Arc, and concludes with the desecration and destruction of the cathedral by the Germans. The vision is magnificently conceived and superbly carried out.

The Jackdaw of Rheims, the famous old story reproduced by the Ingoldsby Legends, furnishes the theme for some spirited drawings by George Wharton Edwards. His diagramatic version of the west front, however, gives somewhat the impression of a church with five portals, instead of three as is actually the case.

Vive la France by E. B. and A. A. Knipe is a novel dealing with a young girl of Reims and largely centered in that cathedral. As a story it has real interest, but the authors are not always quite accurate in their chronology. They represent Cardinal Luçon, the archbishop of Reims, as present at the time of the first bombardment, while actually he was not in the city. This, however, is a slight blemish in a well written tale.

L'Art pendant la Guerre by Robert de La Sizeranne reproduces a number of articles contributed to various periodicals by the author. They cover a considerable range of topics, from caricature to the new esthetic of battles. Two notable chapters are concerned with Reims, one on the famous tapestries and the other on the cathedral.

La Destruction des Monuments sur ie Front Occidental by Auguste Marguillier treats of a very large subject within modest scope. It includes chapters on artistic destructions in Belgium, Italy and France. The notes on France relate to Senlis, Soissons, Reims, Arras and other places. The author has space only for the most important facts, but these are admirably grouped, and his book forms an excellent handbook to one of the most horrible phases of the war. Forty-nine photographs of destroyed monuments supplement the text.

Pour Relever les Ruines by Joseph Dassonville is a discussion of what steps may be taken to repair the unnecessary ruin wrought by the Germans on French soil. One may not always agree with the author's proposals, but he presents a serious discussion of a very difficult subject. His book includes a chapter on the cathedral of Reims, and some other matters relating to the same city.

Now that the war is over many books on the devastated regions may be looked for. One of the earliest is Mlle. Noelle Roger's *Terres Dévastées et Cités mortes.* The author is a newspaper woman who seems to have had some exceptionally favorable opportunities to make early visits to the destroyed regions. She offers interesting chapters on Rheims, St. Dié, and Verdun, the cathedral cities especially noted in her survey.

The interest attached to *La 56ᵉ Division au Feu* by General F. de Dartien, is not wholly due to the fact that it is by the Commandant himself, although this is not inconsiderable. It treats of the earlier days of the war, from August 1 to October 2, 1914; but in that limited time the Division saw service from the Woevre to the Ourcq and from the Aisne to the Oise. Some interesting pages are given to the battle of Senlis in September, 1914.

Prés des Combattants by André Chevrillon is a miscellaneous collection of papers on various aspects and periods of the war. He visited the front from the Argonne to Champagne in May, 1916, and spent the following month with the British troops. He chronicles his impressions with the skill of a trained observer. The book includes chapters on Arras and Reims. Another volume by a newspaper correspondent is *Sur les Champs de Bataille* by André Tudesq, which likewise covers a wide territory. *Leur Calvaire* by Benjamin Vallotton is specifically dedicated to the refugees of Cambrai, Noyon, Lille and St. Quentin. The author is a Swiss; he makes no effort to differentiate between the experiences of the refugees from these various places, but summarizes the experiences of these unfortunate folk as a whole. *Dans Paris Bombardé* by Lucien Descaves is a brief summary of bombardments in 1871 and from 1914 to 1918. *St. Dié sous la Botte* by Ernest Colin describes the remarkable adventures of the author in seeking the return of the women and children taken away by the French as suspects when they left the city, a return demanded by the German general. It was an episode that constituted one of the most painful experiences of the German occupancy of this city.

Out of the Ruins by George B. Ford, of the American Red Cross Reconstruction Bureau in France is a rapid survey of what must be done to reconstruct the devastated regions. The author is not so much concerned with the ruin accomplished by the Germans as with what must be done to bring about restoration. He presents a graphic summary of what the French government has already accomplished and what still remains to be done.

THE CLASSIC FACTOR
IN FURNITURE DESIGN

BY WALTER A DYER
Photographs from the Metropolitan Museum of Art

SO large a proportion of modern furniture is being designed in the period styles—or what purport to be such—that the average person feels the need of knowing enough about their essential characteristics to enable him to discriminate between authentic reproductions and slipshod adaptations. To be ill informed on this subject is to be—well, ill informed.

But information is not the whole of education and culture; one of our American defects lies in our worship of facts. To train the powers of appreciation is more important than to store or impart mere information, for therein lies the whole question of our relation to the arts. One may be informed about the arts and still remain uncultured. One may memorize for useful or conversational purposes many interesting facts regarding musical composition or schools of painting and yet remain untouched by the enlightening power of the arts. There is a criterion of taste which transcends information.

We are speaking of furniture design, which, as I see it, is one of the applied arts. A finely wrought chair, for all its utilitarian purpose, may be as much a work of art as a painting or a poem, a sonata or a cathedral. Working upward through the ages the craftsman spirit has expressed itself through the medium of those things which are intended for homely uses, and civilization may be measured to a large extent by this glorification of our home life by the craftsman's art. To the Chinese potter, to the rug weaver of Ispahan, to the metal worker of old Granada, to the cabinet maker of sixteenth-century Florence we are indebted for much of the beauty which warms and illumines our twentieth-century homes, but which has become so familiar to us as to be almost commonplace. We observe our furniture and that of our neighbors less critically than we observe our paintings or our books, and yet since the dawn of civilization the spirit of the artist has been wrought in the form of household furniture.

Let me not be misunderstood as disparaging information; I am simply maintaining that in the realm of art information is not sufficient, does not carry us far enough. The facts regarding the historical development of the furniture styles are essential as a basis for understanding and appreciating those styles. Poverty of information is but another name for ignorance, and we none of us like to appear ignorant.

Let us have the facts, by all means. But in that we have been making some progress. A great deal has been written and read about the facts of furniture design. Most people are more or less well informed nowadays. Most people have some idea of who Buhl and Chippendale were and know that Jacobean furniture is older than Georgian. Perhaps we have reached a point where we can safely take another step in advance. The collecting of old furniture is a pretty universal hobby, though too often its indulgence displays a sad lack of discrimination. Why not make something more than a hobby of it? Why not let it become a study, a part of our education? For there is no short cut to culture; we must give more than a passing thought to these things.

In short, perhaps the time has arrived when we should begin to advance beyond the stage of collecting furniture and facts and begin the training of our powers of appreciation and discrimination. Perhaps we may hope for a keener vision that will enable us to recognize artistic merit without the help of a guide-book, to know inwardly and with conviction why a thing is good, and to tell the good from the bad. For not all old furniture is worthy of equal consideration. How, then, are we to know? What are we to look for? By what criterion are we to judge?

The first step for one genuinely desirous of acquiring a critical knowledge of the furniture styles is the accumulation of the essential information and the arrangement of the essential facts in their relation to each other. Assuming that this labor is at all worth while, we may then proceed to the cultivation of the appreciative and discriminating faculties.

As to the facts, it may be useful to marshal them briefly in review, partly as a basis for discussion and partly in order to note how the art impulse in furniture design has persisted through the centuries.

In the earliest periods furniture was either rude and lacking in artistic expression, or else it was architectural or sculptural in form. Furniture design as a distinct art can hardly be said to have emerged from architecture and sculpture until the period of the Renaissance. But Greek and Egyptian furniture is not to be ignored on that account, for the best of what followed constantly harked back to the classic for its inspiration. In the Roman and Pompeiian chairs and tables we discover the first signs of a mobiliary art in which the

Fig. 2. Italian Renaissance chair, late sixteenth century, of the curule type. Excellent in line and proportion.

classic feeling was evidently paramount.

About the year 1400 began that extraordinary movement, that awakening of the creative impulse, that emergence from the conditions of the Dark Ages that we have called the Renaissance. It expanded to its fullest flower in the sixteenth century, having its genesis, focus and highest development in Italy and spreading over most of the rest of Europe. All the arts flourished luxuriantly, and cabinet making and furniture designing became one of the honored crafts. The Greek spirit found a recrudescence in furniture design, to which the age added its own priceless contribution. The art of wood carving and joinery was perfected, and the homes of the nobles of Florence, Milan, Rome and Venice were furnished with elaborate and handsome chests, cabinets, tables and chairs. Design features, based upon the classic, became fixed and a definite, recognizable period style was evolved.

To attempt to catalogue the distinguishing features of this or any of the succeeding styles would be to exceed the limits of the present discussion. A description of them may be found in any good book on furniture. Suffice it to say that no education is complete, in the field of decorative and applied art, without some knowledge of the best work of the carvers and cabinet makers of the Italian Renaissance.

During the seventeenth century the Italian furniture styles suffered a decline or decadence, with a tendency toward confusion of ideas, over-ornamentation, and the lavish use of baroque and rococo details. Meanwhile, both in England

358

and on the Continent, the Gothic style in architecture had left its impress on furniture design, and some of the French and English Gothic furniture of the fourteenth and fifteenth centuries, while distinctly architectural in character, displayed a genuine feeling for design, particularly in the exquisite carving.

Then, in France, Spain and Flanders the Gothic influence in furniture design gradually disappeared before the resistless tide of the Italian Renaissance movement, and in each of those countries a Renaissance style was developed, based very definitely on the Italian, but undergoing some changes through force of environment and national character. In France the reign of François I (1515-1547) was one of the high-water marks in the history of French furniture design. A decline followed, succeeded in turn by a rise in the artistic curve during the reign of Louis XIII, when Cardinal Richelieu was prime minister and Simon Vouet was a leader in the art world.

The contemporary styles of Germany, Holland, Flanders and Spain were all closely related, though in Spain the virile Moorish elements, always stronger there than the Gothic, persisted and modified the style of the Spanish Renaissance.

The Renaissance movement, strictly speaking, was less marked in England than on the Continent. England was slower to respond to the almost universal impulse, but there was a gradual development of styles during the Tudor period which parallels the Renaissance movement elsewhere. Roughly, English furniture may be divided into that of the age of oak, lasting until about 1660;

Fig. 1. French Gothic chair stall, fifteenth century, illustrating the stiffness of line with delicacy of ornament.

the age of walnut, 1660 till about 1725; and the age of mahogany, 1725 to the beginning of the nineteenth century.

During the reign of Henry VIII (1509-1547) English furniture styles emerged from Gothic crudities, largely because of the monarch's anti-Papist and hence anti-Gothic predilections. Decorative details were imported from the Continent, but the Renaissance spirit was not fully felt in England until the reign of Elizabeth, during the last half of the sixteenth century. The styles were still not strictly Renaissance in type, but they were freer, more imaginative, and more fully expressive of an art impulse. New furniture forms were introduced, the plain trestle table gave place to something more pleasing, chairs became more common, and distinctive decorative details in line and carving were introduced. The classic influence was felt, though remotely.

The Jacobean period, properly speaking, extended from 1603 to 1649. The styles showed a continuation of the Elizabethan along what may be termed native British lines in spite of numerous importations. New forms and new ornamental details were introduced, but the styles remained natural and virile, tending even toward a greater austerity than those of Elizabeth's day rather than toward anything more effeminate or elaborate. These were the days of Inigo Jones and the beginnings of an English architecture.

With the restoration of Charles II to the throne of England in the year 1660, there came an era of greater luxury and of imported ideas. Walnut became the popular wood and a greater ornateness came into vogue. With the historic influences what they were, this might easily have been a period of decadence but for the fact that the styles then borrowed from Spain and France and Flanders still possessed beauties inherited from the Renaissance. It was a borrowed but not a decadent style. The chairs were patterned directly after

more distinctly. British product in which the purely classic motifs, doubtless due to the influence of Sir Christopher Wren, became more and more evident.

And so, without any serious slipping back into the inartistic errors of either slipshod crudity or wanton overelaboration, the English styles gradually de-

Fig. 3. Late sixteenth century Italian Renaissance chairs. Proportion good, lines stiff, carved and inlaid ornament.

those of Spain and Flanders, but there were still some heritages from the Jacobean period, notably the gate-leg table.

Following the abdication of James II, in 1689, and the accession of William and Mary to the throne, the Dutch element, brought over by William, entered strongly into the English styles, together with borrowings from the French of Louis XIV, which, in turn, had been adopted by the Dutch through the agency of Huguenot exiles like Daniel Marot. Here again we find in England a borrowed, almost a mongrel, style, which might easily have slipped into degeneracy had not the designers of the reign of Queen Anne, which followed, seen fit to engraft upon the Dutch elements a

veloped into those of the Georgian period, when mahogany became the popular wood and when, in spite of many whimsical lateral tendencies, the classic tradition was kept alive.

From the time of Queen Anne the furniture styles developed through the early Georgian transition period until, about the middle of the eighteenth century, the influence of Thomas Chippendale became paramount. Chippendale's styles show a strange mixture of good and bad. He was a master carver and a master of ornament. Unquestionably his feeling for line and proportion was highly developed and he was nothing if not original in spite of his many borrowings. But he suffered from too much versatility, from too great a desire to outdo himself in the matter of novelty, so that while his best work stands supreme as typical of the Georgian golden age, his poorest work is so lacking in consistency and restraint as almost to seem decadent. And between these two extremes there was not a little mediocrity. But I shall have more to say of Chippendale presently.

There followed the later Georgian period in which the work of Adam, Hepplewhite and Sheraton predominated. Robert Adam was not a cabinet maker, but as an architect, interior decorator and designer, he exerted a powerful influence on the furniture styles of the day. Adam's style was almost purely classic, based upon his study of Roman and Pompeiian antiquities and affected, no doubt, by the contemporary classic spirit of the Louis XVI period in France. What it lacked in virility was more than compensated for in its chastity, delicacy and restraint.

Hepplewhite's style was influenced by this classic revival, but not entirely so. Many of his details were his own, or the product of native fashions; but his lines, proportions and decorative details all show the classic influence.

Sheraton was the truer classicist in his earlier work, and his wonderful feeling for line and proportion was that of a born artist. He never, in those early days, allowed himself the extravagance of an unnecessary curve and his touch was delicate. But Sheraton was unfortunate in more ways than one, and gradually he allowed himself to be engulfed by the vulgar wave of popular taste that demanded something more ornate and showy, so that his later work, in the early years of the nineteenth century, was distinctly decadent. And with

Fig. 4. Late Renaissance, Switzerland or North Italy, lacking all the essential qualities of good design.

him there came to an end all that may be truly termed artistic in English furniture until the present generation.

Returning now to France, we find in the period of Louis XIV (1643-1715) a recrudescence of the art impulse as applied to furniture design. France spoke her own language in this and the following periods. The Louis XIV style is marked by dignity, grandeur, bold effects, lavish but not excessive ornament, and faultless workmanship. It was too voluptuous to be called truly classic, and yet many of its motifs were of classic derivation. The details were symmetrical and balanced.

But French exuberance was not long to be restrained. Even the great cabinet makers and designers who flourished at that time succumbed to the movement of popular and royal taste. Rococo ornament became more and more lavishly employed and details became unbalanced to the point of eccentricity, till we find, during the reign of Louis XV (1715-1774), a veritable riot of florid ornament and gilded luxuriousness, by no means lacking in decorative merit but often sadly overdone.

Then came the reaction. The style of Louis XVI (1774-1793) shows a return to simpler lines, a more restrained and delicate ornament, and a classic feeling. Grace, restraint, daintiness, refinement and excellent workmanship distinguished the period, with a preference for straight lines and simple curves and the abandonment of the rococo.

The Empire style (1799-1814) is more difficult to characterize, for here we are considering less a natural style evolution than the whim of an egotistical emperor. The style was based on the classic Roman, and at its best it was worthy of being classed as a classic style. But

Fig. 5. The Louis XIV. style was marked by dignity of line, proportion and ornament.

Fig. 8. The best of the furniture of the French Empire was dignified, if somewhat formal and severe.

Fig. 6. Excessive ornamentation and gilding and unbalanced details were characteristic of Louis XV. furniture.

Fig. 7. A return to simpler lines and more delicate ornamentation marked the Louis XVI. style.

Fig. 9. The late Empire styles were
often grotesque and decadent.

Fig. 10. The Wainscot chairs of the
Tudor period in England were not
without decorative distinction.

Fig. 13. A domestic simplicity, combined with pleasing curves and good proportions, distinguished the style of the Queen Anne period.

Fig. 14. The best of the Chippendale designs show a harmony of line and exquisite ornament.

Fig. 11. A certain grace of line and carving saved the high-backed chairs of the Restoration from over-ornate degeneracy.

Fig. 12. The chairs of the William and Mary period partook of the qualities which distinguished those of Louis XIV.

in its usual manifestations it was stiff, formal, heavy and sombre, and but poorly adapted to domestic needs. At its worst it was decadent, and it ushered in decadence.

So much, then, by way of a brief survey of the historic facts of the development of the furniture styles. They may easily be committed to memory, but that is not the final test of understanding. The more subtle realm of appreciation stretches ahead of us still.

Some of us are born with this power to a certain extent; we have natural taste, as the saying is. But whether we are born with it or not, our taste, our powers of appreciation, the responsiveness of our reactions may be trained and cultivated. Most of us do not appreciate classical music when we first hear it—though we may insist that we do; our musical tastes must be cultivated. In the same way we may cultivate our powers of appreciation of

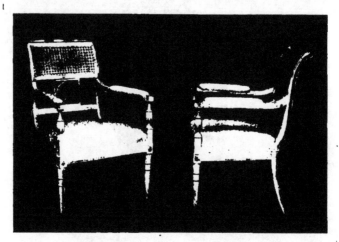

Fig. 17. Robert Adam introduced a classic simplicity and grace which displays a kinship with the Louis XVL style.

During all these centuries both good and bad furniture was produced, but the art impulse persisted. Always there were sincere craftsmen who sought to impart the artistic touch to their designs, and usually there were some who succeeded. We may accept this statement without question or we may seek to comprehend and believe it. If we are honest, we will ask ourselves whether we really see anything beautiful in a piece of old furniture, or whether we merely say that we do because it is the fashion. Do our natures pleasurably react to the element of beauty in these things? For that is the ultimate test—the personal reaction. It is the indication and measure of our powers of appreciation.

what is fine and beautiful in applied art, in furniture. And if the attempt is to be honestly made, perhaps I can give a helpful hint as to its direction.

In the first place we must learn to discriminate. Perhaps we have taken it for granted that all old furniture is equally worthy; or perhaps we have been a bit skeptical about the whole of it. It was not all of it good, and we may hope to learn to discriminate between the good and the bad and so to establish a criterion of excellence. To some extent this is a matter of taste, with opportunity for honest differences of opinion. To take a concrete example, there are friends of mine who prefer Chippendale's work to that of Sheraton. They find his sweeping curves more

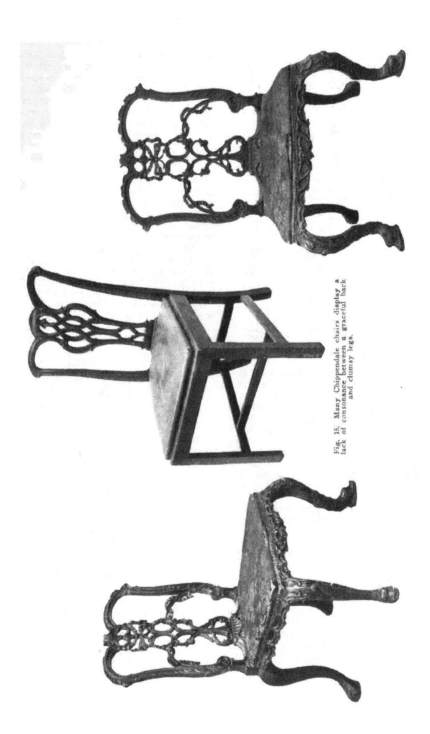

Fig. 15. Many Chippendale chairs display a lack of consonance between a graceful back and clumsy legs.

Fig. 19. The early work of Sheraton shows a rare perfection of line, proportion and workmanship, and restraint in the use of ornament.

portion, too, which some experts have endeavored to express in mathematical terms, but which must be appreciated with the senses rather than measured with a rule if we are to understand it fully. The fact is that certain proportions of length, width and thickness produce a pleasanter impression on the human eye than do others, just as certain color and sound combinations are pleasanter than others. The masters had a feeling for this, and proportion is a criterion of excellence in all furniture design. As for ornamentation, it is partly a question of quantity. The over-elaborate has always been bad. Ornament should never obscure line or proportion. Yet ornament, finely conceived and wrought, adds to furniture beauty and softens the harshest lines. It is where cabinet makers have forgotten the principles of line and proportion in their desire to decorate that we have the ornateness that characterizes many of the decadent periods.

Let us now examine the historic styles and discover, if we may, how and where

pleasing than Sheraton's sometimes austere simplicity. To me, on the other hand, there is something so refined and perfect in Sheraton's best lines and proportions that he rises quite above Chippendale's level. So far we may set it down to a matter of taste. There are, however, certain fundamental principles of design that are as inflexible as the notes of the scale, and the designer who proposes to ignore them invariably goes astray.

These basic principles have to do with line, proportion and ornamentation. There is a rhythm and harmony of line which is as elementary as that of poetry and music. It is something that can be understood only through studious observation. Sheraton, for example, never used strikingly different forms of the curve on the same piece; while Chippendale did not hesitate to place a back full of sweeping and reversed curves upon a chair with almost clumsily straight, square legs, and he produced a discord. There is a criterion of pro-

Fig. 18. Hepplewhite, at his best, had a fine feeling for line and ornament.

these principles are manifested. It is not surprising to discover in the furniture of the Greek an Attic perfection of line and proportion, and that grace and restraint of ornament which characterized Greek architecture and which causes us ever to hark back to it when we feel the need for a draught of pure inspiration. The best of the furniture of the Italian Renaissance, while sometimes clinging to stiffness of line, exhibits beauty of proportion and the feeling for the skillful placing and execution of ornament. The same is true of the best of the Gothic. During the period of the late Renaissance there may be detected a tendency to greater freedom of line, but this was counter-balanced by the taste for over-ornamentation, and the popular appreciative faculty suffered a decline.

In Tudor England harsh lines persisted after the craftsmen of the period had begun to display a feeling for proportion and ornament; during the Jacobean period the lines became gradually freer and more graceful. The Restoration brought almost a superabundance of ornament and a tendency toward unusual proportions, particularly in the high-backed chairs; but there was a certain excellence in the carving and a certain grace of line which saved the period from decadence. To a certain extent this is true of the William and Mary period that followed, when the beds, for example, were smothered in a superfluity of draperies. But the Queen Anne period followed promptly to save the day, and here a softening domestic element crept in to lay a restraining hand on the tendency to exaggeration, and in ornament Greek elements were introduced, as in the broken arch pediment.

The cabriole leg was graceful in itself, and Chippendale developed and perfected it. He had a wonderful feeling for ornament, and he knew where to borrow the best that was to be had, but he overdid his borrowing. He not only produced in some cases a sad mixture of Dutch, French, Chinese and Gothic elements, but he confused his lines and proportions as well. At his best he was a master of the art; at his worst, to my way of thinking, he verged dangerously close upon the decadent.

But again the impulse of a classic revival, fostered by Adam, stepped in to preserve the dignity of English furniture design, and England held true to its conservative principles until the nineteenth century, when even Sheraton went mad and Hope introduced his atrocious novelties, and line, proportion

Fig. 20. The American Windsor chair is sometimes remarkable for the grace of its lines and proportions.

and harmony of ornament all went by the board.

In France a steady development of ornament is to be detected from the time of the Renaissance. The Louis XIV style was dignified and even majestic; but the Louis XV style mixed its curves, gloried in lack of symmetry, and sought for the appearance of luxury in gilt and rococo over-ornamentation. The Louis XVI style was a sharp reaction from this, and the principles of good proportion, moderate ornament, and simple, graceful lines were restored. The Empire style was a strange mixture of excellences and defects, and it ended in decadence.

American furniture styles reflected so closely those of the mother country that they need not be considered separately, with one or two exceptions. Here we developed the wonderfully graceful Windsor chair, with its often perfect lines and proportions, through some remarkable genius of the Yankee craftsman. Here, too, Duncan Phyfe kept alive the Sheraton tradition after Shera-

Fig. 21. In America Duncan Phyfe held to the best traditions of Sheraton and the French Empire.

ton had lost his grip. Here we softened the asperities of the Empire style through the medium of a sort of domestic moderation. And here, finally, we fell into our own forms of decadence in the black walnut and Japanese and Eastlake periods.

Thus, throughout the history of the development of the furniture styles, we can trace waves of taste, a curve sometimes ascending, sometimes descending, now gradual, now abrupt, but always coincident with the state of popular taste and the artistic aims and ideals of the craftsmen. There were times

when men followed false gods, forgetting the fundamental principles of design and seeking for novelty and deceptive elegance. And there were times when men shook off convention and fashion and false standards and got back upon more solid ground.

To me it seems perfectly clear that the spirit of the Greek, the original discoverer of the principles of design—of line, proportion, and ornament—runs like a musical motif through it all. And wherever it is most in evidence, there we have the high points on our curve. It was the classic spirit that invigorated and dominated the Renaissance movement. It was a revival of the classic spirit that produced the Louis XVI and Georgian periods. In this classic instinct a wonderful vitality has ever resided. It is this classic factor in the evolution of the period styles that has served as the sure foundation for our artistic faith throughout the centuries, and whenever man has turned aside from it he has failed.

There is a lesson for us in this consideration of history. Today we stand at the parting of the ways. There is a school among us that demands novelty, that affirms that the past is dead, that calls for an American style based upon a new national consciousness that should be creative, that would cut loose forever from the trammels of tradition. If this movement is successful it will run counter to all the teachings of history, for it has been the collective experience of mankind that the worthiest and most permanent developments of decorative art have not arisen at the call for novelty, like the late lamented L'Art Nouveau, but have invariably been built upon the solid foundations of the past. The classic factor has been weighed and found not wanting. It will persist and survive; we cannot get away from it. And if now, after the war, we are to experience a new Renaissance, it is my belief that it will be but another classic revival. And in that case our study of the historic furniture styles, our effort to appreciate their merits, and our recognition of the classic factor inherent in them will not have been in vain.

THE
SLAV TEMPERAMENT IN ARCHITECTURE

BY LEON V. SOLON

HISTORY shows civilization following the sun in its progress from east to west; its illumination, however, has not shone with the same impartial prodigality. From the Orient, the land of genesis, it spread with infinite slowness westward, skirting great tracts in fickle progress, which it left fallow amidst neighboring luxuriance. Russia for centuries was such a tract, in comparatively close proximity to the highly matured cultures of Greece, Byzantium, Persia and Mongolia.

During the latter half of the nineteenth century we became conscious of the power and subtlety of the Slav temperament in music and literature, when, satiated by the stilted works of would-be classicists, and surfeited with the forced efforts of the Romantic School, the study of psychology became the directing impulse in certain phases of imaginative art. We found Scandinavians and Slavs masters where we were students, through their racial habit of introspection.

In the order of our enlightenment, Slav music preceded their literature; possibly because so many virtuosi were of the race, or because no translation is necessary to make Slav music intelligible to other races, a uniform system of structure governing all European music.

The subsequent translation of the great Russian authors created a deep impression and a vogue among intellectuals almost equal to that of Slav music among musicians; Turgenief and Tolstoy influenced the direction of a new school in writing as radically as Chopin and his followers had done in music.

In European music, previous to the Slav influence, the emotions chosen for harmonic expression might be designated as the "elementary sensations"; with the new basis of psychic selection, infinite new gamuts of human vibrations were revealed for symphonic interpretation.

The literary world was correspondingly fascinated in seeing the psychic problems of life handled with the fatalism, susceptibility to color, and ruthless dramatic instinct of the Orient; the musical world heard for the first time, in tones and semitones it could not comprehend, the songs, passions and plaints of the East. It was a revelation to discover the arts of a nation exercised primarily for their capacity to express sensuousness—to find purely intellectual objectives subordinated to uncurbed racial instincts which had developed during centuries, untouched by our standards of taste and morals.

The general and professional public has a casual acquaintance with Russian craftsmanship and would experience no hesitation in identifying the enamels, metalwork, embroidery or jewelry; the architecture, on the other hand, is a closed book to the majority, who would probably dismiss it from consideration as a type of bastard Turkish, with gaudy buildings surmounted by gaudier cupolas.

The scarcity of data on the subject, the many calls on the traveler's attention in more easily accessible lands, may account for past indifference towards a strongly characteristic and original method of construction and design, although a simple and obvious deduction should have produced the inference that the strong racial temperament which we

371

find so deeply impressed with such true artistic judgment in literature and music, would reveal itself in some unforeseen manner in buildings.

The greatest enthusiast for the various Slav manners of architectural treatment could not state with truth that any one ranks with the fine types of Greek, Roman or Gothic; they contribute, however, a number of interesting and characteristic features which our racial instinct and our history would prevent us from evolving spontaneously.

The Slav made his debut in building as a pupil of Byzantium, the influence of which, although it left an indelible stamp, was submitted to the modification occurring in the architecture of all northern races when finally freed from the Roman domination, namely, the instinctive tendency to build in height rather than in breadth.

In conformity with the tradition of the Aryan races, the early Slav buildings were made of wood; this continued until the tenth century. In the eleventh century dressed stone came into general use, and vaults constructed with it were inspired by the Byzantine, but the plan of the churches conformed to the type created by the Greek Christians of Peloponnesus. One of the earliest stone churches is that of the Intercession, built in the province of Vladimir in 1165, the central cupola of which rests on four massive columns.

The Tartars, who had conquered and ruled the country previous to this, left no mark upon the arts, adhering to their invariable policy of non-interference in the national customs of subjugated races, exacting heavy tribute only. Slav builders trained in Byzantium were in great request with their conquerors, and together with their brother craftsmen were sent for periods to the Khan's court in Asia, to execute work; those who returned to their native land are credited with introducing a part of the Oriental character prevailing in the later Slav buildings.

It was only in the fourteenth and fifteenth centuries that the Slavs made contact with the influence that proved most fertile in stimulating their inventive faculty. At that period Persian and Arab civilization was reaching its apex, and the Slavs, fascinated by the *tours de force* performed by those great builders, learned certain systems of construction which ultimately became the keynote of their style. The construction of the cupola consisting of superimposed tiers of arches built out on corbels, attracted them most; but their adoption of this principle was not a literal copy. Instead of the plain, unbroken surface of the exterior finish of their masters, they saw great decorative possibilities in making these tiers of arches penetrate to the exterior, which developed into their most characteristic feature. To this origin we can trace the friezes of arches of varied types which cluster round the roofs, and in a variety of other places where their appearance is often justified only by their excessive popularity.

A good example of the almost affectionate use of this feature is seen in the church tower of Medkevoko, in which the arches cluster even round the base of the lantern. It will be noted that two types of arches are combined, the semicircular and a type of ogival arch, essentially Slav, differing in combination of curves from the Gothic ogee. The oblong windows in the tower are characteristic and are always placed in effective contrast to the arches and tapering spires.

During the seventeenth century Slav ingenuity developed a new treatment of the penetrating arch, a typical example of which is illustrated in the Church of the Ascension at Kolomenskoe. Here this treatment of the arch is made a prominent feature in the general scheme; the alternate sides of the octagon are squared in a very ingenious fashion.

The use of bricks was productive of much individual work unlike that of any other race or nation. The belfry sketch represents a type of design created for execution in that material, which is most impressive in scale and proportion; a great decorative quality is extracted from the brick, and an added richness of color obtained by the simple method of recessing a number of panels, on-

BELFRY, TYPICAL OF EARLY SLAV BRICK-BUILDING. RECESSED PANELS, ONE BEHIND ANOTHER, CONSTITUTE THE MAIN MOTIF OF THE DECORATION.

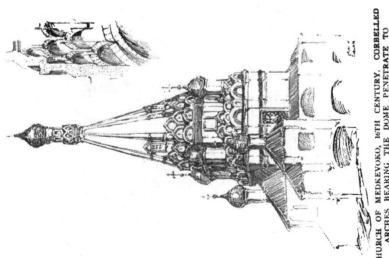

CHURCH OF MEDKEVOKO, 16TH CENTURY. CORBELLED ARCHES BEARING THE DOME PENETRATE TO THE EXTERIOR AS A DECORATIVE FEATURE.

CHAPEL OF THE CONVENT OF ST. NICHOLAS, 17TH CENTURY. THE STRUCTURE AND
ARCHITECTURAL MEMBERS ARE OF BRICK.

CHURCH OF THE PRESENTATION OF THE VIRGIN, 16TH CENTURY, IN ENVIRONS OF
MOSCOW. IT IS DECORATED WITH POLYCHROME FAIENCE, COMBINED
WITH STONE EMBEDDED IN STUCCO.

CHURCH OF THE ASCENSION AT KOLOMENSKOE, 17TH
CENTURY. SHOWING A LATER DEVELOPMENT
OF THE PENETRATING ARCH.

within the other. The great balustre shaped columns at the angles are admirably designed for execution with small units. In this and in many other brick structures there are unusual arrangements of the units which it would well repay the designers of brick buildings to study.

The Chapel of the Convent of St. Nicholas is a much later brick building, dating from the seventeenth century. It is typical in detail and general treatment, though it would be difficult to find any two churches which nearly resemble each other. The frieze of arches still survives, but another type is used over the windows, composed of two sectors of a circle penetrating a right angle. This style of opening is found in a considerable number of edifices.

Another type of structure is shown in the Church of the Presentation of the Virgin, built in the environs of Moscow in the sixteenth century. A polychrome frieze of birds with outstretched wings girdles the building, perched on inverted stone arcs which are supported on long bands of stone simulating pilasters, all on a stucco field; a polychrome band of faience ornament runs below the roof. The builder succeeded in doing without any rows of penetrating arches in this instance, but was faithful to the bulbous

dome, which is surmounted in the usual Russian manner with the emblem of Christianity reposing snugly in the crescent of Islam.

From the aspect of polychrome architecture, almost all Russian buildings are of interest, more for the lavish use of vari-colored materials to produce a gorgeous result than from any scientific principle underlying their disposition. The domes were of copper, frequently gilt. Tympanums, soffits and corbels were treated in color, both on the exterior and interior. Mosaic on gold ground, polychrome, faience and paintings of ornamentation and symbolic figures were lavishly used.

This brief glance at Slav architecture touches a very few of a great assortment of varying types, nearly all of which embody peculiarities differing greatly from our routine of practice. In such subjects our appreciation is handicapped, accustomed as we have become to submission to set canons; long ago we signed our indentures of apprenticeship to the workshop of method, and see precedent rather than digression. Precedent is the aesthetic insurance against errors of taste; but creative power depends for its stimulation on an element of novelty, be it from the unknown or from an unaccustomed angle of consideration in the familiar object.

Daniel Chester French's New Lincoln.

For several years there has been under construction on the banks of the Potomac in the National Capital an imposing marble structure of Greek design, the work of Henry Bacon. This is the National Memorial to Abraham Lincoln, an edifice so vast and splendid as to evoke the admiration of all who delight in classic perfection, so admirable indeed that it vies in architectural excellence and impressiveness with the Capitol itself and the Washington Monument.

Many have been the speculations regarding the character of the statue which is to be the chief sculptural feature of this magnificent edifice. Little, however, could be learned concerning the work. It was stated that to Daniel Chester French, foremost of American sculptors, had been entrusted its execution.

Owing to very strict rules laid down by the National Committee in charge of the work, it was a long time before any one was even permitted to see the preliminary studies in the artist's studio and all requests for photographs of the statue were refused. During the war the work on the Lincoln Memorial was largely suspended and owing to the extreme difficulty of importing huge blocks of marble, there has been some delay in completing the statue. Now, however, the ban has been lifted and photos of the statue are for the first time released for publication.

What shall be said of this latest interpretation of Lincoln in sculpture? In these days, after nearly two hundred statues of him have been created, when the man has been depicted in practically every phase of his eventful and picturesque career, it would seem that anything approaching originality must be manifestly impossible.

And yet we feel fully convinced that in this, which is certainly the most imposing of all his creations, Daniel Chester French has accomplished the impossible and given us a new Lincoln thoroughly original and quite unlike any other statue. Lincoln is presented to us at that moment of his life most appropriate to be represented in the splendid structure which shall for all time shelter it. "Lincoln Triumphant" is one title suggested for it.

Mr. French is the author of two statues of Lincoln. Unstinted has been the praise of his earlier work "Lincoln in Thought," which adorns Nebraska's Capital City. In that statue the president is portrayed in deep meditation, perhaps a bit perplexed. But in the latest creation there is nought of perplexity on that calm benign countenance. This is not the triumph of a Marcus Aurelius extending an imperial scepter over the Roman populace. This is the great President and Executive, a reformer rather than the Commander-in-Chief of armies, who having accomplished his epoch-making task, sits down at last, weary but satisfied, to contemplate the tremendous work which he has wrought. This is the triumph of the prophet who realizes the fulfillment of his dreams.

The lover of good sculpture will revel in the fine pose of the majestic figure. He will study the masterly handling of its planes and lines. Most of all he will enthuse over the marvellous technique of the surface modeling and those remarkable hands. The lover of Lincoln will feel a thrill at the depth of feeling which emanates from this great statue, from the face so full of contentment yet bearing the deep furrows wrought by a tremendous struggle.

The casual observer will of course be impressed by its huge bulk, for this statue is a veritable colossus. Although it represents the seated figure, the head is nineteen

STATUE OF ABRAHAM LINCOLN, IN GEORGIA MARBLE,
OCCUPYING THE CENTER OF THE LINCOLN MEMORIAL,
WASHINGTON, D. C. DANIEL CHESTER FRENCH, SCULPTOR.

THE LINCOLN MEMORIAL, ON THE POTOMAC EMBANK-
MENT, WASHINGTON, D. C. HENRY BACON, ARCHITECT.

PROPOSED BRONZE DOORS FOR LIBRARY OF NEW YORK UNIVERSITY
IN MEMORY OF STANFORD WHITE

feet above the pedestal and thirty feet from the floor. It was utterly impossible to take from the quarry, much less to import, a block of Carrara large enough for the entire work. The piece from which one leg was cut weighed between twenty and twenty-five tons. The head is five feet from the chin to the top. French's "Lincoln Triumphant" is probably the largest marble statue ever carved. Its very magnitude alone impresses one. The carving was done by Piccirilli Brothers.

Mr. French has given the world such a vast and varied number of estimable works of art that it would require a masterpiece indeed to add anything to his fame. In "Lincoln Triumphant," however, he has added to his fame a transcendent work of art worthy its creator, worthy the unsurpassed locality where it stands, and we believe more nearly representative of America's present conception of Abraham Lincoln than any other statue hitherto created

FRANK OWEN PAYNE.

Stanford White Memorial at New York University. The memory of the late Stanford White is to be perpetuated through the erection of a pair of bronze doors which the friends of the distinguished architect and art lover will present to the New York University. The memorial will be installed at the entrance to the Library of the University, which was designed by Mr. White. The trustees of the University have formally signified their acceptance of the gift and the Committee in charge of the memorial will begin at once the work of collecting subscriptions to cover the cost. It is the purpose of the Committee to appeal for funds from the friends and admirers of the late architect; and subscriptions from the general public, while they may not be refused, are not desired.

As a delicate attention from the men in charge of the memorial, the work of designing it has been entrusted to the son of Stanford White, Mr. Lawrence Grant White. The doors will be of bronze, and will be unique in that they will contain a number of medallions symbolizing art, the originals of which will be contributed to the memorial by eight or ten sculptors formerly associated with Stanford White. It is the purpose of the Committee to have the doors ready for dedication on the opening of the academic year, this autumn.

Funds for the memorial may be addressed to W. Francklyn Paris, 7 West 43rd street, New York.

Literature and Sworn Testimony. Spanish civil architecture during the late Gothic and early Renaissance periods was the subject of my proposed researches. I had gone at it valiantly, undaunted by the warning Mr. Royall Tyler sounds in his *Spain: Her Life and Arts.* His is a good-natured complaint, but much to the point, as all will agree who have had to rely for their data on the writings of Spanish archaeologists. "To take advantage of the writings of these diligent men," says Tyler, "is quite a different affair from pillaging the Englishman Street with his terse style and careful index. The Spaniard who has spent fifteen or twenty years in unearthing and deciphering documents does not propose to leave the fruit of his toil within the reach of every passer-by. He writes a book, yes; but he makes it as long as possible, never by any chance includes an index, suppresses all page headings that might give a clue, and, when he has spun out as much artistic rhapsodizing as he has in him, leads one an endless game of hide-and-seek before he will relinquish the architect's name and date—if he really has them. His idea is that anyone who wishes to use his book shall have to work as hard as he did to write it."

There is, however, one important, even monumental, work recently written on Spanish architecture that is all one could desire in conciseness and arrangement (except for the index). It is neither poetry nor "fine writing"; just a straightforward exposition of the theme; but that theme happens to be religious, not civil architecture. As to this latter, the author himself could refer me to nothing more concrete than the occasional articles that had been published in various periodicals, especially in the Bulletin of the Spanish Society of Excursionists. Now, a bulletin being, according to Webster, "a brief statement of news to the public from one specially authorized," and the Excursionists being the most noted archaeological body in Spain, the humble searcher is justified in expecting a rich haul. For years it had been the custom of these learned gentlemen to make a monthly trip to some historic monument, of which one of their number then published an account.

"*Excursion to Alcalá*" was the first title that attracted the eye on turning over an early number of the *Boletin*. Knowing that in Alcalá Cardinal Cisneros built a great university, and Archibishop Fonseca, the princely art-patron of the early sixteenth century, an episcopal palace, I began eagerly. The excursionists, I find, met on the morning appointed in the railroad station; they bought their tickets; they took their seats in the train; the train pulled out; they conversed en route; they were received in Alcalá by the priest of the Collegiate Church, whose courtesy is extolled to the skies. Then, with one bound, the chronicler informs us that "beautiful portals, splendid patios, artistic stairways, a magnificent sepulchre with beautiful recumbent statue" (I knew he meant that of Cardinal Cisneros), "all served the sculptors as a field in which to leave the stamp of their various impressions." And after these edifying lines we learn that "there was also time to dedicate to exhausted nature, and in the beautiful residence of Señor F. the Excursionists recuperated from the deep emotions produced by the sight of so many artistic jewels. The lunch table was presided over by Miss F., as pretty as she is educated, and in whose consummate discretion could be divined, from the first moment, a young lady of great culture who had visited the principal countries of Europe and had lived in England, appropriating all that was best and most noble in said countries."

To encounter the foregoing in the most serious journal of art and archaeology was amusing, but also a bit disheartening; one began to understand what Tyler meant by Spanish rhapsodizing; but perhaps the Excursionists had been particularly unlucky that month in their chronicler. Let us see if next month's outing will be better reported. On that occasion they went to Guadalajara. We had read elsewhere that the feudal lords of that place, the mighty Mendoza family, built there one of the most sumptuous Renaissance palaces in Spain. We glow in anticipation. The writer appears to be a man of sense, for he wastes no time in tiresome preliminaries of ticket-buying, etc., but puts us at once *in medias res*: "We visited first the superb palace erected in the last years of the fifteenth century" (he could hardly have avoided the date since it is inscribed in the patio) "admiring the pomp and splendor of its façade and its principal patio, where the exuberant ornamentation of the Gothic decadence still boldly held its own. The magnificent *alfarjes* (decorated carpentry ceilings) of the various salons also enchanted us, recalling: first, the beautiful assembling of Saracenic geometric interlacings, so exquisite and varied; second, those stalactite ceilings whose entirety, so rich in lovely effects, is nevertheless composed of three simple prismatic elements whose lower portion, cleverly perforated, gives place to seven stalactite elements with which are produced combinations as elegant and diverse as those obtained in the most sublime melodies by means of the seven notes of the musical scale."

From this poetic simile we drop abruptly to the vulgar: "Physical necessities obliged us to suspend the contemplation of so much beauty and we hurried to the Casino, where an excellent and economical lunch was served to us and in measure as we repaired our lost bodily force we consecrated our conversation to an exchange of impressions on the history of Guadalajara." (If anything of historical value was said the author carefully omits it.)

"Our comfortable lunch terminated, we visited the superb mausoleum erected by the Duchess of S——, etc., etc." (Let us interject that this is an atrocious modern work.) "The visit to this splendid pantheon accomplished, and the hour for the departure of the Madrid train approaching, we took leave of our kind guide and returned to our homes joyous and satisfied, but regretting that our worthy president had been prevented by his many occupations from accompanying us."

Thus ended the story of Guadalajara and its palace, and I was none the wiser. Not even the name of the *genius loci* had been mentioned. Fortunately I had known it beforehand, as already stated, and it recalled to me that another member of this same Mendoza family had built a Renaissance palace near Granada. For this information I was indebted not to a Spaniard, but to the German, Professor Carl Justi, who had gone to Genoa and unearthed contracts and correspondence between Don Rodrigo de Mendoza, natural son of the Great Cardinal, and his Genoese architect. Surely, with this preliminary drudgery done by an interested foreigner, some Spaniard must have devoted himself to the same subject. Yes, the Bulletin contained an article on the Castle of Lacalahora (which the present owner, by the way, insists on calling the Castillo de la Monclova). The author of this article is really instructive, but alas! he does not love us, for he opens with a Bolshevik cry of rage against the Yankees and their money.

"In 1890," he says, "the enthusiasm of Professor Justi induced certain Spaniards to visit LaCalahora and publish articles on it." (Innocent omission!) "On learning of its worth there rushed to buy it one of those Yankee millionaires who corner the historic and artistic glories of other countries because they have none in their own; and when the sale was nearly consummated, a Spanish nobleman who has united to the prestige of distinguished birth that acquired by his own personal effort" (the gentleman has a popular brand of wine on the market) "succeeded in preventing this iniquitous despoiling of our country and thus saved for Spain the jewel of La Calahora."

He who wrote the above is the same who recommended the Bulletin to me. He knows well the vast sum of . American money spent in reclaiming for Spain historic monuments which the natives themselves have shamefully maltreated. Likewise he knows that if Spanish art is sold out of the country it is Spaniards themselves who implore foreigners to buy it, charging, always, a fantastic price for their wares. As for the "Jewel of La Calahora," which is, on the exterior, a bare-looking dungeon, the only part of artistic merit is the patio and stairway, carved in Genoa and sent piece by piece to Granada in the early sixteenth century. The titled wine merchant, we have heard recently, is about to remove the carved doorways and balustrade and bring them to Madrid to be incorporated in his house here; in which case the so-called jewel will be bereft of all its lustre.

Happily, spite is not a prominent Spanish characteristic, and most of the Bulletin's articles are amiability itself. The Excursionists invariably shower gratitude on the *cura* (village priest) who meets them at their destination and shows them his historic church; or if it is an ancient palace, still inhabited, that they inspect, its owner is made immortal in the printed pages. "The possessor of all these artistic treasures received us in that house which, more than house, is a veritable museum, and did the honors like a person perfectly familiar with the uses and customs of high society. For each one of us he had a charming phrase pronounced with his exquisite courtesy, and he never tired answering our many questions." Could any host ask more than to have it set down, for all time, that he is "familiar with the uses and customs of high society?"

Always on their way back to Madrid the Excursionists indulge in poetic reflections—chiefly on Spanish grandeur that has been, for that is the traditional ideation of the race. Seldom does it occur to the chronicler who tells all this to mention one pertinent fact concerning the monument visited—date, architect, subsequent modifications, or whether it is of real merit. And if the place of pilgrimage lies off the railroad, of course he scorns all mention of the manner of reaching it. We turn dejectedly from these earnest but prolix Pickwickians, and their "publication of news to the public." Much valuable information it undoubtedly contains, but Spanish information is like Scotch humor—it must be dug out. Perhaps the imposing row of volumes entitled "Spain and Her Monuments" will be better. The first that comes to hand treats of Catalonia. The author is himself a Catalan, one of that hard-working, methodical race despised for these very qualities by the lofty Castilian. (Without which qualities, incidentally, the national treasury would not be so full.) In antebellum days, the Castilian used to say scornfully of the Catalan that he was the German of Spain; but when the war came it was the Castilian who hugged the Teuton to his heart, while the so-called German of Spain went valiantly to the battlefields of France to fight for the Allies. But this is a digression. Let us see what we can learn about architecture in Catalonia.

The first sentence that greets us, on the first page, shows that when it comes to his own native soil, the shrewd Catalan is as abstract as the more poetic Castilian, the only difference being that he warns us, in the first breath, not to expect mere facts. "In the articles on monuments and famous works of architecture, our observations are made principally with relation to the poetic and philosophical aspect of the subject." Even our Catalan is hopeless.

We recall how, once in Salamanca, which is the Renaissance city, *par excellence,* of Spain, we were ransacking the University Library for data, when a distinguished member of the faculty offered a pamphlet written by himself. "But where did you get your information?" we asked innocently. "We have perused every available document without discovering a single fact, except in the case of the Cathedral, and its history has been published." "Information?" he repeats with hurt expression.

"Facts? Why, this is a literary appreciation of our beloved Salamanca."

Clearly, to the Spanish author, literature and facts are as opposed as the two poles. He believes, with Augustus Birrell, that literature is one thing and sworn testimony another. How different from Carlyle, who spoke of his love of facts as his "stubborn realism," and who said of Harriet Martineau's book on American travel that her one page on the way Daniel Webster used to stand, hands in pockets, before his grate fire, was worth all the poetry, politics, philosophy and economics in the many remaining pages. "Give Carlyle a fact," it has been said of the great historian, "and he loaded you with thanks; theorize or indulge in abstractions and you were rewarded with the most vivid abuse." One dreads to think of the malisons the choleric Scotchman would have heaped upon Spanish rhapsodists and theorists had his fate been to prepare a history of Spanish architecture, gathered from Spanish sources, instead of a history of Frederic the Great, gathered from German.

MILDRED STAPLEY.

The Old West Church.

In looking up some material in regard to the Charles Street Meeting House, Boston, I came across some notes on the West Church, which was built at about the same time. In "The Georgian Period" the authorship of the West Church is attributed to Asher Benjamin, and in the reprint of Asher Benjamin's work is a design almost identical with the façade of this edifice. I referred to this in a talk I was giving on architecture and architectural books at the Public Library, and shortly afterward Mr. Buckley, of the Library, brought me a copy of the Columbian Centinel (spelled with a C!) of Nov. 29, 1806, referring to the laying of the corner stone on April 4 of that year, and to the completion on November 27, giving the names of the building committee, and Asher Benjamin as the architect.

The Charles Street Meeting House was built in 1807, but so far I have been unable to find the name of the architect, although

it is a simple and good example of the style used by Charles Bulfinch and Asher Benjamin.

FRANK A. BOURNE.

Artificial Daylight Achieved by a British Invention.

According to the American Chamber of Commerce in London, a light has been perfected in Great Britain which surpasses any existing arrangement of artificial light, and is a very close approximation of actual daylight. The apparatus consists of a high-power electric light bulb, fitted with a cup-shaped opaque reflector, the silvered inner side of which reflects the light against a parasol-shaped screen placed above the light. The screen is lined with small patches of different colors, arranged according to a formula worked out empirically by Mr. Shoringham, the inventor, and carefully tested and perfected in the Optical Engineering Department of the Imperial College of Science and Technology.

The light thrown down from the screen is said to show colors almost as they appear in full daylight. A test was made with such articles as colored wools, Chinese enamels, pastels and color prints, each being subjected successively to daylight, ordinary electric light and the new Shoringham light. Under the new light delicate yellows were quite distinct, indigo blues were blue, cobalts had their full value, and violets lost the reddish shade which they display in electric light.

The American Chamber in London says a great future is expected for this invention in such uses as the lighting of show windows and art galleries, studio work of all kinds, dye-works, tea and tobacco blending, and many other industries. Color photography will also probably benefit. As is to be expected, a proportion of the illuminating value is lost in the process, and higher candle power has to be used, but 60 candle power bulbs were satisfactory for the experiments mentioned.

The memorial flagpole base illustrated on page 121 of the February issue is in Duluth, Minn., not in Minneapolis, as stated in the caption.

Vol. XLVII.   No. 5   MAY, 1920   Serial No. 260

Editor: MICHAEL A. MIKKELSEN   *Contributing Editor:* HERBERT CROLY
Business Manager: J. A. OAKLEY

Yearly Subscription—United States $3.00—Foreign $4.00—Single copies 35 cents. Entered May 22, 1902, as Second Class Matter, at New York, N. Y. Member Audit Bureau of Circulation.

PUBLISHED MONTHLY BY

THE ARCHITECTURAL RECORD COMPANY

115-119 WEST FORTIETH STREET, NEW YORK

F. T. MILLER, Pres.   W. D. HADSELL, Vice-Pres.   J. W. FRANK, Sec'y-Treas.   E. S. DODGE, Vice-Pres.

GARDENS OF CHARLES M. SCHWAB, ESQ., LORETTO, PA.
CHARLES WELLFORD LEAVITT, LANDSCAPE ENGINEER.

Evergreen Court, with Bronze Group of Orpheus by John Gregory, Sculptor.
Planting of Boxwoods, American Arbor Vitae and Native White Pine.

THE
ARCHITECTVRAL
RECORD

VOLVME XLVII  **NVMBER V**

MAY, 1920

The GARDENS OF
CHARLES M. SCHWAB, E^SQ.
LORETTO, PA.

CHARLES WELLFORD LEAVITT, LANDSCAPE ENGINEER
BY ROBERT IMLAY

THE gardens of Mr. Charles M. Schwab at Loretto, Pennsylvania, are of unusual interest among monumental American gardens. In creating them, Mr. Leavitt has done something more than display high professional skill. Skill indeed his design possesses; but it has a larger merit, for the gardens are finely expressive of the landscape of the locality and of a quaint settlement in the Alleghanies of western Pennsylvania.

One cannot praise enough this aim of capturing the spirit of a locality in garden art. It is the quality which too often is missing in great gardens in America.

This is unfortunate, because only through such intimate local expressiveness can arise an American style of garden design. Expressiveness and symbolism in a garden are not simply a matter of using local tree and plant forms; they should be carried imaginatively into all the elements of the whole design, in all its features of architecture and sculpture. It would seem as if designers have become so immersed in the task of trying to equal the extraordinary technical skill in design of the historic European gardens, concerning themselves with researches into motives of technique, that they have overlooked the quality of the extraordinary local expression of these same gardens. Those of Italy are wonderful, not simply as masterworks of the technique of garden design; much of the real art of each of them, as in the case of d' Este at Tivoli, Lante at Bagnaia, the Boboli at Florence, the Farnese at Caprarola, lies in their remarkable neighborhood expression, whether it be the spacious, worldly majesty of a suburban villa of Rome in the Campagna, luxurious, sensuous, southern; or the simpler, more countrylike situation on a northern hillslope, sequestered and homelike, in exquisitely delicate scale; or the palatial urban surroundings of the City of Florence; or else the bold, bleak setting on the mountainside, perched high above the valleys that extend away to the southward, amid the oaks and pines tossed by the great winds, rustic, rugged, even a little stern. Although these gardens are characteristically Italian, the local expression of each would be totally out of harmony in the setting of the others. In fact, they are all the more Italian, because they are so intimately rooted in their own locality. This same local fitness is evident in the gardens of France and England, though perhaps to a lesser extent, since these countries do not have the wide range of landscape found in Italy.

America, in a like way, must attain the same local expressiveness, in our great variety of landscapes. Our gardens should symbolize local conditions of land and light and atmosphere and color, trees and shrubs and flowers and rocks, and they should also contrive to gain some of the human flavor and whatever background the district may have come to possess in the passage of years. Until such local personality is expressed, our gardens will be more or less arbitrary arrangements of geometrical forms. Their geometry will be unimaginative; and, in art, there is nothing more uninspiring than geometry that is without meaning. Particularly is this true of planting. Such intimate elements of nature can hardly take on the form of human art unless it be pecularly appropriate and harmonious. Perhaps this perfunctory use of the mathematics of form in gar-

dens explains why some landscape designers have gone to the other extreme, which is that of seeking a freer, more naturalistic arrangement. They have sought a sincerer treatment through ignoring or slighting the geometry, avoiding formality by skimping the architecture and sculpture and arranging the planting in a naturalistic manner. But designs of this type are just as superficial in their way as the other type. They are weak in form and they lack character and contrast.

Thus the great need of garden design today—like architecture, be it said—is traditions of local expression; traditions which will develop personality and craftsmanship in our garden art. And, since big things grow from little beginnings—a truth that is particularly evident in the matter of background and traditions—such a local, vernacular expression will arise in any district through long experience in the simple gardens of small houses, in the planting of farms and along roads and in pastures. Much of this experience will be unconscious, and the keen designer of a great garden, searching for local flavor, may somewhat anticipate the evolution of a local garden tradition by observing, in the neighborhood where his garden is to be located, such characteristic use of stone and plant and flower in sunlight as will aid him in gaining the local landscape expression in his design. Then he will further try to incorporate in it the human atmosphere local in the place.

Such appears to have been the purpose of Mr. Leavitt in this great garden. In a large measure he has attained it. To understand his success, an idea should be had of the landscape and human character of the district.

Loretto lies about one hundred miles east of Pittsburgh, in the Alleghenies. It is in a district of broad rolling hills and wide valleys, of no great differences in heights, though all of it is high in elevation above the sea. Thus, notwithstanding its rather gentle hill slopes, its great elevation gives it the climate of mountains. It has turns of mist, swift changes from bright sun to clouds, with gusts and squalls playing over the woods and farmlands and pastures—a characteristic landscape of eastern America. With such a rugged climate go the trees and plants of the district—white pines and sugar maples, native thorns with their gnarled branches. On the hillsides years of the eighteenth century, when, in 1799, Vallié Gallitzin, a Jesuit missionary, dedicated the first church of St. Michael's there. Fr. Gallitzin was a Russian nobleman who came to this country, entering the ranks of the So-

VIEW FROM MAIN ENTRANCE GATE ACROSS THE PIAZZA AT THE
INTERSECTION OF THE STATE HIGHROAD WITH .
THE VILLAGE STREET.

and in the pastures are wild crab-apples, fragrant, and, when in blossoms, intense with hues of pink and white against the evergreens. Mr. Leavitt has made good use of these native trees, and besides has brought in cedars from Massachusetts, near Cape Cod.

The human characteristics of this locality are unusual, of much romantic charm. Loretto was founded in the last ciety of Jesus, and, at the order of Bishop Carroll of Baltimore, went into western Pennsylvania. Loretto is, therefore, on the edge of that pioneer America, stretching westward from the Appalachians, which was reclaimed during the nineteenth century. Even before that, however, in colonial times, it was not far east of the route of the French voyageurs of Canada as they traveled

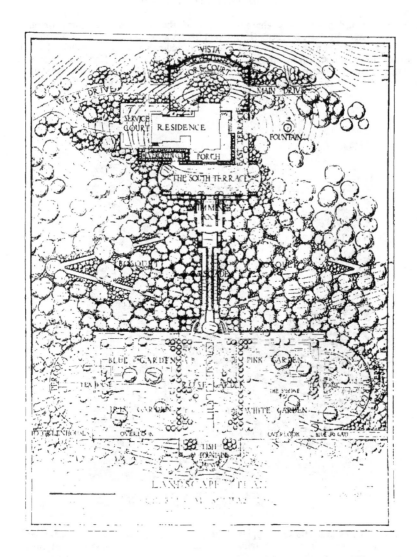

PLAN OF HOUSE AND GARDENS OF
THE ESTATE OF CHARLES M. SCHWAB,
ESQ., LORETTO, PA. CHARLES WELL-
FORD LEAVITT, LANDSCAPE ENGINEER.

LANDSCAPE PLAN OF THE ESTATE OF CHARLES
M. SCHWAB, ESQ., LORETTO, PA. CHARLES
WELLFORD LEAVITT, LANDSCAPE ENGINEER.

from Quebec to St. Louis and Louisiana by way of Lake Erie, Forts Presque Isle and Duquesne—now the cities of Erie and Pittsburgh—and on down the Ohio river. In the sixteenth, seventeenth and eighteenth centuries it was a country disputed between the Indian tribes and the French and English trappers and hunters and soldiers; a region of resolute, hardy spirits, whose lawless ways were mitigated only by the unflinching courage of the missionaries, Such was the romantic birth of Loretto, which remains, to-day, a tiny, undisturbed, unambitious American village, of Catholic atmosphere and un-English ancestry. It is thus unique, though had it not been the birth place of Mr. Schwab, it would no doubt have continued to slumber unvexed by any undue attention from the outside world.

This distinctiveness of the humanity of the countryside Mr. Leavitt has well expressed in the architecture of the estate. It is seen in the village cross road, with its tall cross, out of which the road to Mr. Schwab's house leads; in the buildings and walls and entrance gates of the estate, particularly in the charming farm group which Messrs. Murphy and Dana cooperated with Mr. Leavitt in creating. It also shows in touches in the garden, in the lower level, and one seems to feel it in the planting. Since the gardens are our main interest, the rest of the estate, including the house, may be only mentioned. It consists of seven hundred acres, mostly old farmland, woods and pasture, and contains, besides the house with its terraces, service appurtenances and roadways, an immense vegetable and fruit garden, two farm groups, greenhouses, a small open air theatre, a little rustic cottage used as a retreat solely by the owner, a golf links, and the great garden itself. The design of such a work was a varied enterprise, and in accomplishing it Mr. Leavitt called in many artists to cooperate with him, particularly Messrs. Murphy and Dana, the architects.

The house lies on the crest of a low hill, about sixty feet above the cross roads of Loretto. Its wide, simple greensward expanse, with balustraded terrace, looks toward the south, affording a superb view over the country. A smaller, more secluded terrace, lies along the service wing of the house a few steps lower, and with slightly more planting and garden furniture. To the east is an open lawn on the top of the hill, with a flagpole on the axis of the great terrace. Down from the terrace, alongside its retaining wall, lead steps to the water feature which carries down the slope to the great garden. To build the garden a cut was made into the hill, a retaining wall constructed against it, and a fill brought into the valley, where another retaining wall lifts the garden above the main highway that runs from Pittsburgh to Philadelphia. The course of the highway was changed at this point. Thus the garden lies protected on the south slope of a hill, yet overlooking another valley. The space between the garden and the house is wooded with white pines, forming a bosquet through which is cut the main axis of the water feature and cascade. All this arrangement is evident in the plans.

One may gain an idea of the size of the whole from the following dimensions: The distance from the great terrace to the garden is 247 feet, the drop in level being fifty feet in this distance. The main garden is 190 feet wide and 600 feet long. The width of the lily pools which centre across the garden is twelve feet. The highway is ten feet or more below the garden. The design, therefore, derives much character from these decisive changes in level.

Here, then, are the main features of the design—the southern hillslope and the three grand divisions of the garden lying parallel across it. They include the great terrace of the house, the bosquet and the formal garden, all tied together chiefly by the water treatment of fountains, cascade, garden pools and fish fountain at the end, with steps and ramps forming a vista from the house over the landscape. The effect from the house is therefore not so much that of a garden cut out of the landscape, a thing apart from it, but, instead, that of a beautiful view of sky, hills, woods and open spaces, in the centre of which is the

CASCADE, WITH DOUBLE STAIRCASE DESCENDING
FROM THE RESIDENCE THROUGH THE BOSQUET
OF WHITE PINE TO THE ROSE GARDEN.

garden, the heart of the whole landscape scene. The thick planting of the bosquet at the sides of the water treatment furnishes a frequent enframement of this splendid vista.

This able scheme of design has been

tremely architectural and monumental; while the rest of the garden is more naturalistic, contains less architecture, and that architecture—for the most part of walls and colonnades of the great rounded ends—is less sophisticated and more

THE EAST "GRIFFIN," IN LIMESTONE, AT THE LOWER BASIN OF THE CASCADE, PAUL MANSHIP, SCULPTOR.

worked out in a highly interesting fashion. The basis of it all is the geometry, the mechanism of the design, seen both in the pattern of the plan and its relief in walls, stairs, water and other architectural elements.

One may say of the mathematics of the plan that they are well thought out, well proportioned, and, on the whole, well balanced. The water feature is ex-

rustic in character. It might be thought that this contrast has been carried almost too far; that more harmony and co-ordination in design between water feature and main garden would have resulted if more water elements had been introduced into the main garden.

In respect to the minor details, the fuller shapes and great round ends of the flower garden seem slightly at vari-

THE ROSE GARDEN WITH ITS THREE LILY POOLS AND LONG GRASS WALKS, AND PLANTING OF RED CEDAR.

VIEW ALONG THE MAIN AXIS, LOOKING FROM THE SWIMMING POOL LEVEL DOWN THE CASCADE.

TWO OF THE LIMESTONE "CARYATIDES," HENRI
CRENIER, SCULPTOR, ON THE BALUSTRADE
OF THE ROSE GARDEN ABOVE THE VALLEY.

FISH FOUNTAIN IN ROSE GARDEN, WITH LIMESTONE "CARYATIDES" AND BRONZE FOUNTAIN. HENRI CRENIER, SCULPTOR.

DETAIL OF THE CASCADE WITH RAMPS
OF GRASS AND STONE AND PLANTING OF
LAUREL BORDER AND SPREADING EVER-
GREEN (JUNIPERIS TAMARICIFOLIA).

ance with the sharper, more angular shapes of the cascade. This slight inharmony extends to the design of the bosquet, although the owner did not care to develop the bosquet. On the design as presented, nevertheless, it is well to remember that the bosquet hardly serves as an interesting contrast to the open garden and a relief from its openness and sun and winds, nor does it serve as a transition from the highly abstract geometry of the garden to the naturalistic design of the rest of the estate. Except for two ramps, it is undeveloped. Thus, in its general features, there is a slight inconsistency and disharmony in the design.

The details of the scheme are of the highest excellence. Again the water treatment figures prominently in this part of the achievement. The photographs show the splendid execution, the interest and charm, the monumental character, at the same time expressing the locality. The color aids in the effect. There is a small amount of smooth faced ashlar of limestone, but most of the stone is local, a warm, rich, light tawny yellow of unusual beauty. It has been excellently handled, as the details show. In the balustrades and in the cascade and fountains of the water treatment the limestone appears. Here again in the water feature is a slight disharmony of lines and slopes in plan and in relief. The angularity and segments of the steps and walls and balustrades is not altogether suited to the sinuous, subtle curving of the cascade. Lower down the uncompromising rectangles of the lily pool, with their flat, unmoulded curbs, harmonize neither with the sinuosity of the cascade above nor with the fish fountain at the other end. This rectangularity, if I may use the word, deserves comment, because it is one of the most persistent minor faults in present day design, of all types, where the most complex, delicate, graceful forms are often brutally marred by having rectangles thrust among them. It may be noticed in the exterior of the office of J. P. Morgan & Co. on Wall street, New York—a fine building, indeed, almost Greek in refinement and elegance of form; but its walls are cut with

huge rectangular windows, great holes without any relieving forms of architecture or chamfer or panelled splay to harmonize them with the wide flowing curve of the base below or with the luxurious, Corinthian-like cornice above, This particular fault is also common in interiors. It should be made clear, however, that the faults in the Loretto garden are those of detail, and that they do not greatly mar the excellence of the whole. All that may be said is that the design has not quite that extraordinary consistency and closely woven harmony of the old Italian models, nor of the designs of Mr. Platt or of Mr. Stanford White in this country.

One excellence the architecture of Mr. Leavitt's design embodies to a high degree. It has the true garden scale. This is a virtue not so well understood in garden art in this country. One may not easily define it. However, garden scale is quite different from the scale of buildings, particularly of buildings in the city. It is peculiarly expressive of the country, of the garden, and this is perhaps its secret. Robustness and heaviness are not necessarily its characteristics, though often these are noted in it. It is bound up with natural aspects of color and of sunlight, of great play and contrast and vivacity of light and shade, of sculpturesque and dramatic qualities. It is in harmony with outdoors, of the earth and growing things, often rocky instead of stony. Besides this intimate harmony with nature in the architecture of the garden, it has a human element no less distinctive. It symbolizes the country— the rural, the rustic, the romantic, even with touches of the fantastic, and the grotesque, the jovial, the burlesque and a hearty country humor.

It is the character of Twelfth Night rather than of the Merchant of Venice.

All these qualities belong in the expression of the architecture and sculpture of the garden, in varying degrees in the different parts of the garden. Often the terraces near the house may partake of it to the extent of forming a transition between the garden and the more sophisticated, quieter architecture of the buildings. In the more open and frequented parts of the garden, the scale and the architecture is primmer, but distinctively expressive of the country, and only in the bosquet and in the outlying features may it yield to pure fancy. All the old European garden architectures have this sensitive expression to the highest degree; but in America it is neglected, even in our best gardens, where the scale is apt to be more like that of buildings, or is too delicate, or else too citified to be in keeping with the country.

Of course, such unusual expression in architectural design is almost too difficult for the modern architect. He is too occupied with buildings, too carefully trained in academic form and rigid, puristic taste for such phantasy of design. For him, form is bound up too much with the functional expression of construction, to feel it almost as pure modelling in light and shade. In truth, the architectural elements in a garden are hardly architecture at all, as we know it in its modern specialized form. It is only slightly constructional. It is rather sculpture. Of course, the architect may best conceive the scheme of design and its main garden features; but he can hardly work out so well as could the sculptor the details, not of statuary only, but of pedestals, fountains, water motives, even stairs and balustrades and walls and stonework—that is, and here is the drawback, if the modern sculptor were enterprising and had fitted himself to cover the whole range of sculptural design, and had not gone to the extreme of specialization by absorbing himself in the study of the human figure. The human figure is the apex of the sculptor's art; but he might not be harmed if he cultivated a broader interest and did not feel obliged to call upon the architect to design the pedestals or settings or even the lettering—purely a sculptor's task—of his figures, as is now the practice. There is talk of the painter's too great concentration upon "easel painting"; so one may think that the sculptor is too devoted to the gallery piece.

However this may be, Mr. Leavitt, all things considered, has successfully bridged the gap left by the sculptors. For the purely figure side of the sculpture at Loretto he was fortunate enough to have Mr. Schwab call in a group of well-known American sculptors. Mr. Paul Manship supplied some characteristic statues, particularly the bronze of the east fountain and the stone griffins at the foot of the cascade. Mr. John Gregory did the exquisite bronze of Orpheus at the Evergreen Court. Here also are works by Miss Ann Hyatt, Mr. C. A. Heber, and animal reliefs by Mr. Fred S. R. Roth. But perhaps the figures that have best caught the spirit and scale of a garden of the country are the remarkable caryatides of the fish fountain. These are bold vertical elements of design placed at the end of the vista from the house down the main axis of the water treatment. Among these the male figure deserves special notice for its rustic character, vigorous modelling, splendid light and shade, which the artist has obtained without losing refinement. They are the creation of Mr. Henri Crenier, a young Franco-American.

There is not, however, one jovial imp or satyr in the whole collection. Nor do we note our American counterpart of these antique terrors of the landscape, the Indians. Indians would well express the legendary history of Loretto, of its old pioneer-voyageur country. I mean real, deliciously ugly, wicked-looking redskins—such as used to fascinate us in "Buffalo Bill." Indians might give us Americans a moral equivalent for satyrs in our gardens. Besides, the Indian has one advantage over the satyr in claiming admission to our gardens. The school legends, no matter how harshly they treated his character, never attacked his morals. So far as we know to the contrary, in that respect he was always a knightly gentleman, and hence he could easily pass the American censor. So may our sculptors create some warlike Indians for us! We need a garden mythology badly. Unfortunately, all the sculptured Indians are handsome, gentlemanly appearing young men, who could not bear to tomahawk a chicken. They are too respectable even to be schoolbook heroes. One fears that many of our sculptors are a little too *précieux*

DETAIL OF THE ROSE GARDEN,
WITH ONE OF THE FOUR ETAIN
OIL JARS, PAUL MANSHIP, SCULPTOR.

PLANTING IN THE ROSE GARDEN OF
RED CEDARS AND OLD BOXWOODS.

THE NORTH LILY POOL IN CENTRE OF GARDEN
ON MAIN AXIS. PLANTING OF SUGAR MAPLE,
AND, IN FRONT, BORDERS OF HELIOTROPE
SURROUNDING ORANGE TREES IN STONE VASES.

for the hearty atmosphere of the country.

No description of the art of Loretto could end without calling attention to the planting. Indeed, it merits more notice than anything else. Unfortunately the maples and native thorns have been used, re-inforced by the stately cedars brought from Massachusetts pastures. These trees mainly, and shrubs have been grouped with great skill and with a fine taste too seldom found. Everyone

BLUE JAY GATE, OR THE VEHICLE ENTRANCE TO THE WHITE
GARDEN. MASONRY OF NATIVE PATTON SANDSTONE
IN WARM LIGHT-BROWN TINTS.

one finds it nearly impossible to convey clear ideas of planting in photographs or text. The picture of the landscape, the light, and the variety of growing things must be seen to be felt in reality. In the dilemma few observations must suffice.

I have referred to the characteristic trees of the region and how Mr. Leavitt has used them in the design; how the white pines especially and the hemlocks, knows of the stilted planting of evergreens; of the use of spotty, fussy, flower beds and paths. These may be harmonized in European gardens by the soft mellow light, often misty, of England or France; but in our light, such self-conscious design shows up clearly, every detail baldly revealed. We have not dramatic statuesque tree forms like the Italian stone pines and cedars, and we cannot succeed with exaggerated efforts to rival these. At the other extreme is the type of planting which is more naturalistic, scarcely designed at all, and utterly out of keeping with the strict geometrical shapes of the garden. Thus of the Loretto garden points the way, as a careful study will show. The photograph of the lily pools illustrates the wonderful design and modelling of the planting. Here you notice the tall cedars of the background, the vertical elements

THE EAST TERRACE OPENING ONTO THE FORECOURT AND THE MALL, WITH BACKGROUND OF GIANT WHITE PINE.

in American garden design there seems to be two conflicting practices in planting. One slights design; the other exaggerates it. Neither understands the possibilities or limitations of our hard sunlight, or the way to use native plant forms as elements of design, at once reinforcing and softening the geometry of the garden. Clearly much experience is to be gained here, and the planting carefully composed, but not too obviously so; the rounder, fuller shapes of the box filling the angle between the cedars and the low shrubs—again not too obviously, nor too solidly, affording big depths of shadow; and the lower, flatter shrubs and patches of flower beds and greensward. The whole is an extraordinary arrangement of design in contrasting shapes and planes, in striking

405

SHRINE IN THE WHITE FLOWER GARDEN,
WITH MARBLE STATUE, "THE SPIRIT OF
THE GARDEN." HENRI CRENIER, SCULPTOR.
PLANTING OF SUGAR MAPLE AND BOXWOODS.

but subtle artistry. It is not often that one sees such personality and such character in planting. It shows a true appreciation of how to use growing forms in the arrangement of art. Effective also .is the use of this planting in connection with the architecture, much as furniture is arranged in a room. Examples of this are the shrubs of laurel that fill the space between the ramps and the troughs of the cascade, the vines at the base of the caryatides, the trail-

ing juniper planting at the fish fountain, and lastly the exquisite simple planting of the east terrace near the house.

Such design points the way towards obtaining character in planting; not only character of technical skill, but the local flavor of the neighborhood. It is the expression of locality in a formal garden that alone may make its rigid geometry seem entirely appropriate, or even endurable in our bold, rough landscapes and clear, vivid sunlight.

SMALL CIRCULAR PERGOLA AT THE INTERSECTION OF THE FRUIT
GARDEN AND THE CUT-FLOWER GARDEN, WITH BRONZE
FIGURE OF "ABUNDANCE." C. A. HEBER, SCULPTOR.

RENAISSANCE ARCHITECTVRE AND ITS CRITICS

By A.D.F. HAMLIN

PART IV - *Construction & Expression*

YOU were aware, Sire, that we do not care for the things about which we are ignorant, and that one must know what architecture signifies, to esteem it as it deserves." In these words, addressed by the great Blondel to Louis XIV, we may find one explanation of the attitude of the hostile critics with some of whose charges against Renaissance architecture I have tried to deal in previous papers of this series.* They are hostile to the Renaissance, because they do not understand it. With all their scholarship, which is often thorough and sometimes profound, they have failed to grasp its real character or penetrate to its true inner content and significance.

This failure is due to one or more of several causes. The first is a strong prepossession in favor of Greek or Gothic architecture resulting from long previous preoccupation with the study of these styles, combined with an inability to approve a style differing so widely as does that of the Renaissance from those which have previously absorbed their interest. The second cause is the fact that, with hardly an exception, these critics are untrained in the profession and practice of architecture. Thus one critic commends Michelozzi's shallow window reveals in the Riccardi palace, "since the farther out the glass is placed the less will be the shadow thrown upon it, while the interior reveal . . . reflects light into the interior." That is, the amount of light depends upon the position of the glass! These critics are literary critics, scholars, specialists in other forms of art, who approach their sub-

*The Architectural Record for August and September, 1917, and July, 1919.

ject from the outside, with little or no experience of the psychology, of the processes, the conditions and methods of architectural design, and without technical training in practical construction. Having first assumed as axiomatic certain philosophical maxims and criteria of their own, and illustrated these by carefully selected examples from Greek or Gothic art, they apply these maxims and criteria in their own way to carefully selected examples of Renaissance architecture for its condemnation. In this criticism those facts, features and aspects which might count against this condemnation are generally overlooked or minimized. Underlying this procedure there seems to be a fundamental misunderstanding of the true purpose and function of architecture itself. It is treated as a symbol, as a philosophy, as an expression of sentiments, religious ideas, morals, social character and movements, as almost anything except what it really is—an art based on practical needs, serving utilitarian purposes by the use of available materials, under the limitations of climate, environment and tradition, by the application of human science and common sense inspired by the love of beauty. Race, religion, social and political changes, the great movements of human thought, all have their influence on architecture, but they are not architecture, and architecture "expresses" them only in so far and in such manner as these forces act upon the architects who try to solve these very practical problems, and on their clients or employers who provide the problems and the means for their solution. The expression of moral, religious and social ideals in architecture is real, but incidental. It is a confusion of ideas to unload upon architecture—that is, upon the architects—the praise or the blame of the forces under which they work, except in so far as they—the architects— have rightly or wrongly used or resisted these forces. And that is to be determined not by *a priori* reasoning, but by the testimony of the works themselves.

A third reason for the inadequate comprehension of the architecture of the Renaissance by these critics may be found in their too exclusive preoccupation with façades and details, which is in turn due to their general approach to the subject from the outside. The details are treated as if they were the architecture, instead of the form-alphabet by whose means the architectural conception is expressed. They are an essential part of the architecture; they constitute one of its criteria, but only one, and the

architecture of the Renaissance is something behind and under its details and much bigger than they. The form and mass of the building, the scheme of its plan, the interior effect, the structural design, even in many cases the façade composition as distinguished from its details, are slighted in these criticisms in order to concentrate attention on the orders and decorative details.

One of the most impressive interiors of modern times is that of Alberti's church of San Andrea at Mantua. It illustrates perfectly what Alberti meant by "restoring the good ancient manner." for its grandeur of scale, its simplicity of scheme and its system of internal buttressing are all thoroughly Roman; yet it is a wholly original conception, copying as a whole no assignable Roman example. Yet the hostile critics, even when they grant a few words of praise

THE CERTOSA AT PAVIA: WEST FRONT—EXTERNAL DETAILS EMPLOYED AS SURFACE ORNAMENT.

PALAZZO DEL CONSIGLIO, VERONA. DESIGN APPROACHED FROM THE SIDE OF
DECORATIVE EFFECT.

to this superb interior, generally devote most of their criticism to the west front, in an effort to prove it a copy of a Roman arch of triumph. The marvelous variety of plan and almost invariable success of effect, of the North Italian types of domical church, are hardly even alluded to by these critics; or if the allusion is made it is usually coupled with fault-finding with details of the orders, external or internal.

Fergusson, as we have seen, denies to the Italian Renaissance architecture the quality of truthfulness. This is, next to the charge of copyism, the accusation most frequently laid against the Renaissance; it has been in different forms reiterated by Ruskin, by Moore, by Porter, by Statham and by others. The accusation is based upon the fact that, as a general rule, Renaissance buildings do not, externally at least, "express construction"; that their external details were not designed to perform any essential function in the structural scheme of the building; and that many of them, designed originally for one or another structural function, are employed solely as surface ornaments, suggesting a structural framework which does not exist. The words "sham" and "make-believe" are applied to this practice, and the classic orders, above all the combination of the arch with an order, come in for especial censure.

Fergusson, moreover, contends that such buildings as St. Peter's at Rome and St. Paul's at London are examples of untruthfulness, because, though dressed in Roman details, they are not Roman (that is, antique Roman) buildings. Just what he means by this charge —just wherein the untruthfulness lies— is not quite clear. Probably Fergusson's idea would have been better expressed by reversing the order and charging that

410

these two great buildings and others like them, not being ancient Roman buildings (which of course they could not possibly be), should not have been designed with ancient Roman details. If this was his meaning, it was merely another form of his charge of "reviving a dead style" or "designing in a dead language." I briefly answered this charge in my last paper (July, 1919); I will only add to that answer that I can think of no reasons in the domain of artistic "morals" or of common sense to forbid one's using Roman architectural forms whenever they serve better than any other forms to express and carry out the architectural conception. Considering the fact that in Italy there never was a time when they were not in use, from the days of the Roman Empire down to the present day, we may rightly call them the traditional architectural vernacular of the Italians. Fergusson admits this on an early page of his "History of Modern Architecture," but seems to forget how absurd it renders his charge that the use by the Italians of their traditional architectural vernacular was "designing in a dead language." It would be about as reasonable to say that we write in a dead language when we use the Roman alphabet.

II.

What do the critics mean by "the truthful expression of construction"? The words in themselves are clear enough, but what is their application by the critics? Apparently they mean (a) that the structural system of a building should be expressed in and by its external design; and (b) that no decorative forms should be employed that do not reveal, suggest or express this structural framework or in themselves perform a definite structural function. Any architectural design, therefore, that fails in either respect is not a truthful design and should be condemned.

The contention I have above tried to analyze has, by virtue of its constant and insistent reiteration, obtained such wide and unquestioning acceptance that to attack its validity must seem to many a reader a surprising piece of philistinism, almost of artistic immorality! Moral catchwords have great power with the multitude, and when a critic can use the words "untruthful" and "false" of a design, the average reader accepts its condemnation without question. But it behooves the thoughtful student to examine carefully into the basis, the origin and the applications of the criterion of "truthfulness in the expression of construction" before he yields absolute assent to the condemnation pronounced by the critic. For to accept its absolute and universal validity is to assent to the whole mass of sweeping condemnation visited by the hostile critics upon nearly all the architecture of the Renaissance as well as upon nearly all ancient Roman architecture. They are quite correct in claiming that in these two architectures the external dress rarely expresses the construction in any such way as that in which the forms of Gothic architecture express its structural system; while the decorative details of these styles seldom perform any real structural function in the edifices they adorn.

But the reader who reflects on the implications of this contention, who considers the significance of so sweeping a condemnation of human activity in creative art, who meditates upon this imputation of fundamental error, of untruthfulness and love of sham and pretence to one of the most active-minded and progressive of peoples through two periods of centuries of extraordinary productiveness in architecture, who moreover recalls his own impressions of wonder and delight in the contemplation of many of the works thus visited with artistic censure—such a reader may wisely question whether the premise from which it flows is correct.

This premise is closely connected with the assumption that Gothic architecture, especially that of the thirteenth century in Northern France, should be the norm and criterion by which to judge all architecture; and since in that architecture the structural system is clearly expressed by the exterior form and decorative details, all architectures which

411

conform to this principle are good architectures. The Romans violated it often, the Renaissance builders very often; therefore these are bad architectures.

Whether the contention in this premise results from the assumption that the French Gothic is the norm for all styles, or this exaltation of the French Gothic is the result of the assumption of the premise as an axiom, makes little difference. Both contentions are pure assumptions and must be tested by the facts. Both are open to question and must be defended by reasoning based on adequate observation and discussion of all relevant considerations.

Both assumptions are defective because based on too narrow a field of observation. So far as they rest on facts they appear to be derived from the study of one class of buildings—those for religious worship—comprising two main groups: the antique temple, especially the Egyptian and the Greek, and the medieval cathedral. All the buildings in these groups were erected for a like general purpose; each is an isolated monument, standing in the open, built of stone, which was the only material generally available, and under certain definite conditions of society, government, religion, race, situation, climate and resources. It was inevitable that the Egyptian, the Greek and the medieval builder should have built as each did; and the frank expression of the structural system was almost equally inevitable, given the material employed, the purpose of the building and the conditions under which the style was developed.

But it is a universal and inescapable law of artistic and peculiarly of architectural progress, a law rooted in human nature, that after the evolution of structural forms to meet practical necessities, and the development of their decorative treatment, have culminated, the force of tradition continues the use of these forms as decoration, even when and where they are no longer needed structurally. To claim that this is false art is to set up a purely transcendental kind of criticism which ignores the inescapable laws of human psychology in design. In every age, in all the arts, in all styles, one may trace the operation of this law. The sloping walls of the Egyptian temple do not express construction, but are obvious traditional reminiscences of primitive mud building. The quite useless cavetto cornice preserves the memory of the papyrus stalks which formed part of the primitive structural framework of papyrus and mud; it serves a purely decorative purpose. The flaring capitals of the Egyptian campaniform columns perform no structural function whatever; they are purely decorative survivals of forms which once had a definite use and function. The triglyphs, mutules and guttae of the Greek Doric temple and the useless volutes and dentils of the Ionic order are further examples of the use as ornament of details whose structural origin has been forgotten. So also the deep coffering of the Greek pteroma ceilings, a treatment quite foreign to stone construction but preserving the tradition of panels framed in wood, is as deserving of the opprobrious term of "sham" as many of the Renaissance decorative details to which it has been applied by some critics.

The whole history of Gothic architecture is likewise a record of continual successive transformations of structural forms and members into mere ornaments. Gables, pinnacles and tracery are thus converted from purely structural to purely decorative uses—not in the decline of the style but in the very hey-day of its culmination in the middle period; from the very first the vaulting-shaft was made an essential part of the decorative system of the interior, although, as I have shown in a previous paper* it was always a superfluous member, seeming to carry the vaulting which is really supported by the masonry behind it. It is exactly as "false," as truly a "sham," as the engaged columns of Roman and Renaissance architecture,

*See the Architectural Record for January, 1917, page 11.

against which the transcendental critics lay so heavy a charge of insincerity and deception.

The decorative use of structural members is thus seen to have always been a matter of taste. The assumption that it is *per se* to be condemned is not supported by the facts of architectural history. Every case of its occurrence must be judged on its merits. Is the use of the pilaster, the column, the vaulting-shaft, the decorative pediment, the entablature dividing the stories, the open-work gable, the pinnacle, the coffered ceiling, justified by the value of its decorative effect? Opinions may differ as to any specific case, but the critic cannot in-

voke against it an alleged law founded, after all, on a pure assumption.

Whatever may be the merit of the contention we are discussing as an abstract proposition, it would be found inapplicable to many classes of buildings, for many systems of construction and many

BAPTISTERY OF FLORENCE. DOME CONCEALED BY WALL OF DRUM
CARRIED UP TO SUPPORT PYRAMIDAL ROOF.

details of construction cannot be expressed externally. They constitute the hidden anatomy of the building, which, like that of the human body, although shaping it, is not revealed by it to the eye. The Gothic system of the stone skeleton, externally buttressed because the interior structure is too light, lofty and weak to stand alone, can hardly avoid being expressed externally. But

413

even in a Gothic building the vaulting—for whose sake the whole structural system has been contrived—is not expressed externally, but is concealed under a steep roof of timber and slate or lead. A building constructed with horizontal ceilings and with floors carried by beams instead of vaults cannot well express this construction either directly or indirectly on the exterior, except as it is suggested by the fenestration. In a building of complex plan, not a unitary or one-room edifice like a temple or church, the interior construction—all that does not abut in the external walls—is of necessity invisible. In a building between party walls the façade is perforce reduced to a practically flat composition of voids and solids which can only rarely be made to tell the story of the interior. It is evident in all these cases, as in many others, that the law of structural expression cannot be applied in a hard-and-fast manner; it must be variously interpreted, variously modified, even in many cases excepted from; in other words, it is open to discussion and amendment, and may prove to be not a law at all, but a variable criterion, perfectly just in some cases yet quite invalid in others.

Having reached this conclusion, the inquisitive reader who refuses to take his criteria ready-made may now go further and ask: "Why must an architectural design express construction? Is a building designed for the purpose of showing its construction, or the construction designed for the purpose of producing the building? Is construction the end or the means, the mistress or the servant of architecture?

These are questions that go to the very root and core of architectural criticism. They are not to be lightly brushed aside nor answered offhand.

If architecture may be properly defined, as I think it may, as "the art of building beautifully" or "the art of designing beautiful buildings," then the primary purpose of architecture is beauty, the giving of pleasure to the esthetic sense through visible form, and construction is the means to this end,

the servant and not the mistress of architecture. To design a building with primary reference to its beauty of visible form and to make the construction serve the purpose of giving stability to this form is at least as logical as to make the structural framework dominate the design, and subordinate the decorative treatment to the display or expression of that framework. Either procedure is logical in itself. Whether a given problem should be approached primarily from the side of construction, or from the side of beauty of form and detail and decorative effect, must depend upon the conditions of the problem—the purpose and nature of the building, the materials and resources available, the site and environment and other like conditions. There is no law of esthetic "morals" to compel the display of the internal structure, that is, of the means by which stability is effected. But it is imperative that a building shall *look* secure, capable of standing up; that the eye shall see an adequate support for every visible supported feature. The doctrine that the hidden strains, the invisible forces at work in a building, ought to be suggested or revealed and to be resisted by visible means is a pernicious doctrine, without basis in common reason. Only when the visible form of a structure itself suggests to the ordinary spectator the presence and action of some disruptive force does it become imperative to provide a visible resistance to that strain.

This objectionable doctrine is invoked with a certain plausibility by the hostile critics in condemnation of the most brilliant and original of the architectural inventions of the Renaissance—the lantern-bearing dome on a drum. They contend that the thrust of such a dome demands an external design having sufficient abutment to resist it with no aid from concealed chains or belts; or that failing this, the drum should be carried high enough to provide a vertical load sufficient to ensure the stability of the whole, and that the whole should then be covered with a protective roof up to the lantern. This was done, we are reminded, with the dome of the Florentine

Baptistery; and although this arrangement would have entirely concealed the magnificent dome for whose stability it should have been provided, Brunelleschi should nevertheless have made this sacrifice in the interests of "truthful" construction! And by parity of reasoning Michel Angelo should have done the same with the dome of St. Peter's!

and beautiful form possible, both lofty and spacious, with which to cover the vast unencumbered space where nave, choir and transepts meet. Not only would the proposed huge cylinder topped by a cone or pyramid have been a most

DOME OF CATHEDRAL OF FLORENCE. DESIGN EXPRESSES STRUCTURAL SYSTEM; INVISIBLE STRAINS RESISTED BY CONCEALED BELTS.

I think we may rejoice that these two Renaissance architects were wiser than their latter-day critics. Their purpose was indeed not to express construction, but to express the majesty and glory of the Church—a much nobler and loftier purpose—by the most imposing

woeful sacrifice of beauty to construction, but it would have produced an architectural solecism, one of the very "falsehoods" against which the critics are so severe. For it would have completely hidden the essential structure—the dome; and would have given to the lantern the appearance of resting on a low pyramid or cone of slate or lead! Such are the dilemmas into which we

DRUM OF ST. PETER'S. BUTTRESSES OF DRUM PRODUCE SATISFACTORY EXPRESSION OF STABILITY.

are sometimes led by the rigid application of this alleged axiom of esthetic morals to the masterpieces of the Renaissance.

This sort of criticism Mr. Geoffrey Scott, in his suggestive and informing book on "The Architecture of Humanism," has called the Mechanical Fallacy. "Why," says he "are we to conjure up the hidden forces of the dome and refuse to think of the chains which counteract them?" In other words, why may not a concealed resistance be opposed to a hidden force? What sense is there in forbidding the use of any rational, practical means that is effective in securing stability, provided the structure in its masses and details suggests stability and sufficiency of means to ends? Is a chain or belt esthetically immoral? Then surely all cramping and doweling of masonry, and all the elaborate medieval systems of concealed metal *chainages* described by Viollet-le-Duc, must be esthetically immoral, as being concealed devices for stability.

III

But the critics have another charge to make against both Roman and Renaissance architecture. The decorative forms employed, both on the exterior and interior, particularly the structural forms used for ornament, such as engaged columns and pilasters and wall-arcades, and pediments over doors and windows, are false, because they suggest a construction which does not really exist, at least as a part of the essential structure of the edifice. It is a fictitious construction, applied as a dress, and to strip it away would not endanger the real structure.

This is alleged, for example, of the entire system of façade decoration by pilasters and entablatures introduced by Alberti in the Rucellai Palace at Flor-

416

ence, and further developed by Bramante in his Roman works; of the similar use of pilasters in the interior of the Pazzi Chapel; and of the arch-and-order combination as a whole, wherever used. If the objection is well taken and is as serious and fundamental as the critics would have us believe, it condemns a very large part of the architecture of the Renaissance throughout Europe, as well as of the architecture of more modern times, and is, therefore, deserving of the most careful examination. This sweeping verdict, however, is just what some, at least, of the hostile critics intend, and they are not at all disturbed by the havoc it works among the masterpieces of whole ages and the reputations of great and famous men; nor do they hesitate at the slap it administers to all the multitudes of educated people, supposedly possessed of good sense and taste, who have admired and even still admire the artistic product of what

Ruskin calls "the foul torrent of the Renaissance."

But alas, this verdict does far more than this, for it condemns also the authors of a large part of the product of the Middle Ages, and sweeps away such a vast mass of gables, pinnacles, vaulting-shafts, and utterly "useless" moldings, traceries, false gargoyles and non-structural carvings, and then working back into the ages wrecks so much of Roman architecture, not sparing the Egyptians nor even the sacrosanct works of the Greeks, that the critics may themselves be inclined to cry Halt!

Is it not conceivable that the objection is after all not well taken, and that there may be a real justification for that whole extensive category of forms of decoration against which it has been raised?

A critical analysis of the objection seems to show that it contains two implications: that such pseudo-structural decoration is *useless* structurally, and

COURT OF FARNESE PALACE, ROME. EXAMPLE OF RENAISSANCE ARCH-AND-ORDER DESIGN.

417

that it is *deceptive*—a sham, as the critics like to call it. Or we may state these implications conversely thus: all decoration of an architectural character must be a part of the real structure of the edifice, and there must be no deception nor illusion in decoration. All this sounds plausible, and the reference to deception seems to imply some sort of moral dereliction. We hate most kinds of fraud, and are thus easily led to believe that we ought to be shocked at any and all artistic deception.

To this the rejoinder may be made that deception, or that kind of deception which we call illusion, is of the very essence of certain forms of art, and that such "deception" is enjoyable and not in the least objectionable. This, however, is not a sufficient reply, nor indeed, a fair one; for the illusions we enjoy—like those, for example, of the theatre—are illusions which we expect and desire. It can hardly be said that we particularly *desire* to be deceived by architectural forms; we certainly would not go out of our way for the purpose of experiencing an architectural illusion, as we do to experience the illusions of a theatrical stage and of the performance upon it. But it is fair to say that the alleged deceptiveness or falsehood or dishonesty (to use the language of the critics) of the architectural forms of the Renaissance is of no consequence whatever. That is to say, if these forms and designs do produce the illusion of a non-existent construction, the illusion does no harm whatever; it wholly fails to shock our moral sense, and I doubt whether, even when the "deception" is revealed to the spectator, his sense of intellectual propriety is disturbed in any appreciable degree. He accepts the design for what it was intended to be—an effort to decorate a wall, a structure, to enrich its surface and make it interesting or beautiful; and it makes no difference to him whether the pilasters or columns are an essential part of the wall or not, or whether the entablature is carried by the wall or by the columns which to the eye support it. As a matter of fact, it may be doubted whether

FAÇADE OF MONASTERY AT PIEDRA, SPAIN. ORDERS EMPLOYED FRANKLY AND OBVIOUSLY AS A WALL DECORATION.

the alleged deception, the illusion of a non-existent construction, has any real existence outside of the minds of the purist critics themselves. The decorative purpose of the forms and features under criticism is so obvious, and their into the criticism of the decorative apparatus of a style or of a building, next to the inquiry whether it performs satisfactorily its primary function of decorative effect, is the question of its propriety, of its fitness for its place in that

S. MARIA DELLA SALUTE, VENICE. LANTERN CROWNED DOME ON A DRUM.

decorative effect so successful, that it is perfectly natural and proper to accept them and enjoy them without even a tincture of shame or vexation at the supposed effort to fool us. We are not shocked at the gilding of a picture frame, nor fooled into thinking it of solid gold; we know there was no intent to deceive, and we accept, as of course, the purely decorative purpose of the thin layer of gold.

The real question that ought to enter particular design, of its harmony with its environment, with its material, with the scale and character of the building. The great pother raised by Fergusson and his followers about the "truth" or "falsehood" of Renaissance design has too often obscured the really valid and significant factors of a just criticism. When one devotes one's attention to asking whether each detail is a "useful" part of the construction and whether it does or does not deceive by simulating a fictitious construction, one is apt to forget the essentials of design—good proportion, correct treatment of scale, the proper balance between variety and unity, beauty of line and of surface, the harmonious distribution of voids and

tinction betwen Gothic and Renaissance architecture which is worthy of notice. Gothic architecture, he says in substance, is *organised* architecture; Renaissance architecture is *arranged* architecture. There is a measure of truth in this dis-

COURT OF BEVILACQUA PALACE, VERONA. TYPE OF THE
RENAISSANCE ARCADED COURTYARD.

solids; these and other like considerations, to say nothing of the planning and general conception of the building.

IV

Mr. Claude Fayette Bragdon, who has written entertainingly and suggestively on architecture, the fourth dimension, projective ornament and other subjects connected directly or indirectly with design, has more than once drawn a dis-

tinction, if we correctly understand the meaning of the two words "arranged" and "organized" and rightly limit the field of their application. In both architectures there must of necessity be both organization and arrangement, for no building can stand unless it is structurally organized, and no designer ever produced a work of architecture or of any other art without arranging the elements of his design. But it is quite fair to say that the Gothic builders started with construction, which means organization, and proceeded from that to decoration or the arranging of the design or of its details for the production of decorative effect; while the Renaissance architects started with the decorative effect they had in mind and arranged their organized construction so as to serve that purpose. The two elements of organization and arrangement are present in both cases, but their relative order of importance and their order in thought are reversed.

This distinction, thus understood and thus limited, is closely related to one of the three fundamental differences between the two styles which I pointed out in the first paper of this series. I venture to quote from that article :*

"In all classic and neo-classic design the architect expresses his conceptions by means of an alphabet of element-forms already perfected, wrought to a species of finality by centuries of experimentation. The types of these element-forms are fixed: the designer reveals his artistic quality in the way he composes his design with these elements, in the refinement of his proportions, in the infinitely varied subtilties of his profiles, the variations of the details, the harmony and rhythm of his *ensemble* and of its decoration. In Renaissance architecture these fixed or conventional type-forms are adapted to an infinite variety of kinds and types of buildings, utterly diverse in plan, mass, proportions and purpose. In Gothic architecture, on the other hand, it is the general type of the building that is fixed—that of the several-aisled cruciform church with high vault and towers—and the form-elements that are endlessly varied."

In the marvelous skill with which the Renaissance made use of its alphabet of form-elements, creating with the old and long-familiar characters a new language wherewith to utter new thoughts, in the dignity and nobility of the new conceptions and the beauty of the dress in which they were presented to human view, the Renaissance displayed artistic gifts and a measure of creative inspiration no whit inferior to those of the

*The Architectural Record, August, 1917.

medieval church-builders, though differing in kind. They bequeathed to humanity an inestimable gift of loveliness and delight in builded form and decoration, and it betrays a strange blindness to the rightful claims of artistic beauty when a critic allows himself to be misled by fine phrases and the jargon of a transcendental mixture of morals with esthetics, into the attitude of a general and all-including contempt of the Renaissance and its works.

To call Renaissance architecture an "arranged" architecture, if this is meant as a general condemnation and signifies anything else than what I have above suggested or implied (the arrangement or disposing of the superficial decorative features of the design upon the organic core of the structure), is therefore a misleading and an unfair use of terms. To quote once more: "The broad-minded critic makes the necessary distinctions, recognizing that in the world of architecture there is room for both kinds."

V.

In these four papers I cannot claim to have answered all the animadversions, or exposed all the fallacies, of that criticism which starts out with the allegation, direct or implied, of the essential wrongness, the fundamental objectionableness, of Renaissance architecture in general and particularly of that of the Italians. I have only touched its high points, the basic errors and assumptions which vitiate its judgments. To meet in detail its various attacks upon scores of masterpieces, which somehow continue to win the admiration of the majority of mankind, including many persons in learning and culture quite equal to the assailants, would require a volume, and even those which most tempt one to rejoinder must be passed over.

If in this and the foregoing papers of this series I have given the impression of an undiscriminating partisanship for Renaissance architecture, of blind admiration and refusal to recognize patent faults, the impression is a mistaken one, due to the necessity of defending that architecture against the sweeping verdicts and apparently fundamental hos-

THE MINT AND THE LIBRARY OF ST. MARK, VENICE.

tility of the critics. A blanket indict-
ment seems to demand a blanket defense.
I do not pretend to praise all Renaissance architecture nor to defend all its
practices and devices, but I do wish to
protest against any condemnation of the
entire product of a great age of wonderful architectural activity, on the
strength of criteria based on fundamental assumptions which are, in my judgment, wholly untenable. I feel that a
protest should be entered against that
conception of construction which requires it to dominate instead of serving
beauty of form; that attitude which leads
even the usually sympathetic Professor
Frothingham to say of the Italians that
they were "the least constructive nation
in Europe"—the Italians, who in ancient
days built the Pantheon, the Baths of
Caracalla and the Basilica of Maxentius,
and in later times reared the unrivaled
domes of Santa Maria del Fiore at Florence and of St. Peter's at Rome, over

two of the mightiest temples ever built
by Christian hands!

No, I would object as strenuously to
an uncritical and sweeping laudation of
the Renaissance architecture of Italy as
to the sort of fault-finding with which
I have been finding fault. I ask only
that this architecture be judged upon its
merits, with clear understanding of its
problems, its conditions and its purposes.
I ask of its critics the laying aside of
prejudice or dislike springing from the
study of other styles, and a sincere effort to approach their subject sympathetically, to penetrate to the real
spring and inspiration, the ideals and
aims of the Renaissance designers. I
ask that full justice be done to the beauty
of the product, the excellence of the
planning, the nobility of the interiors,
the splendor of the ensembles, the loveliness of the decorations of the Renaissance. I ask recognition of the marvelous way in which it solved the host of

new problems with which the blossoming of a new culture confronted it. I ask its acquittal of the charges of copyism, servile imitation, untruthfulness, fraud and sham laid against the style as a whole or against its great masterpieces, I call attention to the originality and beauty of the two great contributions of the Italian Renaissance to architecture —the lantern-crowned dome on a drum and the arcaded palace-courtyard, each based on age-old elements yet none the less splendid new creations.

If we can get rid of the notion that somewhere between 1400 and 1500 the Italians suddenly threw off all honesty and principle in design, becoming at the same time the most extraordinarily prolific producers of beautiful works of art and the most servile copyists of a long dead style, designing false buildings which are base deceptions, frauds and shams, although marvelously beautiful; if we can for a time forget the preaching of those who, from their pulpits of assumed esthetic superiority of judgment, so loftily magnify the errors and minimize the merits of this architecture, we may then approach it with a fair chance of appraising it with tolerable correctness. We shall learn to distinguish between the formative Quattrocento, the culminating Middle or High Renaissance, and the gradual but progressive decline thereafter, through the various stages of the Barocco to the really imitative age of the eighteenth and early nineteenth century, each period having its own differing merits and defects. We shall recognize both the excellences and the failures of Renaissance design, its great strength, its versatility in decoration as well as the mistaken ways in which it sometimes sought to produce decorative effect—as in making church fronts mere screens unrelated to the church behind them.* We shall ap-

preciate the soundness and good sense of much Renaissance construction, while recognizing in certain cases the failure to extract from the construction itself the full measure of its decorative possibilities. We shall be free to enjoy to the full the nobility of its palace façades, the swelling majesty of its churchly domes, the magnificence of its courtyards, the dignity of its interiors, the beauty of its ornament. We shall feel equally free to condemn the stucco shams of the Baroque Jesuit churches and the infelicities of any design that offends us by inappropriate detail, unhappy proportions, wrong scale or any other fault. In short, we shall try to judge each work according to the problem it presented to the architect and the solution he adopted for it, using such common sense as God has endowed us with and such measure of good taste as we may have been able to acquire. And we shall refuse to call Brunelleschi, Bramante, Peruzzi, Sansovino and Michelangelo, either directly or by implication, copyists, liars or frauds.

Such I believe to be the program and such the fair and proper attitude of the critic of architecture, whatever the style or period with which he deals.

The derivative Renaissance architectures of France, Spain, the Low Countries, England, Germany and other countries, sprung from seeds of the Italian carried West and North by various agencies and currents, the critic should examine in the same spirit, applying such criteria as seem relevant in each case and giving full weight to those considerations of race, climate, previously existing traditions and the like, which were concerned in the evolution of each style. Only by such sympathetic study, free from bias and preconception, examining each development in the light of the conditions out of which it grew, can we rightly read the lesson of the Renaissance or of any other great period of art. "With malice toward none, with charity to all" is an excellent motto for critics in dealing with the styles.

*This is not, however, a fault especially of the Renaissance, but of Italian practice generally through the entire Middle Ages as well as in the Renaissance. Nor is it unknown even in French Gothic architecture, as Mr. Roger Gilman has shown in a penetrating article as "Gothic Architecture and Shell Fire" in the April Journal of the Archaeological Institute.

DECORATED PLASTER CEILING IN
THE CASTELLO SANT' ANGELO, ROME.
RENDERED DRAWING BY ARTHUR BYNE.

ARTHUR BYNE'S RENDERINGS
AND WATER-COLORS

By Mildred Stapley

WE are considering in this article the drawing and painting of Mr. Arthur Byne, whose Spanish scenes have been appearing for some time past as covers to the Architectural Record. Trained in the School of Architecture of the University of Pennsylvania, Mr. Byne continued his studies in the American Academy in Rome. On returning to New York, he entered the office of Messrs. Howells and Stokes, where he remained until 1914, when he undertook some special work for The Hispanic Society of America. At this he is still engaged, spending most of his time in Spain.

Nothing more unexpected could have befallen a practical young architect who up to that time had been chiefly occupied with modern American building; but it happened that he and his wife, after making a trip to Spain in 1910, determined to seriously study the archtecture of that practically unexplored country. Their guide-book was George Street's *Gothic Architecture in Spain*. In tracking down Gothic monuments, however, other and more racial phases of the great art as practiced in Spain attracted them. The Plateresque, or Renaissance period, they found, bore a very individual stamp, yet had ·not received the attention it deserved, foreign or native. They decided on annual visits for the purpose of studying it and gathering material for a book on the subject.

As the preparation of this work advanced, such a wealth of accessory products—woodcarving, ironwork, silverwork, furniture, textiles, etc.—beckoned that even these most earnest students of the Plateresque Style could not resist the temptation to tread frequent by-paths. Long before the matter originally designated had been prepared, innumerable photographs and measured drawings of other subjects had been amassed,

chiefly ironwork. These last, coming to the attention of The Hispanic Society of America, were published with descriptive text by Mrs. Byne under the title of *Rejeria of the Spanish Renaissance* (Number 87 of the Society's publications, 1913). The *Rejeria (iron screens)* was followed by a general handbook on Spanish ironwork. Next came the book first planned, *Spanish Architecture of the Sixteenth Century*, and quite recently, *Decorated Wooden Ceilings in Spain*. These, along with other volumes still in the making, have temporarily banished the practice of architecture.

The great value of all these works is their unstinting graphic presentation. Mr. Byne loves to draw. He takes delight in examining a monument down to the last detail; then equal delight in making a straightforward transcript of what he has seen. It is this liberality of personal illustration, if one may thus differentiate drawings from photographic reproductions, that widen the scope of the Byne books beyond that of any others yet published on Spanish architecture. It is Mr. Byne's manner of presenting such drawings, as well as others made recently, that we propose to discuss here.

No attempt has been made to collect the more conventional architectural renderings done during his ten years' office experience with Messrs. Howells and Stokes, New York. During that time and in collaboration with Mr. Henry Deville, numerous competitive drawings were rendered, including those for the Municipal Building and the Court House. In work of this nature, academic in character, where the rules of the competition or the concensus of office opinion often determined the method of procedure, it would be difficult to lay finger on the personal quality. It seemed preferable to select, therefore, some of the less restricted efforts dating from student days in Rome. Such are the Arch of Titus appearing as cover to the August, 1919, Record, and the ceiling in the Castello Sant' Angelo illustrated in monotone with the present article. With these to compare with recent work one may study the natural progress of an open mind and facile hand. In the Roman water colors made some fifteen years ago, the line so dear to every modern-trained architect is carefully preserved and the color dexterously but cautiously applied. In recent work the drawing, or disposing of the pattern on paper, is a matter of a few minutes. Line is subservient to color; and color is no longer a mere matter of staining the paper pleasantly, but of building up impressive masses, for instance, as the ancient bridge of San Martin at Toledo.

However, while still working as an architect only, Mr. Byne tried in the ceiling plan just mentioned to get away from the conventional line drawing and express the texture of the surface he was trying to represent: namely, decorated stucco. True, the outline was all laboriously inked-in, though very lightly; then it was just as laboriously washed down so that the delicately modeled highlights should not be overpowered by assertive lines. It is no attempt at sparkling line work, which was decidedly a fad with students of that day; a fad which, according to many observers, was responsible for the lack of sentiment in subsequent executed work. It is quite believable that if a little more sentiment were encouraged to creep into architectural renderings the interpretation in stone and wood might be more sympathetic.

The drawings reproduced from The Hispanic Society's publications, some in line, some in wash, are as varied in treatment as they are in subject. The frontispiece of the Rejeria is the painted heraldic panel over the central doors of the mighty iron grille in the Royal Chapel of Granada. The drawing measures sixteen inches by twenty-four inches. It is in pencil and is rendered in color and gold, being remarkably faithful to the original, which, it is claimed, has never been repainted or gilded since its erection in 1523. Enough of the surrounding bars and embossed horizontals have been included in the composition to give an idea of the splendid quality of Spanish smithing. The descriptive lettering, Mr. Byne's own contribution to the page, adds not a little to its charm. It seems hardly necessary to remark, in passing, that there would have been half a dozen less attractive ways of rendering a bit of painted ironwork.

Very much smaller in spite of the wealth of detail they contain are the Plateresque drawings. To one accustomed to the repose and fluent line of Italian ornament it required some readjustment of mind and hand to interpret the agitation and nervousness of the Spanish style. The drawn line could not be coldly uniform throughout, but had to be itself modeled in order to express the robustness of the carved stone or wood. Hence the special character of line used for the portal from the Archbishops' Palace at Alcala; or the combination of pencil and india-ink wash on rough paper to express the façade of the Casa de las Muertes, Salamanca, where there is much fine carving in coarse local sandstone. On the other hand extremely delicate penwork, especially considering that the drawing is only seven by twelve inches, is seen in the tomb of Ferdinand and Isabella, at Granada. This is strictly an architectural drawing, in that nothing is left to the imagination. Yet it is not merely line for line's sake; it is not flat, but suggests a certain amount of modeling, even more evident in the original than in the reproduction.

In entirely different vein are the two monotone drawings made several years ago to illustrate a tale of medieval France. The architecture, while carefully delineated, is used decoratively, making the *mise en scène* for an incident told by the figures in the foreground; but they would be easily recognized as an architect's work, although their special technique would probably never be recommended in any course on architectural rendering.

Some six years ago while still busy preparing books Mr. Byne began to paint

TOMB OF THE CATHOLIC SOVEREIGNS IN THE CAPILLA REAL, GRANADA.
From "Spanish Architecture of the Sixteenth Century." By Permission of
The Hispanic Society of America.

the irresistible Spanish landscape. Leisure for this sympathetic task came only at rare intervals; in fact during his last two visits to Spain no opportunity whatever presented itself for continuing a work so promisingly begun, so that his output thus far has been necessarily small. In Madrid and New York he has held one-man shows, and at the Panama Exposition his envoi was accorded a separate alcove and received a silver medal. The medium is pure water color free from gouache or Chinese white, and the manner of using it is most unusual and interesting. In technique, in the choice of subject, and in the large scale of the pictures, the temperament of the man is revealed as it never could be in the more limited field of architectural draughtsmanship. As is natural, masonry figures largely in his pictures—Roman aqueducts and bridges, Moorish gates, Spanish castles, all make special appeal, particularly when they stand, as so many great monuments do in Spain, abandoned, yet strong and defiant. Without feeling a great interest in the locality Mr. Byne never paints, and thus far the locality that has most interested him has been

stern Castile rather than smiling Andalusia.

Of first essays in painting the Architectural Record has published the Portico de la Gloria of Santiago Cathedral (September, 1917), a view of Segovia (August, 1917), and several others, while the Tarragona Cloister appeared January, 1920. These were straightforward painting, high in key, with the medium fluid and the brush kept full. It is surprising how little line preoccupies the artist. Even so architectural a subject as the famous Santiago portal is seen not so much with Street's joy in discovering one of the architectural glories of Christendom, as with a painter's delight in finding aged marble turned sea-green. The sketch represents a matter of two hours' work on the spot and was never touched afterwards. It recalls Philip Gilbert Hamerton's phrase, "the genius of elimination," without which, he said, no etcher could be a good etcher. What Mr. Byne put into this composition of naive twelfth-century figures is only a hundredth part of what he left out; but there is no doubt that had he sat before the subject as an architect, bent on mak-

427

ALCALA DE HENARES
A DOORWAY IN THE ARCHIEPISCOPAL PALACE

SCALE OF 12 0 1 2 3 4 5 6 7 FEET

A DOORWAY IN THE ARCHBISHOPS'
PALACE, ALCALA DE HENARES.
From "Spanish Architecture of the
Sixteenth Century." By Permission of
The Hispanic Society of America.

CASA DE LAS MVERTES · SALAMANCA

CASA DE LAS MUERTES, SALAMANCA.
From "Spanish Architecture of the Sixteenth
Century." By Permission of The Hispanic
Society of America.

CHÂTEAU OF AZAY-LE-RIDEAU, FRANCE.

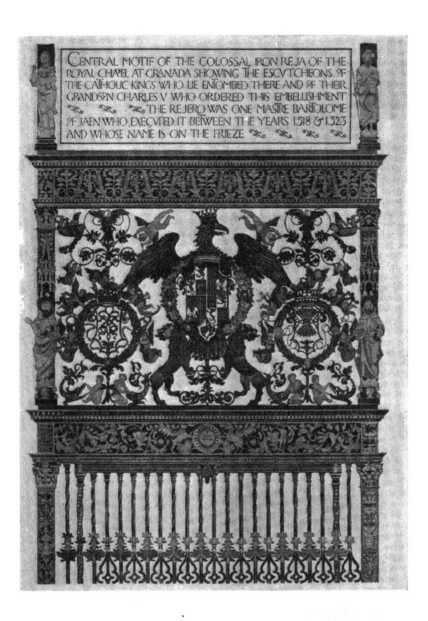

CENTRAL MOTIF OF THE COLOSSAL IRON REJA OF THE ROYAL CHAPEL AT GRANADA SHOWING THE ESCVTCHEONS OF THE CATHOLIC KINGS WHO LIE ENTOMBED THERE AND OF THEIR GRANDSON CHARLES V WHO ORDERED THIS EMBELLISHMENT THE REJERO WAS ONE MASTRE BARTOLOME OF JAEN WHO EXECVTED IT BETWEEN THE YEARS 1518 & 1523 AND WHOSE NAME IS ON THE FRIEZE

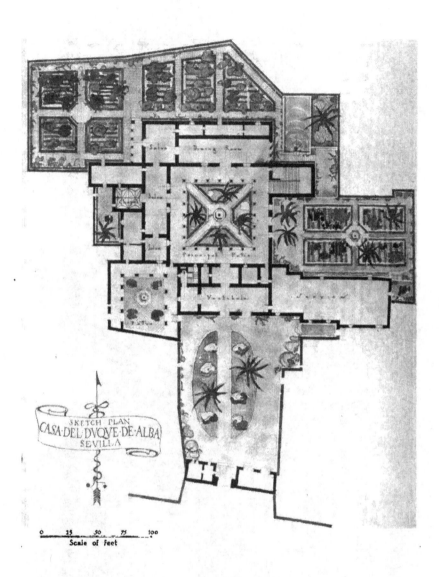

PLAN OF THE CASA DEL
DUQUE DE ALVA, SEVILLE.
From "Spanish Architecture of
The Sixteenth Century." By
Permission of The Hispanic
Society of America.

BRIDGE OF SAN MARTIN, TOLEDO.

ILLUSTRATION FOR "THE
BLACK HERMIT OF PONTOISE."

ing a pen-drawing, the omissions would have been very few.

Later paintings, of which unfortunately there have been too few, grew richer in pigment, broader in handling, and larger in size. The Aqueduct of Segovia measures two feet by three feet; the Walls of Avila, three feet by six. All were executed in a few hours on the spot, recorded while the impression of their massive beauty was fresh in the mind; and, likely as not, that very same night the painter became architect again and devoted several hours to an almost meticulous rendering in pen and ink of some bit of Spanish Plateresque ornament. While the color here in the Aqueduct is applied thick, in short definite strokes instead of in the limpid fluent manner of earlier work, the medium ever loses its

brilliancy. "If you can handle paint like that, why not use oils?" ask the painters; and the reply is, "Because I want to show that water color is a facile, rich medium of great possibilities. Moreover I love its mat texture so like the old frescoes, also the precision of touch it requires. One has to paint the entire picture in his mind before starting, for there can be no bungling or changing afterwards. It must be a single impression, quickly interpreted and then left for better or worse."

Critics have been kind enough to think that it has been for better; and it is to be hoped that Mr. Byne, now that he is again in Spain, may be able to devote more time to painting that curiously picturesque land before he comes back to New York.

WOOD CORNICE OF THE LONJA, ZARAGOZA.
From "Spanish Architecture of the Sixteenth Century.
By Permission of The Hispanic Society of America.

435

REAR VIEW—"RIDGEHANGER," EALING, MIDDLE-
SEX, ENGLAND. ROBERT ATKINSON, ARCHITECT.

SOME PRINCIPLES OF SMALL HOUSE DESIGN

By
JOHN TAYLOR BOYD, JR.

Part VII   Interiors

THE interior of a house should embody the highest expression of the art of the home. Although the environment of the neighborhood outside may dictate the arrangement of land and the practical side of the house plan and may influence the elevations, and although the influence of these externals may penetrate the interior, still the interior is the place above all others where is symbolized the ideal of the family. The interior is the hearth itself. If art is to be sacrificed anywhere in the small house, let the interior be the last part of it to suffer.

Since the interior is the essence of the home, it is most unfortunate that, at such a critical point in the intricate process of designing a small house, there should be a rift, a cleavage in design, which too often brings down failure upon the whole project. I refer to the cleavage made by dividing the field of interior design between the two specialties of architecture and interior decoration. The two arts overlap or sometimes leave a gap between them that is evident in the completed work. That is why you will often see interiors which are two separate designs—one, the work of the architect who has conceived the plans and shapes and the details of the shell of the interior, who has wrought them with one clear picture in mind; and the other, the design executed by the decorator in the finishing touches of color, furniture, fixtures and hangings, thus planting on the first design a secondary one of an entirely different pattern. Such an interior is twins—twins, but with no family likeness between them, sometimes not even a racial one!

At this point I wish to avoid any misunderstanding. The criticism does not apply to a minority of houses in which the break in design does not appear— in which the primary design of architecture and the secondary design of furnishings are one, as they should be. Nor is it meant personally as an argument against interior decoration. Interior decorators have put forth fine efforts in the development of a discriminating national taste in interiors. In this they have been aided by an excellent press, which has rendered valuable service in leadership. A difficult, patient task it is, and one that too many architects have avoided. Only a minority of men have followed the example first set by Charles A. Platt and Stanford White, although the last few years have seen a rapid increase in the ranks of architects who are skilled in the art of interiors.

But, in spite of the progress in standards, many architects still design houses with practical plans and excellent exteriors, the latter carefully wrought in every line; but in which the interiors show scarcely a trace of any definite artistic conception. The ablest decorator, if called upon, could not rescue such a design from mediocrity.

Another fault of the architect in interior design has been mentioned in previous issues of this series; that is, the perfunctory use of types of plans particularly of the stock plan. I have mentioned how this stock plan has deadlocked interior decoration as well as other features of house design—lot plan, house plan and elevations. With the incessant repetition, common in small houses, of box-like rooms and spaces, all about alike in size, shape and character, alike even in details, and fitted together always in the same way, individuality is stifled, and inspiration seems visionary to think of. As a very able decorator said to me recently: "When I pass by these little houses in the suburbs I know exactly what is in them. I can tell you the shapes and dimensions of the rooms, even to the dimensions of the openings and fireplaces; how the rooms are located; what kind of furniture is in each room; how it is placed—yes, and I can even tell you the dimensions of the furniture!" Although he said this in a jocular mood, the decorator hit the nail on the head. In many of our houses, instead of an art of the hearth, we have a few set formulae of design, repeated in the routine manner of custom and habit.

Like the architects, the decorators suffer from this division between the two specialties in household art, with its consequent lack of responsibility and of mastery of technical knowledge. Perhaps from a worthy desire not to interfere with the architect, interior decoration tends to emphasize finish and furnishings—those final touches in interior art—at the expense of the fundamental design of walls and ceilings and shapes of rooms. This error of over-emphasis of secondary design is encouraged by many of the writings on interior decoration. Such limitation is natural enough, perhaps some of it is unconscious; but it inevitably broadens the rift that has come about in the art of interiors. There are now some excellent books on interior decoration, which contain illuminating discussions of principles of color design and arrangement of furnishings; but they give too little thought to the architectural geometry of the interior, which is the foundation of art and interest in interiors. One may perceive this limitation in some of the illustrations in these books. These are pictures, entitled "Italian style," "English Renaissance room," "Louis XVI boudoir"; but really portraying—what? A design in some historic style of furniture, tapestries, hangings, art objects,

etc., all imposed on another design of a typical American room-shell, undisguised in its American character of shape, size, ceiling height, window and door openings and lighting effects. It is as if a simple, sober American citizen had been dressed up like an early Italian or an English aristocrat or a Parisian gallant! Such an effect, one may believe, confuses the art of the home with the art of the masquerade ball. Though the author of such an anachronism as that described above may urge that it is published as an illustration chiefly of furnishings, and that historic styles should not be copied literally—the vice of the "period" room—nevertheless, two different expressions are contained in such design, which split it into twins. And many people, particularly beginners, will take the writer literally.

One may, therefore, conclude that the need of interior design to-day is something more than a knowledge of how to apply aesthetic principles. The need is also to avoid some common errors that are due not to causes in art, properly speaking—though they may have unfortunate consequences in art; but which are provoked by the economic and technical complications of the times, and which have injured the arts through the vice of specialization. Both architecture and decoration suffer through the division of the field between them. As a result the primary or architectural part of the design is apt to be neglected, not only in its essentials of mass, shapes and coordination and expression, but in the smaller technical details of architecture that mean as much in interiors as in any other portion of the home. The perfunctory use of the stock plan has aided in this confusion. While again it should be observed that, although neither the most gifted architects nor decorators fall into these errors, yet a general tendency to commit them runs through the design of small houses. What is necessary is to recapture the unity of design, to treat the art of interior as a whole. Whether it be designed by one or more persons is a matter of no consequence;

438

LIVING ROOM—RESIDENCE OF FRANK A. COLBY, ARCHITECT, HARTSDALE, N. Y.

the fundamentals of interior design, the architectural shaping of the interior are the essentials to seek. If they are understood and applied, interior decoration will show to better effect—beautiful clothing on a beautiful body. Interior decoration will be less likely to be deadlocked in formulae and thoughtless habits of design. Then, as a result—carrying the conception of co-ordination further —interior art will not only be improved in itself, but will be better harmonized with the elements of the design outdoors and in the elevations. Only in this way may the art of interiors be rescued from the mediocrity and confusion that now enshrouds it.

Fortunately, it is not difficult to determine what are the fundamentals of interior design. Here one is simply entering upon a region that has long been explored and was richly cultivated before. The trouble with the art of interiors is a matter of neglect and indifference towards well known principles, rather than a hesitation to go forward. For if in lot design there is

much to learn, much to learn also of gardens and planting and form and color and style of architecture; and if in plan new arrangements will evolve in special conditions and as the result of economic changes—in interiors, the essentials are clearly established. If they are practised, progress in styles will easily be adjusted to the tradition.

In any attempt to determine the essentials of the art of interiors, it would seem that the first requirement is to picture the interior of the house as a whole. This should precede consideration of the design of separate rooms and spaces.

In previous articles of this series, there were noted at length many of these essentials of the artistic expression of the interior as a whole. At this point it is well to recall all that has been said in favor of a flexible conception of the house plan, both artistically and practically. The need of creative design to fit each individual case of site and situation and family circumstances; of combining elements of the plan, eliminating

439

STAIRWAY—RESIDENCE OF FRANK A.
COLBY, ARCHITECT, HARTSDALE, N. Y.

others and adding new features to complete the design in the effort to meet practical requirements and to maintain some air of spaciousness and ease in the small house; how this process should center around the design of the living room, which might thereby be enlarged and developed into greater artistic importance than before—all these principles will stimulate art in the interior as nothing else will. They are the true foundation of interior design. And it is the further development of those principles with particular reference to the artistic expression of the interior that is sought in these pages.

Proceeding with this development of the conception of flexible planning, one of the chief considerations is the proportioning of rooms and spaces. I have pointed out that, with the stock plan reduced to fit small houses, such proportioning—which is mainly the harmonious contrast of large and small, and the design of the space relationships—is nearly impossible. If we carry this idea further we shall see that this design of shapes resembles the design of measures in the plan. There is much room for a flexibility of shapes in the house plan. Nothing adds more to the art of interiors than the taking of this step which immediately breaks the deadlock of the box-shaped room. Curiously enough, many small houses show the paradox of too much variation of shape and form on the exterior, and almost none at all in the interior. In this connection a further exaggeration is to be noted. Some designers have imitated the British house in exterior design, which is exactly that part of it least suited to American conditions; but they have neglected the example set by British interiors, which is much more significant. For Americans, the value of modern English design lies in the tradition of wonderful Gothic variety in shapes of rooms and of the flexible way in which they are combined. This Gothic precept also bids English architects take account of the variety in classic planning which is not at all inconsiderable. The result is a character and consistency in planning in British houses that cannot

be too highly praised. It appeared in the English house at Biddenham, that was illustrated in the third article, and in the charming little house by Robert Atkinson shown herewith. The first was a plan of freer shapes, of a flexible

DETAIL OF ENTRANCE HALL—RESIDENCE OF FRANK A. COLBY, ARCHITECT, HARTSDALE, N. Y.

Gothic type; while the second shows a more formal, more severely geometrical arrangement in the Renaissance manner. Considered merely as paper diagrams, these plans reveal unusual character and interest, which is a surface indication, at least, of the art of their interiors.

Flexible design of shapes need not be confined to walls, and this truth explains another cause of the excellence of the

DINING ROOM—RESIDENCE OF FRANK A. COLBY, ARCHITECT, HARTSDALE, N. Y.

VISTA FROM FLOWER ROOM INTO DINING ROOM.

LIVING ROOM—RESIDENCE OF FRANK A. COLBY, ARCHITECT, HARTSDALE, N. Y.

VISTA FROM RECEPTION ROOM INTO LIVING ROOM.

best English plans, as well as the weakness of some of our own. It is, of course, only a matter of *section*, a technical part of design well known to American architects in the design of large buildings. In small houses, the artistic shaping of the section is usually omitted, and we have instead the custom of three equal planes of first and second and third floors cutting rigidly through the house and joined together by the stairwell. When it can be accomplished without artificiality, there are few elements of design which afford greater interest and character—as well as that unexpectedness and vivacity that make for charm—than differences of floor and ceiling levels, and of ceiling shapes. In respect to changes of floor level, I recall an old house in Holderness, New Hampshire, that straggled down a gentle hill slope in a series of large rooms in a line, each two or three steps below the one above. The vista through the rooms was striking indeed, and I have never forgotten it, though I saw it when a boy. This is an extreme case, and I cite it only to emphasize the possible picturesquesness of effect to be gained through changes of floor level. Changes of level appear best when they are a natural result of an uneven site.

In regard to design of ceiling, restrictions of cost forbid elaborately decorated ceilings. It is not, however, generally known that ceilings of simple, vault-like forms, such as flat segments of circles in section, or barrel vaultings, or even simple penetrated vaults, do not add greatly to cost, perhaps not so much as a simple running cornice at the top of a box-like room. The best English designs, and a few American designs of large residences, show a beautiful use of these simple ceiling forms. There are, in addition, many fine examples of rooms of a story and a half such as fascinate beholders in studios, which have the angles replaced with oblique planes, giving a shape to the ceiling of half a hexagon. These larger variations of ceiling shapes may be infinitely varied and enriched by minor details of simple beams or differences of level, linked together with a beam at the juncture of the ceiling of a main room with the ceilings of alcoves or bay windows. There are endless possibilities on this line of thought on which a volume itself could be written.

It is well, however, not to push this theory of variation of interior shapes and sizes too far; otherwise, interiors will be overdone just as exteriors are often overdone. Variety of itself will not ensure picturesqueness or charm, unless it is expressed in the terms of art. In American houses, too much elaboration on Gothic models will be out of keeping with our simpler American ideals. There are other factors which counsel moderation. With the softer light and mellower atmosphere of the English climate, there is less emphasis of variations and of details in English houses, and this is aided by the English practice of small windows. The late Frank Niles Day explained this principle of the use of small windows, with the window heads kept well down from the ceiling, by saying that it is often desirable to cut down the amount of daylight admitted to a room in order that the ceiling have a slight mellowness and air of mystery. This conception has its value in America, which shall be considered further in detail. The point to be made, here, is that the greater illumination in America makes less detail advisable than in England, where details are less prominent in the mellower light. In our small houses, one or two picturesque motives may be all that is necessary to achieve unusual character in an interior. In walls too much variation of shape should be avoided. In large rooms it may preferably take the form of alcoves or bays, or corners cut off as a sort of bay; and only in minor spaces, such as vestibules, stairs, may the walls be rounded. It is in these minor spaces and elements, especially in fireplaces, that picturesqueness counts for so much. They aid in vistas also, which are a matter of the relationship of the interior as a whole. They are apparent not only as the spectator stays in one spot but as he moves about the

VISTA FROM DINING ROOM—RESIDENCE OF
HERBERT S. DREW, ESQ., BELMONT, MASS.
GRANDGENT & ELWELL, ARCHITECTS.

house or enters or leaves it. This last consideration, in the technical language of architecture, belongs to communication and circulation, which, it should be remembered, has an artistic as well as a practical side.

The proper lighting of the interior has a greater bearing on the flexible design of the interior than is generally appreciated. Again one is obliged to call attention to the superiority of British houses, particularly of those designed in the Gothic vernacular tradition. The control of daylight in design, contrasting dim light, or moderate light, in some parts of the house, against a huge beam of sunlight flooding in through a bay or through a tall mullioned window, is one of the most beautiful devices in the whole range of interior decoration. When we think of the recent progress in artificial illumination, of the distinction in interior effects that has come through using table lamps and portable lamps on standards, which light up that part of the room where centers the chief interest of the art of interiors (which is none other than the humans) throwing it into high relief and leaving the rest of the room in gloom through which the color and gilt of decoration glows and gleams—we have ideas for pictures that might apply to daylight illumination. But somehow, our best light of all, sunlight, is too little considered on the side of design. There is, however, less flexibility of control with daylight, which is fixed in position. Artificial light may be moved about, so to speak, thus varying the centre of interest of design and maintaining it always on people. Light may be colored, both sunlight and artificial light, using curtains or transparent shades in each case, although this color needs to be slightly roseate, to meet the wishes of the ladies.

With daylight, some of the same design is possible, as we have seen. It should be adjusted to American conditions of glare of sunlight and to the fondness of Americans for this light, together with the requirement of great window ventilation in summer. Some English houses seem extreme, under-il-luminated, with principal rooms lit by windows that are hardly more than slits. On the other hand, many of our houses are equally over-illuminated, pierced with windows everywhere, as many as two in one wall in a small room. The windows are evidently too large, a fact proved by the attempt to cut them down with various sets of curtains or hangings, or the unbecoming window shades. Furthermore, there is no proportion in the distribution of such lighting; it is diffused everywhere alike until the house is illuminated like a factory. Some of the houses that have been published in this series are excellent examples of artistic lighting of daylight in well proportioned volume and intensity. Mr. Colby's living room is illuminated through a small window on the long outside wall and through a large south window casting a great beam of light across the room, behind which is revealed a fine fireplace nearly as high as the room. No effect could be more simply obtained, yet it is really dramatic. It is, however, not theatrical, for, naturally, the spotlight of the stage hardly belongs in the home.

All these considerations of lighting influence color design in interiors. This is a chapter in itself and its importance need only be mentioned to be realized. Light is the source of color. The effect of light on color, through emphasizing it, harmonizing it and modifying it, is really the whole secret of color in art. Color is really designed by means of light. Designers follow this principle when they work out the color schemes of rooms "on the job" itself—mixing colors of surfaces and trying them on the walls and ceilings of the rooms they are to decorate and testing samples of hangings against them. If one could try the experiement of changing the amount and quality of light in some of the most beautiful interiors by changing the design of openings in the walls, he might witness a great change in the value of the color and decorations. Some designs would lose emphasis and interest in a subdued light or if the light were closed off in a certain direction; while other

STAIRCASE WALL OF BOOK ROOM—RESIDENCE OF FRANCIS V. LLOYD, ESQ.,
EDGEMONT, PA.

DINING END OF LIVING AND DINING ROOM—RESIDENCE OF FRANCIS V. LLOYD, ESQ.,
EDGEMONT, PA.
Mellor & Meigs, Architects.

447

designs, in a strong light or with light added from additional sources upon dark surfaces, would be rendered crude.

This principle of lighting and of color in lighting has still another sequel; that is, the problem of how many sides of a rectangular room should have windows. Dr. Denman W. Ross once pointed this out to me, as he pointed out many another truth in design. In his remarkable researches into the mysteries of color and painting, he experimented for years in portrait studies, painting models seated in his studio, which is a large room, in different effects of daylight, of "hot" or "cold" light, of light coming from different sources. As a result of this long experimenting he came to these interesting conclusions about the placing of windows in a room: Too much cross-lighting is to be avoided, hence light from windows on three sides of a room may be undesirable; also, a fireplace in a wall with windows each side of it causes confusion of lighting and a diffusion of interest. I have never accepted this precept without reservation; but I have seen many a room which would have been the better for following it.

Incidentally, windows have another relation to interior design. Just as in the case of exteriors, they should be contrasted with wall spaces; they should not cut up the design; there should not be too much variety of size and shape and of pattern of window panes. If small panes are desirable in the exterior of a small house, they are particularly needed when seen from the inside. In the stock plan, the custom of placing two windows on each side of the centre entrance in each room, where one would usually be better, leaves too little wall space both inside or outside. In some small old houses I have seen rooms, 14 feet square, amply lighted by three windows 4 feet 6 inches by 2 feet 4 inches, two of them in one wall and one in a wall adjacent. The arrangement provided ample cross ventilation, maintained the scale of the rooms, and afforded more space for furniture and decorations. In very small rooms, a single window in a wall, particularly in an end wall, has the virtue of furnish-

ing but one source of light instead of two, thus making less cross-lighting; also it avoids emphasis of the corners of the room which have less illumination. This concentration of light into one large window motive, of grouped windows, of a "battery" of casements, or in a bay, has the additional merit of making the window an interesting feature of design in itself rather than a mere utilitarian opening in the wall.

One more application of lighting principles should be noted before the reader wearies of the subject. As in other parts of the design, the proportioning and variation of amount of light is apt to be most sound when it has a practical reason behind it to reinforce a purely artistic one. Certain spaces in a home, like the dining space, need more light than others. Even certain parts of a large living room may have stronger sunshine than others, particularly around the fireplace. Lighting helps establish the transition between the most sheltered and secluded parts of a house and the outdoor world; that is, glazed loggias or enclosed porches may have most light of all. Often, however, this principle is exaggerated. One sees an enclosed breakfast porch all glass panes, hardly with any appearance of firmness of walls or points of support, giving the effect of a greenhouse. Likewise, in the relation to the exterior, bay windows or projections such as alcoves may jut out from the interior to take advantage of a landscape view or serve as a transition to the garden; and, as viewed from the exterior, such a bay or large window may appear at the end of a vista through some part of the garden or through the lot.

Such proportioning of illumination with regard to the relation to the exterior runs parallel with the design in space relations, as described in previous articles of the series. It also affects the design of the shapes of plan and of section, as noted above. In this connection, porches are important. In the north, porches are useful only during part of the year unless glazed in, in which case they are often better designed to be enclosed at the beginning. In New England and

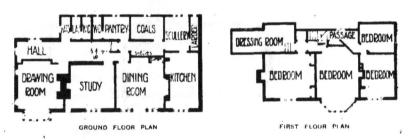

GROUND FLOOR PLAN

FIRST FLOOR PLAN

Reproduced by permission from "Country Cottages," by J. Elder Duncan; John Lane Co., Publishers.

COTTAGE AT SILCHESTER COMMON,
NEAR READING, ENGLAND. MERVYN
E. MACARTNEY, ARCHITECT.

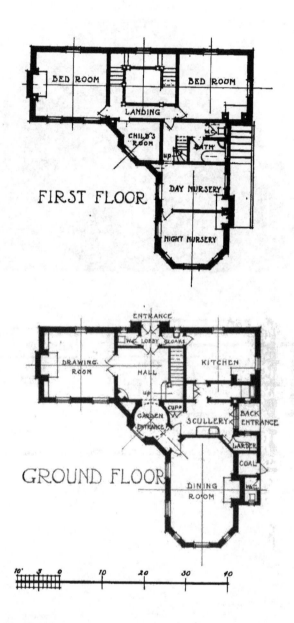

FLOOR PLANS — "RIDGEHANGER,"
EALING, MIDDLESEX, ENGLAND.
ROBERT ATKINSON, ARCHITECT.

"RIDGEHANGER," EALING, MIDDLESEX, ENGLAND. ROBERT ATKINSON, ARCHITECT.

ENTRANCE HALL — "RIDGEHANGER,"
EALING, MIDDLESEX, ENGLAND.
ROBERT ATKINSON, ARCHITECT.

VISTA FROM ENTRANCE HALL INTO DINING ROOM—"RIDGEHANGER," EALING, MIDDLESEX, ENGLAND. ROBERT ATKINSON, ARCHITECT.

DRAWING ROOM. "RIDGEHANGER," EALING, MIDDLE-
SEX, ENGLAND. ROBERT ATKINSON, ARCHITECT.

the far north, the porch can be used for only about four months in the year, and in many cases it may be better if it is replaced by a terrace and an awning on uprights that may be unrolled during the heat of the day. Here, too, the effect on the illumination of the interior by the porches is often overlooked.

One further aspect of the art of the interior taken as a whole deserves notice; that is, the linking together of the rooms and spaces. If one studies small house plans, he will often see cases that give evidence that the designer has become confused between two conflicting principles. One principle is the separation of rooms to preserve individuality and privacy; and the other is the throwing of them open in order to gain that effect of ease and spaciousness which is so desirable and is particularly expressive of the tradition of hospitality. Each principle is valuable, according to circumstances, and both may be used in the same house. The fault to avoid is that of trying to use both at the same point. This makes a plan loose, poorly jointed, and robs the interior of character or contrast. It may be well to remember that spaciousness and hospitality have been valued in the past, and have been obtained without sacrificing the individuality of rooms. Even in the old Italian palaces, planned for lavish entertainment, a room was usually entered through a rather small single door, sometimes through a double door in great rooms. In France, this separation is to be noted, particularly in the smaller rooms, even in the Palace of Versailles. The French doors, divided into two leaves, each leaf with three or four panels, are most successfully used in the principal rooms of the small house. They look very well with one leaf open, and give ample effect of space and ease when both leaves are opened.

On the other hand, if rooms are thrown open to one another, they should be boldly joined together with but little wall space dividing them. It is the wide, squarish, sometimes doorless openings that wreck so many small house interiors. These, or else the use of doors all glass, which, added to the glass of too many windows in the other walls, do irreparable damage to the walls of any room, plastered as it thus becomes with panes of glass on every side, usually too big. This always seemed to me one of the curious minor faults of contemporary house design; yet I do not know of a designer who was not in some respects addicted to this device. The early American interiors were always beautifully co-ordinated in the design of openings. The right sort of opening was usually chosen for each case, and it is always beautifully proportioned and shaped, in harmony with the other forms of the rooms. In old houses one sees hardly any of those impossible fat, rectangular openings combined with delicate Renaissance proportions of other surrounding elements, such as are found to-day. This is a common fault of design and extends even to elevations and to gardens. Where double doors are used, an opening 4 feet wide is usually wide enough and 3 feet 10 inches may be better.

All these elements of the design of the interior as a whole can hardly be successful unless framed in one consistent scheme. The scheme should express singleness of purpose. The whole expression should be formal or informal, though a certain judicious combination of the two schools is possible. If flexibility is sought, it should not be loose or careless, or capricious. It should be firm and it should be sound. It is apt to be better if it is direct and simple. This is the field of interpretation and expression and is the peculiar province of the personality of the artist.

455

J. S. BACHE MAUSOLEUM, WOODLAWN, N. Y.
DAVIS, McGRATH & KIESSLING, ARCHITECTS

J. S. BACHE MAUSOLEUM, WOODLAWN, N. Y.
DAVIS, McGRATH & KIESSLING, ARCHITECTS

J. S. BACHE MAUSOLEUM, WOODLAWN, N. Y.
DAVIS, McGRATH & KIESSLING, ARCHITECTS.

J. S. BACHE MAUSOLEUM, WOODLAWN, N. Y.
DAVIS, McGRATH & KIESSLING, ARCHITECTS.

J. S. BACHE MAUSOLEUM, WOODLAWN, N. Y.
DAVIS, McGRATH & KIESSLING, ARCHITECTS

J. S. BACHE MAUSOLEUM, WOODLAWN, N. Y.
DAVIS, McGRATH & KIESSLING, ARCHITECTS.

STAIRCASE, SHOWING FRIEZE—ROYAL COLLEGE
OF SURGEONS. SIR CHARLES BARRY, ARCHITECT.

English Architectural Decoration
Text and Measured Drawings by Albert E. Bullock

Part XIV-2. Staircases (Continued).

THE eighteenth century in architecture and decoration opened with a burst of literary activity, which was largely retrospective when the classical revival may be said to have definitely developed with a far-reaching effect.

During the first decade Sturt published a translation of Pozzo's "Principles of Perspective," the proofs being read by three eminent architects, Sir Christopher Wren, Sir John Vanburgh and Nicholas Hawksmoor. Volumes upon allied subjects were produced by James Gibbs, Colin Campbell, William Kent and many another well known architect. These books consisted of drawings giving accurate dimensions and measurements of examples of the best buildings of their predecessors, indicating that research in architectural matters was sought after; while several designs for current work were frequently included. The chief source of their efforts comprised many of the more important buildings erected by Inigo Jones—Colin Campbell including in his three large folio volumes, "Vitruvius Britannicus," the two designs for the Palace at Whitehall, the Queen's House at Greenwich, Wilton House and many other later works.

Towards the midde of the century the number of firms of cabinet makers and joiners increased until Sheraton—who was famous for his seaweed marqueterie—published in 1793, with the assistance of Adam Black, his "Cabinet Makers' and Upholsterers' Drawing Book," to which was added a list of over 450 of the principal cabinet makers, etc., of his day. Chippendale's "Director" had hitherto held sway as a standard work of reference in furniture; while John Grunden, Ince and Mayhew and a few others produced books of varying merit.

The close of the previous century had witnessed a purely naturalistic tendency in the carvings for decoration. Hugh May, the friend of Evelyn, is associated with the early portion of Cassiobury Park, Herts., which contains much carving of the Grinling Gibbons school in this famous house of the Earl of Essex. The staircase at Sydenham House is of Charles I period, having pierced balusters carved with Ionic capitals; while at Westwood, Worcestershire, the staircase newels are carried above the level of the handrail with lofty Corinthian columns, each terminated with a ball finial.

At Rushbrooke Hall, Suffolk, the staircase is also of the time of Charles I, having turned balusters, closed strings and panelled newels. The balusters at Norton Conyers are of Italian type, similar to Burton Agness in Yorkshire, only that the latter example contains more members in the moldings.

At Gifford's Hall the balusters are twisted similar to the example given from Forbes House, Gloucester. At Wakehurst Place two types of baluster are used, one being twisted and the next plain in alternation.

The type adopted by Inigo Jones at Ashburnham House occurs with slight variation at "The Vyne," Basingstoke. Hants., with its Palladian entrance hall by John Webb, and also at Coleshill in Berkshire.

Panelled risers occur in the elaborately carved Charles I work at Dunster Castle, Somerset, of which the balustrade is pierced and carved after the manner of the work quoted from No. 25 High Street, Guildford, and a house in the Close at Winchester. Another instance of panelled risers is to be seen at Ladybellegate House, Gloucester, where the balusters are twisted, the newel being formed of a group of four balusters clustered together upon a carved acanthus bulb-shaped base. The carving to the top landing frieze appears to be somewhat later than other details of the house and is obviously applied. Although the general features are of late Charles I period, the front room ceiling has the character of the work of the time of James Gibbs.

Carved balusters of massive type exist at Cobham Hall, Kent, which are richly treated with Ionic capitals and acanthus leaved bases. The twisted baluster was introduced before the close of the reign of Charles I, as is evidenced by the work at Dawtrey Mansion, Petworth, which is dated 1652 upon one of the newel terminals. The finials or drops in this instance are pierced, giving an interesting effect of lightness to an otherwise heavily molded feature.

In some cases the newel was carried up above the level of the balustrading as a column to support the landing above,

often being treated in similar character to the baluster, as occurs at St. Georges, Canterbury, where the twisted form of the baluster is repeated in a slightly thicker form. This example is illustrated in Mr. W. H. Godfrey's book upon "The English Staircase," where also may be seen a photograph of a unique circular stairway with twisted balusters from The Friars, Aylesford.

Before the treatment of ramping the handrail became common practice, the projection of the first stair to a flight appears to have created some difficulty, which was met in certain instances by a carved scroll projecting from and attached to the base of the newel. The main staircase at Cobham Hall is a good solution of this problem.

With the introduction of the cut string, the nosing moldings were returned around the end of the stair, which offered an opportunity to carve brackets at the stairs ends for enrichments. An early instance of this exists at Messrs. Bruton & Knowles's premises at King Street, Gloucester, and No. 51 Conduit Street, London.

STAIRCASE—UNLAWATER, NEWNHAM-ON-SEVERN, GLOUCESTERSHIRE.

STAIRCASE—BEACON HOUSE,
PAINSWICK, GLOUCESTERSHIRE.

It is possible that staircases having molded soffits of the type at the Victoria Hotel, Newnham and Unlawater in the same Severn Valley village are of early origin within the period, the idea of panelling the spandril being adopted later to avoid the expense of this alternative. Soffit panelling was sometimes resorted to in lieu of the usual plaster, plain or enriched.

Later examples include Saltram at Plympton in Devon, which has three balusters to a tread, two of which are twisted and the center one fluted; while the staircase at Beacon House, Painswick, previously referred to, is similarly treated to the latter and to a staircase at the Conservative Club in Gloucester, formerly belonging to a wealthy tanner of that city. Bearland House, Gloucester, now occupied as the telephone exchange, is one of the finest examples of the time. The care with which the stairs at the landing level are shaped to the bend of the well and the double turned stairs at the foot, known technically as the "curtail," as shown on the accompanying plan, indicate a high grade of craftsmanship, not to speak of the carved archway in the hall or the adjoining panelled room, which latter has, however, suffered some vicissitudes of fortune since its origin.

At North Pallant House, Chichester, the newel differs from the baluster in being formed of a small fluted Corinthian column with similar pilaster upon the dado to correspond. The stair ends have a carved panel and adjacent carved bracket under each second stair. The combination of spiral carving or twist with the molded base reflects two previous periods. The simple turn of the handrail over the abacus of the column is noticeable, also the character of the ornament introducing the continuous bead indicating George III period.

Among the exceptions may be mentioned the staircase at No. 5 John Street, Bedford Row, London, which is a type of work practiced by John Grunden, an exponent of lath work and a contemporary with Thomas Chippendale. The style is of Chinese origin and continued late into the following reign. A simi-

lar treatment from Beacon House, Painswick, has already been illustrated, and a simpler type exists at Flaxley Abbey, the rooms of which house were designed by J. Leck, aftesr the fire there of 1777, in the Adam manner. Little seems to be known of this architect except that he flourished in 1783 and left the designs for the alterations to this house. The present owner, Sir Francis Crawley-Boevey, has taken a great interest in its historical associations and kept a record of the alterations effected from time to time by his ancestors. I shall hope to deal with the reception rooms from that house in a detailed way when treating of the Adam school in a subsequent article. Several of the examples cited in this and the last number have already been illustrated by photographs, such as "The Pynes," Devon, and the wrought iron staircase of Pembroke House.

Staircases of cast iron and stone were not uncommon in the Adam period, such an instance existing at Eastgate House, Gloucester. The idea of molded soffits to timber built staircases was doubtless obtained from stone examples, such as the staircases at Chatsworth, St. Paul's Cathedral and Hampton Court Palace.

Lady Paget's house at Newnham is a good type of domestic stair with considerable play in the effective treatment of the half landing steps, which are supported in lieu of solid filling by tiny balusters. In addition, the ends of the stairs are finished with a flush inlay carrying down the line of the baluster; the carved brackets coming under the second stair in each case.

The inlaid staircase at Claydon House, Bucks, is a very elaborate work of mid-Adam period, with inlaid veneered treads and risers and wrought iron balustrading.

Much elaboration was displayed in some of the Scottish staircases, of which the square turned and carved work at Hopetoun House is typical.

Late George IV work is notable for the importance given to the entrance hall. Henry Holland's scheme at Dover House, Whitehall (now the Scottish office)—in which he was doubtless assisted by his assistant (Sir) John Soane

HALL AND STAIR-
CASE—CIRENSTER HOUSE,
GLOUCESTERSHIRE.

THE HALL, BEARLAND HOUSE, GLOUCESTER.

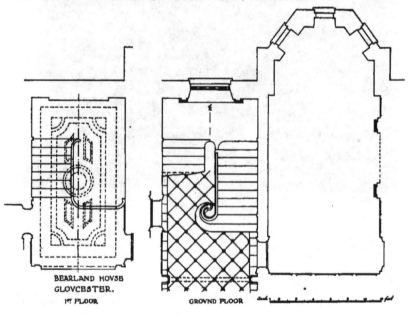

BEARLAND HOVSE
GLOVCESTER.
1ST FLOOR.

GROVND FLOOR

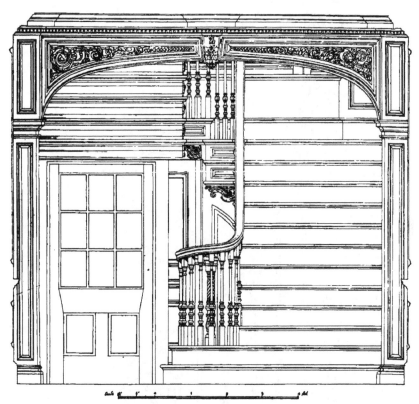

BEARLAND·HOVSE·GLOVCESTER·

BEARLAND HOUSE,
GLOUCESTER.

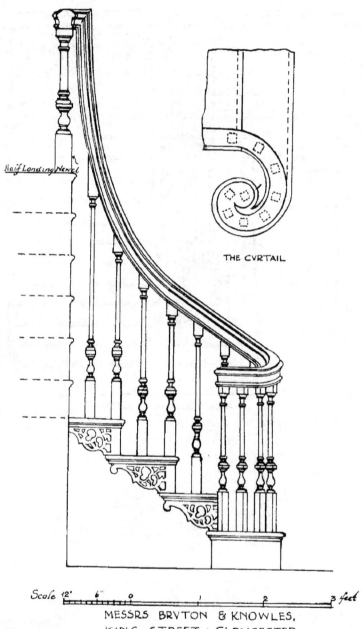

Half Landing Newel

THE CVRTAIL

Scale 12" 6" 0 1 2 3 feet

MESSRS BRVTON & KNOWLES,
KING STREET : GLOVCESTER.

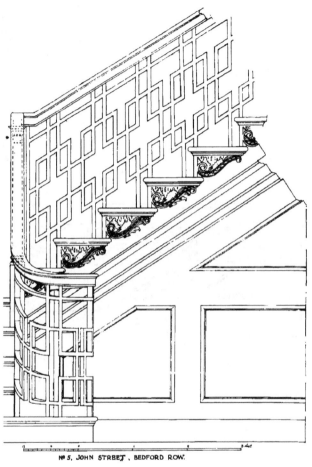

Nº 5, JOHN STREET, BEDFORD ROW.

NO. 5 JOHN STREET,
BEDFORD ROW, LONDON

BRACKET TO STAIRS
BEACON HOVSE,
PAINSWICK . GLOS⁵

SCALE OF INCHES

STAIR BRACKET—BEACON HOUSE,
PAINSWICK, GLOUCESTERSHIRE.

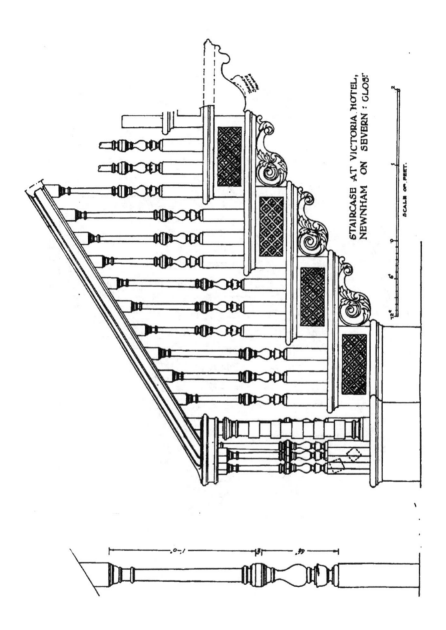

STAIRCASE AT VICTORIA HOTEL,
NEWNHAM ON SEVERN : GLOS:

SCALE OF FEET.

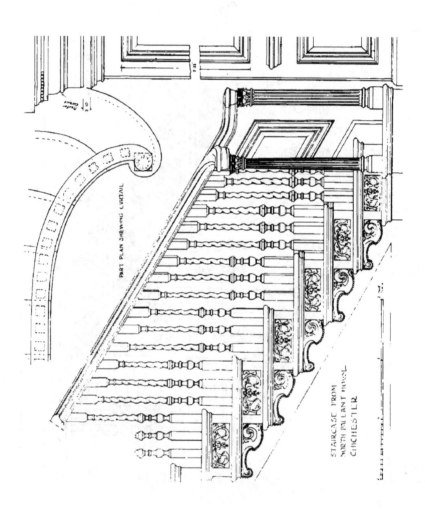

PART PLAN SHEWING CURTAIL

STAIRCASE FROM
NORTH PALLANT HOUSE
CHICHESTER

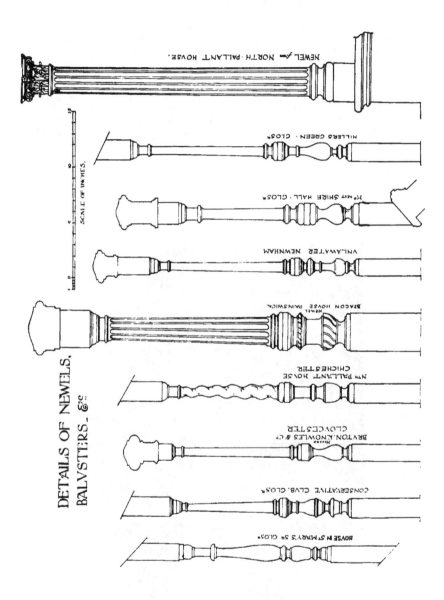

DETAILS OF NEWELS,
BALVSTERS. &c

NEWEL ƒ⁻ NORTH PALLANT HOVSE.

MILLERS GREEN · CLOSᴬ

Nᵒ 17 SHIRE HALL · CLOSᴬ

VNLAWATER · NEWNHAM

NEWEL
BEACON HOVSE PAINSWICK.

CHICHESTER
Nᵒ PALLANT HOVSE

GLOVCESTER
BRYTON, KNOWLES & Cᵒ

CONSERVATIVE CLVB, CLOSᴬ

HOVSE IN STMARY'S Sᵗ CLOSᴬ

SCALE OF INCHES.

—consists of a circular court, with domed light over, supported upon iron columns with a porte-cochére without and main central flight within giving access to the principal apartment. The Insurance Office at Exeter, executed about 1837, has a variation of the same conception; while Sir Charles Barry at Bridgewater House, the Surgeons College in Lincoln's Inn Fields and in his Club Houses in Pall Mall introduced in addition to the hall a central lounge or winter garden with large ornamental glazed light over. The planning seems to be an adoption of the Italian cortile, by covering the latter from the weather and thus bringing it within the habitable portion of the house. Barry rarely made a great feature of the staircase itself, relegating it to a secondary place in the plan; from which time it is noticeable that staircases in large buildings were frequently constructed of marble.

UPPER LANDING—LADYBELLEGATE HOUSE, GLOUCESTER.

Saxon Architectural Styles.

Scarcely a century has passed since Rickman began the first adequate study of historical architecture in England. His researches enabled him at once to classify almost everything known as an ancient important building into the groups named by him Norman, Early English, Decorated and Perpendicular. Of course there are relics of the Roman time, as at Wroxeter, and even pre-Roman, such as Stonehenge; but he found so little of the Saxon period that his disciple J. H. Parker, in one of his early editions, stated that, except for part of the crypt of Westminster Abbey, built just before the Conquest by Edward the Confessor under immediate Norman influence, the only well authenticated Saxon structure in England was the tower at Earl's Barton in Northamptonshire. Later Parker recognized other buildings as undoubtedly Saxon, but he classed most of these as so like Norman as in most cases not to be worth distinguishing from it.

Rickman and Parker by careful study of archives overthrew so many traditions that it is not strange they came to be regarded as almost infallible. Nevertheless, such occasional study as I have been able to give to this hobby, in the few days which I have been able to steal from other affairs in the course of a dozen trips to England on entirely unrelated business, has convinced me not only that there is much unrecognized Saxon architecture in England, but also that this can be divided into three styles as distinct as Early English, Decorated and Perpendicular.

The first of these is shown by a small group of churches of great irregularity. Of these I have seen but three, namely, Brixworth in Northamptonshire, St. Martins at St. Albans and the church in Dover Castle. The others are mainly in the extreme North, where I have never had time to go. It is at least twelve years since I have seen any of them, so that I must ask some indulgence.

These have often been considered as of the Roman period, and they are built in part of Roman bricks; but I cannot imagine their being either of this period or the period after the Romans departed and before the Saxons came, for the British masons must have kept up in general the Roman practice until disturbed by the Saxon invasion, and the Roman was essentially the child of law and order. Occasionally he departed from strict regularity as in the arch of triumph at St. Rémy in Provence, where one jamb of this most formal building is four inches wider than the other, but the reason of this is plain. It is a late work (date unknown) for which the reliefs were probably stolen, and the frames for them had to be made to match. The mouldings around them are similar, and I had no idea of the discrepancy until by way of testing out my theory that the fundamental unit of a building generally can be deduced from its principal dimensions, I tried a steel tape on it.

But the irregularities of such of these churches as I have seen are wild. St. Martins has three bays on one side of the nave and four on the other. The church in Dover Castle has one wall of the nave a foot longer than the other. I was disturbed in my measurements of this by an officious sergeant, who finally, after his other objections had been answered, stated that this was in a fortress, and that no measurements could be taken without an order from the Commander. I had only the time between trains, so that I had to give it up, but not until I had convinced myself that the building was based on a unit of eight Roman feet. If I remember aright the chancel arch had this span and twice this length, while the nave was sixteen Roman feet wide and sixty-four long. The individual discrepancies were large, but they averaged up well. I believe this to be a seventh century building erected from the wrecks of former Roman structures by men engaged on their first venture in important masonry and trying to follow the description of a Roman church.

At Brixworth I had only a foot rule

shown in the adjoining sketch. The tangential angles were very sharp at the top, being generally less than 60 degrees, but sometimes the stones were merely laid perpendicular to the lines of the opening, with a cap at the top. A tower at Much Wenlock Abbey in Shropshire shows this style. There is a record that Leofric, the husband of the Lady Godiva, did some building at this place, but I am inclined to assign this to a century before his time. Perhaps he built the nave of the church of which the roof joint still shows on the tower wall. This had the sharp pitch

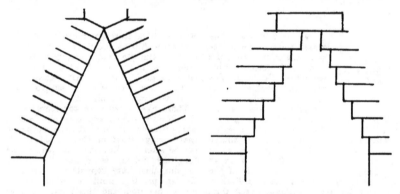

THE ANGLO-SAXON STYLE IS CHARACTERIZED BY OPENINGS COVERED WITH OVERLAPPING STONES LAID HORIZONTALLY.

and the back of an envelope for my measurements. Here again no two piers or spans agreed; but again it looked like a reminiscence of the Roman foot, though the correspondence did not seem so well defined as at Dover. The irregularity was so great that it seemed impossible to accuse of it a skilled builder in any style.

The Britons must have had what churches they needed in the Roman time, and it is difficult to conceive of their beginning to build stone churches, if before they only had wooden ones, in the terrible time of panic which marked the coming of the heathen. There is one stone church in England now recognized as of the Roman period. It is quite different from these, though I believe that all have round arches. I cannot imagine how such different arch centers came to be built as those at St. Albans.

The second Saxon style is characterized by openings covered, not by arches but by overlapping stones laid horizontal, as is

which seems to have characterized most Saxon churches, even of the latest date.

The straight sided, sharp pitched openings in Saxon architecture, instead of having either overlapping stones to cover them or stones laid at right angles to the pitch, sometimes had a single bar of stone extending over the full length of the sloping side, so that two such stones meeting at the top closed the opening just as two wooden beams would have done. These stones also in many cases corresponded with what is known as long and short work in Saxon architecture, namely, upright bars of stone of the same kind which made the ornamentation of the corners, whereas the intermediate spaces filled in with rubble. Occasionally one of these bars was laid horizontal extending well out into the rubble. The stones thus laid bore a very strong resemblance to the wooden constructions known as half-timbered work today in England, and is, I believe, a reminiscence of the time when

478

Saxon huts were mainly built in this half-timbered style, with the openings filled with clay and wattle instead of with brick work, as in present day construction.

There are in Colchester quite a number of windows of this type in ancient houses, and if I remember these are mainly of Roman brick, which abounded there. Possibly some of these may have been built later, as cheap substitutes for arches. The Saxon Chronicle records that Eadward the Elder, son of Alfred the Great, rebuilt this town in 921.

My copy of the Saxon Chronicle, published before the day of Rickman and Parker, has a lot of cuts of Saxon coins. Among those ascribed to Eadward the Elder (901-925), several show the apses of stone churches, and the Chronicle itself tells how under this Eadward was built the new minster at Winchester and the towns of Chester, Witham, Bedford, etc., were rebuilt. Doubtless this included rebuilding churches. Most of these I believe to have been in the general style of Western Europe, known as Byzantine. This would agree with the representations on the coins; and also on the jamb of the door of the unquestioned Saxon tower of Earl's Barton there is a low relief, nearly gone, but still unmistakable, representing an arcade of round arches with (if I can trust my memory for twenty years) fillets around the shafts supporting the arches. I believe Eadward the Elder to have introduced this style into England in rebuilding churches in the region from which his father had finally driven out the Danes. These heathen hung on for a long time in East Anglia, and the hold of the sons of Alfred was somewhat precarious, so that probably the new style, involving high technical skill, was slow to spread and lapped over for a long time on the older, especially in the wild no-man's land of the Welsh marches, so that possibly the Much Wenlock Tower may be Leofric's work in spite of his following a century after Eadward the Elder, although there are in that neighborhood a number of churches in the more finished later Saxon style. One of these, at Stotesden, has a feature which I have never seen in any other building. This is some beautiful low relief carving on the under surfaces of the square caps between the tops of .the shafts and the springing of the arches. Otherwise this sufficiently resembles Norman, so that Parker can be excused for classing it as such if he ever

saw it. In several other churches which I think surely Saxon there is remarkable carving; and I am inclined to think (in which I am not alone) that it was extraordinary if in the troubled reigns of the two Williams, of Henry the First, Stephen and Matilda and Henry the Second the immense amount of, so called, Norman architecture could have been erected, which is commonly credited to them, and especially by masons without previous experience; while it would not be at all exceptional to have any man who added to a building speak of the whole as his work.

I have found specific reference of earlier date than Rickman in one or two cases to churches as having been built by the Saxons, for instance, St. Johns at Chester, though probably in this case only the foundations are so early. On the other hand in Chester Cathedral there is one arch of an arcade, otherwise considered Norman, which is there represented as Saxon because of an interlacing pattern on the jambs. This I think is a mistake, for I remember seeing forty years ago a very similar pattern in Norman work at Monreale in Sicily, where the Saxons never were. On the other hand in Church Stretton is a doorway of which I believe the east jamb to be Saxon and the west Norman. The moulding is different. The break comes near the top of the arch and a piece of that on the east jamb is built into the wall above. Apparently the west end of the church had been destroyed and rebuilt in the Norman style. The earlier part may have been Norman also; but I believe it to have been late Saxon, as there are a number of late Saxon churches in the neighborhood, and the name is Saxon.

N. T. BACON.

Is Architecture a Simultaneous Art?

Somewhere, in a school of fine arts, one reads on the door of the studios for life drawing and modeling the words "Simultaneous Arts." What these words mean every one knows. I need only call attention to them in contradistinction to the "successive arts," which include literature, music, dancing, etc. While the latter unfold their creations by degrees, the former are supposed to show theirs at a glance.

It seems right to say that when an object is presented to your eye you see its whole at once, especially if the object is of a small size. But a little consideration will prove this statement to be only partly true. To see even a minute object, say, a small ring, the eye must travel from one point to the next if it is to focus equally on all parts. How much more this holds good when the object of our inspection happens to be such a work as St. Peter's or the Parthenon, in which the most we can gather from the first general impression is just an idea of the silhouette.

There is as much successive perception involved in the examining of works of architecture or sculpture as in the examination of any of the works of the "successive" arts. Those particularly interested in the subject will find the book on Rodin by Gsell extremely interesting. The master helps us to enjoy not only the masterpieces of his own art, but of painting as well. In speaking of a famous painting, "Le voyage a Lutece," he explains how the artist succeeded in suggesting motion by having the various attitudes of a movement performed by different groups of figures. Thus, in this picture, the foreground figures are hardly determined to rise, while the very last in the perspective are rushing for the boat. How could such a reading of a picture take place, but for the successive work done by the intelligent eye. The same master, explaining the meaning of "The Bronze Age," one of his own creations, says this conception represents the awakening of man to a higher knowledge. In it the master endeavored to suggest the very idea of awakening. "The feet and legs are still slumbering." It takes Rodin's power of observation to detect such a delicate thing as the slumbering of a leg. Probably the most backward Indian is in this respect far more advanced than his civilized brother, for people living in a primitive way are trained by observation to judge the mental and physical states from the mere motion of a single muscle in the body. "As the eye rises on this figure the forms begin to assume more definiteness, becomes sharper and suggestive of life, until on reaching the head we see the young man taking hold of his hair as if endeavoring to shake himself and throw off the last vestiges of sleep." It is needless to dwell on the necessity of the successive steps required to discover all these qualities in a masterpiece.

Turning to architectural conceptions, let us ask: What are the various phases to be considered in the examining of, for instance, a small inspection pavilion in a park? We have seen that our art partakes of the successive and the simultaneous, according to the distance of the observer from the work in view. Let us, then, stand at a respectable distance from our little pavilion, especially on a misty day. Hardly anything will be seen but a clear silhouette detaching itself against the sky or wood. This silhouette is enough to take hold of us, if the structure was designed with this particular consideration in view. Should it prove well done, it would invite closer inspection. We slowly approach till we detect masses of lights and shades. Though we may not perceive a single detail, if the work is successfully carried out, we shall be impressed by the harmonious distribution of these masses and their rhythm. The interest is increasing and as we approach closer we begin to distinguish details, to the examining of which we apply the same process of "thorough seeing" as we did in noting the distribution of the masses. Our progressive advance will finally take us so close to our object as to focus the very texture of the material forming the background of the ornaments. Thus we have seen the gradual unfolding of the qualities of the artist's conception: beauty in features big and small, and beauty in their relationship.

A great work of architecture must present the same qualities as the life of a great man. The latter must appeal to the historian through the hazy perspective of centuries, when nothing but general facts are perceived indicative of power or inspiration; likewise any structure of merit, be it ever so small, should present to the eye more than a mere display of details. It is the artistic arrangement of materials and details that gives the whole conception all its merit—that keeps the eye constantly interested from the moment it discovered it in the distance till one could almost touch it.

The foregoing contains a hint as to the real method of studying design. We have to satisfy the various stations of the onlooker, even the most remote. Here is where the study begins. We start with our silhouette, the prelude of our composition as it were; then gradually we pass on to the study of the main proportions of the masses and their relationships, until we reach the study of details, the nature of which must be related to the desired effects from the distance.

DAVID J. VARON.

THE ARCHITECTVRAL RECORD

CONTENTS

Vol. XLVII. No. 6   JUNE, 1920   Serial No. 261

Editor: MICHAEL A. MIKKELSEN *Contributing Editor:* HERBERT CROLY
Business Manager: J. A. OAKLEY

*Yearly Subscription: United States, $3.00; Foreign, $4.00; Single Copies, 35 cents. Copyright,
1920, by The Architectural Record Co. All rights reserved. Member Audit Bureau of Circulation.*

PUBLISHED MONTHLY BY

THE ARCHITECTURAL RECORD COMPANY

115-119 WEST FORTIETH STREET, NEW YORK

T. S. MORGAN, Pres.   W. D. HADSELL, Vice-Pres.   J. W. FRANK, Sec'y-Treas.   E. S. DODGE, Vice-Pres.

DINING ROOM—RESIDENCE OF LAWRENCE
F. ABBOTT, ESQ., CORNWALL, N. Y.
PARKER MORSE HOOPER, ARCHITECT.

THE ARCHITECTVRAL RECORD

VOLVME XLVII   NVMBER VI

JUNE, 1920

SOME PRINCIPLES OF SMALL HOUSE DESIGN

By
JOHN TAYLOR BOYD, Jr.

Part VIII   Interiors-Continued

THE interior of a house should be viewed as a picture rather than as a technical effort of design. Broad unity and a harmony of effect are particularly essential, yet are not easy to attain, because the interior is a many-sided conception, in which most of the arts and crafts have a place. Amid all the variety of technique art itself is often neglected.

There is, of course, no new idea in asserting unity in art. No one questions the precept; nevertheless too few designers realize it to the full in practice. When unity is missing in interiors, usually one cause is at fault: the variety of technique which has fostered an un-symmetrical cultivation of the whole field, as described in Part VII. Architect and decorator divide the field of the art of interiors between them, developing two different spheres of influence, which overlap at some points, and at others leave gaps for which neither feels responsible. In this division it is the architectural part of the design that suffers most. How the bad effects of this cleavage operate in many designs and how they might be avoided if the art of interiors were treated as a whole, and then properly related to the exterior part of the small house design, of lot and of elevations—all this was set forth in Part VII. However,

Part VII emphasized the side of technique, which, important as it is, should not dominate. So it might seem as if much of the confusion of the art of interiors would disappear if attention were centered on the meaning of unity. There might then be more inspired design in interiors, instead of the too usual technical formulae. That is why, in order to make the idea of unity more vivid, it is here presented as the effect of a picture.

But even the idea of a picture has its limitations when applied to the interiors of a small house. A broader conception is needed. In addition to the painter's desire for a harmonious, beautiful effect in color and form and light, there is the organic structural art of architect and of furniture designer—the foundation of the whole—and then also the more abstract, sensuous art of the decorator, which is largely the art of pure design. Still more than these, a fourth viewpoint enters into the conception of unity. The art of the sculptor has a place, with its modelling in planes and relief and light and shade. The sculptor's art has always played an essential part in most of the historic styles; has, in fact, even been supreme in certain unusual episodes, such as the baroque in Italy and the later rocaille in France. Thus all four points of view of the fine arts are combined in the design of interiors, and to them must be added the whole range of the handicrafts which were developed almost entirely for interiors.

The perfect combination of the varied arts and crafts in an interior, first one and then the other predominating in different incidents of the design, ensures the unity—the picture—that is sought. It is because of the presence of the several arts in the same design that the technique of interior art in small houses is many-sided, even though it be not very complex in each one art. What is required of the designer is a breadth of view rather than an extraordinary specialist ability in any one line.

The process of design in interiors is therefore a long one. It begins with the architectural shell, pictured as a whole

and in its relation to the outside world; it passes through the planning and modelling of this shell of rooms and spaces, as described in Part VII; through the intermediate stage—part architecture, part furniture, of subordinate motives like doors, windows, alcoves, bay-windows, stairs, fireplaces—into the stage of furniture, and only ends with the finishing touches of the abstract art of hangings, art objects and other decorations. In all this process, rightly considered—a truth which cannot be remembered too often—there is no true line of division, no real classification into separate parts. It is one thing, and that only a part of the house as a whole.

The purpose of this chapter is to set forth some of the ways in which these different viewpoints, particularly those of the four major arts, combine in the varied process of interior design.

The interior of a small house, then, is best conceived as a picture painted in colors and light and form, which in addition bears the imprint of the conditions of site and situation outside, and which, inside, symbolizes the human interest of the family. In a sense it is a link between man and his neighborhood. Being thus a crucial point in the design of the house, it presents another reason for maintaining a delicate balance of relationships. Hence much depends upon the character of the picture, and it is evident that a theatrical quality, such as overpowering effects and the lavish display of self-advertising, however they might impress in a decoration in a public building, do not belong in the home. In other words—here is another essential which is probably the key to it all—the expression of harmonious restraint, of a fine taste, should penetrate every detail. As much as any other quality, good taste is needed in a home.

Good taste cannot be exaggerated in interiors. Even an illiterate peasantry may appreciate its value. It helps unravel the snarl of technique, especially when complexity threatens to ensnare the design. It has a bearing on the decision as to the degree of variety, of boldness, of imagination, that the artist

LIVING ROOM—RESIDENCE OF JAMES A. BURDEN, ESQ., SYOSSET, L. I.
Delano & Aldrich, Architects.

LIVING ROOM—RESIDENCE OF JAMES A. BURDEN, ESQ., SYOSSET, L. I.
Delano & Aldrich, Architects.

will seek. Thus good taste may decide the question of how much flexibility of design is desirable. In fact, any advice to seek variety or boldness in a design is a matter of degree, and this good taste decides. And since it is one of the most difficult decisions in art, it is worth further illustration.

At this point the reader should recall the many remarks in previous pages, asserting the value of a more flexible system of design, of originality, of the necessity of freeing interior art from formulae—particularly of the stock plan—in short, of the need for inspiration. Of an opposite sort were comments on the side of moderation, advising that art be simple and harmonious. It would seem that these offhand statements, to the effect that interest should be counteracted by restraint, were not enough. We should attempt a more specific understanding of the compromise which combines conflicting principles in proper proportion.

Some people will be surprised at the idea that principles may be connected with good taste. Good taste has been often viewed as a mystical, personal quality of the artist that could not be analyzed. There is some truth in this view; but it was held in extreme form in the nineteenth century when art was concerned with the "major" arts and preferred to dwell on the work of genius or of highly specialized talent. But now that these literary mists which have veiled art are blowing away, it may be well to examine this theory. May one not believe that good taste is evolved in a proper interpretation of the conditions of a problem, more than is sometimes admitted? The fact of the matter is, if the design be direct and expressive, it will probably be in good taste. To say this is not to rob the artist of his personal prerogative, because expressiveness in a design depends more on a clear, imaginative understanding of the deep-lying, intangible factors of a specific problem, than on an easy reading of the surface indications, which are often dangerous and deceptive. As everyone knows, the greatest achieve-

ment of the artist is to interpret the intangibles.

All this would seem obvious enough—the principle that good taste depends much on grasping the intangible factors and conditions of design in a problem. Style, as we are beginning to understand it, depends on these intangibles, and we take a great step forward, I think, if we further realize that good taste is closely bound up with style. If once we understand style as the principle of design that native conditions and national temperament force upon us, as set forth in the previous issues of this series, almost inevitably conceptions of good taste become clearer. They seem akin to those of style. We then are furnished with criterions of judgment, of perception, which all of us can firmly grasp. On the other hand, as long as we hold to the older notion that style is a more or less arbitrary set of intellectual forms, either developed in the brain of the brilliant designer, or else borrowed by him from a foreign art, we have no real basis for judgment. Agreement is hardly possible, because the intangibles either do not exist, or, if it is a question of an imported art, the intangibles and conditions are not found here or can not be understood by Americans. In such a method the real props that support style and good taste have been knocked out. Certainly art-styles, which can reach the perfection of form and good taste only as mental feats of extraordinary gifted men, cannot be worth much to a people. If the theory of style and good taste as a personal prerogative, an abstract set of forms, were correct, that would rule out the whole field of craftsmanship, the work of humble men. Unfortunately, for the caste theory of style and good taste, these qualities are never so imaginatively perfect as in the best craftmen's art. Craftsmen's art is the despair of the academic book-and-paper trained designer in these as in other of its qualities.

Thus it seems just to believe that the only serviceable style and good taste are those of a vital national tradition, its judgments and instincts, the common property of all designers. This tradition helps determine the intangibles which must be expressed in design if it is to be sound. It is no drawback to the true master, since it relieves him from the heavy intellectual task of inventing abstract forms, or of establishing the fundamentals of good taste; and sets his full energy free in creative art. In other words, he is entirely an artist, instead of partly a mathematician or a philosopher. And there is another benefit in such a conception of style and good taste, which is this—that in expressing native conditions and thus establishing a tradition,

art runs along in the same channels with the rest of the life of society and becomes an intimate part of it. Unless the American public can instinctively recognize in a work of art the same fundamental native characteristics that it knows in other experiences in life, it has no basis of appreciation. Not only each of the many arts, but also literary, musical, and intellectual activities will have no relation to the native temperament and its environment, nor to each other, and the existing confusion in art and letters and music will never be cleared up.

An illustration of this principle may

RECEPTION ROOM—RESIDENCE OF JAMES A. BURDEN, ESQ., SYOSSET, L. I.
Delano & Aldrich, Architects.

LIVING ROOM—RESIDENCE OF MRS. E. EGERTON WINTHROP, SYOSSET, L. I.
Delano & Aldrich, Architects.

be desirable. For instance, if in decorating an interior, an American housewife is advised to acquire certain furniture and hangings and to arrange them in a certain way, because Madame du Barry once approved this scheme, she hardly knows what to say to the suggestion. But if she is told that our strong sunlight—which, like other Americans, she delights to see flood into the house, bringing out every detail clearly—almost of itself requires that certain colors and designs of form be used, she has been offered a basis for decision which rests on knowledge and not on whim. She is deciding the question on a viewpoint of pure art, in principles of good taste and style. Likewise, when an American home owner is asked to live in an ornate, oppressive house, his common sense makes him ill at ease. But when the designer informs him that both the necessities of clear light without atmosphere, and of the native temperament and of American society require a simpler pattern, he

easily grasps the principle. He sees the basis for the design and he may trace its development throughout all details. His interest in art awakens.

This relationship between style and good taste may be carried further in order to help explain certain doubts that have caused great controversy. These concern the tiresome argument as to the classic versus the picturesque, the symmetrical versus the unsymmetrical, the formal versus the informal. There is no need to refer to them here except to remark that, under the nineteenth century conception of style and good taste as mostly arbitrary intellectual symbols, such discussion was altogether in order. Where, however, these factors in design consist in meeting conditions of specific problems, instead of avoiding them, certain valuable truths emerge. One is that extreme classicism or formality hardly meets the needs of the American of today, or his desires, neither does extreme picturesqueness. Neither extremes are apt to arise as the natural result of

ENTRANCE HALL—RESIDENCE OF DR. E. J. CURRY, FALL RIVER, MASS.
Parker Morse Hooper, Architect.

conditions. Exceptions will be rare, and then will occur only under such distinctive conditions that there can be no doubt as to the taste. But where conditions are not forced too far, the proportion of formal and informal, or the choice between the two, will be settled by a close reading of the conditions of the problem.

Particularly is it necessary to establish a clearer idea of the picturesque. To do so, it is necessary to refer to the exterior, because its character influences the character of the interior. One of the worst tendencies in small houses is the indiscriminate use of picturesque, free motives of design, often of North European origin. They overload many houses. In former pages it was noted how these forms did not suit American conditions in respect to light, color, modeling and national temperament. Without repeating these, it may be remarked again that

much of the beauty of the picturesque North European architecture comes from the mellowness of the gloomy, misty light there. A film of atmosphere has been drawn across the picture made by the architecture, harmonizing its variety and complexity of form. In our light the same architecture looks restless and spotty. There are southern types of picturesque, which, though equally striking, have greater unity—or the kind of unity—suited to our southern conditions. Such a type has simplicity and repose in mass and surface and outline and form, pure proportion, and careful distribution of centres of interest, which are emphasized. Because the eye is strained in intense sunshine, it should be rested by effects of broad, plain surfaces. Any widespread pattern of decoration of architecture, like windows spotted closely together, or a wall of bright brick

489

joints, defeats this purpose. Ornament is better if used sparingly, not scattered either, but concentrated, with differences in relief, so that any hardness or line or shape is softened by shadows and shade broken across it. In southern art color doors and outdoors, between the buildings, old and new, of the University of Virginia, where Thomas Jefferson and his craftsmen obeyed a principle of color that later architects ignored, among them even so great an artist as Stanford White.

DINING ROOM—RESIDENCE OF E. L. TAYLOR, ESQ., NEW HAVEN, CONN.
Parker Morse Hooper, Architect.

is a requisite; without it form crops out hard and naked. Color of a kind that brings unity through being clear and sparkling is needed, which the bright light makes richer and mellower and warmer, instead of bleaching it gray and cold.

Proof of this lies in the difference, in-

As a result the newer buildings, though finely designed in the same form as the old, have other colorations that are either dark or neutral, and are decisively out of key of the sunshine and of the vivid green foliage. It is a striking evidence that key of color is as important as form is in architecture.

Besides conditions of light and color there are also the character of the landscape that influences style and good taste. Our landscapes are broad, usually rough and often bold. They require a more solid, a broader, simpler type of design than that suited to the more delicately shaped, more finished parklike landscapes of England or of the garden country of France. lie deep at the roots of that great division in art between the Classic and the Gothic. It really seems to be the difference between the art of the south, of the sunlit Mediterranean with its bold dramatic outdoors on one hand; and on the other the art of North Europe, of dimmer light and softer nature. Geography dictates that one shall be in form simple,

LIVING ROOM—RESIDENCE OF E. L. TAYLOR, ESQ., NEW HAVEN, CONN.
Parker Morse Hooper, Architect.

France. If there is any truth in the principle that architecture should be consistent with the setting that nature furnishes it, it is evident that here are fundamental imperatives of taste and style which determine art in America, of which the art of the interior is only a part.

Thus it would seem that we are committed to a southern type of art in the United States. At least an art that is different from that developed by the special conditions of Northwest Europe. In fact, I am inclined to believe that these differences of climate, light, landscape, color—and the type of art they evolve— robust, full, reposeful, even when dramatic; the other complex, more delicate, subtle, mystic. A different series of rhythms are required in each. Geography ordains that in the south the color be light, clear, vivid, perhaps with centres of intensity; and in the north that it be more neutral, or deeper, or murky. Energy and life and imagination are apt to be found in the form of northern architecture; and in southern architecture, in its color and contrasts of bold, full geometrical shapes. And if there be any who associate an idea of decadence or weakness with the south, it is only necessary to point out to them that in the

491

whole world no art has ever been more virile, freer, more boldly monumental, more vibrating with energy, than the art of Spain. Needless to say, also, that one can hardly afford to patronize Greek or Italian art as ineffective.

Such differences seem more fundamental than any distinctions that are made between southern and northern art

Even in spirit our art can hardly be the same, because racial and social conditions are different with us, and even our geography is not identical with any part of Europe. As I endeavored to prove in previous articles of the series, we have our own type of American tradition, which was developed through two centuries far along towards evolving an art

DINING ROOM—RESIDENCE OF THOMAS W. RUSSELL, ESQ., HARTFORD, CONN.
Parker Morse Hooper, Architect.

on the basis of classic symmetry as opposed to free, picturesque art. It should be remembered that the south has a characteristic free, picturesque type of its own, which is akin to the symmetrical "classic" type in the qualities just mentioned. It does not resemble the picturesque types of the north in spirit. Natural conditions in the south and north dictate a difference in spirit that extends to all types of design, whether symmetrical or not, formal or informal.

Of course, although the style and taste of our art should be southern, that does not mean that we copy literally the art of the Mediterranean in the United States.

that suits our peculiar needs. It marks out the road to be followed with energy and purpose, and style and good taste are more eloquently taught in its models than is possible in any writings.

This idea of a southern or classic mean —or vein—that runs through American art, imposing restraint yet allowing expression to the energy of our race and time, helps fix the degree of flexibility in design. If there is necessity for a flexible conception of design to meet conditions, it should be realized that it is only of value for that purpose, and should not be pursued for its own sake. It should not in its turn become a recipe for design.

Specific instances of this have been pointed out in former pages and they need not be repeated here.

These are some of the principles of style and of good taste, two factors which are so closely identical. Such a concep-

at any rate, whatever its sources, it is known over the world and in France as *le gout francais*. *Le gout francais* saturates the work of any Frenchman, whether he be an impossible radical or a reactionary, drenching it in Frenchi-

STAIRWAY—RESIDENCE OF WALTER H. CRITTENDEN, ESQ., CORNWALL, N. Y.
Parker Morse Hooper, Architect.

tion is held among the French, the one people in the modern world which is the most easily artistic. The French maintain an uninterrupted tradition, yet are always reinterpreting it freely and freshly in the spirit of the times. How much of it is the result of nature and how much

ness. It simply means the French taste and style.

This ends the consideration of the principles that, it may be conceived, in some measure form our ideas of style and good taste. As stated above, although they pertain largely to the exterior of the

STAIRWAY — RESIDENCE OF WALTER H.
CRITTENDEN, ESQ., CORNWALL, N. Y.
PARKER MORSE HOOPER, ARCHITECT.

terior, because they are so fundamental, because the interior cannot be divorced from the rest of the household, and because the intimate humanness of the house interior make them so vital there. It remains to set forth some of the ways in which they are incorporated into the interior design.

Where the four major arts and most of the handicrafts are combined in a design, as they are indoors, they do not all necessarily operate in the same way. Some or one of them may symbolize the main interest; while some, or one, may embody most of the unity. For instance, where the architectural shell is simple and severe, the interest may be emphatic in minor architectural motives or in furniture and furnishings. Where the architectural shell is more diverse in form, too much interest in details might make it split into parts, appearing restless; hence the details may be most harmonious, even inconspicuous, or very sparingly used, just enough to prevent bareness. Countless examples of these ideas can be presented.

There is the case of many of the interiors of Mr. Charles A. Platt in great houses, where big, simple, almost squarish rooms are splendidly decorated with monumental motives of architecture on walls and ceilings, and a fine display in decorations. Besides, the big squarish shapes and the scale of the rooms are repeated in the architectural motives and the furnishings. Mr. Colby carried out this scheme in a way expressive of the small house in his living room illustrated in Part VII. This is a squarish room, appearing large, and its fine character lies in the south window, with its concentrated light, also—which should not be forgotten—in the long plain wall surface opposite, which offers a contrast and a background; in the beamed ceiling and in the interesting furniture and decorations. On the other hand, Mr. Parker Morse Hooper's interiors, of boldly designed architectural shell, are tempered with simple harmonious furniture and decorations. Among rooms of irregular shape none are more beautiful than the living room in the home of Mr. A.

Stewart Walker, the architect, illustrated in The Architectural Record of last July. It will repay thorough study to perceive the ways in which the unusual variety of plan of the room was harmonized by the furnishings and architectural details, which prevent it from seeming loose in form and dividing into parts. It is such a room as would appeal to a painter.

Of the place of the sculptor's art of light and shade and modeling in planes and relief, there are not so many striking examples in the houses of today as there were in some of the historic styles, like the baroque or rocaille, where the sculptor, even if an architect, held sway throughout the design, repeating his imaginative, sensuous shapes and curves in walls, ceilings, architectural motives and details, and in the furniture and all the art objects and decorations. Naturally such exuberance hardly comes within the field of the American small house, but the principle of the sculpturesque qualities in design is a good one, and it may often be well worked out in minor details of architecture and furnishings.

Always, in this union of the arts and crafts in the interior, the balance should be kept. If one art leans far toward variety, the others may set up a counteracting restraint, yet not aiming to conceal or to negative the expression. If all were equally bold and imaginative in the same room, the unity of the design might become theatrical or exaggerated in one direction.

All these principles of design have dealt with the interior as a whole. Next to them in importance are the considerations that appear in the design of individual rooms and spaces of the small house. One of the first of these is the expression of function in a room. Decorators understand this well in their part of the design when they declare that a dining room should appear as a place for eating, that a reception room should have the expression of a place where guests are received, and so on. This is, of course, a sound principle; but its first application should come as much as possible in the architectural shell of room or space. This again reveals a further

ENTRANCE HALL—RESIDENCE OF ANDREW
M O R R I S O N, ESQ., MONTCLAIR, N. J.
WILLIAM EDGAR MORAN, ARCHITECT.

defect in the unvarying use of the box-like room in the stock plan, which too often makes impossible any distinctive character in the room and reduces decoration to formulae.

It is not necessary to enter at length into the ways in which each space of the interior may take on character, but one may point out certain features of the process. This is a principle of planning and has been treated to a large extent in former issues.

The position and arrangement of the entrance stairs were referred to at length in Parts IV and V. The possibilities of interesting, expressive and more compact arrangement were covered. Here also the need for proper circulation comes into play. If the stairs are to ascend from the living room, they may well be near the front entrance, otherwise the path of circulation from entrance to stairs will cut across the living room, where people will wish to gather undisturbed; that is to say, the function of hallway must not be overlooked in combining stairs with other rooms. The stairs may also be planned for access to service portion or a secondary outside entrance leading to garage. Whatever be the arrangement, the stairs affords many interesting opportunities for design.

It is the design of the living room, in combination with or relation to the dining room, that may yield great possibilities. The linking of spaces together, to gain effect of space or to preserve individuality, described in Part VII, should be recalled here. The essential in this flexibility is, of course, the plan, which may express function in many ways through the use of technical motives, such as stairs, stair landings, bay windows, alcoves, fireplaces, etc. Even an ordinary living room has functions of lounging or reading or entertaining which may appear in the plan and in the architecture of the room. Where other functions, such as dining, are added to the living room, they may also receive expression in its design, at least so much as will not destroy the unity. Excellent examples of this manifold expression of functions of a living room in plan, and

therefore in shape, are the living room, in Part IV, of the house of Dr. T. J. Abbott, designed by Mr. Parker Morse Hooper, and also the living room in the cottage in Connecticut designed by Murphy and Dana, in Part VI, in each of which was planned a place for meal table, and service to it, for entertaining visitors, for lounging—every function kept distinct from the others. A living room as large as 18x30 contains great possibilities in providing for all sorts of human use in its shape, even to quiet corners or retiring spaces, where one person may be apart while others are gathering elsewhere in the room.

The relationship of living room to outdoors through transitional spaces, such as bay windows, porches, or breakfast rooms, was mentioned in Part VII. Here is another case where much commonplace, perfunctory design occurs, in their resemblance to greenhouses or even to a factory, a resemblance which extends to the tiresome use of lattice, though this latter practice is not so much followed as formerly. Such transitional spaces should have a well developed character, expressed in various ways—in the design of glass in relation to wall spaces and piers so as not to lose solidity or acquire looseness; in use of rougher textures, brighter colors, greater contrasts, bolder shapes, change of materials; more charm and vivacity of details, like iron or brass, and the use of plants and flowers.

These principles of functional expression extend to all parts of the house, even to design of bedrooms and of service portions. In bedrooms, good taste at least is well established, in a simplicity of design and decoration that only needs more interest and charm of shape of room and proportioning of window illumination to make these chambers one of the best parts of the home. Often they are too much cut up with doors and windows to have all the air of repose that is desirable: although, in this connection, it must be remembered that the heat of our summers calls for cross-ventilation from windows in two walls wherever possible. As to the service portion, that will be dealt with in a later article;

but it may be remarked here that there is much room for good taste and interest of design in such parts of the house without encroaching upon the strictly practical character of its dispositions. Since of recent years grim economic pressure has forced the housewife to spend more time in the service part of the house, she has found means to make it take on attraction in an artless way. Kitchen and service are not only much more practical now, but they are not so shop-like as formerly.

Leaving these many ideas of design of individual rooms and spaces, the more subordinate aspects of details of interior architecture come next in order in this examination of the progress of design. With this, a wide field opens indeed. It is a crucial point in the design of a room, for it forms a transition, a linking in design between the architecture of the room shell and the furniture and furnishing. The same principles of design are found in these minor motives as in the larger features of the house, and they are now well handled by American architects. They furnish endless opportunity of interest and charm, and, in a rectangular shaped room, they furnish a large part of the character, if not all of it. Such an example was the living room of Mr. Frank A. Colby's house in Part VII. One may call attention, however, to two great faults in the details of American interiors. One is inconsistency in shapes; and the other is overemphasis of lines, rectangles and other angles.

The disharmony of shapes in American interiors is, I am forced to believe, largely a matter of faulty, even careless, practice in design. This assertion seems proven by the fact that it is found less in rooms that are elaborately designed with paneling and similar architectural motives, where the designer has been obliged to make careful detailed drawings. Too often smaller rooms are designed by proportioning the windows with regard to the exterior solely, and merely figuring sizes of doors and other openings on the plan.

Had the designer taken the trouble to make even a rough scale drawing of the rooms of the wall, he might have noted an inconsistency in its shapes that could have been easily remedied with perhaps only slight changes. Fat, rectangular shapes, without real proportion, inharmonious with other shapes of decoration, easily creep into design. While one should avoid the error of laying down dimensions in design, it seems clear that, in the living portion of a house, a double doorway, 6 feet 8 inches high and 4 feet or less wide, is apt to yield a better shape of casing and pattern of door paneling than one 5 feet wide, or even 4 feet 6 inches wide. Such fat rectangularity is particularly hard when emphasized by a color contrast, and it is at its worst when used side by side with flowing curves, like ellipses or ovals or semi-circles, or else with complex architectural motives such as the orders. The basis of most architectural design is the purpose to depart from crude, primitive angularity, and it must be thought that the attempt to use these two extremes in the same design shows a lack of sensitiveness to form and a perfunctory comprehension of the real meaning of motives of design. Yet this fault runs all through American architecture; it may be seen in elevations and even in the design of gardens, and in the shapes of pools and fountains.

In small houses consistency of shape and harmony of measures and change from straight line to curve are extraordinarily important, because small house interiors are usually simple and disharmony is only too easily noticed in them. This quality really marks one of the distinctions between the amateur and the professional. It is seen at its best, as far as the small house is concerned, in the early American rooms. Any comparison of a drawing of the elevations of the walls of an old room, even a simple one such as a kitchen, with some modern rooms that somehow seem to lack sureness and harmony, is apt to show distinct superiority in mass, shape, proportion and line in favor of the old model. The reason is that the old model was designed by craftsmen—right "on the job"—by men who knew instinctively the difference that an inch or two in height, and espe-

LIVING ROOM—RESIDENCE OF ANDREW MORRISON, ESQ., MONTCLAIR, N. J.
William Edgar Moran, Architect.

cially width, of a window or door meant before they built it into the walls of the room.

The other vice of contemporary design, excessive lines and hard lines and angles, is everywhere apparent. It stands ruthlessly revealed by our clear native light, even in interiors. This is where the sculptor's ability to soften hard lines and edges, by his modeling in light and shade, is of great value, as well as the technique of the painter who knows how to blend over edges. It is an evidence of the need of color and of texture in interiors, if any were needed.

Texture is, of course, important in an interior. Nothing adds more quality in design, provided it be not overdone, as it often is at the hands of certain designers, where it partakes of sophistication, or an extreme affectation for the rustic or the antique. At any rate, we are getting away from hard, machine-like surfaces. Another fault of current design in interiors may be noted: that is, the use of brick surfaces whose coarse texture and crude checkered pattern of joints are at variance with all the rest of the room. Often a brick fireplace facing is the most aggressive feature in a whole room. Only seldom have I seen brick used successfully indoors, and then only where it is done boldly and consistently with certain other materials, in broad masses, largely in semi-outdoor spaces like sun-rooms or loggias.

All this architectural detail should harmonize, even combine, with the furniture and decorations. The modelling and texture and scale of cornices, belt courses, casings on walls and ceilings and the details of features, like bookcases, window seats, mantels, cupboards, alcoves, should be wrought with the furniture in mind. Indeed, some designers prefer to talk of them as furniture rather than as architecture, and hold that they should portray a freedom and fancy of form —within proper limits—which take them far from the sober appearance of more strict architectural forms. This flexibility, leading to a sculptor's viewpoint of

499

pure form, is all the more permissible, since these features, even if fanciful, are bound to derive solidity in any case from being incorporated in the walls, the bold planes and angles of which they relieve, aiding in the effect of transition from architecture to furnishings. Again, for illustration, one must point to the early American craftsmanship whose wealth of fancy and sense of exquisite form yield richest inspiration in these details.

This tradition of American craftsmanship is now so well re-established in design in the eastern part of the country, that it needs no further illustration. I would, however, except the fireplace, yielding it at least a brief remark. The fireplace is the ultimate symbol of the home, the hearth itself. The oldest human interest in the world centers in it. The home owner who appreciates its significance, as so many do, takes the keenest pleasure in the design of his hearths, with their chimney breasts and mantels. In no feature of the home is there more opportunity for design, and art has always been lavished upon it. If one may explain the keynote of its design, he may say that it is wholly a frame, a setting for the fire on the hearth, with light and flames playing against gloom and darkness. However complete a unit the mantel or enframement may be, it should always enframe the fire. The American tradition has a bewildering variety in hearth design, now well known, that is replacing the perfunctory types still too often found. Some designers still feel that small fireplaces are required in small houses. Distinctly this is not true. In some old houses the fireplace will occupy almost the whole wall of a small room. In Part VII, Mr. Colby's towering living-room fireplace shows another model. This is of Italian inspiration, offering a large black background for a small fire, if desired, in scale with the room. In contrast to this is the commonplace formulae of living room fireplace, 3 feet by 4 feet opening, with mantel shelf slightly over 4 feet high and bedroom fireplaces somewhat smaller. In fireplace design too much emphasis cannot be placed on the facing of the opening. This is an integral part of the fire enframement, and one of the crudest devices in interior design, as remarked above, is to make this of brick with strongly marked joints. If a better material cannot be had, the brick may be painted a dark deep color, black or even a rich purple red, such as I once saw in an old fireplace on Nantucket. In fact, if I were asked to name the three worst minor faults in house design, I would list them as strip panels, glass panes in interior doors, and brick fireplace facings. Yet who of us has not committed them at some one time or other?

It is not necessary to go further into this architectural detail of interiors. Interior decoration, so-called, will occupy the next issue of this series. Here one may conclude by saying that the tradition of beautiful interior design in our early American provides us with more ideas than can be set down in volumes. We need only to learn its vocabulary through a study of its best models, and then learn to apply it imaginatively and expressively and accurately in the houses of the day. We may well incorporate into this tradition our American notion of modern ideas of color and design that are coming back into civilization with a fresher spirit. But the older American tradition is needed to supply the foundation of firmness and consistency and vigor, to give both life and purity to the pattern of form and color of all the arts and crafts that is woven into the unity of the interior. Only in that way may the picture have taste and style. Taste and style are the channel through which the art of a people flows.

The MODEL FOR THE BAHAI TEMPLE, CHICAGO

LOUIS J. BOURGEOIS, ARCHITECT

By J. R. Reid

THE model designed by Louis J. Bourgeois for the great Bahai Temple to be built in Chicago is attracting much attention from architects. It is of unusual interest from several points of view. The Temple is a new and original form in architecture—"the first new idea in architecture since the thirteenth century," according to Mr. H. Van Buren Magonigle. Beautiful in the harmony of its proportions, it has in addition a singular charm in its symbolism; and to the psychologist it is noteworthy, because the creator declares: "It is Baha Ollah's temple. I am only the channel through which it came."

In form the temple is a nonagon, or nine-sided structure, and its lower

LOUIS J. BOURGEOIS.

story offers a complete innovation in architecture in the use of nine inverted half circles, with a great doorway in the centre of each, so that from whatsoever side one approaches the edifice it seems to extend its arms in welcome. From dome to foundation it is a unique creation and unlike any building in existence, yet one reads in its curving beauty the story of the architecture of the world. The first floor in its simplicity of line suggests the Greek and Egyptian temples; while the treatment of the doors and windows is Romanesque in form, and both Gothic and Arabic in the intricacy and beauty of ornamentation. The second story is Renaissance in line and Gothic in the interlaced arches of its openings. The third is restful, quiet and Renaissance in treatment. Above it rises a lovely dome, suggestive of Byzantine forms; but above the closed top rise other beams of the dome itself like hands clasped in prayer, so that the dome gives the feeling of ascension and aspiration found previously in the Gothic towers alone.

In the geometric forms of the ornamentation covering the columns and surrounding windows and doors of the temple, one deciphers all the religious symbols of the world. Here are the swastika cross, the circle, the triangle, the double triangle or six pointed star (or *Solomon's seal,* the magic symbol of mecromancers of old); but more than this, the noble symbol of the spiritual Orb, or Sun behind the Saviour of mankind; the five pointed star, representing the man saviour—Christ or Buddha or Mohammed; the Greek Cross, the Roman

501

or Christian Cross; and, supreme above all, the wonderful nine pointed star, figured in the structure of the temple itself, and appearing again and again in its ornamentation, as significant of the Spiritual Glory in the world today.

The nine pointed star reappears in the formation of the windows and doors, which are all topped by this magnificent allegory of spiritual glory, from which extend gilded rays covering the lower surfaces, and illustrating, in this vivid and artistic limning, the descent of the Holy Spirit.

Curiously enough this *Descent* of the Holy Spirit was the first thing Louis J. Bourgeois pictured in his drawing of the temple. He said, "I did the doors and windows of the lower story first, and then I got the entire form."

The numbers 9 and 19 recur again and again in the structure of the temple, illustrating its basic principle of Unity—9 being the number of perfection, containing in itself the completion of each perfect number cycle, and 19 representing the Union of God and man, as manifested in life, civilization and all things.

His description of how he made the model is as interesting as the structure itself; but in reading it one must remember that Bourgeois is an architect of long and wide experience. He built Gothic churches in France; then he built them in Canada. His buildings are found in Chicago, in California, where he erected and planned the well known house and garden of Paul de Longpré, the flower painter, and also in New York.

Twenty-five years ago he had a remarkable spiritual experience, through which he came into a knowledge of his spiritual self, as well as his physical man. Then he was told that some day he would build a great temple, and he made a sketch of a circular twelve sided building, at that time. Henceforth he dreamed of his temple, and tried to make a drawing of it, but could not. He became interested in the Bahai Movement, and nine years ago made an architectural drawing of a temple, in order that he might be represented in the competition spoken of at that time for the erection of a Bahai

temple in Chicago; but he said then, "This is not my temple, I am only putting it in to get a chance in the competition. If I win, I can draw the real temple."

But the competition never materialized, and four years ago, when he returned from the Bahai convention in Boston, Bourgeois suddenly, in an hour's time, sketched the lower story of his temple. But he could get no further, and half dazed by the ornate splendor of this fragment realized that he must model it, because he could never express on a flat surface the many-faced beauty of its plan. He endeavored to cut into the plaster the intricate tracery of ornament he saw; but he had never done such work, and he was obliged to ask the help of a friend skilled in the art, and after half a day's training he went at his task successfully. He did each successive story in this way, modelling the beauty in plaster as it was revealed to him, never seeing the whole, yet saying to himself constantly, "How do I dare go on? Because this is so wonderful; and how can I make a dome wonderful enough to complete it?" And then always the thought would come, "The Power that is giving you this will give you a dome the most wonderful of all!"

So he did the first story with its welcoming arms, and the second with its Gothic elegance, and the third with its Renaissance quiet and beauty. One morning he wakened suddenly at three o'clock and knew that he was to draw the dome. He was very happy; and as his fingers flew on for a rich hour, he knew that the dome was the most wonderful of all. That is why he says, "It is Baha Ollah's temple. It is not mine!"

There is another side to this temple story, which is both human and appealing. It has to do with love and comprehension and faithful service. The architect is not rich, and he realized that if he worked at his model the family income would cease, and perhaps no one would ever build his mighty temple. His wife is also an artist, but she bought a little notion store in West Englewood; and while he worked on the model, she sold ice cream and candy. When he needed

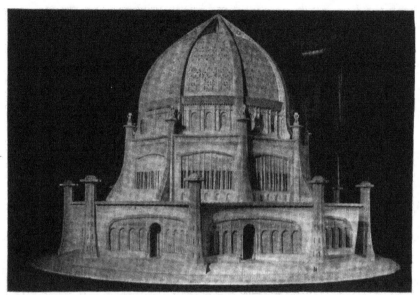

MODEL OF THE BAHAI TEMPLE, CHICAGO.
Louis J. Bourgeois, Architect.

clay for his first modelling he was out of money, so he went into the garden, filled his wife's clothes basket with Dorothy Perkins roses, which covered the arbor. He took them to New York and sold them for five dollars, with which he bought his clay.

He though he could make the model in three months, but it took him three years, and he says his wife is really the temple builder, for had it not been for her sympathy and cheerful sacrifice he never could have carried to completion the gigantic work.

The model is now on exhibition at the Kevorkian gallery in New York City. It was chosen for erection in Chicago by the delegates to the Bahai Convention, held recently in New York. Its original plan demands a building 360 feet in height, and 450 feet in diameter; but these figures will be halved for the Chicago structure, making a dimension of 180 by 225. The building constructed in this size will cost somewhere near a million and a half dollars.

One naturally asks what is behind such a conception and what it means for humanity. The Bahai Movement, which is planning this stupendous creation, is the great international movement of Unity and Brotherhood, which arose in Persia in 1844 and extends its branches and its influence everywhere at the present time. It was first taught by Ali Mohammed, who was presently given the title of Bab or Gate, meaning a door opened between heaven and earth. He foretold the coming af Baha Ollah, who he said would appear in nineteen years. and would be the *Glory of God* for all mankind through the nobility of his life and teachings. Baha Ollah means the *Glory of God,* and his influence, penetrating all mankind in the Glory shining through him, will at length unite all religions, all nations, all races—banishing hatred, rancour, partisanship in the great love which rises through realization of the Fatherhood of God and the true brotherhood of mankind.

Baha Ollah died in 1892 in the prison town of Acca, Syria, to which he had been sent by those persecutors who, as in the case of all the Prophets, could not distinguish light from darkness. He left

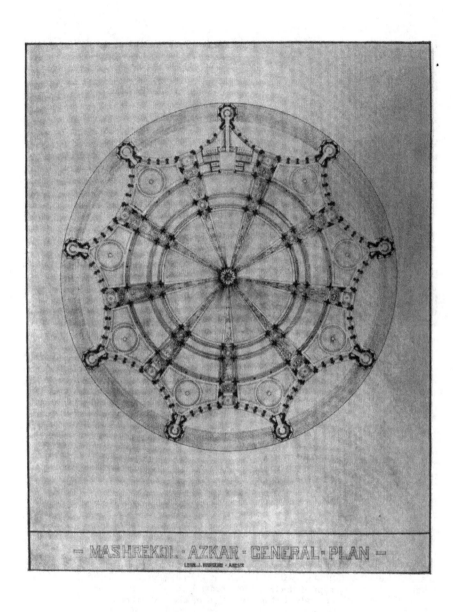

PLAN OF THE BAHAI TEMPLE. LOUIS
J. BOURGEOIS, ARCHITECT.

ONE OF THE NINE ENTRANCES, BAHAI TEMPLE.
Louis J. Bourgeois, Architect.

the leadership of the movement in the hands of his son, Abbas, also a prisoner, saying, "I have established a new covenant between God and Man, and my son is the centre of that covenant."

His son took the title of Abdul Baha, or *The Servant of God*, literally, the *Slave of the Glory*, and the name of Abdul Baha has already become known everywhere, the synonym for service, love and wisdom. He was freed from imprisonment in 1908, through the action of the constitutional revolution in Turkey, and since then has travelled in western countries, visiting America in 1912.

The Bahai Revelation, as it is sometimes called, inspires a movement, not a sect. It has a very slight organization embodied in a *Unity Board*, which manages the Temple fund. The temple will be a great place of worship for all mankind. Its doors will never be closed; no priesthood will ever officiate within its walls; about it will be gardens and fountains; and beyond these, a series of buildings devoted to the application of true religion to life, a hospital, an orphan asylum, a hospice or house of hospitality, a guild house, a university, etc. Only worship can be voiced in the temple itself; but the results of such worship are to be evidenced in these surrounding buildings, where all activities of the community will meet in the comradship inspired by mutual counsel from which criticism and politics shall have been banished.

505

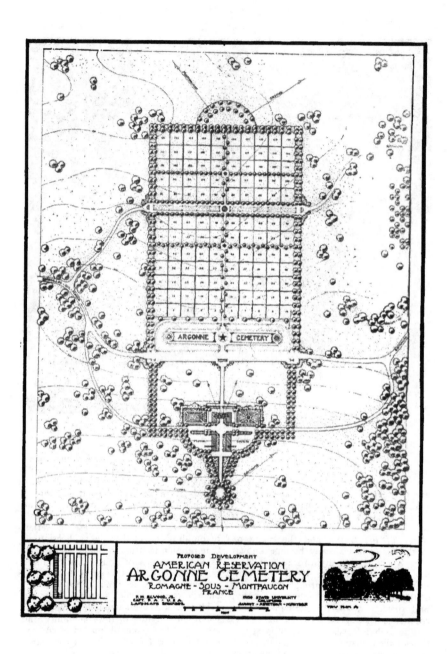

PROPOSED DEVELOPMENT
AMERICAN RESERVATION
ARGONNE CEMETERY
ROMAGNE - SOUS - MONTFAUCON
FRANCE

THE ARGONNE CEMETERY OF THE A. E. F. AT ROMAGNE-SOUS-MONTFAUCON, FRANCE

BY P. H. ELWOOD, JR.

CARING for the dead is one of the most trying tasks to be performed by an army in the field. However, the problem was not so complicated for the American army as it had been earlier in the war, when large areas frequently changed hands several times during the active fighting. Ground once gained by the Americans in France was never relinquished to the enemy except for most temporary retention. The duty of identification and burial of our dead was assigned to the Graves Registration Service of the Quartermaster Corps, whose burial parties followed closely upon the heels of the advancing soldiers, often under heavy shell-fire.

During and immediately following an offensive, graves were necessarily shallow and hastily located near where the body fell. One of the two identification tags carried by every soldier in the field was buried with the body and the other attached to the temporary cross marking the grave.

One thing that made the later work of complete identification and rechecking difficult was the fact that, before going into the front lines, the man's organization was usually scratched from his identification tags to prevent this information from falling into the hands of the enemy. This, coupled with the circumstance that among the army in France literally hundreds of men bore the same name, made definite identification impossible in many cases. The personnel department at the Central Records Office has some exceedingly interesting and almost unbelievable figures on this subject.

Soon after the armistice, the recheck began of all American bodies buried in the battle areas. The temporary crosses were painted and complete identification made where possible.

Small metal tags with all available information, such as organization and time of death, were placed upon the crosses and the graves arranged carefully and mounted neatly. Detachments of engineers were called upon to assist in definitely locating each grave by coordinates and making sketches drawn to scale, showing just where each body was in the sector. Blue prints were made of these sketches and a complete file was kept for the future work of the concentration parties.

The work of concentrating the bodies into several large cemeteries was begun early in 1919. The location of these main concentration cemeteries was largely a problem of transportation and convenience to the majority of individual graves. The British Imperial War Graves Commission chose to bury their dead in small units of a few hundred bodies, thereby gaining a degree of seclusion; and in some cases the little burying grounds may be seen surrounded by groves of fruit or other trees protected by a low wall.

It was decided early in the work to concentrate as many as possible of the American dead into large cemeteries, in view of the possibility of having to remove the bodies later to America. Therefore, Lieutenant Gove S. Wright, Chief Concentration Officer, after supervising the building of the cemeteries at Château-Thierry and Belleau Wood, located the three main American cemeteries at Beaumont, Thiacourt and Romagne-sous-Montfaucon. Romagne, the subject of this article, to be known as the Argonne Cemetery, lies practically in the geographical center of the Meuse Argonne sector, north-west of Verdun and south-west of Dun-sur-Meuse.

The site of the cemetery is on the edge of the little village of Romagne, on a gently rolling hill opposite a more abrupt slope partly covered with old apple trees. The neighborhood witnessed some of the severe fighting of the later days of the

Argonne offensive. Cunel, a hamlet within sight of the cemetery, was taken by the 5th American Division with difficulty. The ground on which the cemetery now rests was filled with shell holes made by American 75s and 155s.

Historic Montfaucon with the famous observing tower of the Crown Prince is just to the south-east and within full

the work was well under way, it became necessary to call in all the available German prison labor in the sector to assist in building camp roads, laying water pipes, grading, laying sod, building walks, and planting. The supply of coffins from Paris ran short due to limited rail transportation, making it necessary to construct the coffins on the spot. This was

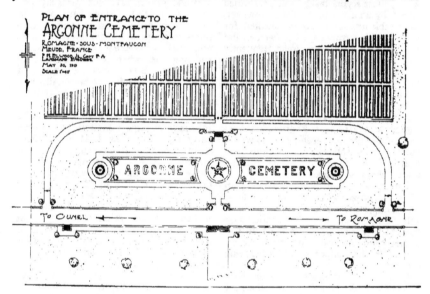

PLAN OF ENTRANCE TO THE
ARGONNE CEMETERY
ROMAGNE · SOUS · MONTFAUCON
MEUSE, FRANCE

ARGONNE   CEMETERY

TO CUNEL ←   → TO ROMAGNE

view from a part of the reservation. Of course, practically all buildings for miles in every direction are now in ruins or unfit for habitation, though as soon as work on the cemetery began the long-suffering French peasants began plodding back to the remains of their former homes.

It soon became evident that the most important problem was transportation for moving the bodies to the cemetery. In response to urgent calls from the Camp Commander, Col. Chapman, the Motor Transport Corps ordered over 500 trucks with the necessary repair units to Romagne, all under the Camp Motor Transport Officer, Capt. John C. Cashman.

When this force had been obtained and

done by setting up several portable saw mills and combing the country for lumber. At the end, the local box output nearly supplied the demand.

Materials of every sort used in modern warfare were to be had in any quantities at a huge German supply dump at Brieulles, a few miles away. From this dump we obtained all our wire and iron posts for fencing the reservation and for the fence around the cemetery itself. Every fourth post was set in concrete, also obtained at the same dump.

Until nineteen days before General Pershing's visit of dedication, we had bent most of our energies toward concentration and on camp work; but from then on we used practically the entire force of prisoners, at times over 4,000,

besides several hundred pioneer Infantry troops from the 815th and 816th regiments, upon the engineering and landscape construction work.

Much grading and draining, as well as removing of temporary buildings and accumulated debris, were necessary before any finished landscape work was possible.

The design for the approach roads and the landscape setting having been made and accepted, its execution was rushed with all possible speed in order to have the cemetery ready for inspection and dedication on Memorial Day by the Commanding General.

When he arrived, he found a white wooden cross, a spray of evergreen and a small American flag at every grave on the hillside. Two large grass and gravel panels, with twenty-foot turf letters spelling the words "Argonne Cemetery," stood out prominently on either side of a central circular pansy bed with a thirty-foot star of bright golden pansies. It had been necessary to make several trips to Luxemburg to obtain these plants. The evergreen trees used were obtained from the French near Verdun.

Interesting features of the design are a rising grade toward the main central walk or drive, from both sides, and a

Central pedestrian entrance, showing the forty-foot pansy bed with its gold service star of yellow pansies. The stone walls with concrete coping were built by German Prisoners of War.

German Prisoners of War policing the Cemetery after decorating each grave with an American flag and a spray of evergreens for the dedication services, Memorial Day, 1919. Each grave is marked by a four-foot wooden cross with the name and organization of the soldier.

sunken entrance-garden in the area between the public highway and the cemetery proper.

For miles in every direction there was nothing but waste and destruction, and the cemetery as it neared completion seemed to those of us who had been in the devastated area since early fall, something in the nature of an oasis in a desert.

As to costs no record was kept, as nowhere in civilian practice would like conditions be encountered where labor and materials were to be had for the asking and motor transports doing the work of the railroad and men the work of horses and machines. As an example, no plow was available; so several gangs of troops, some 500, were set to work spading up a field of several acres. When this was done the improvised drag pulled

by a mule team was found ineffective and too slow, so more troops with picks and shovels were ordered and a clod crushing race started across the field.

As an illustration of the pressure and speed of the work, the main entrance steps to the cemetery proper, seven in number and twenty feet long, were erected in one day from the foundations, and they were built to last in heavy concrete and stone.

After May 30, much finishing and polishing was done, the front wall constructed and the roadways resurfaced, giving the whole area a much more finished appearance, so that when the last troops broke camp the morning of July 4, they left with a feeling that they had given the brave boys buried there a worthy resting place as a lasting memorial to the real sacrifice of America.

The GUARDIAN SAVINGS AND TRUST COMPANY'S BUILDING

CLEVELAND, OHIO

WALKER & WEEKS, ARCHITECTS

By Philip Lindsley Small

THERE are many institutions in the commercial life of a large city, which, by reason of the nature of the business they transact, are limited in their location to a certain definite area—that area in which they can transact their business with the greatest degree of efficiency. Thus we very often find, as distinctly segregated districts, the Wholesale District, the Market District, the Newspaper District, the Retail District, the Financial District; and, in a well-organized and comparatively stable community, whatever expansion takes place must take place within that district or otherwise encroach upon the territory of another. A general readjustment on a large scale of all the elements is seldom possible at the present stage of development in most of our cities. Hence, when an institution like a large banking and trust company has outgrown its present accommodations and must expand, something within the so-called Financial District must give way to this expansion; and, with the high property values of such a district, and the difficulty of finding purchasable property at all, the problem is indeed not easy to solve.

In the city of Cleveland all of the larger banking institutions are located on Euclid Avenue, within a space of a couple of hundred yards, the busiest and most congested portion of the city; a fact which would seem to indicate that these institutions consider it indispensable that their main entrances at least should be accessible from this portion of Euclid Avenue. Thus they are, and always will be, confronted with a very difficult problem. They are all rapidly outgrowing their present accommodations and are in more or less urgent need of enlarged space and yet it is within this short reach of two

hundred yards that they will all, no doubt, remain. This will sooner or later mean one of three alternatives for each of them: (1) tearing down one of the comparatively modern office buildings of the district to make room for an entirely new plant; (2) enlarging their present building, or, (3) converting the lower floors of some other building to their needs.

This last alternative has, in a measure, been adopted by the Guardian Savings and Trust Company, which institution solved the problem of expansion in rather a unique manner, adding to the district one of Cleveland's largest and most complete banking plants, without disturbing the functioning of the business already located on the property utilized. In their plan of improving this property they have acknowledged that the main issue was largely centered, not in a broad Euclid Avenue frontage, but in an entrance on that thoroughfare. They have consequently utilized for the most part the rear end of their property, at the time occupied with very poor structures, and by so doing have carried out their project of expansion without displacing any of the stable business enterprises on Euclid Avenue.

The New England building, with one hundred and thirty-three feet of frontage on Euclid Avenue and covering the front sixty feet of depth of a plot extending two hundred and fifty feet to Vincent Avenue, was sixteen stories in height and every office occupied. The west half of the building and a two-story extension to Vincent Avenue was occupied by a small department store, which was on the point of moving to larger quarters. The east half and a one-story extension to Vincent Avenue was occupied by the largest book store in the city.

It was determined to leave the exterior of the old building unchanged, except for a new monumental façade to the lower four stories; to provide a public arcade from Euclid Avenue to Vincent Avenue, giving to the bank the west and larger portion of the plot, to include a basement, the entire first floor and parts of the second and third floors; allotting to the book store the east portion to the depth of one hundred and forty feet and including a basement, first and mezzanine floors. On Vincent Avenue and in the north end of the arcade were to be several small shops. In addition, the building was to extend the full height of two hundred feet allowed by the city, from Euclid to Vincent Avenues.

This, in general, was the problem that was confronted at the outset.

The existing building greatly hampered the development of the plan, which would have been difficult of solution at best, considering the irregularity of the lot (page 517), the difference of levels and the requirements laid down by the bank. In fact, from the commencement of the preliminary study to the final completion of the building it was a series of adjustments and readjustments—shifting, restudy, and the surmounting of one obstacle after another, in exemplifying which it might be mentioned that the plans of the old building showed steel columns throughout, and yet, when wrecking was commenced, the columns supporting the second floor were found to be cast iron and much larger than those they had anticipated finding. Upon excavating, it was found that the footings of the adjoining building projected from five to twelve feet beyond the property lines, so that the steel framework, already completed in design, had to be changed and the party walls supported on cantilevers. Such changes in the steel framing in most cases necessitated a complete restudy of the interiors affected. How serious these changes were it is now impossible to judge, in view of the fact that the final result gives no evidence of having been worked out under any than the most ideal conditions. It is, however, easy to imagine how serious it must have been to the mind of the designer who had already been confronted with more than a just share of difficulties. Among other things the exigencies of the new general plan necessitated other locations for the elevators, with continuity of service during the change; a complete rearrangement of the heating, lighting and plumbing equipment during maintenance of continuous service; establishment of adequate entrances to the offices and bookstore during reconstruction of the main façade, and the protection of the tenants from any annoyance or inconvenience. With a clear understanding of the problem in all its many intricacies, the few features of the result which are open to criticism from an artistic point of view are more than forgivable.

The Euclid Avenue façade is very successful in its proportions and detail. The spacing of the columns was predetermined by the existing steel columns, and of themselves would have been too far apart to have been dignified; but the device of the broad Corinthian-capped pilasters, engaging the columns of the same order, has enabled the designer to obtain an effect of narrower spacing that gives the sense of verticality necessary to the dignity of the façade. The very harsh mechanical sketch (page 513) does not give an adequate idea of the grace of line or well-studied detail that is so pleasing in the original. The Vincent Avenue façade is even more successful. It is of grey limestone throughout its height, and all of the mouldings, architraves, pilasters, cornices and belt courses have been kept in very low relief—a very intelligent bit of design, as it is entirely free from that heavy overpowering effect so general in façades on very narrow streets, such as the one in question.

On entering the main banking quarters from Euclid Avenue one passes through a vestibule into a transverse circulation, which leads to the arcade on the right and, on the left, to the stairway and elevator to the President's and Directors' suites on the floors above. To the right of the vestibule, on the main façade, is the women's room, panelled in satinwood and decorated in fine painted ornament, from which room a private stair leads

DETAIL OF EUCLID AVENUE FAÇADE—GUARDIAN
SAVINGS AND TRUST COMPANY'S BUILDING, CLEVE-
LAND, OHIO. WALKER & WEEKS, ARCHITECTS

PERSPECTIVE SKETCH FROM EUCLID AVENUE—GUAR-
DIAN SAVINGS AND TRUST COMPANY'S BUILDING,
CLEVELAND, OHIO. WALKER & WEEKS, ARCHITECTS.

MAIN BANKING ROOM FROM EUCLID AVE-
NUE ENTRANCE—GUARDIAN SAVINGS AND
TRUST COMPANY'S BUILDING, CLEVELAND,
OHIO. WALKER & WEEKS, ARCHITECTS.

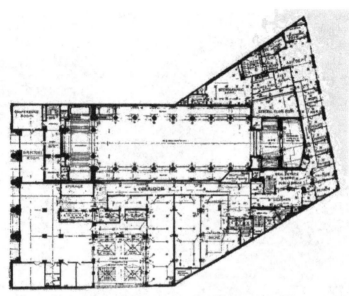

SECOND FLOOR AND BANK MEZZANINE—GUARDIAN SAVINGS AND TRUST
COMPANY'S BUILDING, CLEVELAND, OHIO.
Walker & Weeks, Architects.

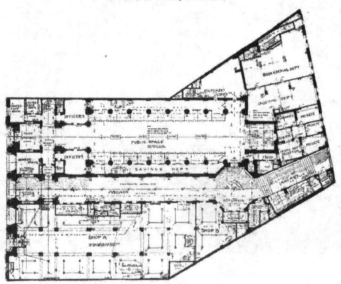

MAIN BANKING FLOOR—GUARDIAN SAVINGS AND TRUST COMPANY'S
BUILDING, CLEVELAND, OHIO.
Walker & Weeks, Architects.

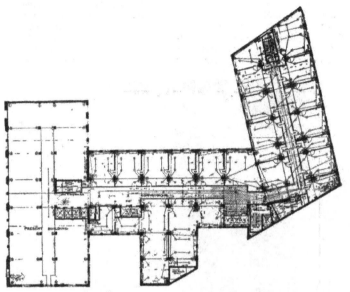

TYPICAL FLOOR PLAN—GUARDIAN SAVINGS AND TRUST COMPANY'S
BUILDING, CLEVELAND, OHIO.
Walker & Weeks, Architects.

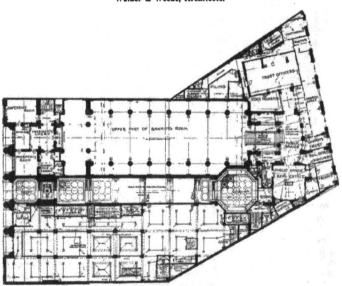

THIRD FLOOR (TRUST DEPARTMENT)—GUARDIAN SAVINGS AND TRUST
COMPANY'S BUILDING, CLEVELAND, OHIO.
Walker & Weeks, Architects.

517

to dressing rooms and toilets in the basement; to the left of the vestibule is a consultation room. The transverse circulation or lobby is low-ceiled, and rightfully so I think, as it gives an added air of dignity and spaciousness to the main

proportioned, with a peristyle of Corinthian columns, and pilasters of the same order, the capitals of which set the pace for every bit of detail in the room. All of the detail, in line and form and relief and color, is in harmony with these

MAIN BANKING ROOM FROM MEZZANINE LEVEL—GUARDIAN SAVINGS AND TRUST COMPANY'S BUILDING, CLEVELAND, OHIO.
Walker & Weeks, Architects.

banking room that opens out to its full height immediately beyond. To the right and left before reaching the banking space proper are the officers' platforms, railed off by balustrades of Georgia marble. These occupy the rear bay of the old building, and are the full height of the main banking room—are in fact part of it.

The room is long and high and finely

capitals. The bronze screen of the wickets, a very delicate and chaste bit of design. has fortunately not been affected by the scale of the detail above, being treated as part of the furnishings and not as part of the architecture. The fact that these wickets hide the bases of the columns may or may not be open to criticism, but certainly they give to the banking space a greater degree of effi-

MAIN BANKING ROOM FROM VESTIBULE—GUARDIAN
SAVINGS AND TRUST COMPANY'S BUILDING, CLEVE-
LAND, OHIO. WALKER & WEEKS, ARCHITECTS.

DOORWAY IN MAIN BANKING ROOM—GUARDIAN
SAVINGS AND TRUST COMPANY'S BUILDING, CLEVE-
LAND, OHIO. WALKER & WEEKS, ARCHITECTS.

ciency than had they been sacrificed to some artistic effect. The columns to the necking, the check desks, the base of the screen, the pilasters and walls to eleven feet high are all of tooled Georgia marble; and the color effect thus obtained

city are efficient only for a very limited time, if they can be made so at all. At the base of a high light-well they transmit very little light at best, and in the course of a very few months will have collected soot and dirt and refuse to the

DETAIL OF BANKING ROOM—GUARDIAN SAVINGS AND TRUST
COMPANY'S BUILDING, CLEVELAND, OHIO.
Walker & Weeks, Architects.

is admirable—soft and warm and pleasing in the contrast of light and shade. The ornamental plaster of the ceiling is tinted to match the marble below and picked out in metallic colors which harmonize with the bronze of the screen and the lighting clusters.

The lighting is the most noteworthy feature of the room, being entirely artificial and yet deceiving the most careful observer. Skylights in a large and dirty

extent that they are worse than useless. Here, although the roof of the room forms the bottom of the light-court, the usually futile attempt to make use of natural light was very wisely abandoned, and a scheme of artificial lighting installed, which not only approximates natural light in color, but gives the entire room an evenly distributed flood of light that would be impossible to obtain with natural light. The major portion of the

521

STAIRWAY TO TRUST DEPARTMENT LOBBY FROM MAIN BANK-
ING ROOM — GUARDIAN SAVINGS AND TRUST COMPANY'S
BUILDING, CLEVELAND, OHIO. WALKER & WEEKS, ARCHITECTS.

TRUST DEPARTMENT LOBBY AT HEAD OF STAIR FROM MAIN
BANKING ROOM—GUARDIAN SAVINGS AND TRUST COMPANY'S
BUILDING, CLEVELAND, OHIO. WALKER & WEEKS, ARCHITECTS.

WOMEN'S ROOM—GUARDIAN SAVINGS AND TRUST COMPANY'S BUILDING, CLEVELAND, OHIO.
Walker & Weeks, Architects.

direct light is obtained by means of three large ceiling clusters in bronze and glass, very beautiful in design and workmanship. In all, it is the most effectively lighted banking room I have ever seen.

On the main axis at the rear of the banking room rises a monumental stair to the semi-circular public space of the Trust Department. The difference of level between Euclid and Vincent Avenues is such that, though the Trust Department floor is just a short easy flight above the banking room floor, it is a full story height above the shops on Vincent Avenue. At either side of the stair at the top is a free standing column, and between each of these and the pilaster at the wall is a marble parapet or balustrade, the top of which serves as a check desk, a very unique feature. The far wall, in which are four Trust Department wickets, is slightly curved, masking the turning of the axis at this point. The detail of both the stair, with its bronze railing, and the lobby is very refined and chaste, and the transition from the large scale of the banking room through the stair well to this lobby has been very skilfully handled. To the left is a small vestibule and beyond the Trust Officers' public space and conference rooms; to the right another small vestibule and the Real Estate Department. The salesmen's rooms and most of the working space of this department are on the floor above, reached by both stair and elevator from the lobby on the Trust Department floor.

At the front of the building, at the same level as the Trust Department, reached by a private stair and elevator, is the President's suite, comprising a lobby, a Secretary's platform railed off from the lobby, the President's private office, a small consultation room, a toilet and a large committee room. The President's office is panelled in walnut, and is very simple in detail and furnishing. From the lobby of this suite leads a balcony overlooking the main banking room and beyond to the stair and Trust Department lobby at the far end. Directly above this is the Directors' suite, similar in plan and treatment. The plan and design of both of these suites was largely determined by the existing structure of the New England building. It was found necessary to retain the second floor framing construction at a level three feet below the Directors' suite floor level; hence, the low ceilings, doors and windows and the large beam in the President's lobby.

is the inner or Safe Deposit lobby, which forms the public circulation to the three vaults. Facing one on entering is the door to the main safe deposit vault and at either end are the small lobbies leading to the other vaults for silver and furs.

LOBBY OF PRESIDENT'S SUITE—GUARDIAN SAVINGS AND TRUST
COMPANY'S BUILDING, CLEVELAND, OHIO.
Walker & Weeks, Architects.

At the rear of the banking room, on either side of the stair leading to the Trust Department, is a flight descending to a low vaulted lobby in the basement. Directly ahead, as one descends the stairs, and screened off by a very beautiful grille in Benedict metal and color,

Here is one unit of the plan, treated as a unit, a small plan problem in itself, subordinate to the more important units on the floors above, but worked out with care and intelligence—just one more item of evidence that, though the artistic side has been well studied, the practical efficiency of the layout has been, as it should always be, the dominating factor.

Each department has its own public

525

GRILLE OF SAFE DEPOSIT DEPARTMENT—GUARDIAN SAVINGS AND TRUST COM-
PANY'S BUILDING, CLEVELAND, OHIO.
Walker & Weeks, Architects.

lobby, easily accessible and all inter-communicating; its own points of contact with the public; its own separate working space, and its own administration. At the same time all of these departments are connected by a circulation entirely separate from that of the public, by means of which money, papers and the bank personnel can pass from one department to another. This circulation is greatly assisted by a system of pneumatic tubes, working from a central, with outlets at all the wickets of each department.

Working out a plan to satisfy all of the requirements of the circulation chart is one of the most exacting phases of bank design. In the plan in question the architects have arrived at an admirable solution.

Of late we hear much of the "Art of Democracy" and progress toward a truly American Art; and whether or not we can see evidence of any such progress is open to a great deal of doubt. All agree that it is an aim worthy of the highest

effort; but in setting our minds and our hearts upon the coveted goal we must not close our vision to those works that may not, it is true, take us ahead, but surely are evidence that the high level of our architectural traditions is not on the retrograde.

In the Guardian Savings and Trust Company's new building, Messrs. Walker & Weeks have not created an artistic masterpiece in any sense of the word. It is neither a step toward the coveted "Art of Democracy," nor is it evidence of a new era in American architecture. And yet it is good architecture, better than ninety-nine per cent. of the other buildings being erected in Cleveland. It is graceful, dignified; fits well into its setting; is well-studied in detail. In color and proportion, it is extremely pleasing to the eye; and, above all, it fulfills to the highest degree of efficiency its mission as the home of a large, twentieth-century banking and trust company. It is an admirable solution of a modern problem.

English Architectural Decoration

Text and Measured Drawings by Albert E. Bullock

Part XV. The Adam Period.

IT has been truly said that without a knowledge of preceding work one cannot pretend to be inventive in architecture. Whether this emanated from Sir William Chambers or from Sir John Soane is of little moment; it was, however, a famous statement of the latter.

The work of the Brothers Adam was similar to that of John Wood of Bath, the architect of Buckland House, Berkshire, now the residence of Lady Fitzgerald; in addition, he executed many works in Bath and the surrounding districts.

During the latter half of the eighteenth century, a number of eminent men were contemporary with the Adam school, of whom we should not lose sight in surveying the decorative work of the period. Thomas Chippendale, of the firm of Chippendale, Haig & Company, carried out a considerable amount of furniture and decoration in several different styles, including certain furniture to the designs of Adam for David Garrick in 1760, some of which was housed at his suburban residence at Hampton and the residue at his house No. 5 Adelphi Terrace, London. A story is told of Chippendale to the effect that he conceived the notion of arranging tea parties at his house as an incentive to the selling of his various examples of carved furniture. He hailed from Worcester and with his father, before 1727, settled at Conduit Street, having workshops at Long Acre.

The activities of Sir William Chambers included many temples in the gardens of Kew, in addition to Somerset House, London, and many another notable residence for the nobility of his time.

Abraham Swan flourished in 1758; while J. C. Kraft, W. Thomas and Robert Manwaring are among the joiners and decorators who vied with Sheraton and Ince & Mayhew for the honors of competing in the cult of artistic expression in furniture, chimneypieces and other objects for interior use. With John Carter, Robert Wood, Nicholas Revett and James Stewart we have to deal with the school of antiquarian research, which produced the Greek revival under Sir John Soane and James Cockerell in the opening years of the nineteenth century.

Josiah Wedgwood stands apart as the epitome of all that is good in the design and execution of pottery and jasper ware, and whose style was developed by sculptors of the type of John Flaxman and Chantrey.

In contemporary sculpture William Cheere and John Eckstein exhibit the prevailing characteristics, respectively, of the Chippendale and Adam schools of design, their method being more clearly discernable in the nature of the mural tablets and cenotaphs at Westminster Abbey.

Instances of the influence of the Adam cult in varying degree of efficiency are to be found in many districts of England. Their authentic work includes Kedleston, Sion House, Nostell Priory, Lansdowne House; The Orangery, Bowood, Wiltshire; Harewood House, Yorkshire; Harewood House, London; Stratford House (now Derby House), and the Admiralty screen in Whitehall, London.

Isolated examples of Adam rooms in older mansions exist in many places, among which may be mentioned the library at Belton House, near Grantham, and the small drawing room at Forde Abbey; while the influence of their work is exemplified at Boodles Club, St. James's Street, London, as designed by John Crunden; the later work at Flaxley Abbey by J. Leck; the chinoiserie plaster work at Beacon House, Painswick,

THE CHAPEL, ZAVERIAN COLLEGE, BRIGHTON.
Shows Influence of Adam, Although Built Middle of Nineteenth Century by Sir Charles Barry.
Room Probably Decorated Towards End of Century, After Barry's Death.

Gloucestershire, and the typical decorations at Clayton House, Buckinghamshire.

Throughout the realm of furniture, silversmiths' work and the manufacture of chinaware the typical features of the Adam school prevails in a very definite and marked manner. The smallness of detail, its repetition and the reduced projection of the main cornice and subsidiary features are characteristics of the productions of this era, whether relating to external or internal work. The stone front to Eastgate House, Gloucester, is a pertinent subject, having motifs which suggest the possibility of the direct influence of John Wood or J. Leck.

The general effect of the authentic ornament accompanying the decorations of the Adam period is the attempt to give a definition to texture. The fine detail, with its repeating note of either fluting, beading or leaf enrichments, is noticeable in work existing at all the best houses treated during this era, the manner of which is very marked in the

ornament to the walls of the long gallery or library at Sion House.

The merit of the style of Robert Adam lies chiefly in the temerity with which he inaugurated an heretical cult in art at variance with former convention, which, although exhibiting pagan motifs, was adaptable to the successful treatment for interiors of modern residences.

His so-called "Etruscan taste," as executed for the Countess of Derby, is simply the style which he himself evolved from the material acquired during his travels and researches at Spalato in Dalmatia (a palace built by Diocletian in A. D. 304); his studies at Rome and his tours in the northern province of Etruria. which latter district became subject to Rome in B. C. 330 and was thereafter intermingled with the traditional character of Roman work. Early Etruscan work does not appear to have been so highly decorative as the more southern practice at Pompeii and Herculaneum. It was of a rather primitive nature

528

compared with Pompeiian examples, being largely confined to mural paintings within the tombs and some sculptured work and exceptionally good masonry.

The late Mr. Phené Spiers has pointed out that certain tombs at Rome in the combined with bas-reliefs and fine floral designs in stucco attached to the tufa backing.

In point of fact, the tombs of Rome and Pompeii must have provided the Adam Brothers and their colleagues with

OVERDOOR IN THE VICARAGE, HAMMERSMITH.

Via Appia recall early Etruscan types; but the detail was apparently more advanced in point of design and execution, as one example in the Via Latina indicates. This latter has a character much more in keeping with the general style of the usual Adam period, ceilings being worked in geometrical squares and circles much of the detail they subsequently incorporated into their peculiar style, in which, from a critical standpoint, one may readily trace the origin of many distinctive features.

The ornamented pilasters are obviously based upon the Raffaelian types existing in the galleries of the Vatican.

ADAM PERIOD STEEL GRATE. IN VICTORIA AND ALBERT MUSEUM.

Historically, the Adam Family are a very important link in the progress of English and Scottish architecture.

William Adam, the author of "Vitruvius Scoticus," was a renowned architect of Scotland, practising in the early years of the eighteenth century. If he was not actually an assistant of Sir William Bruce of Balcaskie, there is little doubt that he was largely influenced by the latter, as his designs show a refined and skilful handling with a chastity comparable with much later work. Had he never executed another edifice than Drum House, Gilmerton, this alone would suffice to merit his distinction. This building is described as "Sommervel House" in his monograph, being erected originally for James, the 13th Baron Somerville. There is an air of refinement about this residence almost equivalent to that which pervades the Petit Trianon at Versailles, where Marie Antoinette sought seclusion from the excitement of the French Court and the distractions of the later years of her troubled life

William Adam, however, made many additions to other mansions, including Mellerstain, near Kelso, and Hopetoun House, a large building originally designed by Sir William Bruce.

The dining room of Yester House exhibits a fine sense of architectural knowledge similar to the English Georgian manner. As the house was incomplete upon the death of William Adam in 1748, some of the additions may be attributable to his son, Robert, who is known to have succeeded his father about 1760, and remodeled a portion of the façade in 1789.

Robert Adam was born in 1728 and commenced his travels in 1754; but he had an elder brother, John, who was doubtless his father's right hand when Robert was in his teens. John Adam remained in Scotland, succeeding to his father's business, being also the latter's sole executor. His practice does not appear to have been as extensive as that of his younger brothers. There is no record of his having traveled abroad; he was apparently content to remain where he was born and maintain his father's connections.

James Adam went traveling with

Clerisseau and Zucchi in 1760-62, visiting many of the haunts previously traversed by his elder brother. He returned to London in time to render assistance upon the reconstruction of the Duke of Northumberland's residence

ing never been executed. A stateliness and charm pervade the decorations of the interior; and although all the schemes were not realized, the majority are very successfully treated.

After the stately hall, the dining room

ADAM PERIOD SHOP FRONT, CORNHILL, LONDON.

(Sion House, at Isleworth), by far the most famous of the Adams' productions.

The plan here given will be seen to be unique in several particulars. The long gallery or library has a width of only fourteen feet, at the back of which are the sleeping apartments of the Duke and his Duchess, facing the internal court, the hatched-in walls of the rotunda hav-

is as satisfactory an apartment as any, being plainer and freer from repeated ornament than the library, which is too harried with motifs to give repose of effect, a most essential element in all interior designing. In justice to Robert Adam it should be remarked that the walls of the long gallery were fixed to a width of which he did not approve and

TEMPLE OF THE SUN, KEW GARDENS. SIR
WILLIAM CHAMBERS, ARCHITECT. ABOUT
1760. DESTROYED BY STORM IN 1916.

Demolished 1914

PORTIONS OF CEILING IN 9 ARGYLE
PLACE, LONDON. DEMOLISHED IN 1914.

SION HOVSE.

Scale

LEFT HALF OF DRAWING. RIGHT
HALF ON OPPOSITE PAGE.

PART OF LONG GALLERY.

RIGHT HALF OF DRAWING, LEFT
HALF ON OPPOSITE PAGE.

SION HOVSE.

Scale ⊢┴┴┴┴┴┴┴┴┴┤

LEFT HALF OF DRAWING. RIGHT
HALF ON OPPOSITE PAGE.

PART OF LONG GALLERY.

RIGHT HALF OF DRAWING. LEFT
HALF ON OPPOSITE PAGE.

Section of one End of the Hall, next to the private Apartment. Coupe du Vestibule au Côté des Apartements particuliers.

PRINT SHOWING ONE END OF
THE HALL IN SION HOUSE.

Section of one End of the Hall, next to the great Apartment   *Coupe du Vestibule au Côté des grandes Apartemens*

Scale   *Feet*

PRINT SHOWING ONE END OF
THE HALL IN SION HOUSE.

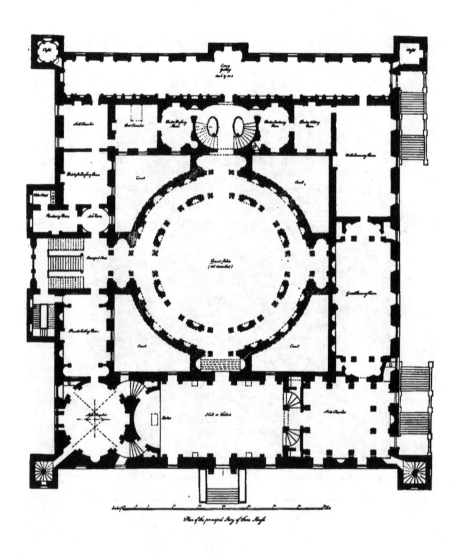

PLAN OF THE MAIN FLOOR
OF SION HOUSE, ISLEWORTH.

FLAXLEY ABBEY.
DECORATIONS
by
J·LECK c 1784
(ADAM PERIOD.)

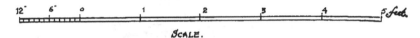

12˝   6˝   0   1   2   3   4   5 feet.

SCALE.

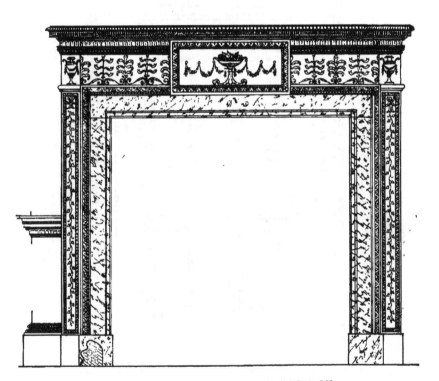

DRAWING ROOM CHIMNEY PIECE.

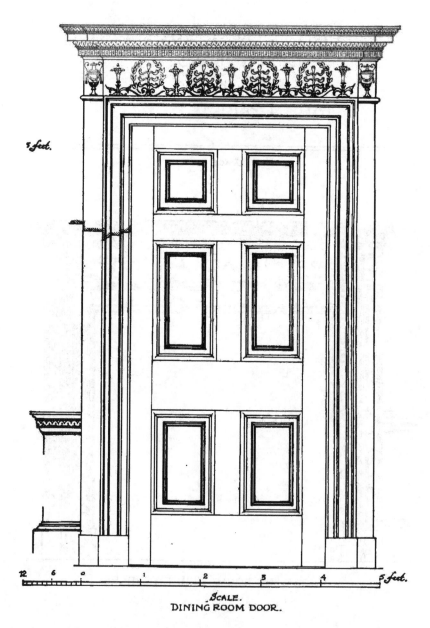

SCALE.
DINING ROOM DOOR.

FLAXLEY ABBEY, GLOUCESTER. DECO-
RATIONS BY J. LECK, ABOUT 1784.

SCALE.
DRAWING ROOM DOOR.

FLAXLEY ABBEY, GLOUCESTER. DECO-
RATIONS BY J. LECK, ABOUT 1784.

THE HALL—FLAXLEY ABBEY, GLOUCESTER.

the ceiling of a height which limited his sphere of operations. The great length of one hundred and thirty feet by a narrow width naturally called for a treatment of pilasters which would break up the horizontal perspective of converging lines that would otherwise be inevitable.

The screen on the Brentford Road is a fine composition, of a trifle less solid nature than what he designed for the Admiralty at Whitehall.

The library at Ken Wood, Hampstead, for the Earl of Mansfield, has a barrel vaulted or concave ceiling with semicircular end screened off by a trabeated columnar treatment. The effect of this is to keep the continuous bookcases at one end, leaving freedom in the center for the disposition of furniture and wall space for pictures. The usual oppressive feeling of the stuffy, over-volumed library is largely absent in this instance.

At Belton the cases project into the room at intervals, leaving little space for furniture, giving the effect of a public library rather than the reception room in a private house where study can be indulged in at leisure.

Antonio Zucchi executed some of the paintings at Ken Wood, for which his account exists; while Thomas Chippendale and his son provided silvered French plate glass for certain definite purposes, and doubtless some furniture.

At Bowood, for Lord Lansdowne, Robert Adam remodelled the dining room and built the Orangery, which contains also a library and breakfast room; the whole placed on a balustraded terrace with formal garden in front, which latter was probably laid out when Sir Charles Barry made his additions in the middle of the nineteenth century.

CHIPPENDALE PERIOD BENCH. IN VICTORIA AND ALBERT MUSEUM.

JACOB DOLL & SONS' BUILDING, NEW YORK
CITY.   ALFRED C.   BOSSOM,   ARCHITECT.

JACOB DOLL & SONS' BUILDING, NEW YORK CITY.
Alfred C. Bossom. Architect.

JACOB DOLL & SONS' BUILDING, NEW YORK CITY.
Alfred C. Bossom, Architect.

6

TITUSVILLE TRUST COMPANY'S BUILDING, TITUS-
VILLE, PA. ALFRED C. BOSSOM, ARCHITECT.

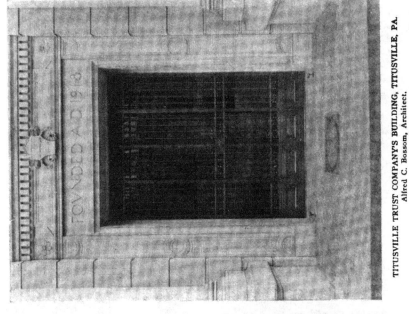

TITUSVILLE TRUST COMPANY'S BUILDING, TITUSVILLE, PA.
Alfred C. Bossom, Architect.

TITUSVILLE TRUST COMPANY'S BUILDING, TITUSVILLE, PA.
Alfred C. Bossom, Architect.

TITUSVILLE TRUST COMPANY'S BUILDING, TITUS-
VILLE, PA. ALFRED C. BOSSOM, ARCHITECT.

TITUSVILLE TRUST COMPANY'S BUILDING, TITUS-
VILLE, PA. ALFRED C. BOSSOM, ARCHITECT.

KANAWHA BANKING AND TRUST COM-
PANY'S BUILDING, CHARLESTON, W. VA.
DENNISON & HIRONS, ARCHITECTS.

ALTERATION TO MERCHANTS' NATIONAL BANK, NEW HAVEN, CONN. DENNISON & HIRONS, ARCHITECTS.

ENTRANCE DETAIL—NEW BRUNSWICK TRUST
COMPANY'S BUILDING, NEW BRUNSWICK,
N. J. DENNISON & HIRONS, ARCHITECTS.

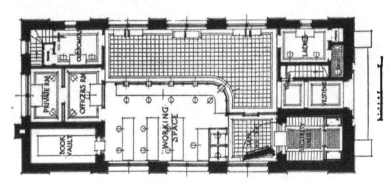

PURCELLVILLE NATIONAL BANK, PURCELLVILLE, VA.   DENNISON & HIRONS, ARCHITECTS.

DETAIL OF INTERIOR — FULTON COUNTY
NATIONAL BANK, GLOVERSVILLE, N. Y.
DENNISON & HIRONS, ARCHITECTS.

GARAGE OF EDWARD C. GUDE, ESQ., WHITE PLAINS,
N. Y. WILLIAM LAWRENCE BOTTOMLEY, ARCHITECT.

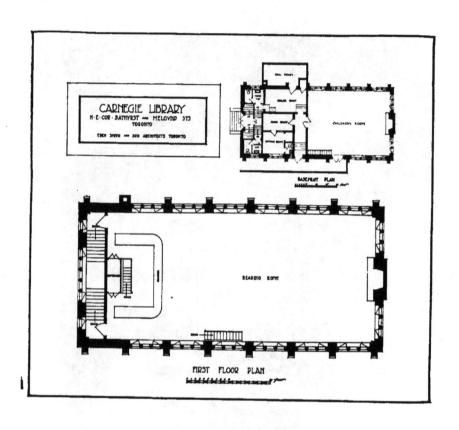

CARNEGIE LIBRARY
N · E · COR · BATHVRST and MELGVND STS
TORONTO
EDEN SMITH and SON ARCHITECTS TORONTO

BASEMENT PLAN

CHILDREN'S ROOM

READING ROOM

FIRST FLOOR PLAN

WYCHWOOD BRANCH OF TORONTO PUBLIC LIBRARY. ERECTED IN
COMMEMORATION OF THE TERCENTENARY OF SHAKESPEARE.
GEORGE H. LOCKE, CHIEF LIBRARIAN. EDEN SMITH, ARCHITECT.

WYCHWOOD BRANCH OF TORONTO PUBLIC LIBRARY.
Eden Smith, Architect.

WYCHWOOD BRANCH OF TORONTO PUBLIC LIBRARY.
Eden Smith, Architect.

557

Planning the Farmhouse.

In November and December, 1919, I conducted, through The Farm Journal, a prize contest for "The Farmhouse I'd Like to Have." This was strictly limited to actual farm folk—chiefly farmers' wives and daughters. Rough sketch plans (no elevations) were required. From a circulation of one million, pretty evenly spread over the United States, we got 3600 contestants. The great majority of the plans were remarkably well worked out, and followed certain definite lines. I know now, beyond all question, what the program is for designing a real farmhouse; and I'll try to state that program. Naturally, particular local conditions will alter it somewhat; but here are the general requirements.

To illustrate, I'll take one of the prize-winning plans, sent in by a Nebraska woman. It will fit almost any other section equally well. The sketches showed a semi-bungalow; the second floor plan was not especially interesting, so I will not reproduce it. The first floor, however (Figure 1), covers nearly every needed feature; it would serve equally well in a two-story scheme, and the dotted portions show how a straight bungalow may be developed.

1. The kitchen is the most important room in the house. It must be well lighted, well ventilated, and of an average size of about twelve feet by fifteen. The family eat breakfast here; other meals are usually (but not always) served in the dining room. The sink should be directly under a window; the drain-board is frequently expanded into a work-table, and set at a height of three feet two inches, or thereabouts. Maple flooring seems to be the favorite for the kitchen, although magnesite or other plastic floorings, with integral cove base, are beginning to appear.

The dumb-waiter is universal. Because of the ice problem, a farm refrigerator is often out of commission; so perishable foodstuffs are put in the dumb-waiter, and lowered down to the cool cellar. Sometimes a shallow well is dug in the cellar floor, so that the whole affair can be kept still cooler. The dumb-waiter also serves to lift fuel, winter vegetables, etc.

Elaborate cupboards and kitchen cabinets are in great demand; indeed, probably fifty per cent. of the farm women do not want a pantry, preferring to keep all their groceries and supplies right at hand, in the cabinets. The other fifty per cent. want the pantry, but merely as a reserve magazine.

The little "breakfast alcove," with two settles and a fixed table, is very popular, but not universal.

A fuel box near the stove, arranged to be filled from outside or from the cellar, is called for by hundreds of farm women, and many of them say: "I want my kitchen set where I can get a view of the road, and see what's going on, as I stand washing dishes or making mince pies."

2. Next in importance comes the dining room. It must be big enough for "threshing dinners" (though on a very large farm, a second table would be set in the living room). The size depends entirely on the probable number of men that must be taken care of; a dairy farm will not need so large a room as a wheat farm, for instance.

The buffet should always be built-in; and usually it should be placed as I've shown, with glass doors on the dining room side, and panel doors in the kitchen. Food, dishes, etc., are placed on the shelves in one room, and taken off from the other; anything that will save steps and save labor is eagerly welcomed by the farmer's wife.

The dining room is also the general sitting room of the farm family; so bookcases, boxed window seats to hold work, toys, magazines, etc., bay-windows for flowers and so on, are very desirable, although not all of these features are shown on this particular plan.

Hardwood finish and hardwood floors are wanted here; never make the mistake of suggesting white-painted woodwork to a farmer's wife. "Do you want me to spend an hour every day, washing the paint-work clean, after the men-folks have messed it up?" she'll ask. We are too apt to forget that farmwork is particularly dirty and that from two to twenty-five workmen, in their working clothes, invade the farmhouse at least three times a day.

3. The living room is somewhat smaller than the dining room; it's more of a "company room," though it is actively used now-adays, and not shut up like the old-time "parlor." In most cases, the front door opens directly into this living room; the reception hall is very seldom wanted west of Ohio. In the East, perhaps fifty per cent. of the plans show this arrangement. As a matter of fact, a reception hall is very little used in a farmhouse; the family always enter and leave from the back of the house, because that is nearest the barns, fields, and chicken-houses. "Neighbors always drive up to the rear of the house, because that's where I'm usually to be found," says one farm woman.

4. The stairway is almost always at the back of the house, convenient to the kitchen, etc. Hired men can come in and go directly up to their rooms. This particular plan is not quite typical, in that it does not show a main stair with "grade door," which is by far the most popular sort.

5. The wash room (or some substitute) is absolutely vital. Practically every plan showed it, in some form. "The men come from work, and go right into the wash room, from the porch; they take off their muddy rubbers, shed their wet and smelly old coats, and wash up. Then, by way of

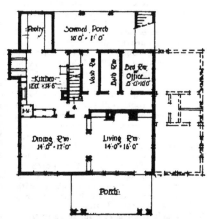

Fig. 1.—First Floor Plan of a prize-winning semi-bungalow from *The Farm Journal* Farmhouse Contest. The Second Floor had three Bedrooms, Sleeping Porch, Sewing Room (or Bath) and storage space. The dotted portion shows how a pure bungalow could be developed.—Courtesy of *The Farm Journal.*

the hall, they pass right to the dining room without going through my kitchen." So says one woman; and her sisters all agree. The idea is that men track dirt into the kitchen; worse still, they invariably get on a flustered woman's nerves, when she's hurrying to serve a meal.

Sometimes the washroom is so placed that a porch connects it with the dining room; or the wash room is in the basement. This is particularly desirable where hard winters prevail; the men enter the grade door, go directly down, and leave their wet and snow-covered wraps to dry, around the furnace. Then, coming upstairs, they go to the dining room, or to their own rooms, especially the hired men. I think that the average grain farmer would be much interested in metal lockers, industrial shower-baths, ranges of lavatories, etc.

6. The downstairs bathroom occurs in seventy-five per cent. of the plans, at least —often to the exclusion of any other bath. One reason is, the farm water pressure is frequently too low to supply any upstairs fixtures; indeed, there may be no power pressure at all, but just a hand pump in the kitchen. But a still more cogent reason exists: the farm woman spends at least three-fourths of her time in or near the kitchen; and she wants a toilet close at hand, not only for her own use, but for the small children. A lavatory, with toilet, may

Fig. 2.—A very popular and convenient first-floor layout. The bay-window is wanted to hold winter flowers, provided it has a sunny exposure. The grade entrance to the stairway is an extremely good feature.

answer to some extent; but not altogether. The baby must be bathed, the children's bath supervised, and, at the same time, the cooking must be watched.

7. There is nearly always at least one downstairs bedroom, no matter what the type of farmhouse. "When Johnny's sick in bed in green-apple time, I don't want to be trotting up and down stairs, whenever he wants a drink of water." When Johnny gets well, the room will probably serve as a farm office; or maybe as a sewing room.

8. A large screened back porch, at least ten feet wide, is very necessary indeed; meals are often served on it, and almost all the kitchen work, etc., done out here, in the cool. Quite often this porch is weatherboarded up about three feet; in winter time, the open spaces are glazed with temporary sash. This porch may or may not have a concrete floor.

9. An ample front porch, set so as to catch the breeze, goes without saying. A concrete floor is probably the favorite. Screening is not necessary, except in mosquito neighborhoods; since (as sometimes happens) this front porch is used for sleeping.

10. Upstairs, several good bedrooms are needed, depending on the size of the family and the number of farmhands. Very large closets (preferably with windows) are wanted.

11. A sleeping porch may or may not be required; but at any rate there must be an upstairs balcony, for shaking rugs, airing bedding, and so on.

12. Ample storage space sometimes for seed-corn, etc., is necessary.

13. The basement always has a heater room; also a large room, shut off from the heat by solid partitions, where apples, potatoes, and other perishable crops may be kept, free from frost, yet not too warm. Often these are commercial crops, intended for sale, not merely the family's supply. A laundry room, too, is usually down here, all fitted with the latest equipment of electric washing machines, and so on. Sometimes there is drying-space here, for stormy weather; often, however, the dumb-waiter runs up to the attic, where a store room serves as drying-room at need. And finally, an engine room, workshop, etc., is almost always located in the basement.

I believe this completes the ordinary inventory, but there are a lot of reservations. For example, a small office, distinct from the downstairs bedroom, is growing in favor.

A very small sewing-room, near the kitchen, is suggested by several women; the idea is, that an eye can be kept on the cooking, and every spare moment utilized.

Instead of being in the basement, the laundry very often adjoined the kitchen or the back porch; it is large enough to hold separator, feed-cookers (for heating hog-feed, etc., in winter), men's washing equipment, lard boilers, butcher tables, scalding kettles, and so on. Sometimes this laundry is in a separate building.

Where possible, the garage is in the basement.

A small greenhouse is sometimes built on, and heated from the cellar; it is used to start early vegetables, etc.

The type of house varies in different sections. A semi-bungalow, or a square two-story affair, seems to be the choice in the Middle West; the Eastern farmer rather prefers a colonial two-story scheme; the South is a general jumble; the Far West is all for bungalows. Indeed, the straight-out bungalow is very popular everywhere.

WILLIAM DRAPER BRINCKLOE.

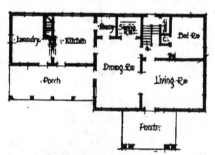

Fig. 3. — Another satisfactory solution. The laundry serves as a wash-room for the men, and may possibly have a shower-bath and frost-proof hopper in it. All sorts of miscellaneous work, like lard-rendering, poultry-dressing, etc., is done here.